KISSING THE WILD WOMAN

Art, Beauty, and the Reformation of the I
in Giulia Bigolina's *Urania*

Kissing the Wild Woman explores the unique aesthetic vision and innovative narrative features of Giulia Bigolina's greatest surviving work, the prose romance *Urania* (circa 1552). Here Bigolina re-examines the concept of the Italian prose romance as it had existed since the time of Boccaccio, fashioning a new type of narrative that combines elements of both the romance and the novella, as well as a polemical treatise on the moral implications of portraiture and the role of women in the arts.

The study demonstrates how Bigolina challenges cultural authority by rejecting the prevailing views of the *paragone* between painting and literature. In the face of the pervasive apotheosis of portraiture that was extensively promoted by Bigolina's sometime antagonist Pietro Aretino, she reveals how painting constitutes an ineffectual, even immoral, mode of self-promotion for women, who are better served by creating their own 'portraits' in the form of literature.

This study also shows how Bigolina orients her defence of women toward a rejection of the cult of visualized female beauty that predominated in the rhetoric and artistry of such figures as Aretino and Titian. It concludes with a discussion of Bigolina's innovative treatments of certain romance topoi, especially those of the grief-stricken protagonist who resists madness in wild places, as well as the encounter between civilized characters and wild folk living at the margins of society.

(Toronto Italian Studies)

CHRISTOPHER NISSEN is an associate professor in the Department of Foreign Languages and Literatures at Northern Illinois University.

CHRISTOPHER NISSEN

Kissing the Wild Woman

Art, Beauty, and the Reformation
of the Italian Prose Romance in
Giulia Bigolina's *Urania*

UNIVERSITY OF TORONTO PRESS
Toronto Buffalo London

© University of Toronto Press 2011
Toronto Buffalo London
utorontopress.com

Reprinted in paperback 2021

ISBN 978-1-4426-4340-6 (cloth)
ISBN 978-1-4875-2622-1 (paper)

Toronto Italian Studies

Library and Archives Canada Cataloguing in Publication

Title: Kissing the wild woman : art, beauty, and the reformation of the Italian prose
    romance in Giulia Bigolina's Urania / Christopher Nissen.
Names: Nissen, Christopher. author. | Container of (work): Bigolina, Giulia, –1569.
    Urania, nella quale si contiene l'amore d'una giovane di tal nome. | Container of
    (expression) Bigolina, Giulia, –1569. Urania, nella quale si contiene l'amore d'una
    giovane di tal nome. English.
Series: Toronto Italian studies.
Description: Series statement: Toronto Italian studies | Paperback reprint. Originally
    published 2011. | Includes bibliographical references and index. | Includes Giulia
    Bigolina's last will and testament in Italian, followed by its English translation.
Identifiers: Canadiana 20210285419 | ISBN 9781487526221 (softcover)
Subjects: LCSH: Bigolina, Giulia, –1569. Urania, nella quale si contiene a l'amore
    d'una giovane di tal nome. | LCSH: Italy – Civilization – 1559–1789. | LCSH:
    Painting in literature. | LCSH: Aesthetics in literature. | LCSH: Beauty, Personal,
    in literature.
Classification: LCC PQ4610.B58 Z65 2021 | DDC 853/.4–dc23

This volume has been published with the aid of a grant from Northern Illinois
University.

University of Toronto Press acknowledges the financial assistance to its publishing
program of the Canada Council for the Arts and the Ontario Arts Council, an agency
of the Government of Ontario.

 Canada Council **Conseil des Arts**
for the Arts **du Canada**

 ONTARIO ARTS COUNCIL
CONSEIL DES ARTS DE L'ONTARIO
an Ontario government agency
un organisme du gouvernement de l'Ontario

Funded by the   Financé par le
Government   gouvernement
of Canada   du Canada

Contents

Acknowledgments

Inasmuch as this book has profited to a great extent from the same body of research that led to my 2004 critical edition of Bigolina's works, it is appropriate that I acknowledge once more the two grants that made that edition possible, those of the Research and Artistry Committee of the Graduate School of Northern Illinois University and of the Gladys Krieble Delmas Foundation. I also extend my thanks to certain staff members of the State Archive of Padua for their invaluable assistance throughout these many years of study, especially Rossella Consiglio, Renzo Sgarabotto, Luigi Sangiovanni, and Adriano Zattarin, as well as to the archival researchers Francesco Piovan and Elda Martellozzo Forin for their welcome advice pertaining to manuscripts and paleography.

I would like to acknowledge *Italian Quarterly*, wherein some of the substance of this book has appeared in the form of an article, '*Paragone* as Fiction: The Judgment of Paris in Giulia Bigolina's *Urania*' (42.165–6 [2006]: 5–17). In addition, I have cited here various passages from my translations of Aretino's letters to Bigolina, which have recently been published in their complete form in volume 58 of The Other Voice in Early Modern Europe series, *In Dialogue with the Other Voice in Sixteenth-Century Italy: Literary and Social Contexts for Women's Writing*, edited by Julie D. Campbell and Maria Galli Stampino (Toronto: Centre for Reformation and Renaissance Studies, 2011).

I remember with gratitude the recommendations of a number of people who have made essential contributions to my research, among them Patrizia Bettella, David M. Stone, Mary Lee Cozad, Julie D. Campbell, Cristelle Baskins, Laura Keyes, Dennis McAuliffe, and Laurie Riggin. I am particularly grateful to Lori Lawson for her inspiration and encouragement during those times when it seemed the work would never end, and for the love and support of my sons, Alexander and Cameron, who have scarcely known a time when Bigolina was not an invisible member of our household.

Finally, I remember with fondness Ruggero Stefanini, one of my professors at the University of California, Berkeley, who was lost to us as I began to write this book, and whose voice I will continue to hear as long as I read and ponder and write: 'ut te postremo donarem munere mortis.'

Introduction

Urania, nella quale contiene l'amore d'una giovane di tal nome is the oldest Italian romance, in prose or verse, known to have been written by a woman.[1] It has also languished in all but total oblivion for 450 years. Although these facts alone surely help to make it a worthy object of critical study today, my purpose in writing this book has not merely been to point them out, but also to demonstrate that *Urania* ought to be regarded as a unique literary creation of great importance, ranking among the finer works of imaginative prose produced by the Italian Renaissance.

Romance, a literary form but also to some extent a mode of expression that transcends the limits of form, contributed much to the rise of the modern novel; this fact is well known, and often repeated.[2] It is also well known that great romances of the Middle Ages and early modern period tended to inspire numerous forgettable imitations – it was not always a genre that attracted keen minds with something original to say. We cannot be blamed for assuming that books that lie about unread and unmentioned (yet in plain sight) for centuries must somehow be deservedly overlooked, as the early nineteenth-century antiquary Bartolommeo Gamba, one of the very few people known to have examined Giulia Bigolina's work before the present day, thought this one had been.[3] After all, Bigolina's miserable experience with posterity is scarcely unique, and in fact it may be compared to that of one of her contemporaries, Lodovico Corfino, whose prose romance also lay forgotten in a single manuscript for centuries, until at last it was discovered and published just a hundred years before *Urania*.[4] However, Corfino's somewhat unremarkable *Phileto* has essentially remained a literary curiosity since its reappearance, scarcely read more now than it was in all those centuries when it slept on a dusty shelf.

I would argue that Bigolina's *Urania,* now beginning its second life in a new millennium, holds the promise to become something quite different. The author was clearly unwilling to imitate her predecessors slavishly in either the novella or romance traditions, with the result that in *Urania* she consistently exhibits a desire to create a new and unique work of art, one that merges elements of both novella and romance in unprecedented ways.[5] In Bigolina's hands, the Italian prose romance becomes a more versatile vehicle than it had ever been before, subtly crafted to depict a wide range of human perspectives and experiences; thus her version of the genre points more surely towards the modern novel than any other of her time and place. On occasion, it even aspires to present certain revolutionary social notions, as Valeria Finucci has observed in regard to Bigolina's defence of women: Bigolina anticipated by a generation, at least in Italy, the polemical appeals of Moderata Fonte and Lucrezia Marinella that women be accorded moral and intellectual parity with men.[6]

The present study seeks to add new dimensions to this image of Bigolina as literary innovator and defender of women, by taking note of ways in which she deliberately challenges several predominant notions of her time. Bigolina's overtly rhetorical defence of women, presented so forthrightly in Urania's lecture to the five men she meets in the woods near Naples, is accompanied by a much more subtle one in the treatment of the *paragone* (comparison) between the arts of painting and literature.[7] Bigolina re-examines the contemporary rhetorical debates on the arts in a completely original way, deftly weaving them into the plot of her romance, and making them into the very substance of a work of art that depicts the triumph of the written word over painting. Out of this grows her audaciously provocative rejection of the cult of physical beauty, as well as her dismissal of the apotheosis of the sight of such beauty, cultural commonplaces that flourished in so much of the writing of her time, especially in the context of the discussion of women. *Urania,* replete with references to the moral implications of women's posing for paintings or gazing at paintings, as well as the account of Urania's multiple male disguises and the powers they confer upon her, is built around a sort of crisis of the visual, a tour de force of the moral consequences of seeing and being seen. Ultimately what emerges is a lesson that is meant to inspire women to take control of the way they are to be put on display, in terms of both their bodies and their talents.

Bigolina undertakes her task of communicating these things in part by slyly appropriating two modes of discourse that were particularly meant to reaffirm the cultural and intellectual hegemony of males: the treatise and the epic.[8] I say slyly, because of all the literary forms she might have adopted as a vehicle for her magnum opus, she chose the prose romance, the one that was perhaps least likely to attract the critique of the patriarchal voices of society because it did not tend to be the preferred genre of the more distinguished writers of the Cinquecento, and thus was perennially overlooked by critics and literary theorists.[9] Bigolina shows her skill at exploiting the expressive potential of this eclectic and even occasionally amorphous literary form, to the extent that *Urania* may indeed aspire to be something of a treatise, with its didactic passages on the arts and the perception of beauty, as well as on the role of women in society. At the same time it also contains elements of the medieval and early modern chivalric epic, with its heroine fleeing society while in anguish over lost love, only to take up a quest to overcome the challenge of a fearsome creature, so that in the end she may liberate and claim her imprisoned lover (the male equivalent of 'a damsel in distress') and live happily ever after. The ways in which Bigolina artfully combines these elements in *Urania,* with the aim of enhancing the communicative powers of her chosen genre, will be one of the subjects of this study.

The first chapter, 'The Reformation of the Prose Romance,' begins with an overview of Bigolina's cultural formation, inasmuch as it may be reconstructed from her surviving works and contemporary references to her. Subsequently I proceed to a close examination of *Urania,* noting the elements that link the work to ancient Greek romances, medieval chivalric romances, the Italian novella, and the early modern Italian romance in prose; in the last category I emphasize the works of Giovanni Boccaccio, Iacopo Caviceo, Niccolò Franco, and Lodovico Corfino. Here Bigolina departs from a long-established tradition, when she orients her romance away from the patterns for the amatory prose romance that had prevailed ever since they were established by Boccaccio more than two centuries earlier. Instead, she prefers to write a sort of hybrid work that displays many characteristics of the novella. She also sets out to write a romance that differs markedly from the grand example set by Ludovico Ariosto, especially in her use of the motif of the protagonist's wandering (*errare*), and in her creation of a plot driven by the alternation of bad and good judgments made by characters. Ultimately I conclude that Bigolina does not model *Urania* on the works of any specific predecessor, even though she chooses a genre that thrives on imitations of great bygone narratives; hers is essentially an original work, to match its original system of messages. This is borne out by Bigolina's unique reshaping of the established didactic genre of the defence of women, which I discuss at the end of this chapter, with special emphasis on the influence of Christine de Pizan's *Livre de la cité des dames*.

It is my contention that Bigolina's literary innovations are meant to be seen as provocative, and that *Urania* is to a certain extent a polemical book, albeit a discreet one, presented in the guise of a conventional love story. Her innovations are couched as challenges to the literary, artistic, and intellectual status quo of her day, and seem to have derived at least in part from her fleeting brush with two of the greatest figures of her time in the realm of the arts, Pietro Aretino and Tiziano Vecellio (Titian), as I describe in the second chapter, 'Writing a Portrait.' Aretino and Titian are the only truly famous personages who are known to have had a direct connection with Bigolina. Aretino published Book 5 of his monumental epistolary collection, the *Lettere*, in 1550, including therein three letters to Bigolina. Each of these acknowledges an item that Bigolina had sent to Aretino over the space of two months in 1549; nowhere else in all of his voluminous writings does he make any reference to her. I present evidence indicating that in all likelihood Bigolina, who had barely attained any degree of fame as a writer even in her native Padua at this time, initiated an acquaintance with Aretino as a means of advancing her career, as many other writers and artists are known to have done during the decades in which Aretino, famous throughout Europe, was a dominant presence in Venetian print culture. Although a superficial glance at Aretino's three letters would seem to indicate that he regarded Bigolina highly, a closer examination, in conjunction with an overview of the attitudes that Aretino continually presents in the *Lettere* and other works, reveals his dismissive or even mocking rejection of her importance both as a writer and as an individual. Aretino's close friend Titian is specifically mentioned in two letters as an onlooker in these proceedings.

By all evidence, Bigolina began to write *Urania* not long after seeing Aretino's letters to her in print. I seek to demonstrate that her romance contains a subtle, profound, and carefully conceived rejection of certain opinions that Aretino expresses not only in his letters to Bigolina but also throughout the *Lettere* as a whole. Drawing from Luba Freedman's research on Aretino's views of portraiture, I describe how the Paduan author's ideas concerning the prevailing cult of the adoration of female beauty and the ethical implications of portraiture as an art form are diametrically opposed to the attitudes that Aretino trumpets throughout the *Lettere,* especially in conjunction with his constant exaltation of Titian. In effect, *Urania* takes on the appearance of a polemic when (to borrow a metaphor from the title of Luba Freedman's book) it is viewed through the lenses of Aretino's writings and Titian's paintings. Moreover, it can be argued that one of Bigolina's most fascinating characters, the disreputable painter who tries to cause the Prince of Salerno to fall in love with an aristocratic widow by having her pose in a painting as Venus, is meant to be seen as an unflattering caricature of Titian. Bigolina seeks to reject the idea that a woman's principal mode of self-promotion lies in the sort of public display of her physical beauty that male artists and writers were ever inclined to depict. Instead, she urges women to express themselves through their own artistic creations, which ideally should take the form of literature. As Bigolina states explicitly, in writing *Urania* she writes her own portrait.

Chapter 2 concludes with a reference to Donald Maddox's notions of how characters in medieval romance modify their self-image through 'specular' encounters with allegorical or supernatural informants. Again I compare Bigolina's own such encounter in the proem of *Urania* with that of one of her principal models, Christine de Pizan's *Livre de la cité des dames,* noting that both authors employ mirrors as metaphors for moral self-examination in their defences of women. Bigolina's proem dramatizes the strategies of a woman endowed with artistic talent who wishes to take control of the way she is to be portrayed in the arts; she must resist being depicted as a generic, nameless icon of beauty, as painters so often presented women. I note parallels between these strategies in *Urania* and those of Bigolina's contemporary, the artist Sofonisba Anguissola. Anguissola defied the limits imposed on women portraitists by applying Leon Battista Alberti's concept of *istoria,* the dramatic, narrative aspect of painting, to portraiture, a category of painting that was supposedly unable to aspire to such heights of expression. I compare Anguissola's efforts in this regard to Bigolina's own grand conceit: the latter writes a literal *istoria* (one of her terms for *Urania*) about a woman who refuses to pose for a portrait, and who instead invents a story that includes a fictional painter's failed *invenzione* ('invention,' another of Alberti's rhetorical terms applied to painting). Bigolina describes a painter who creates a woman's portrait that has a dubious moral purpose, one that is calculated to present her as a soulless icon of beauty – the very thing the authorial persona has learned to avoid. In diverse and contrasting art forms, Bigolina and Anguissola have set a similar task for themselves: to enhance the expressive potential of their aesthetic media, and to take charge of the way they are to be given life in the arts.

I begin chapter 3, 'Ekphrasis and the *Paragone*,' with an overview of the ways in which works of visual art have been described in ancient, medieval, and early modern Western literature. This overview serves as an introduction to my discussion of the treatment of the motif of painting and the visual arts in *Urania*, with emphasis on Bigolina's unique treatment of the *paragone*, the traditional comparison between the arts. I outline how the author adapts terminology appropriate to the art of painting in an allegorical proem which is meant to reject that art in favour of literature, the art form most suited to express a spiritual portrait of the individual, especially the female individual, who could not easily expect in this period to receive the requisite training to be able to express herself in the other arts. As the narrative of *Urania* unfolds, this concept is evoked yet again as an element of plot in the contrast between the work's two Venuses: Urania (who represents the Celestial Venus, and is a writer) and the duchess (the Carnal Venus, since she poses as Venus in a painting of the Judgment of Paris). Alone among the writers of her time, Bigolina associates the two Venuses with contrasting art forms, and weaves their depiction into an ornate fiction of the *paragone*. As a result, she rejects the Horatian doctrine of 'ut pictura poesis' (poetry is like a painting) that was so prevalent in contemporary theories of the arts. I also describe how she satirizes the established motif of the poetical description of the beautiful woman (*descriptio mulieris*) in a unique way, avoiding the typical satirical methods of the poet Francesco Berni and his followers, who contented themselves with parodies of *descriptio* terminology in order to depict an unattractive woman, the opposite of Francesco Petrarca's Laura. Instead, Bigolina places an ironic description of a truly lovely woman in the mouth of a character whom the reader is supposed to dislike, a painter who is moreover highly skilled (rather like Titian, in fact) at portraying lovely women. By these means, Bigolina adopts the description of the beautiful woman for her own ideological purposes, as a subtle means of rejecting the cult of feminine beauty in the arts. Whereas the standard blazon of the woman was meant to be a homage to visual art, a high-flown and often surreal literary motif that tried to reproduce the descriptive powers of painting, Bigolina converts it into a triumph of ironic literary expression by reducing it to a mundane plot element in the service of a work of realistic prose fiction, and by having it evoke a painting created for the purpose of deceiving others. Bigolina demystifies the *descriptio* instead

of revelling in it, and shows its true colours as a vehicle for the objectification of women through her description of the wily painter's scheme.
In order to emphasize the uniqueness of Bigolina's attitude towards the
standardized description of the beautiful woman, I describe extensively
the prevailing notions of woman's beauty as they appear in contemporary popular dialogues on love and beauty, especially Leone Ebreo's *I
dialoghi d'amore*, Niccolò Franco's *Dialogo dove si ragiona delle bellezze*, and
Agnolo Firenzuola's *Dialogo delle bellezze delle donne*.

Although Bigolina was doubtless influenced to some extent by Counter-
Reformation attitudes, as could be expected for any creative person of
her time and place, I assert that it is hard to identify the true spirit of
the Counter-Reformation in Bigolina's challenge to the cult of female
beauty and painted erotic mythology in *Urania*, a work almost wholly
deprived of overt references to religion. Instead, her rejection of the
validity of visual art, as well as her distrust of her culture's continual
exaltation of the sight of a woman's beauty, serve an overall purpose
that is essentially at odds with Counter-Reformation sensibilities; her
book consistently teaches women how to create valid artistic personas
for themselves, amid a culture that tended to diminish the importance
of women's contributions to aesthetic endeavour.

At the conclusion of the third chapter, I observe that Bigolina rejects
the central irony of the Boccaccesque amatory prose romances, which
appear to promote erotic love even though their stated task is to emphasize the dangers of such love. This is most evident in the motif of the
book as 'galeotto' (pander) in Boccaccio's *Filocolo*. Even though Bigolina
shares Boccaccio's interest in describing the peculiar genesis of her narrative, and is likewise inclined to discuss her book as a physical object
that may be given as a gift, she neatly avoids all the irony that Boccaccio
creates when he postulates that a book describing the dangers of erotic
love might also serve as a pander on behalf of its author. For Bigolina,
the 'galeotto' is not her book, nor indeed any other book; instead it is
the art of portraiture, the power of the visual arts to reduce the human
image to an object calculated to move a person to lust.

In the fourth chapter, 'The Sight of the Beautiful,' I explore another
of Bigolina's challenges to contemporary voices of cultural authority:
her rejection of the primacy of sight in the process of falling in love and
appreciating true beauty. I begin with a description of the passages in
Urania that describe the roles of the senses and the intellect in the appreciation of beauty, which Bigolina mostly derives from the popularized
versions of the neo-Aristotelian theories of her age, with some admixture

of Neoplatonic terminology. However, Bigolina quickly parts ways with a contemporary Neoplatonic commonplace: the notion that love and the appreciation of true celestial beauty start with the sight of physical beauty. Instead of emphasizing the direct contemplation of physical beauty, Bigolina stresses the role of the contemplation of artificial images of that beauty, specifically paintings, which for her take on a role similar to that of the *species sensibilis,* the essential go-between that served to communicate the appearance of material objects to the immaterial soul in neo-Aristotelian psychology. Bigolina's emphasis on the detached artificiality of painted images becomes a stratagem that allows her to question the role of sight in the process of cognition of both beautiful objects and the true beauty of the soul. In order to illustrate the uniqueness of her viewpoint, I provide a survey of the role of sight in the cognition of beauty in the most influential theoretical texts of the Italian Renaissance, including those of Marsilio Ficino, Giovanni Pico della Mirandola, Francesco Cattani da Diacceto, Pietro Bembo, Baldassare Castiglione, Mario Equicola, Leone Ebreo, Niccolò Franco, Sperone Speroni, Giuseppe Betussi, Tullia d'Aragona, and Bartolomeo Gottifredi. Flying in the face of such doctrinal solidarity, Bigolina sets herself the task of writing a romance on the topic of love that defies this imposing tradition by greatly diminishing, even regarding with suspicion, the role of sight in the love process. She stresses the materiality, and ultimately the very artificiality, of beauty by describing paintings that are meant to stimulate a morally inappropriate love desire. Thus, when the senses are discussed in *Urania,* the emphasis is always on the arts, either on painted images of physical beauty, or else on literary works that communicate far more effectively the spiritual beauty of the soul.

Throughout *Urania,* Bigolina consistently rejects corporeal display in art, symbolized by the sight or depiction of nude bodies, in order to demonstrate in metaphorical terms her dismissal of the attitudes expressed by authors such as Gian Giorgio Trissino, Agnolo Firenzuola, Niccolò Franco, and Federigo Luigini, who sought to present women as iconic art objects for the delectation of male eyes in their popular dialogues on beauty. I demonstrate her main point in terms of her overriding polemic: women who seek to memorialize themselves by posing for paintings, by relying entirely on a sort of passive visual display of their physical essence, will ultimately fail to make a lasting or worthy impression. However, I stress that this is not merely a colourless exercise in prudery. Bigolina makes a point of rejecting not bodies per se but rather the artistic rendering of bodies for the sole purpose of giving pleasure to the sense of sight. For Bigolina, gazing at bodies means gazing at art, and in this context I explore intriguing parallels between certain episodes in *Urania* and the psychoanalytic theories of Jean Jacques Lacan, especially as they are interpreted by the cultural critic Harry Berger. Berger postulates that Renaissance portraiture involved the painted subject's conscious act of giving himself or herself 'to be seen' (akin to Lacan's *donné-à-voir*), so that the subject seeks to provide, with the active complicity of the painter, the visual aspect of self-representation and the portrayal of the psyche according to sociopolitically correct (in Berger's terms, 'orthopsychic') norms. Berger calls this 'the fiction of the pose.' I argue that Bigolina provides an ironic dramatization of this artist-subject-viewer relationship in her narrative, with the aim of casting doubt on the ability of portraiture to communicate a proper representation of the self. Therefore, she provides us with a sort of 'fiction of the fiction of the pose,' a dynamic rendering in narrative form of the moral pitfalls inherent in the acts of posing for, and gazing upon, works of art. I conclude this chapter with a discussion of Bigolina's motif of the writing woman who proposes to offer a portrait of herself as a gift to a man she admires, a motif that also appears in the works of the poet Veronica Franco, who flourished a generation after Bigolina. Although at first glance the two writers appear to occupy divergent ideological camps with regard to their use of this motif (Bigolina quickly rejects the validity of the portrait as gift, whereas Franco appears to revel in it), I seek to demonstrate how their uses of this motif are essentially congruent: each exploits the portrait gift as a symbol of the *paragone* between the arts, with the aim of exalting the literary woman's creative abilities as well as diminishing their society's nearly obsessive glorification of the sight of a woman's physical beauty.

The final chapter, 'Kissing the Wild Woman,' deals with the varied forms of literary wildness that appear in *Urania*, starting with the pun on the name of the man to whom Bigolina dedicates the book: Bartolomeo Salvatico, whose very name means 'wild.' Since the book she writes will be her gift for the 'Wild One,' part of her literary task inevitably becomes the depiction of wildness: wild behaviour and wild people emerge as persistent elements in this extensive exploration of the metaphorical potential of marginalization and savagery. The theme of wildness permeates this romance more completely, and in more varied ways, than in any other romance I have seen. Citing especially the essential studies of literary and folkloristic wild folk by Richard Bernheimer and Roger Bartra, as well as Cesare Segre's analysis of wild behaviour in the chivalric romance, I trace the origins of Bigolina's manifestations of wildness, including the authorial persona's sight of her own 'wild' aspect in the mirror-like eye of the allegory of Judgment in the proem, as well as Urania's cross-dressed flight into the wilderness to avoid lapsing into insanity for lost love, which is modelled on the episodes of wild exile that characterize such romance protagonists as Chrétien de Troyes' Yvain, Tristan and Lancelot of the *Roman de Tristan en prose,* Boccaccio's Beritola, and Ariosto's Orlando. Moreover, *Urania* culminates with the protagonist's need to kiss the captive Wild Woman in order to free her lover from a sentence of death. I focus especially on three texts that provide intriguing antecedents to Bigolina's episode of the Wild Woman who must be kissed by a woman disguised as a man: the anonymous romance *Lestoire de Merlin,* Master Heldris's *Roman de Silence,* and Giovan Francesco Straparola's tale of Costanzo (*Le piacevoli notti,* 4.1). Here, as elsewhere, Bigolina adapts established literary motifs to suit her own purposes: although cross-dressed women are frequently seen to capture and tame wild men in older depictions, only Bigolina builds a narrative around the conflict between a cross-dressed civilized woman and her wild female counterpart, with the aim of showing how women must learn how to mimic the 'wildness' of men on occasion in order to achieve their legitimate desires, as well as make daring choices and overcome their own less civilized impulses. Urania only triumphs in her nearly impossible quest when she herself takes on the guise of a wild man by donning putrid men's clothing, showing that she has learned how to exploit fully the knowledge of the hierarchy of the senses that she has already displayed in an earlier doctrinal passage on the roles of the senses in the cognition of true beauty. When she tricks not only the Wild Woman's sense of sight but also her sense of smell, she shows the benefits of her superior ability in what I have termed 'the game of the senses,' which in turn suggests a link to the continuous Cinquecento discussions of the role of the senses in the cognition of beauty and the *paragone* of the arts. In this way Bigolina commingles the experiences of both her authorial persona and her romance protagonist: Urania reveals the same awareness of the roles of the arts and the senses in the appreciation of beauty that Bigolina herself displays in her account of how she came to write the book. Urania's kissing of the Wild Woman therefore emerges as more than a fleeting homage to older romance motifs: it also stands as a symbol for all the things, be they intellectual, social, or aesthetic, that Bigolina is seeking to communicate through her text. For this reason I have come to regard the episode as emblematic, and thus a worthy title for the book as a whole.

1   The Reformation of the Prose Romance

Bigolina's Cultural Formation

Giulia Bigolina was born in or shortly after 1516, most likely in Padua, then a part of the Republic of Venice. The Bigolin, as they are known in the local dialect, were an aristocratic Paduan family which at that time happened to include among their holdings the house in nearby Arquà that had once belonged to Francesco Petrarca.[1] It is easy to imagine that this intimate connection with the legacy of the famous poet must have been a part of the family lore during Bigolina's upbringing and that it could not have failed to impress her as she formed her own ambitions to become a writer. She is remembered today as the first Italian woman to distinguish herself in the field of prose fiction, and the first known to have written a romance in prose, one of the principal precursors to the modern novel.

Information regarding the author's life is extremely scanty.[2] The only substantial biographical reference to Bigolina during her lifetime, which ended shortly before March 1569, is that of the Paduan priest and historian Bernardino Scardeone (1478–1574), who provides a paragraph about her in his *Historiae de urbis Patavii*, published in 1560.[3] Scardeone describes Bigolina as a woman who was devoted to managing her household, yet who still found the time to write some very fine vernacular stories about love in the style of Boccaccio's *Decameron* (418). Although Scardeone declares that Bigolina's style of writing is as good as any man's, either ancient or modern, he provides only superficial information regarding her works, preferring instead to emphasize that Bigolina's stories are quite moral and proper despite their amorous content (418–19). For the next four and a half centuries, Scardeone's single paragraph remained virtually the sole source for the few literary historians who deigned to mention this author, supplemented only by the limited manuscript research of Bigolina's first editor, Anton Maria Borromeo, who published one of her stories in 1794.[4] No new research was done on her life and literary creations until the present day. However, since the start of the new millennium three modern critical editions and translations into English of Bigolina's two surviving works, the prose romance *Urania* and 'La novella di Giulia Camposanpiero et di Thesibaldo Vitaliani,' have at last been produced.[5]

The circumstances of Bigolina's education and upbringing can only be surmised. The family was not particularly well to do, although clearly the means existed to provide a dowry for the daughter of Gerolamo Bigolin and Alvisa Barbo Soncin, so that she could marry Bartolomeo Vicomercato, a native of the Lombard city of Crema, who studied law at the University of Padua.[6] Three children from this marriage reached adulthood, as is indicated in Bigolina's autograph will of June 1563 (included in the appendix of this book). Vicomercato had died at some point between 1542 and 1554, so it is likely that Bigolina pursued much if not all of her writing career as a widow.[7] Her two surviving works can be dated to the 1550s, the period in which she seems to have attained her greatest renown as a writer.[8]

The Bigolin family home (*casa di stazio*) was in the *contrada* of the Colombini, near the church of the Servi in Padua, but its exact location is not known.[9] The family had long possessed holdings in the town of Santa Croce Bigolina to the north of Padua, as well as a country villa in Selvazzano on the Bacchiglione River a few miles to the west; known as the Villa Bigolin, it still stands today, albeit abandoned and in a rather decrepit condition.[10] According to all evidence, it is quite possible that the writer spent the entire fifty-odd years of her life within these narrow confines, dealing with the typical concerns of an aristocratic wife and mother of the time. In her surviving writings, there are only two places with which she shows any real familiarity: the banks of the Bacchiglione, and Mirabello, one of the Euganean Hills that rise abruptly a few miles south of Selvazzano. The other places she mentions, such as Bologna, Vienna, Salerno, Naples, Rome, Florence, and the shrine of the Virgin in Loreto, seem to be nothing more than names on a map to her.

There is no evidence that Bigolina ever joined any of the grand literary academies of her time, such as the Accademia degli Infiammati in her native city, although she is thought to have participated in the activities of an informal group that met regularly to discuss history and the arts at the villa of the antiquary Giovannibattista Rota at Mirabello.[11] These meetings seem to have inspired the setting for Bigolina's frame story in 'La novella di Giulia Camposanpiero et di Thesibaldo Vitaliani,' and might well have provided a forum for Bigolina to promote her literary works; indeed, as Elda Martelozzo Forin indicates, Rota's wide circle of culturally active associates included Bernardino Scardeone (*La bottega dei fratelli Mazzoleni*, 91). Bigolina's will mentions that she belonged to two religious confraternities but otherwise gives no hint of any wider activity in public affairs.[12]

An unspectacular life, perhaps to be expected for a married woman and widow of the lesser nobility who lived in one of the satellite cities of the Cinquecento Venetian Republic. Opportunities, to say nothing of family encouragement, for education, travel, and public mingling with the male intelligentsia would by necessity have been in short supply. Nonetheless, Bigolina's two surviving works reveal a rich cultural formation, even if she was a very original writer who was only sporadically beholden to literary models. Her interest in the novella and prose fiction in general bespeaks familiarity with the works of Boccaccio, as Scardeone indicates; this is further borne out by her use of the name Panfilo, familiar to readers of the *Decameron*, the *Teseida*, and the *Elegia di madonna Fiammetta*, in the title of one of her lost works.[13] She also reveals some specific knowledge of such works as Francesco Petrarca's *Canzoniere*, Christine de Pizan's *Le livre de la cité des dames (The Book of the City of Ladies)*, Iacopo Caviceo's *Il libro del Peregrino*, Ludovico Ariosto's *Orlando furioso*, and Giovan Francesco Straparola's *Le piacevoli notti*.[14] The influence of Christine de Pizan, from whom Bigolina seems to have derived her interest in the humanistic defence of women, might well indicate that Bigolina had some ability to read French, since no published translation into Italian of the *Cité des dames* is known from her time.[15] Moreover, it seems apparent that Bigolina was an avid reader of the numerous dialogues and treatises on the subjects of love, manners, art, and the beauty of women that were so fashionable in Cinquecento Italy, since the concepts and terminology of these works turn up frequently in *Urania*, as will be noted in subsequent chapters.

But Bigolina's cultural interests were not limited to literary works in the vernacular. As any reader of *Urania* quickly ascertains, she was keenly interested in the art of painting, to the extent that portraiture becomes one of the work's overriding themes. We can only speculate about how she might have acquired knowledge of this art: doubtless she saw paintings in churches and aristocratic houses and was aware of the many contemporary debates on the nature and purpose of the visual arts, but she is not known to have commissioned paintings or to have corresponded with any distinguished artists. We have it on Pietro Aretino's authority that the renowned painter Titian (c. 1488–1576) at least had heard of her, but there is no evidence that the two ever met or corresponded.[16] However, as Vicenzo Mancini attests, another member of Bigolina's family is known to have had a keen interest in the visual arts. Her cousin Dioclide Bigolin (c. 1515–64) commissioned the frescoes in the Villa Bigolin and maintained a close association with the great Paduan scholar Sperone Speroni (1500–88), whose family had married into the family of Dioclide's wife, Gerolama Papafava.[17] Therefore Dioclide had opportunities to meet the distinguished artists in Speroni's circle; and as Mancini notes, he was possibly familiar with the portrait of Speroni by Titian that Speroni kept in his house.[18]

By all evidence, the painter whom Bigolina was most likely to have known personally was a Dutchman, Lambert Sustris (born c. 1515, died after 1560); he was active in Padua between 1541 and 1548 under the name Alberto d'Olanda.[19] As Mancini has determined, Sustris was quite certainly the principal artist who frescoed the walls of the Villa Bigolin, probably around the years 1544–5, while the villa was being renovated by Dioclide.[20] These were works that Bigolina must have seen on numerous occasions, and she might also have been a witness to their creation. Not all of them survive, but those that do reveal images that could have inspired the author of *Urania*, images such as allegorical figures and lively mythological scenes, including a modestly attired Venus (probably meant to portray the Celestial Venus, called 'Urania' by Plato), accompanied by her son, Cupid, as well as a pair of satyrs.[21] Before coming to Padua, Sustris had been active in the group of artists and intellectuals associated with the publisher Francesco Marcolini in Venice, a group that included the writer Lodovico Dolce (1510?–68), the architect and sculptor Iacopo Sansovino (1486–1570), Aretino, and the great Titian himself.[22] Sustris was an avid follower of Titian and was clearly inspired by him, as can be seen from his paintings of reclining nude Venuses (see figure 1.1), which closely resemble Titian's *Venus of Urbino*.[23] According to Mancini, Sustris painted more nude Venus images after his arrival in Padua (91–4). Sustris's works reveal a considerable interest in classical and mythological themes; moreover, at least two depictions of the Judgment of Paris, a subject that clearly appealed to Bigolina, have been attributed to him.[24] Bigolina's interest in erotic

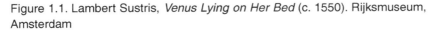

Figure 1.1. Lambert Sustris, *Venus Lying on Her Bed* (c. 1550). Rijksmuseum, Amsterdam

paintings of Venus, so evident in *Urania,* might well have derived from her knowledge of Sustris's work in her native city, if not from direct observation of the works of Titian.

Around the time that Sustris departed from Padua, Bigolina began to acquire a public persona as a writer. She is quite likely the same Bigolina who is mentioned in a poem praising the noblewomen of Padua, written by Giovanni Maria Masenetti in 1548, even though Masenetti does not single her out for special mention regarding her literary abilities or erudition, as later writers were to do.[25] The following year, she took the bold step of introducing herself to Aretino, one of the most famous cultural figures of the age, as will be discussed in the next chapter. By the mid-1550s, contemporary references indicate that Bigolina had become an established figure in the Paduan literary scene.[26]

Padua, as the seat of the distinguished university of the Venetian Republic, was renowned throughout Europe as a centre of learning. Perhaps the most prominent intellectual figure of sixteenth-century Padua was the versatile author and academician Speroni, whose long life completely encompassed Bigolina's own. In the years just before Bigolina's maturation as a writer, Padua attained some prominence for its learned debates on Italian literature and culture: aside from the prestigious Accademia degli Infiammati, which drew several distinguished writers to Padua during the first half of the 1540s, the city was also remembered for the literary salon of Beatrice Pia degli Obizzi.[27] Speroni, who presided for a time over the Infiammati, attracted considerable attention with his controversial tragedy *Canace*, and was moreover the author of several dialogues on a variety of subjects that in time would come to interest Bigolina, including the nature of love and the role of women in society. Under Speroni's guidance, and that of his follower and fellow Paduan Bernardino Tomitano (1517–76), Padua also became a centre for the ongoing debates over which form the ideal Italian literary language should assume ('la questione della lingua'), an issue that Bigolina would have had to take into account as she embarked on her literary career, as indeed did every other Italian writer of the time.[28] This was especially true given the fact that the most famous Paduan writer of the generation preceding hers, the playwright Angelo Beolco (c. 1495–1542), also known as Ruzante, had done much to establish *pavano*, the Paduan dialect, as a literary language in its own right.[29] Bigolina must have laboured under Beolco's shadow throughout her career, since his works had their greatest influence after 1548, the year in which she first gained public recognition, when they began to appear in a series of editions that served to spread Beolco's renown beyond the region of Padua.[30] However, Bigolina's own use of Paduan dialect terms is minimal and quite likely inadvertent.[31] Moreover, inasmuch as Bigolina and Beolco followed very different muses, their works bear little resemblance to one other, apart from an emphasis on Paduan settings and a certain predilection for realistic depictions of characters.[32] Beolco's very theatricality, as well as his general fondness for rustic language and themes as well as ribald bawdiness, place his works in an ideological realm that is removed from Bigolina's stories concerning the deeds of heroic high-born women in love. As will be discussed later in this chapter, by the 1550s Venice had become a centre for the publication of works of prose fiction in Italian, both novella collections and romances, and this seems to have been the literary tradition that most inspired Bigolina as she set about making a name for herself as a writer. She also must have been encouraged by the new trend in the late 1540s for the publication of women's poetry in Venice, a trend that coincided with Bigolina's own emergence on the public scene.[33]

Elements of the Prose Romance

The only contemporary account of Bigolina's literary activities that has
come down to us is Scardeone's, of 1560. Although he says she has
written 'many things worth reading' (scripsit . . . complurima lectu
dignissima), he calls special attention to 'certain comedies or fables in
Boccaccio's style' (quasdam comoedias seu fabulas, ad Boccacii morem);
thus he makes it clear that Bigolina's fame derives from her works in
prose fiction.[34] The terms that Scardeone employs reveal a certain semantic confusion, typical for writers in Latin who found themselves
confronted with literary genres that did not clearly correspond to the
parameters of classical literature. Still, Scardeone's readers would have
gotten the point: if *comoedia* was a fairly broad term that could refer to a
work that began in adversity yet ended in happiness, while *fabula* originally denoted a type of Roman comic farce or staged comedy but eventually acquired other meanings, including simply 'story' or 'narrative,'
the reference to Boccaccio makes it likely that Bigolina had made her
name as a writer of novellas, short prose narratives that descended from
the types of stories that Boccaccio had made popular in the *Decameron*
two hundred years earlier.[35] Such a literary specialty was virtually un-
heard of for an Italian woman of the day, no doubt on account of the
reputation for lasciviousness that many late medieval and early modern novella collections had acquired, both Boccaccio's and those of his
successor *novellieri;* therefore Scardeone makes a point of emphasizing
the moral propriety of Bigolina's works.[36]

So far, no more than two of Bigolina's works have come down to
us, but only one of them, 'La novella di Giulia Camposanpiero et di
Thesibaldo Vitaliani,' may be called a novella; the other, the much longer and more amply developed *Urania,* would be identified today as
a prose romance, or, by some, as a novel. Therefore we may conclude
that Bigolina's predilection for prose fiction must have been considerable, since she tried her hand at two of the predominant prose fictional
genres of her time. Medieval and early modern writers might specialize
in one or the other of these forms, but only rarely in both: Bigolina stands
as one of the few exceptions, along with Boccaccio and Cervantes.

Paul Zumthor has identified two forms of medieval 'nonsung' narrative, to be distinguished from epic, which was typically sung: romance
(in verse or prose) and novella. The novella, Zumthor says, 'tends to produce a meaning which is above all moral,' and has a universal application,

with linear action progressing from consequence to consequence until a largely predictable ending is reached, one that frequently 'corrects' the initial situation in which the characters found themselves (*Toward a Medieval Poetics*, 285). In romance, on the other hand, meaning is historical, implying consideration of time projected into the future or the past. The protagonist's description is revealed only as the story unfolds, the action is usually not linear, and the unpredictable predominates, with an ambiguous sequence of causes and effects (ibid.). Digressions are the norm in romance, providing a wealth of minute details, a 'microscopic fragmentation that amounts to literary myopia,' says Zumthor.[37] A lack of perspective results from this, since each part of the object is described as meaningful in its own right and is therefore susceptible to allegorical interpretation. Boccaccio's *Filocolo* provides a paramount example of these characteristics among the Italian prose romances of the late Middle Ages and early modern period. It is also worth noting that the digressions of the Italian prose romance might sometimes take the form of novellas, brief narrative interludes concerning plots and characters separate from the main action that can be inserted within the larger text when a more exemplary or didactic language is called for. These flourish especially in the context of dialogic *questioni dottrinali* (doctrinal debates), which are occasionally conducted by the characters in a romance: the best examples may be found in the episode of the *questioni d'amore* in the *Filocolo* (4.14–72). Some of the sixteenth-century prose romances, such as the anonymous *Compassionevoli avvenimenti di Erasto* (Mantua, 1542) and Cristoforo Armeno's *Peregrinaggio di tre giovani figliuoli del re di Serendippo* (Venice, 1557), are essentially novella collections set within elaborate frame narratives, while other works that are typically styled as *novellieri* (novella collections) might still have rather inflated frame stories of their own; among these is Girolamo Parabosco's *I diporti* (Venice, 1552).[38] The insertion of novellas within the main plot may also be a feature of the chivalric romances in verse, as in the case of the tale of Tisbina and Prasildo and the tale of Narcissus in Matteo Maria Boiardo's *Orlando innamorato* (1.12, 4–89; 2.17, 50–63), as well as the two stories told to Rinaldo in Ariosto's *Orlando furioso* (43, 10–47; 43, 71–143).

As a literary concept, 'romance' has been the source of considerable controversy, resisting easy definitions.[39] Originally the term *roman* was applied to a series of twelfth-century narrative poems in Old French that recounted episodes from classical epics, such as the anonymous *Roman de Thèbes* and Benoît de Sainte-Maure's *Le roman de Troie*, or else chivalric tales of love and marvellous adventure; the most famous and influential of these were written by Chrétien de Troyes. In the first decades of the thirteenth century some French romances began to be composed in prose instead of verse, such as the prose versions of *Lancelot* and *Tristan*. By the end of that century, similar works in prose had begun to appear in Italian as well; examples include the *Tristano Riccardiano* and the *Tristano Veneto*.[40]

Since the English terms 'novel' and 'romance' have rather distinct meanings in genre studies, Anglo-Saxon critics have had little trouble keeping these notions separate. Novels are said to be realistic, whereas romances have an air of the unreal, imbued with traces of the epic, the poetic, the mythic.[41] Sir Philip Sidney and Lady Mary Wroth wrote things in the sixteenth and early seventeenth centuries that are routinely called prose romances today, whereas the true modern novel is commonly recognized as a product of the eighteenth century; and of course we all imagine we know what modern romances are when we see them for sale in the supermarket.[42] However, such semantic distinctions must be viewed differently in the context of Italian literature, since the word *romanzo* refers to both the novel and the romance.[43] Italian literary histories that focus on the novel typically use the term *romanzo* to describe any long imaginative narrative in prose, with only occasional recourse to *romanzo in prosa* for the medieval and early modern variety.[44] In such a view, there does not appear at first glance to be any substantive difference between Boccaccio's *Filocolo* and a twentieth-century novel, nor indeed between those works and the late classical Greek romances of Longus or Heliodorus: they may all be called *romanzi*. Indeed, this usage may occasionally lead to a confusion of terminology in English studies, as is illustrated by the *Cambridge History of Italian Literature*: here the prose romances of the fifteenth and sixteenth centuries are described in two distinct sections by two different authors, one of whom uses the term 'novel' while the other prefers 'prose romance' or just 'romanzo.'[45]

Boccaccio, whose influence on late medieval and early modern Italian literature is nearly incalculable, established patterns for both long and short prose narratives that were to have considerable influence right up to Bigolina's time and beyond. The Tuscan author wrote ten narrative works in the vernacular between 1333 and 1355, roughly half of them while he was associated with the Angevin court of Naples and the rest after his return to the rather less courtly ambience of Florence. Five of these works are in verse, three are wholly in prose, and two combine both verse and prose.[46] The fact that no two of these narratives are quite alike may testify to Boccaccio's restless creativity and interest in experimentation with pre-existing literary forms, but it may also serve to disguise the fact that a common thread runs through nearly all of these works: a profound fascination with the world of sentiment and the adventures of people in love, elements that tend to bring Boccaccio's creations into the realm of romance. Indeed, those who are drawn to the often risky pursuit of attaching precise genre designations to works of medieval literature have typically found it expedient to refer to certain of his works, especially the *Filocolo*, the *Filostrato*, the *Teseida*, the *Elegia di madonna Fiammetta*, and perhaps the *Ninfale fiesolano* as well, as romances, especially as a means of distinguishing these imaginative narratives of lovers under the sway of fortune, mostly written while Boccaccio dwelt close to the aristocratic Francophile circles of the Angevin court, from such allegorical-didactic works of his Florentine period as the *Comedia delle ninfe fiorentine* and the *Amorosa visione*.[47] Moreover, it is easy to identify the romance elements in the most famous of all of Boccaccio's works, the *Decameron*, which contains a number of longer and more amply developed tales that deal with characters inspired by love while subject to adverse fortune; these are tales that some critics have designated as *novelle-romanzi*, or romance novellas.[48]

However, it is important to note that Boccaccio himself does not designate any of his works as romances; in fact, in fourteenth-century Italy the word *'romanzo'* tended to evoke French tales of questionable veracity and ethical content, the sort of thing that got Francesca and Paolo in trouble in Dante's *Inferno* 5 (vv 127–38).[49] This is evident in certain pejorative references in Boccaccio's own works, among them the *Elegia di madonna Fiammetta*, wherein the narrator wonders if 'li franceschi romanzi' can be trusted to tell actual history (8, 146), and the *Corbaccio*, Boccaccio's scathing indictment of the 'religion' of love. In the latter work Boccaccio describes a widow who keeps 'i romanzi franceschi' as if they were paternosters, despite their inherent lack of truth (74). Boccaccio also condemns romances in canto 12 of the *Amorosa visione*. Here the narrator decides that he will leave off his ekphrasis of a series of allegorical wall paintings that depict figures from Arthurian romance and the *chansons de geste*, again because he is suspicious of their historical value:

> Rietro a costoro assai ched or non metto
> seguien, perchè da dir troppo averei

e contrario al voler seria l'effetto,
   trarmi dal vulgo ancor perch'i' vorrei
delli romanzi e di lor fola scritta,
ch'ombra di istoria sol la conoscei.   (vv 37–42)

[Behind them followed many whom I do not include, because I would have
too much to recount and the result would run counter to my wish; also
because I would like to remove myself from the horde of romances and
their written nonsense, which I knew to be only the shadow of history.]

This sentiment is later echoed by Francesco Petrarca in his *Trionfo d'amore*, when he compares romances to the vanities of earthly life: 'Ben è il viver mortal, che sì n'aggrada / Sogno d'infermi e fola di romanzi' (the mortal life, so pleasing to us, is surely nothing but a dream of sick people and a fairy tale of romance, 4, 65–6). It is one thing for Petrarca, who scarcely wrote anything resembling a romance, to dismiss the genre as 'fola' (fable, nonsense), but quite another for Boccaccio to do so, especially in the 1340s, when he was still quite inclined to produce works that modern critics, in part out of convenience perhaps but also to emphasize the author's clear devotion to an established literary tradition, tend to characterize as romances. Indeed, it was difficult for any writer of the time to completely escape the shadow of romance, which has been called the major secular genre in European literature from the time of Chrétien de Troyes to Chaucer.[50] Boccaccio's most famous and influential work may be a collection of novellas, but he also established an equally enduring pattern for the Italian prose romance as it came to exist in succeeding centuries, especially with two of his earlier works in prose, the *Filocolo* and the *Elegia di madonna Fiammetta*.

The romance has been said to have had 'a vexed treatment' at the hands of many literary historians.[51] The ancient Greeks had romances but no theories to expound about them, not even a ready term to describe them: the Greeks were supposed to have had a word for everything, but their theorists did not make much effort to define the long prose love stories that enjoyed so much popularity among the Hellenized literate masses in the first centuries of the Christian era.[52] By and large, classical theorists disdained them, if they mentioned them at all, and some of that prejudice carried through into the early modern era, even after the late medieval romances of chivalry had risen to prominence, providing new settings, topoi, and vocabulary for the adventurous tale of love.[53] The early modern controversy began with the rediscovery and dissemination of Aristotle's *Poetics* in the 1530s, which led many to condemn the chivalric romances of Boiardo and Ariosto for their violation of classical ideals of unity, verisimilitude, and cohesive structure.[54] Defenders of these works responded vociferously. Two of these, Giovan Battista Giraldi Cinthio and Giovanni Battista Pigna, both published their treatises in 1554, around the time Bigolina was writing *Urania*. Meanwhile, other classical texts were also becoming widely available in Italian translations known as *volgarizzamenti* that were more or less accurate: the Greek love stories of the first centuries of the Christian era, often referred to as novels by modern Anglo-Saxon critics because they are in prose. Annibal Caro's *volgarizzamento* of Longus's *Daphnis and Chloe* appeared in manuscript around 1537, while *Leucippe and Clitophon*, written by Achilles Tatius in the second century, was first published in an Italian version by Francesco Angelo Coccio in 1550. These were followed by Leonardo Ghini's rendering of *Aithiopica* by Heliodorus, often regarded as the best of the surviving Greek romances, in 1556.[55]

Four distinct threads of romance were present in Italy during Bigolina's time: chivalric, moral, pastoral, and amatory. Chivalric romances, descended from French verse narratives of the twelfth century and often dealing with Arthurian legend, classical tales, or the events of the age of Charlemagne, had become immensely popular in the hands of the Italian *cantastorie*, or itinerate storytellers, as well as in the works of poets such as Luigi Pulci, Boiardo, and Ariosto. These long eclectic poems in octaves on chivalric subjects were generally what sixteenth-century Italians had in mind when they spoke of *romanzi*, as Giraldi Cinthio attests: 'io stimo ch'altro non sia dire opere di romanzi che poema et compositione di cavalieri forti' (I consider that works of romance mean nothing more than a poem, a composition that deals with valiant knights; *Discorsi intorno*, 14). The moral type of romance may best be represented by the anonymous and quite popular *Compassionevoli avvenimenti di Erasto* (1542), a prose work inspired by a medieval collection of exemplary tales, *Il libro dei sette savi*.[56] A variety of narratives on pastoral themes that combined prose and poetry, inspired by Jacopo Sannazaro's *Libro pastorale nominato Arcadia* (1504), were also produced in this period, constituting the type of the pastoral romance.[57]

Amatory romance, called variously by Italians *romanzo d'amore, romanzo erotico*, or *romanzo idillico*, is the category to which Bigolina's *Urania* must be assigned, and therefore is of the greatest importance here.[58] Ultimately its origins may be traced back to the ancient Greek love stories mentioned above, but its more immediate presence in European literature derives from the twelfth-century French verse romance *Floire et Blancheflor* and the subsequent works that it inspired: here for the first time in the medieval romance tradition the private lives of young people in love are emphasized, instead of the destinies of rival peoples or sovereigns, or the quest of the hero.[59] This sort of subject matter, set within an intricate and convoluted plot, reflects the influence of the Greek love stories and perhaps such medieval Byzantine descendants as *Hysmine and Hysminias* by Eustathius Macrembolites, which typically recount similar tales of the travails of separated lovers who are ultimately reunited. The story proved popular, as later versions such as the early fourteenth-century Italian *Cantare di Florio e Biancifiore* attest. Subsequently, in the 1330s, Boccaccio recast it in the form of a lengthy prose romance in five books, the *Filocolo*. This book, which was to have considerable influence on later Italian authors right up to Bigolina's time, established the amatory prose romance as a phenomenon that was clearly distinct from the more clamorous romances of Tristano and other prose narratives that adhered to the chivalric romance tradition.

Thus Boccaccio was the first great Italian writer to make extensive use of the amatory romance tradition, both in his *Filocolo* and in the *novelle-romanzi* of the *Decameron*. His *Elegia di madonna Fiammetta* also shares some features with the typical amatory romance, even if it is largely deprived of action and movement, as well as the traditional final union of the lovers. Moreover, Boccaccio's fascination with this literary mode led him to write the novella of Alatiel (*Decameron, 2.7*), which has been called a parody of the old Greek stories in which the kidnapped or shipwrecked heroine must withstand continual threats to her chastity.[60] Boccaccio's influence, conjoined with the model of the Greek romances as they became better known, ensured that subsequent amatory romances would tend to be written in prose, although there were a few exceptions, such as the anonymous fifteenth-century *Istoria di due nobilissimi amanti Ottinello e Giulia,* which was composed in octaves in the fashion of the *cantari*.[61]

The Plot and Characters of *Urania*

Scardeone said that Bigolina made her name as a writer of love stories like those of Boccaccio, but he does not specify if by this he meant only the relatively brief novellas of the *Decameron*, or if he would also include Boccaccio's more elaborate narratives such as the *Filocolo* and the *Fiammetta*. However, during a brief period of renewed interest in

Bigolina's works a few centuries later, for which Scardeone was by far the most useful source, Bigolina is exclusively described as an author of novellas, not romances in prose: for instance, *Urania* is characterized by both Anton Maria Borromeo and Bartolommeo Gamba as nothing more than a long novella.[62] With these earlier assessments in mind, let us now examine the contents and structure of *Urania, nella quale contiene l'amore d'una giovane di tal nome,* to see what kind of work it actually is.

Bigolina begins her book with a first-person introduction that is quite separate from the main narrative; it is addressed to Bartolomeo Salvatico, a Paduan doctor of law. Bigolina's authorial 'I' explains that she would like to leave to Salvatico a token that will help him remember her and her great affection for him. She says her first plan was to have an artist paint her portrait so that she could give it to Salvatico as a gift, but then an allegorical figure comes to visit her and explain that her decision is a mistake. The figure appears as a little naked man with a large head and single large eye like a mirror, who calls himself Giudicio (Judgment). Bigolina's authorial persona sees herself reflected in the shining eye, also naked and with stains on the left side of her body that represent the vices that stain her soul. The homunculus speaks at length, excoriating various human types for their errors in judgment and showing sympathy for the plight of women, who are so often falsely accused of wrongdoing. He tells the author that her decision to have herself painted shows bad judgment on her part, since it would be a vain and useless gesture for communicating the chaste and heartfelt love she bears Salvatico. He pities her a bit for her naive questions, in scenes reminiscent of Beatrice's reaction to Dante's confusion when he reaches paradise,[63] then explains how she would do better to leave the young man something that she has created herself, within her own intellect and by her own powers. At this point the little man disappears in a flash, and Bigolina's authorial persona is left to ponder the significance of the vision. Searching within her mind, or more specifically within her 'basso intelletto' (low intellect), she spontaneously conceives of an *operetta* (little work) that will bear the name *Urania,* since it will describe the adventures of a woman by that name.[64] She offers this narrative to Salvatico as her gift, hoping he will derive some benefit from it and not fall into error himself, as young men are so often wont to do.

The third-person narrative that follows unfolds at considerable length, 154 folios in the manuscript Trivulziana 88, a little over a hundred printed pages; surely longer than anything traditionally called a novella.

Moreover, it is subdivided into six chapters, recalling the subdivision into five books of Boccaccio's *Filocolo*.

Chapter 1 opens in Salerno, in the days when it was ruled by the great Prince Giufredi (who is not a historical figure).[65] Urania is a young unmarried woman who lives there with her mother, renowned for her virtue and indifference to the men who seek her love. A nobleman named Fabio falls in love with her simply from hearing reports of her excellent character, whereupon he contrives to meet her at a party and begin a chaste relationship, consisting of discreet meetings at her house and an exchange of love letters and sonnets. In time, however, Fabio is distracted by another woman named Clorina, who is said to be more beautiful than Urania but less virtuous. In a fit of depression, Urania writes a long letter to Fabio explaining how wrong he has been to leave her for someone of such small spirit and intelligence, for someone who is incapable of communicating her heartfelt feelings through literature and thus can leave no better memorial of herself in her absence than a painted portrait. The text of the letter is over ten folios long in Trivulziana 88 (26r–37v), encompassing nine pages in the 2004 edition (90–106).

In chapter 2, we see Urania dress as a man of high degree and ride out of Salerno alone, resolved to try to forget her misery by subjecting herself to the rigours of travel. Weeping, she expresses herself aloud with heartfelt laments, as her horse wanders where it will. In a beautiful woodland setting north of Naples she meets five young women beside a spring, who awaken her from her reverie and press her to give them advice about how to choose an ideal lover. Since they imagine her to be a man, she tells them that her name is Fabio. She holds forth at length on the requested subject and impresses her hearers with her wisdom; this whole episode is clearly meant to evoke the *questioni d'amore* format that Boccaccio made fashionable for the Italian prose romance. When Urania has finished her discourse, the ladies invite her to join them for a garden party at one of their residences, after which they all turn in for the night. The ladies are quite taken with their disguised guest, who seems to represent the very ideal lover that they all seek; however, Urania herself is still depressed to the point of suicide on account of Fabio.

Chapter 3 begins with Urania resuming her ride, still wandering aimlessly. Before long she meets five young Neapolitan men exercising a falcon in a meadow. They shake her back to her senses very roughly, which offends her, so she lectures them on how gentlemen should act.

By chance these men are in love with the five ladies Urania has met the previous day, so they bring her to a palace in the hopes of discovering what sort of advice she had given the ladies, and what sort of advice she might give to them regarding how to choose the best woman as a lover. This leads to an extended discussion of the worth of women, with Urania (still thought to be a man by her listeners) challenging the men's misogynist beliefs. She lists the accomplishments of famous women of classical history, mythology, and legend, as well as a few from the Old Testament, claiming they can hardly be worse than the wickedest men. She then explains how a wise man may identify and choose a wise and virtuous woman as a mate. Her own words remind her of her miserable state and leave her close to tears.

In chapter 4, Urania rides on alone until she collapses before an inn in Tuscany, emotionally and physically exhausted. She is restored to health by Emilia, a young aristocratic widow who is lodging there. Urania continues to pretend she is Fabio, the young man of Salerno who was supposedly rejected by his lover Urania. Emilia finds herself attracted to this 'Fabio.' The two ride together to fulfil Emilia's vow to visit the shrine at Loreto; then they continue on to Emilia's house in Florence. There Emilia's love for 'Fabio' grows, to the extent that she defies her family by refusing an offer of remarriage. To 'Fabio's' distress, Emilia offers herself in marriage to him instead. Urania can think of no way out of this situation, save to say that, as 'Fabio,' she must return to Salerno to try to restore her relationship with 'Urania,' 'Fabio's' erstwhile lover. Emilia insists on riding along with her beloved, also disguised as a nobleman, and Urania finds she must acquiesce.

At this point the narrative abruptly shifts without a chapter break, to return to the real Fabio back in Salerno. He has been much distressed to read Urania's letter and hear of her sudden departure but still cannot refrain from pursuing the love of Clorina, the woman who is quite attractive but not as accomplished or virtuous as Urania. However, the fickle Clorina is soon drawn to a dashing Sicilian braggart named Menandro. Fabio is dismayed but continues to frequent Clorina's house anyway, unwilling to create a scandal.

Chapter 5 begins with another narrative shift, and the introduction of a whole new set of characters. We hear of the nineteen-year-old Duchess of Calabria, who, upon the death of her husband the duke, has been left to rule her realm alone, with the assistance of an elderly counsellor. She is devoted to religion and virtue. Her greatest passion is collecting portraits of renowned rulers and other individuals, which she displays in a personal portrait gallery. In order to keep her collection stocked, she employs an artist, said to be the most famous of the time, and sends him out regularly to make portraits of distinguished people. However, the duchess's happy existence is soon made miserable by Love, who cannot allow her to resist his power. The duchess's painter happens to go to Salerno, where he secretly paints the portrait of Prince Giufredi and brings it back to Calabria. When the duchess sees the portrait, she falls hopelessly in love with the man shown there and is soon sick to the point of death. She reveals the source of her distress to the old counsellor and asks for his help in gaining the prince's hand in marriage; however, the duchess wants to bring this about in such a way that the prince will have no idea that she is pursuing him. The counsellor is not surprised to hear of her condition, since he knows the power and nature of Love. He consults with the painter and tells him his plan: they will conspire to create a painting of the Judgment of Paris, with the likenesses of various famous ruling women in place of the three goddesses. The duchess herself will be portrayed as Venus giving the golden apple to Paris, whose features will be those of the Prince of Salerno; in this way, the conspirators hope to cause the prince to fall in love with the woman depicted in the painting. The duchess, in her desperation forgetting her usual love of virtuous propriety, agrees to pose semi-nude for the painting, draped in a red mantle. When the work is finished the painter takes it to Salerno to present it to the prince. Once it is unveiled, he describes all the details of how he created it, waxing ecstatic about the duchess's physical charms as they are shown by his artistry. As the prince gazes at the painting, he finds himself moved to lust, but not for the woman whose image he sees. Instead, the painting makes the prince wonder about the body of a certain lady he has long been courting, whom he now wishes fervently to marry. However, the painter does not realize this, and slyly reveals the identity of the woman who posed as Venus even while pretending to be reluctant to do so.

Now the next part of the conspiracy is played out. The old counsellor arrives in Salerno bearing a rose garland, from an exotic bush in the duchess's garden, whose blooms will not fade for an entire year after they have been plucked. He presents the garland to the prince, saying that it is a magical object he has received from a grateful fairy whose life he has saved. The garland, he says, has the power to make any woman fall in love with the man who gives it to her. The counsellor secretly hopes that the prince will want to give the garland to the duchess as a sign of his desire for her. The prince, however, has other plans.

The woman he has been courting, discreetly identified here only as the Wise Damsel (la Savia Damigella), will be returning to Salerno soon, so the prince prepares to receive her, with the garland that he intends to bestow upon her hanging in the palace hall. This causes Clorina to burn with envy, so she subtly encourages Fabio and Menandro to steal it as a means of proving their love for her. The two men both sneak into the hall and end up fighting for possession of the garland, which leads to their capture by the palace guard. The prince now must decide what to do with them. Both deserve death for such a crime, but the prince, sensitive to matters of honour, does not wish to appear to play favourites by sparing Fabio, who is quite popular among the citizens of Salerno. Menandro, on the other hand, is a foreigner and much disliked. The prince decides to let Clorina choose one of the two as a husband; the other will be executed within three days unless some maid loves him enough to risk her own life by kissing the Wild Woman (la Femina Salvatica), a subhuman creature who lives in chains in the palace. The Wild Woman tries to kill any woman who approaches her, convinced that a woman was responsible for the death of her beloved consort, the Wild Man (l'Huomo Salvatico). The prince is certain Clorina will choose Fabio, as her family and the rest of the city urge her to do, but in fact she chooses Menandro. Subsequently, many young women of Salerno make an effort to kiss the Wild Woman, since the prince has offered the handsome Fabio in marriage to anyone who can succeed in doing this, but the ferocious Wild Woman proves to be unapproachable, even when the claimants try to dress as men. The narrative focuses next on Fabio, languishing in prison. He voices a long lament for his lost Urania, whom he now knows to have been the most excellent of all women, then has a dream in which he sees a fantastic re-enactment of his love affairs, with animals or mythological creatures standing in for the participants. As a result, he comes to realize that he truly loves Urania.

In chapter 6, the disparate threads of narrative come together. Urania and Emilia, both dressed as men, ride into Salerno on the evening of the third day of the test with the Wild Woman. When Urania hears that her lover Fabio is about to be executed because no maid is able to rescue him, she resolves to make the effort herself. First, however, she has to explain to Emilia what she is doing and why, and who this other Fabio is. She says the man in prison is the brother of her erstwhile lover, Urania, and if she fails to save him from death, Urania will surely die of grief. Emilia, who knows her companion does not return her love, says she is willing to kiss the Wild Woman herself: if she cannot have one Fabio, she will settle for the other in order to remain close to the one she actually loves. This notion leaves Urania a bit jealous. She pursues her own plan for winning the contest: she changes her aristocratic male costume for another which is filthy and malodorous. When she and Emilia approach the Wild Woman, Emilia is so terrified that she forgets all her former resolve, whereupon Urania lectures her on how true lovers must remain steadfast in the face of all danger in order to save those they love. Urania then approaches the Wild Woman, who is tricked by the smell of the filthy garments into believing Urania is really a man. The Wild Woman is quite fond of men, so she embraces and kisses Urania at some length, in front of numerous witnesses. Urania is brought before the prince; she requests that Fabio be allowed to join her there, so the stage is set for a grand recognition scene, a typical feature of Greek romance. Urania, who still appears to be a man, tells an elaborate story of how she recently wandered north to the regions near Padua, where she met a young woman dressed as a man, who killed herself out of despair for a lost love. Urania pretends, in effect, to have met herself, and to report her own suicide out of grief for Fabio. She gives Fabio her ring as proof. Fabio is moved, and tells the prince of all that transpired between him and Urania and how he realizes only now that Urania was the best of all women. At this point Urania reveals her true identity, to the astonishment of those who are present. She then makes up yet another complicated story to explain who Emilia is and why she is dressed as a man, so that her honour may be preserved. The Prince decrees that everyone is to be married: Urania with Fabio, Emilia with Hortensio, Fabio's brother, and the Prince with the Savia Damigella. The disgraced courtiers from Calabria, who had tried to trick the prince with a painting into marrying their duchess, are sent home; and when the duchess learns that the prince has rejected her she dies from grief. The three married couples live happily ever after.

Bigolina's *Urania* belongs quite plainly to the tradition of the amatory romance. Indeed, it follows the broadest outlines of the typical Greek romance plot, as well as the plot of the *Filocolo*: young people fall in love, become separated, and undergo various trials including a rescue from execution, until at last hidden identities are revealed in a joyful recognition scene and the lovers are united in marriage. Even Odysseus, the oldest romance hero in Western literature, has left a few traces in the character of Urania, who is always ready to use elaborate lies and disguises to further her ends.[66] Northrop Frye has said that the typical romance hero is superior in degree to other men and to his environment, and that he is capable of marvellous deeds (33). This is more easily said of chivalric romance, which Frye doubtless had in mind, than of amatory romance, wherein random fate often plays as great a role as superior ability; nonetheless, Frye's dictum may be comfortably applied to Bigolina's character Urania, who can accomplish great things and succeed where others cannot. She does not end up like Boccaccio's Fiammetta of the *Elegia di madonna Fiammetta*, defeated, ineffective, and miserable, even if she might be said to start out like her.

But Bigolina's romance is also very eclectic and may be seen to employ certain motifs that evoke chivalric romance or epic, such as the heroine's encounter with a monstrous creature, the need to pass a fearsome test in order to win love, and the character of the aristocrat whose true identity is unknown until a dramatic unmasking occurs. Following a standard pattern of movement in the chivalric romance, Urania leaves home on a sort of quest and returns to her prince's court when she has proven herself.[67] As will be discussed in the final chapter, Urania's headlong flight into a life of wandering in isolation reminds us of the actions of such chivalric romance heroes as Yvain, Tristan, and Orlando, even if she is rather more successful in avoiding descent into total madness than is the typical male romance protagonist.

In many ways, Urania resembles the stock romance hero, who is usually a man, but who might also be a woman thought to be a man. As a character, Urania is descended from the doughty heroines of certain medieval narratives who take matters into their own hands and solve problems, such as Nicolette in *Aucassin and Nicolette*, or Boccaccio's Giletta di Nerbona (*Decameron*, 3.9), but also from a gallery of cross-dressed heroines such as Jehanne from the thirteenth-century *Roman dou roi Flore et de la belle Jehanne*, Lionessa from Antonio Pucci's *Cantare di Madonna Lionessa*, and Boccaccio's Zinevra (*Decameron*, 2.9), all of whom use their wits to resolve problems and accomplish grand things while thought to be men. Another such narrative, *Istoria di due nobilissimi amanti Ottinello e Giulia*, not only includes the clever Giulia, who cross-dresses and calls herself Giulio, but it might also have provided Bigolina with the motif of a desperate lover fleeing Salerno in disguise (although here the male character does it).[68] More or less contemporaneous with *Urania* and having some parallels with it is Matteo Bandello's novella of Nicuola Nanni, a girl who must dress as a page boy and infiltrate the household of her wayward lover in order to win him back.[69] Cross-dressed women may also be found in the chivalric context, as in the case of Silence in *Roman de Silence* of the thirteenth century, attributed to Master Heldris of Cornwall, and the women warriors of the *Orlando innamorato* and *Orlando furioso.* These women are not only resourceful, but also capable of fighting as well as men. Moreover, as will be noted in the final chapter, the *Roman de Silence* provides another example of a chivalric motif recycled by Bigolina in an essentially non-chivalric context, that of the test of courage or skill that can only be achieved by a woman. When Urania proves herself to be the only woman capable of passing the prince's test and kissing the Wild Woman, by grace of her male disguise, a parallel can be seen in Silence's capture of Merlin while similarly disguised, thereby fulfilling the sorcerer's own prophecy that he could only be captured by a woman (see Heldris, *Silence,* 271–309). Another old romance motif that influences Bigolina is that of the heroine who rides up at the last minute, sometimes disguised as a man and sometimes not, in order to rescue her beloved from a judicial sentence, as can be seen in *Lanval,* a twelfth-century *lai* (brief verse romance) by Marie de France, as well as in Ser Giovanni Fiorentino's *novella-romanzo* of the lady of Belmonte (*Pecorone,* 4.1), Pucci's *Madonna Lionessa,* and the anonymous *Cantare di Madonna Elena,* all of the fourteenth century.[70]

By Bigolina's time the chivalric romance in verse reigned supreme in Italy, as a result of the great popularity of poets such as Boiardo and Ariosto. On the other hand, the early modern Italian prose romance is a genre famously neglected by authors and critics alike. Even after its distinguished debut in the form of Boccaccio's *Filocolo,* the prose romance scarcely flickered on the horizon of Italian literature throughout the following two centuries. As Alberto Albertazzi notes, Renaissance Italy put far more emphasis on the novella than on the prose romance, whenever it had a mind to generate works of prose fiction.[71] Thus only a handful of Italian prose romances were produced between Boccaccio's time and the end of the Cinquecento, and none of them, unless we consider Sannazaro's pastoral *Arcadia,* which includes passages in verse as well as prose, were written by authors of the first rank. The early modern prose romance often appears amorphous and difficult to characterize, hovering in a tense narrative space where ancient Greek romances, medieval didactic allegory, chivalric romances, and the novella all intersect.[72] In spite of this, or perhaps because of it, critics have tended to avoid comparing or analysing the few works that belong to this category. Now that the recent rediscovery and publication of *Urania* has swelled the ranks of this neglected corner of the Italian literary canon somewhat, the moment seems opportune to re-examine the sources and definitions of the genre, with the aim of creating a literary context for Bigolina's work.

The Prose Romance according to Boccaccio

The phenomenon of the Italian amatory prose romance derives from the literary experiments of Boccaccio, as is the case with so much else in early modern Italian literature. As we have noted, two of Boccaccio's early prose works are said to have provided an essential inspiration to the prose romances of the fifteenth and sixteenth centuries: the *Filocolo* and the *Elegia di madonna Fiammetta*. To a lesser extent, the later romances also reveal traces of the influence of two other works by Boccaccio that are either partly or wholly in prose and likewise deal with the topic of love, the *Comedia delle ninfe fiorentine* and the *Corbaccio*.[73]

It has been observed that Boccaccio does not call any of his works *romanzi*. The only term he actually does apply to the *Filocolo* is 'picciolo libretto' (little book, 1.1, 7–8) despite its sprawling length and numerous digressions, as well as its division into five chapters, which he calls 'libri,' in the tradition of classical epic. Boccaccio's story of the lovers Florio and Biancifiore, told in the third person, is set in the waning days of the Roman Empire. It traces its separated and put-upon protagonists across the Mediterranean, from Spain to Italy, to Greece and to Egypt, then back to Italy and Spain again, ending with their conversion to Christianity and Florio's accession to the throne of Spain. Into this dense narrative, which has been called the first original novel written in Italian, Boccaccio weaves a fantastic account of his own life, veiled within allegorical episodes.[74] In this work, Boccaccio's concept of the prose romance is very eclectic: he includes classical and medieval elements, paganism as well as Christianity, short narratives, etiological accounts, epic battle scenes, and occasional pastoral interludes.

We can only speculate as to why Boccaccio decided that the old story of Floire and Blancheflor, which had been retold often by poets, now required a version in prose. In his first chapter he has his character Fiammetta claim, rather like Chrétien de Troyes at the beginning of *Erec et Enide,* that this fine old story has suffered at the hands of oral storytellers and thus ought to be set down in a superior written version.[75] However, as is well known, Boccaccio subsequently was to display no aversion to writing romances in *ottava rima,* the verse form made popular by the scarcely erudite *cantastorie,* as his *Filostrato* and *Teseida* attest. Moreover, he shows he is fully aware of the novelty of the *Filocolo*'s form when he refers to his work as 'nuovi versi' (strange verses) in his second chapter (1.2, 9). It is therefore difficult to say what prompted him to rewrite the story in prose instead of verse. We can only speculate that he might have been aiming to evoke the atmosphere of the Greek romances in prose, or else he imagined that a prose format would best suit his intention to present a debate on the nature of love, the *questioni d'amore*, which is the doctrinal centrepiece of the *Filocolo*.

On the other hand, the *Elegia di madonna Fiammetta* is a very different work. Since it is relatively short and quite deprived of digressions, it has been described by Natalino Sapegno as a sort of extended novella.[76] The protagonist, Fiammetta, tells her story in the first person, unlike the third-person *Filocolo*, and since the emphasis is on her shifting moods and emotional states while she copes with the disappearance of her faithless lover, Panfilo, it has been called the first psychological novel in the Western tradition.[77] Fiammetta addresses her story to an ideal audience of women, whom she hopes will feel sorry for her when they hear her woeful tale of love and abandonment. Most of the trappings of medieval romance, which are substantially present in the *Filocolo*, are missing here: apart from the oddity of a first-person narration by a woman and the complete lack of quests, adventures, or a happy resolution of the love crisis, the narrative is not set in an exotic realm or in a legendary time but rather in contemporary Naples. Realism is stressed in the *Fiammetta,* since the supernatural is confined to dreams and visions, which mostly centre on epiphanies of Venus as the cruel mistress of Fiammetta's life. A generation ago Robert Hollander demonstrated how Boccaccio's vernacular works had been misread for centuries as exaltations of carnal or courtly love, whereas they actually appear to promote Christian ethics and *amore onesto;* when this perspective is applied to the *Fiammetta,* the protagonist's anguished prayers for the restitution of her beloved Panfilo, directed by turns to both Venus (5, 69) and the Christian deity (5, 100–1), become supremely ironic.[78]

Once more, we must ask: why did Boccaccio choose to write this book in prose, and what are the elements that tempt us to call it a romance today? Despite the contemporary theme and setting, it seems his inspirations were primarily classical rather than medieval: Fiammetta's anguished first-person indictment evokes certain of Ovid's *Heroides,* especially the second, in which Phyllis excoriates her lover, Demophoön, whereas her nurse's extended condemnation of the god of Love (1, 17) is derived almost precisely from an analogous scene in Seneca's tragedy of *Phaedra.*[79] Moreover, Boccaccio calls the work an elegy in the title, which seems to suggest classical pretensions, even if in ancient usage the term only referred to a poem written in elegiac metre that did not necessarily treat a melancholy subject.[80] Although Boccaccio's usage of the term *elegia* likely derives from the *De vulgari eloquentia* (2.4), there Dante simply says that the term denotes a poetic style appropriate to sad subject matter.[81] Thus elegy, for the ancients and for Dante, was a term to be applied exclusively to poetry, although for the ancients it was more a matter of form while for Dante it was a matter of style. However, as Cesare Segre has noted, medieval vernacular translations of classical narratives tended to be in prose, even if the original was in verse; this seems to have been the tradition that inspired Boccaccio to create an original Italian version, replete with chapter divisions as if it were a romance, of one of Ovid's *Heroides*.[82]

Thus Boccaccio presents us with two experimental prose fiction narratives, one of them retelling a medieval verse *roman* in a form resembling that of an ancient Greek prose romance, the other calling itself an 'elegy' and seemingly the author's own invention, although it owes a considerable stylistic debt to Ovid's verse epistles and a tragedy of Seneca. Despite these profound differences, it is clear that Boccaccio regarded these two efforts of his as distinct from his other works. Near the beginning of the *Filocolo*, he provides this explanation of what the work will, and more importantly will not, contain:

E voi, giovinette amorose, le quali ne' vostri dilicati petti portate l'ardenti fiamme d'amore più occulte, porgete le vostre orecchi con non mutabile intendimento a'nuovi versi: li quali non vi porgeranno i crudeli incendimenti dell'antica Troia, nè le sanguinose battaglie di Farsaglia, le quali nell'animo alcuna durezza vi rechino; ma udirete i pietosi avvenimenti dello innamorato Florio e della sua Biancifiore, li quali vi fieno graziosi molto. (1.2, 9)

[And you, loving young ladies, who carry the burning flames of love hidden more deeply within your delicate bosoms, lend your ears and your unwavering attention to these strange verses, which will not offer you the cruel burning of ancient Troy, nor the bloody battles of Pharsalia, lest these things bring harshness to your spirits. Instead, you will hear of the pitiable adventures of the enamoured Florio and his Biancifiore, which will be most pleasing to you.]

Although the ancient world had no trouble distinguishing a prose love story from an epic poem, Boccaccio finds it necessary to define what he is doing in this work of 'strange verses' in terms that emphasize the pre-vailing tension between the *romanzo d'amore* and the various medieval pseudo-epic retellings of the wars of Troy or ancient Rome.[83] Whereas an ancient epic typically began with a lofty declaration of its narrative contents, in the tradition of Virgil's 'arma virumque cano' (I sing of arms and the man, 1 v.1), Boccaccio's new and unusual *Filocolo* must take pains to explain to its reader how it will follow a different course, one dispensing with an emphasis on wars or the destruction of cities.

In fact, Boccaccio inserts a similar disclaimer at the beginning of two of his other works that would prove inspirational to later prose ro-mances, revealing that he was well aware that a narrative in prose on the subject of love would have to be reconciled somewhat with the ex-pectations of his readers. In the first chapter of the *Comedia delle ninfe fiorentine,* Boccaccio uses the same formula to establish the precise mythological context for the work: 'non i triunfi di Marte, non le las-civie di Bacco, non le abbondanze di Cerere, ma del mio prencipe le vittorie mi si fa di cantare' (not of the triumphs of Mars, not of the las-civiousness of Bacchus, not of the abundance of Ceres, but rather of the victories of my prince will I sing, 1, 680). The prince in question is Love, the lord of this narrator's life. The conflict here is not the same as that of the *Filocolo,* between epic (which treats of war) and romance (which treats of love); nonetheless, the phrasing is quite similar and is clearly meant to evoke the passage in the earlier work. Then, in the prologue to *Fiammetta,* the formula is repeated yet again:

> Voi sole, le quali io per me medesima conosco pieghevoli e agli infortunii pie, priego che leggiate; voi, leggendo, non troverete favole greche ornate di molte bugie, né troiane battaglie sozze per molto sangue, ma amorose, stimolate da molti disiri ... (Prologo, 3)

> [I pray that only you ladies, who I myself know to be compassionate and sympathetic to misfortunes, will read this book; while reading, you will not find Greek fables adorned with many lies, nor Trojan battles filthy with much blood, but rather amorous battles, stimulated by many desires ...]

The warfare of love will take the place of the more traditional sort of warfare that the reader of an ancient or medieval epic would have come to expect, suggests Boccaccio; and by coming to terms with the differences between *romanzo d'amore* and epic, he shows he is fully aware of the literary novelty implicit in these prose works, which are otherwise quite dissimilar.

Of the three works by Boccaccio that include this type of 'disclaimer,' two in particular most plainly appear to belong among the ancestors of the Renaissance prose romance, and thus of *Urania* as well: *Filocolo* and *Fiammetta*. (The extensive allegorical trappings and the otherworldly mythological setting for the love story, as well as the intrusion of numerous poems, set the *Comedia delle ninfe fiorentine* in a somewhat different category.) The *Filocolo* has a considerable number of features in common with *Urania*. These include the narrator's opening account of how the book came to be written, the use of the third person for the main narrative, the lengthy episode of love debates or *questioni d'amore*, and the happy ending, which sees Florio and Biancifiore united in marriage. But *Fiammetta*, too, contributes much to Bigolina's romance, most obviously in its emphasis on a female protagonist who suffers great mental anguish after she has been abandoned by her lover, but also in its depiction of a real-world setting in contemporary Italy; in fact, both books are set in the same part of Italy, one in Naples, the other in Salerno.[84] Moreover, as it has been noted, *Fiammetta* resembles *Urania* in that it is much shorter and more cohesive than the *Filocolo*.

After Boccaccio, the prose *romanzo d'amore* nearly disappeared from Italian literature for a time, and through much of the Quattrocento it is difficult to find works to which the term might be applied. Modern critics have employed it in the case of Giovanni Gherardi da Prato's *Paradiso degli Alberti*, a complex work written in the 1420s that begins with the authorial persona's account of an allegorical vision of the nature of love.[85] However, the narrative eventually shifts to a sort of Ciceronian dialogue, a series of erudite conversations held in various Tuscan villas, with luminaries of late Trecento Florence as interlocutors. Much of the text is taken up with novellas recounted by these famous men, and indeed the *Paradiso* has been published in Salerno Editrice's series 'I novellieri italiani' as a novella collection.[86] However, echoes of the *Filocolo* abound in Gherardi's amorphous book, and indeed the *Filocolo*, as a long, digressive work which in turn contains shorter narratives built around *questioni dottrinali*, does provide an essential model for the *Paradiso*, even though the latter work does not describe a love story like that of Florio and Biancifiore, and in fact purports to recount actual conversations between historical figures, to which the author claims to have been a witness.[87] The surest link to the *Filocolo*, and to Boccaccio's concept of the prose romance in general, lies in the disclaimer which Gherardi provides in his introduction: as in the case of Boccaccio's prose romances, Gherardi seeks to define a long prose work in terms of what it is not. The author says the book will not deal with oratory, which is more befitting a work of history, nor will it be a poem, a comedy, a tragedy, or a satire; instead, it will record the happy conversations of a group of kindred spirits (*Paradiso*, 6–7).

In the *Filocolo*, and also to some extent in the *Comedia delle ninfe fiorentine*, Boccaccio established an enduring pattern for the Italian prose romance as a long and frequently erudite work, which in turn could serve as a vehicle for a series of shorter, discrete literary forms such as novella-like narratives, doctrinal debates, and poems. With these models in mind, we may more readily distinguish between prose romances and the longer novellas that became fashionable in the Quattrocento, and which were sometimes not part of novella collections, such as 'La novella del Grasso legnaiuolo' by Antonio Manetti, or the anonymous 'Novella del Bianco Alfani.' Another of these, 'Justa Victoria' by Felice Feliciano of Verona, even includes a proem that resembles that of the *Filocolo*, with a longer and more amply developed disclaimer than any conceived by Boccaccio or his imitators.[88] Nonetheless, despite the length and narrative intricacy of such works, we are much more inclined to refer to them as novellas, and thus distinguish them from the prose romance as defined by Boccaccio's models, for they lack the eclectic diversity and digressive ambiguity of the latter.[89] They also adhere to a certain extent to Zumthor's dictum that a novella should typically end with a sort of moral 'correction' of the initial situation. More problematic are certain longer Latin products of humanistic culture, such as Enea Silvio Piccolomini's *Historia de duobus amantibus* and Francesco Florio's *Historia de amore Camilli et Emiliae*, which offer intricate narratives endowed with certain trappings of romance, and yet are usually regarded simply as longer novellas.[90]

Those qualities that suggest 'true' romance are more evident in three works of the late Quattrocento which signal a renewal of interest in the prose *romanzo d'amore:* these are Francesco Colonna's *Hypnerotomachia Poliphili*, Iacopo Caviceo's *Libro del Peregrino*, and Jacopo Sannazaro's *Arcadia*. Of these three love stories, that of the cleric Caviceo (1443–1511), published in Parma in 1508, has the most in common with *Urania*.[91]

Caviceo's book owes a certain debt to Boccaccio's *Corbaccio*, sharing its anti-erotic, admonitory themes. The book begins, like the *Corbaccio*, with the author falling asleep and dreaming of a ghost who warns him, citing firsthand experience, of the dangers of falling in love (*Peregrino*, 3–4).[92] The ghost, who calls himself Peregrino, recounts to the narrator in three lengthy books the story of his great love for Genevera, a love that eventually led to Peregrino's demise. Although the opening scene might evoke the *Corbaccio,* it also provides a sure link to Boccaccio's prose romances, for we see right away the usual disclaimer, which has become by now a standard topos of the genre:

> Libro mio, se aspernato o reiecto fusti, dire poterai: Lectore, non l'exterminio de Troia, non le fortune di Roma, non li errori di Ulixe, ma de uno pudico amore la historia porto e narro. (*Peregrino,* 3)

> [My book, if you were to be spurned or rejected, you will be able to say: 'Reader, I contain and recount the story of a chaste love affair, not the destruction of Troy, nor the fortunes of Rome, nor the wanderings of Ulysses.']

Once more, we find an author who is supremely aware that he is composing a literary work that will tell a love story, one that must not be mistaken for an epic.[93] There is some irony at work here too, for Peregrino's love story will not always be marked by chastity, despite what the narrator says. This may remind us of a similar sense of irony that has been noted with respect to the disclaimer at the beginning of *Fiammetta,* which promises that the story will not contain 'Greek fables adorned with many lies,' despite its substantial mythological content.[94]

The *Peregrino* has some aspects in common with the *Filocolo*: it purports to be a love story, but it is quite long and digressive, containing a few *questioni d'amore* and several erudite characters who make long didactic pronouncements.[95] It also includes the full texts of numerous letters exchanged by the main characters, an amatory romance convention that can be traced all the way back to Chariton's *Chaereas and Callirhoe* of the first century, and which appears in the *Filocolo,* the *Historia de duobus amantibus,* and *Urania* as well; ultimately this motif will form the basis of the epistolary novel.[96] The *Peregrino* also has features in common with *Fiammetta,* for it is told in the first person, with Peregrino recounting his own lamentable story of misguided love leading ultimately to disaster. His intention is to warn the narrator to avoid the mistakes he made while he was alive. Caviceo's setting is no longer the distant past, as in the *Filocolo,* nor a pastoral or mythological alternative world, as in the *Comedia delle ninfe fiorentine* and *Arcadia,* nor an allegorical dream landscape, as in the *Hypnerotomachia Poliphili.* Instead, as in the case of *Fiammetta, Peregrino* is set in the real Italian cities of Caviceo's own time, and in fact, as critics have determined, numerous parallels can be traced between the life of the fictional Peregrino and Caviceo's own life.[97] Nonetheless, in a tradition harking back to *Fiammetta* and meant to evoke the atmosphere of the ancient romances, the text abounds with names derived from classical literature, such as Briseida, Achates, and the like. Moreover, churches are referred to as temples, and explicit evocations of the Christian religion are often eschewed in favour of references to Olympian deities, an incongruity that is also evident in *Fiammetta*. Caviceo seems keen to operate in the spirit of Renaissance neoclassicism, thereby purging the *romanzo d'amore* of any links to its medieval chivalric predecessors; at one point, we even find that the old Arthurian *corte d'amore* (court of love) has been converted into a *palestra d'amor* (gymnasium of love, 1.40, 110).[98]

Caviceo carries the romance propensity for circular, repetitive plots to an extreme in this long book, which meanders from one crisis and series of anguished laments to the next, with erudite mythological pronouncements scattered throughout. Anti-erotic sentiments tend to prevail, despite Peregrino's endless, obsessive efforts to see and speak to the object of his passion, the Ferrarese maiden Genevera. Various motifs of classical romance are recycled, such as an extended trial scene and the journeys of Peregrino and his friend Achates around the Mediterranean (anachronistically, they are said on one occasion to travel in a 'Venetian trireme,' 3.15, 262). For a time, as sometimes occurred in Greek romances, they are kidnapped and enslaved (2.1, 152). Numerous prophetic dreams provide yet another link to both the ancient romances and those of Boccaccio. Doctrinal debates on love are commingled with a voyage in a dream to a very Virgilian classical underworld, which has been ordained for Peregrino by the ghost of Scipio.[99]

Peregrino is continually presented as a pathetic anti-hero, stubbornly resisting any advice that he give up his pursuit of Genevera. At one point he even tries to sneak into Genevera's house through a sewer, only to arrive at the wrong house, and therefore seduce and deflower the wrong woman in the dark, causing an extended scandal (1.51, 123). His problem is continually said to be one of lust, which leads him ultimately to rape Genevera just before they are finally to be married (3.52–3, 306–8). But the marriage, deferred for more than five hundred pages, leads only to anticlimax: Genevera bears a son, then dies soon after, leaving Peregrino overcome by a combination of grief and guilt for how he has wasted his life in pursuit of erotic passion, until he too dies (3.85–101, 342–63).

Caviceo clearly wants to evoke the world of the ancient Greek romances, even if his anti-erotic message is closer to that of Boccaccio's
works. He adopts the dilatory style of the old narratives, continually
postponing the union of the lovers through a series of misadventures
and wanderings, only to make their final union an anticlimax, an exemplum of the dangers of erotic love. A similar anti-erotic message can be
found in the next Italian prose romance to see print, the *Filena* of Niccolò
Franco (1515–70), subtitled *Historia amorosa ultimamente composta*, published in Mantua in 1547.[100] The influence of Boccaccio is also evident
in Franco's title, *Filena*, which recalls Boccaccio's fondness for titles
that derive from the Greek word for love (such as *Filocolo, Filostrato*).
Franco's subtitle, which may be translated as 'a love story composed in
recent times,' seems to indicate that he too is making a conscious effort
to continue the tradition of the Greek romances. Moreover, it may represent a deliberate effort to create a genre designation, *historia amorosa*,
for the Italian amatory prose romance, which heretofore had lacked
anything of the sort, and also to bestow an erudite air of Quattrocento
Latin humanism on the work, since the Latinized spelling recalls the
title of Piccolomini's *Historia de duobus amantibus*. In any event, Franco's
use of the term in an amatory prose romance seems to reflect a trend:
the term *istoria* had already been used in the title of Lodovico Corfino's
unpublished *Istoria di Phileto veronese*, and would shortly also be applied by Bigolina to her own narrative of the adventures of Urania,
where it appears alongside *operetta*, a less precise diminutive that suggests adherence to the topos of affected modesty (82).

In his introduction, Franco makes it plain he will reject not only the
prevailing sentimental view of love but also the emphasis on extravagant,
even monstrous marvels that characterized the works of so many writers
in the chivalric or epic vein. Referring to his own romance, he says:

> non s'udiranno le maraviglie, con che hanno molti ingrandite le lor pic-
> ciole fiamme. Si che andornatele di mostruose vaghezze, si sono mostrati
> falsi pittori, mentre veri amatori mostrarsi doveano. Et però, lasciati del
> tutto i favolosi et lor vani amori, non di fortunevoli casi, né di incendi, né
> di perigli, né di sanguinosi combattimenti, né d'ogni altra chimera imagi-
> nata per testimone di lunga fede, si vedranno le mie carte pregiate, ma di
> vere doglie et di veri pianti . . . (*Filena*, 4v)

[one will not hear of marvels, with which many have enhanced their tiny
flames, so that once they have adorned them with monstrous delights, they

have shown themselves to be false painters, when they ought to have presented themselves as true lovers. Therefore, dispensing completely with
the fabulous and empty love stories of these people, my pages will not be
esteemed for felicitous incidents, nor for fiery destructions, nor for dangers, nor for bloody combats, nor for any other chimera dreamed up by a
witness of great veracity, but rather for real grief and real weeping . . .]

Once more we find a narrator who feels he must provide a sort of disclaimer in his efforts to define a work meant to be seen as different from
the romance norm. Franco would have his reader believe that one can
learn to be a true lover by suffering along with his text. Misguided people who imagine themselves to be in love habitually write the wrong
sort of stories, full of marvels and monsters to make their 'picciole fiamme' seem greater, but the picture they paint is false. Franco's narrator pretends to recount his actual experiences in the first person and
stresses that he will not tell of made-up adventures or wars in the epic
mode. He is clearly hoping to legitimize his work by steering it away
from the typical romance fare, and by pretending that he has something far more important to communicate in his own work than some
fabricated 'chimera.'

After this, there follows the narrator's dream vision, wherein he
sees a figure representing Love who shows him Filena, the woman for
whom he will suffer an agony of unfulfilled desire. Ultimately his miserable and negative experience of love is meant to provide a lesson for
the reader, and in fact at the end of the book, Sannio, the name that
Love has bestowed upon the narrator, will renounce erotic love for faith
in God.

Franco shared much of Caviceo's message, but not his success: only
one edition of *Filena* ever appeared. It is easy to see why, since its 468
folios and lack of a dynamic plot make for rather difficult reading. Instead
of the marvels and movement of the *Filocolo,* Franco's narrator provides
an unendurably long series of laments and recriminations against the
adverse forces of love and jealousy, rather like a *Fiammetta* expanded
to the tenth degree, interspersed with numerous ponderously erudite
digressions. The book begins with a dream vision in which Love shows
the narrator the woman named Filena with whom he is fated to be in
love (7r–10v). Awakening from his dream, Sannio subsequently meets
Filena in Venice, and their love story, such as it is, begins. As in the
case of *Fiammetta,* there is a strong psychological element in this story,
and most of its 'action' takes place on the stage of the narrator's mind.

He does make the requisite journey of separation from his beloved in Book 9, albeit without any descriptions of marvels or adventures. Little else occurs to break the monotony of interior debate, until finally Sannio turns to God, gives up his quest, and the story ends.

Only one other Italian prose romance is known from the first half of the Cinquecento: Corfino's *Istoria di Phileto veronese*, written between 1520 and 1530.[101] However, as I have already had occasion to note, it was so obscure that it languished in a single manuscript for many centuries, just like *Urania*, until it was finally rediscovered and published in 1899. In some ways *Phileto* reflects the influence of *Peregrino*: it is a first-person narrative, purporting to tell a true story of love set in a real, contemporary landscape of Italian and Mediterranean locales. It also owes the usual very familiar debts to Boccaccio's romances: a protagonist bearing a name derived from the Greek φίλος (love), as well as the standard disclaimer defining the purpose of the work, which will not tell of 'le fatiche di Ulisse, non gli errori di Enea et non le famose ruine dell'antica Troia' (not the labours of Ulysses, nor the wanderings of Aeneas, nor the famous ruins of ancient Troy), but rather of the author's own 'giovanili amori' (youthful loves, 5–6). By now this disclaimer motif, present in all of Boccaccio's prose romances, has become a defining element of the revived romances of the Cinquecento.[102] Like both Caviceo and Franco, Corfino also stresses an abiding 'need to narrate,' a great urge on the part of his narrator to share his experiences with readers so that they might derive some benefit from them (3–4, 6–7, 155–6).

Nonetheless, despite these features, Corfino's work has more in common with the ancient Greek romances, some of which were circulating Italy in printed editions by this time, than it has with either *Peregrino* or *Filena*. It is quite short in comparison to the works of Caviceo and Franco, and also relatively full of action: the narrator, Phileto, falls in love with Euphrosine in Verona but is forced to flee the city with a faithful companion after he kills someone in self-defence (53–4).[103] Living abroad in exotic lands for years, he suffers from the pangs of love until his mother's ghost visits him in a dream and urges him to return home (123–7), whereupon he finds his crime forgiven and is able to marry his beloved (154–5). There is a strong autobiographical element, as Biadego's research has shown: in effect, Corfino is providing a kind of fantasy retelling of the circumstances of his own courtship and marriage (xxi–xxvii). The happy ending, in particular, reveals the influence of the old Greek stories and provides a remarkable contrast with the works of Caviceo and Franco, which follow Boccaccio's *Fiammetta* in using a failed or tragic love story to communicate an anti-erotic message.

Aside from Corfino's occasionally exceptional inclinations, it may be seen that Boccaccio's influence on Italian writers of amatory prose romances was remarkably pervasive and endured in one form or another right up to the time that Bigolina set out to write her own quite innovative contribution to the genre.

Urania in Its Literary Context

By the mid-Cinquecento northern Italy, specifically the regions of Lombardy and the Veneto, had become fertile ground for the production of the Renaissance *romanzo d'amore*, such as it was: Colonna (of Treviso), Caviceo, and Corfino were all natives of those regions, whereas Franco, originally from Benevento, lived for many years in Venice and other northern cities and published his book in Mantua. The Lombard Matteo Bandello published the first three parts of his bulky novella collection in 1554, a work which included some narratives that are essentially short prose romances, such as his tale of the love affair of Don Diego and Ginevra la Bionda (1.27). Another long prose work, the anonymous *I compassionevoli avvenimenti di Erasto*, was first published in Mantua in 1542.[104] This narrative, as has been noted, provides a version of the medieval tale collection known as *The Book of the Seven Sages*. It consists primarily of a series of misogynistic exempla recounted by seven wise men in order to save the young prince Erasto from a false accusation of rape, and thus is best categorized as *romanzo morale*, not *romanzo d'amore*. Nonetheless, it could have served as a model for *Urania* in certain respects, especially in its third-person narrative, which is almost wholly deprived of authorial commentary save in the last sentence (134r). This allows the text to move briskly from one narrative event to the next in novella fashion, without indulging itself overmuch in the workings of a central character's mind. The *Erasto* may also serve as further evidence of the growing interest in longer works of prose fiction during this period: by the end of the Cinquecento, it had gone through no fewer than twenty-six Italian editions, mostly published in Venice.

Bigolina's *Urania*, the next prose romance known to have been written in Italian after that of Franco, was very much part of this tradition of prose romances from the northern regions. Moreover, Bigolina was writing during the early years of the 1550s in the Venetian Republic, a time and place that showed intense interest in the other genre of prose fiction at which she excelled, the novella.[105] In these years, both novella collections and prose romances were frequently published by the presses of Venice. Yet another of the many editions of *Peregrino* had just been published in Venice in 1549, and Giovan Francesco Straparola published the first volume of his popular novella collection *Le piacevoli notti*, which had a demonstrable influence on both of Bigolina's surviving works, in Venice in 1550.[106] Francesco Angelo Coccio's translation of *Leucippe and Clitophon*, the Greek romance by Achilles Tatius, also first appeared in 1550 in Venice, and would see many subsequent editions. Two more novella collections were published there in 1552: *I diporti* by Girolamo Parabosco and *Vari componimenti* by Ortensio Lando, while Silvan Cattaneo, who was closely associated with the University of Padua, composed his own collection, *Le dodici giornate*, around 1553, although, as in the case of Bigolina's own 'Novella di Giulia Camposanpiero,' it was not published until the eighteenth century.[107]

The standard plot features of the Greek romances that abound in *Urania* could easily have been familiar to Bigolina in the form of Coccio's translation of Tatius, if not from other sources. In terms of the broad outlines of its plot, it could also be argued that the story of Urania, as well as the Greek romances and Corfino's *Phileto*, all belong to a remarkably enduring narrative category that still flourishes today in the form of the ubiquitous 'romance novel,' which, as Barbara Fuchs has noted, might well account for more than half of all current sales of paperback fiction in North America. If regarded superficially, *Urania* fits neatly within the Romance Writers of America's parameters of the fundamental requirements of the romance novel, as cited by Fuchs:

A Central Love Story – In a romance, the main plot concerns two people falling in love and struggling to make the relationship work. The conflict in the book centers on the love story. The climax of the book resolves the love story. A writer is welcome to as many subplots as she likes as long as the relationship conflict is the main story.

An Emotionally Satisfying and Optimistic Ending – Romance novels end in a way that makes the reader feel good. Romance novels are based on the idea of an innate emotional justice – the notion that good people in the world are rewarded and evil people are punished. In a romance, the lovers who risk and struggle for each other and their relationships are rewarded with emotional justice and unconditional love. (*Romance*, 124–5)

However, it should be stressed that *Urania* fits this definition only in its broadest outlines. We may note a remarkable convergence here, as well as a testament to the eternal power and attraction of the romance mode across the centuries, without minimizing *Urania's* importance as a unique work of art. When Bigolina's book is examined in its details and not merely in its superficial features, it becomes evident that it defies both tradition and reader expectation and provides a voice for the prose romance that had heretofore not been heard. *Urania* is not a Greek romance, nor is it a chivalric romance, nor is it an 'elegy' in the mould of Boccaccio's *Fiammetta,* even if it adopts certain elements of all three.

The first thing to note is the absence of the traditional disclaimer, which Boccaccio had bequeathed to nearly all of the early modern amatory romances in prose produced in Italy before *Urania.* Bigolina has an implied ideal reader, Bartolomeo Salvatico, but she does not seem to worry what his expectations might be when he picks up her book. She has no interest in defining her literary effort in terms of the age-old tension between epic and romance, or between romances of chivalry and *romanzo d'amore,* as had her predecessors. The early modern Italian prose romance had always wrestled with problems of genre definition, and this manifested itself most plainly in the common recourse to explicit rejections of the motifs of Greek fables and epic warfare. These rejections were not always strictly followed, as can be seen in *Fiammetta,* which persists in employing elements of Greek mythology even after the narrator says she will not include them. Nonetheless, the disclaimers are meant to define the contents of the work, and at the same time steer the reader away from any false expectation: if Homer sang of the wrath of Achilles, and Virgil of arms and the man, these latter-day writers of lofty narratives will sing of something rather less exalted. Even at the conclusion of the *Filocolo,* Boccaccio finds it necessary to apologize yet again for the content and for the type of literary vehicle he has chosen. Addressing the book itself, he humbly reminds us that its youthful author has not intended it to be compared to a real epic:

> con ciò sia cosa che tu da umile giovane sii creato, il cercare gli alti luoghi ti si disdice: e però agli eccellenti ingegni e alle robuste menti lascia i gran versi di Virgilio. (5.97)

> [since you were created by a humble youth, it is unbecoming of you to seek lofty places: therefore, leave the great verses of Virgil to excellent intellects and robust minds.]

Bigolina declares her independence from Boccaccio's romances and their successors, not only by dispensing with the disclaimer motif, but also by doing away with their usual confessional, pseudo-autobiographical rejections of erotic love. Romances in the tradition of *Fiammetta*, such as those of Caviceo and Franco, emphasize quite overtly the errors of the misguided lovers who narrate them. Corfino, in his *Phileto*, retains the Greek-style happy ending for his love story, but still couches it in auto-biographical form, and provides a sobriquet for his narrator that hints at the negative aspects of his troubled 'giovanili amori': as the reader is told, the name 'Phileto' comes from Greek words meaning 'love of grief' (9). Following the Greek romances, Corfino emphasizes the power of random Fortune, which he says is sometimes a 'pietosa madre' (pite-ous mother) and sometimes a 'crudelissima matrigna' (most cruel step-mother, 6); bad luck dogs his narrator, Phileto, throughout the book. It has been noted that the plot of the typical work in the romance mode, such as *Orlando furioso*, is fuelled by errors and confusion on the part of the protagonists, and this can surely be said of the amatory prose romances that precede *Urania*.[108]

Urania, however, is different: its plot is fuelled by judgments, not by errors. Bigolina is more interested in the choices her characters make, often after deep reflection, than in random acts of fate; therefore her plot advances from one judgment to the next, not from one error to the next. Most typically, the ill-advised judgment of one character in *Urania* is set right by the wise judgment of another. The initial separa-tion of the lovers is not a matter of bad luck or unfortunate circum-stance here, as would often be the case in a Greek romance; instead, it is due to Fabio's act of bad judgment when he leaves Urania for Clorina. This in turn is followed by Urania's act of good judgment when she de-cides to abandon Salerno disguised as a man.[109] Fabio's rejection leaves Urania so distraught that she fears she will go insane, which would put her in illustrious romance company, as we will note in the final chapter: Ariosto's Orlando went insane and lived like a wild man in the woods for the same reason. However, Urania consistently takes care-ful, reasoned steps to maintain her sanity. This is most evident in her decision to dress as a man, since the disguise allows her to travel and give vent to her grief without being molested by actual men. It also allows her a didactic interlude, when she dispenses advice to the two groups of young people while thought to be a man; and here, too, her task includes the correction of an error of judgment, since she must set right the misguided notions of the misogynistic males. Ultimately

Urania's return to Salerno shows even more careful reflection and good judgment, as does the prince's decision to reject the duchess and marry the Savia Damigella, a choice that undoes a whole series of misguided judgments on the part of the duchess, her counsellor, and her painter, who together create the painting of the Judgment of Paris.

Bigolina's world view reveals itself to be quite the opposite of Ariosto's, as exemplified by the latter's emblematic declaration of the pervasiveness of fallibility near the beginning of the *Orlando furioso*: 'Ecco il giudicio uman come spesso erra!' (See how human judgment so often goes astray).[110] When human judgment goes astray in *Urania*, an antidote is always neatly provided in the form of another character's wise response, which serves to show up and correct the preceding error in judgment. Even though Urania's anguished laments may be compared to those of the hapless protagonist of Boccaccio's *Fiammetta*, we must note that with regard to the wisdom of her choices, Urania might be called, with a nod to the modern vernacular, a Fiammetta who 'gets her act together': she knows full well how to go about turning useless misery to triumph.[111]

Nor are the events within Bigolina's narrative the only parts of *Urania* to be fuelled by judgments: according to the experiences of the narrator in the proem, the story purports to owe its very existence to an act of judgment. Once Bigolina's authorial persona has heard the pronouncements of Giudicio, the allegory of judgment, she sees the misguided nature of her decision to have herself painted, and thus spontaneously conceives the whole story of Urania in her mind. Elsewhere, I have stressed the uniqueness of this psychogenic origin for the tale: in neither the romance nor the novella traditions are stories normally said to be simply made up in this way, as an act of better judgment, or for any other reason.[112] Romance narrators in the amatory vein frequently claim to ground their narratives in actual lived experience, as can be seen in such examples as *Fiammetta, Peregrino, Filena,* and *Phileto*. In the chivalric tradition, it is typically understood that the narrative substance is supposed to be historical in some fashion, and at times it may be attributed to the account of some illustrious predecessor, as when Boiardo pretends to derive his *Orlando innamorato* from Archbishop Turpin's hitherto lost history (1.3–4). This tradition in turn will be satirized by Cervantes when he claims, quite facetiously, to have transcribed most of *Don Quixote* from Arabic notebooks he picked up in a Toledo market (1.9). Neither the romance nor the novella ever really allow for a purely psychogenic origin for themselves, even if readers might be expected to know better. We are always given to understand that a pre-existing tale, anecdote, or historical event is simply being retold, or that the narrative purports to be an account of lived experience. Bigolina, in effect, cuts through centuries of pretence when she makes her forthright claim to have spontaneously invented a story in her own 'basso intelletto,' a story that therefore cannot be attributed to any source but her own imagination (82). She may present her encounter with the allegorical Giudicio as if it were lived experience, but not the story of Urania that follows. In doing so, she must have been fully aware of how innovative it would appear to the readers of her time.

Therefore it must be stressed that Bigolina does not model her prose romance on that of any specific predecessor: *Urania* is essentially an original work. Although it has been noted that some of Bigolina's episodes were possibly inspired by Ariosto's *Orlando furioso*, precise echoes of earlier romances in prose, even those of Boccaccio, are remarkably uncommon in *Urania*.[113] A few brief passages that seem to derive directly from the *Peregrino* show that she probably knew that very popular work, even if she made considerable efforts not to emulate it otherwise. Bigolina's account of her terrifying encounter with Giudicio may have been inspired by the similar fear that nearly overcomes Caviceo's narrator at the sight of the ghost of Boccaccio in the opening passage of the *Peregrino* (proem, 1). Moreover, the passage in which Giudicio disappears from the narrator's sight seems to evoke the disappearance of Scipio's ghost in Caviceo's book (2.45, 234).[114] Later, when Urania concludes her letter to Fabio, we find her actions described thus: 'Scritta et sigillata c'hebbe la sua lunga lettera, la diede al servo ...' (When she had written and sealed her long letter she gave it to the servant, 108–9). This phrase may be compared to a similar one that appears in the *Erasto* (9v), but it resembles even more a passage in the 1547 Venice edition of the *Peregrino*: 'Scritte, et sigillate le littere me le diede ...' (When he had written and sealed the letters, he gave them to me, 3.2, 175r). The same passage in Vignali's edition of Caviceo's narrative, which reproduces the *editio princeps* of 1508, does not provide a version of this formula that resembles Bigolina's phrase quite as closely (3.2, 243).[115] In any case, these are but small details; they indicate little more than a passing familiarity with a text that otherwise seems to have provided only the most minimal inspiration to Bigolina.

Urania is a prose romance, but it is endowed with numerous traits that remind us of the novella.[116] The main narrative is presented in the third person, the first Italian amatory romance to do this since *Filocolo*; in this regard, it resembles more closely the *novelle-romanzi* of the *Decameron* and Bandello's *Novelle*. It is far shorter, less dilatory and digressive, less cluttered with episodes and apostrophes than such mastodontic works as *Filocolo, Hypnerotomachia Poliphili, Peregrino,* and *Filena*.[117] In terms of factors that advance plot, the shift of emphasis from errors and random fate to characters' choices and judgments shows yet another link to the more moralistic narrative world of the novella.[118]

With regard to characters, we must consider one of Bigolina's most remarkable creations: her painter. I do not know of any other character who is an artist in the romance tradition, unless one considers those references to supernatural seers such as the Cumaean Sibyl, Merlin, or Cassandra, who are said to have created prophetic artworks in the romances of Boiardo and Ariosto, or perhaps Sannazaro's passing comments on the skills of Andrea Mantegna or the unnamed artist who created the temple painting of the Judgment of Paris, as described in *Arcadia*.[119] On the other hand, artists frequently inhabit the real-world setting of the novella, in which historical anecdote may flourish, and they may well be the principal characters of the narratives in which they appear. Novella artists tend to be presented as perfectly normal humans without supernatural qualities, rather like Bigolina's painter: one need only think of Giotto's appearance in Boccaccio's *Decameron* 6.5, or Boccaccio's other painters, Calandrino, Bruno, and Buffalmacco (*Decameron,* 8.3, 8.6, 8.9, 9.3, 9.5), as well as Franco Sacchetti's *Trecentonovelle*, which includes stories about Giotto (63, 75), Buffalmacco (161, 169, 191, 192), the painters Mino (84), Bartolo Gioggi (170), and Andrea di Rico (191), and the sculptor Jacopo da Pistoia (229), as well as a whole group of distinguished Florentine artists who mock women for their 'artistic' use of cosmetics (136).[120] Most of these men, with the exception of Calandrino and Mino upon whom tricks are played, are characterized by quickness of wit and masterful use of jocular or deceptive language, and thus may serve to some extent as predecessors to Bigolina's fast-talking artist.

Later, during Bigolina's time, the tradition of including real historical painters as characters in novellas was continued by such authors as Antonfrancesco Grazzini (*Le cene*, 1.3 and 2.4) and Bandello, who provides anecdotes about Fra Filippo Lippi (as remembered by Leonardo da Vinci) in *Novelle* 1.58, as well as the painter Girolamo da Verona, whose cleverness is extolled in a story laden with references to Boccaccio's own painters in the *Decameron* (2.10). Both Grazzini and Bandello depict these artists much as Boccaccio and Sacchetti had, as men who employ consummate wit and verbal skills to advance their causes or play tricks on others – Bandello's Girolamo even manages to deceive the wise Pietro Bembo with a good-natured *beffa*. However, a tale from the third part of the *Novelle* provides a somewhat different view of the artist, one that suggests not only the equivocal ethics and sense of moral crisis that Bigolina's narrative conveys but also her theme of rivalry between contrasting art forms. In novella 3.23 we read of the musician Galeazzo Valle, who wins the heart of a married Venetian woman by improvising a song to her while accompanying himself on the *lira da braccio*. The two begin a torrid affair, but then are both heartbroken when Galeazzo must move to Padua. As an aid to memory, each promises to provide a portrait for the other. Galeazzo already has one of himself, which he sends to his lover; but since she has none of her own, Galeazzo arranges for a famous Venetian painter to paint the woman in secret (2: 385). Unfortunately for Galeazzo, the strapping young artist falls in love with the woman as she poses for him and seduces her by means of his cleverness of speech, the skill attributed to so many painters in the novella tradition: she falls for his 'favoleggiare' (fable spinning, but here probably closer to 'smooth talk'), since he is 'pieno sempre di nuovi e bei motti' (always full of rare and clever jokes, 2: 386). Thus one artist vies with another to win the charms of the woman, and the painter is the one who ultimately triumphs. This painter, like Bigolina's, is not given a name or a precise identity, although he may well have been historical, as are so many of the characters in Bandello's tale collection. When Galeazzo learns he has lost his love, he strikes the painter in a fit of jealousy and throws him into a canal, earning his own banishment from Venice, whereupon he consoles himself by singing songs about his lost love (2: 386). In his conclusion, Bandello's tale teller indicates that the painter should never have betrayed the man who had trusted him (2: 386). Thus Bandello presents us with a painter who, like Bigolina's but unlike his predecessors in the Trecento novella collections, puts his considerable skills to a nefarious purpose.

Yet another link between *Urania* and the novella tradition can be demonstrated. The duchess's death from dejection at having been outwitted reflects a common motif in the ethical patterns of the late medieval and early modern Italian novella, wherein morally suspect characters are seen to die spontaneously, often within the space of a single sentence as in the case of the duchess, as a form of punishment for having attempted to deceive others.[121]

The Italian novella tends on the whole to describe events that are supposed to have actually occurred in the recent past, in real-world places familiar to the audience to whom the stories are recounted and often describing real people known to that audience; supernatural elements, prophetic dreams, visions, and other marvels usually have no place therein. In novella fashion, *Urania* too is set in the recent past, 'in the days when Prince Giufredi, the most handsome and pleasant lord of his age, peacefully ruled the lovely state of Salerno' (85), most likely a reference, veiled behind a pseudonym, to the recently ended glory days of Ferrante Sanseverino's rule in that city.[122]

To be sure, many of the other amatory romances are supposedly set in contemporary Italy, but they still include numerous unreal elements such as mythological figures, anachronistic references, or outlandish Greek-style names for characters inspired by Boccaccio's romances (Poliphilo, Philena, Phileto, and the like), all things that Bigolina eschews.[123] Bigolina does provide some names that evoke classical figures, but they are less philologically flamboyant than these and at times are endowed with subtle mythological connotations. The name 'Urania,' associated with the Celestial Venus, comes to mind, but we must also consider 'Clorina,' a name that is likely meant to be a diminutive of 'Clora,' and thus could recall Boccaccio's description of the Roman goddess Flora in *Famous Women* (*De mulieribus claris*).[124] Boccaccio, following a euhemeristic treatment in Lactantius's *Saturnalia,* says that Flora was originally a Roman prostitute, not a nymph or goddess; however, when she became a wealthy benefactor of the Romans, they created a mythological identity for her.[125] Boccaccio describes how the Roman Senate, embarrassed by the bawdy nude spectacles in the Floralia games that Flora had instituted, invented the story that she had once been a nymph named Clora, loved by the wind Zephyrus, who had then morphed into the flower goddess Flora. Here Boccaccio, indulging in the same appellative ironies that inspired him to convert his character Ser Cepparello into 'Ser Ciappelletto' in the first story of the *Decameron,* notes that in this way a woman who had been a prostitute named Flora was deified into a nymph named Clora and then accorded all the requisite honours of a goddess, once more known as Flora (269). Titian painted a Flora bearing flowers, 'a woman of indisputable beauty but perhaps dubious morality,' notes Rona Goffen, clearly referring to Boccaccio's story about her.[126] Bigolina was likely familiar with Giuseppe Betussi's popular expanded Italian version of *De mulieribus claris* (Venice, 1545, 1547), which preserves Boccaccio's Latinized name 'Clora' (as distinct from Lactantius's 'Chloris') and thus could have suggested the diminutive form 'Clorina,' an otherwise peculiar name that I have not seen elsewhere in Italian literature.[127] Such an interpretation would be quite congruent with Bigolina's depiction of Clorina as a surpassingly beautiful woman who hides questionable ethical inclinations.[128]

In a nod to the exigencies of the romance genre, the story of Urania does have one prophetic dream imbued with classical imagery, that of the imprisoned Fabio, who sees a sort of allegorical summary of his recent amatory misadventures in which Clorina appears as a serpent-woman and Menandro as a faun (240–4). However, aside from this, Bigolina banishes such stock romance trappings as visions or visitations of classical deities, which are especially common in Boccaccio's romances, from the pages of her more realistic work.[129] This makes the duchess's prayer to the goddess of love, in the hope of gaining the same celestial favour as Pygmalion, all the more ironic (190). The episode is clearly meant to remind the reader of the misguided allegiance of Fiammetta in the *Elegia di madonna Fiammetta,* who devotes herself to a more tangible Venus and likewise prays to her in an effort to succour herself from the sufferings of love (5, 69). However, in Bigolina's hands the prayer to Venus takes on new layers of significance, since the duchess will soon allow herself to be convinced that she must impersonate that very goddess in a vain and ultimately fatal attempt to make her yearning a reality. She will actually 'become' Venus in an effort to fulfil a prayer that she has, in effect, made to herself, as one of the only classical deities actually to appear in *Urania:* those rendered by the artist in his painting of the Judgment of Paris.[130] The ancient gods have assumed a completely new role in Bigolina's fiction, one that looks forward to the banal realism of the modern novel, not backward to the otherworldly trappings of myth.

Bigolina's Defence of Women

One of Bigolina's more startling innovations in this unconventional prose romance is her adaptation of the standard motif of the *questioni d'amore.* Her setting is normal enough, as it was established in the *Filocolo* and continued in later romances following the *Filocolo's* model, such as the *Peregrino:* a beautiful, natural place, originally derived from certain motifs of the medieval lyric tradition, set apart from the civilized world and to some extent standing at odds with it. Nor is Bigolina's initial topic so strange: the women and men whom Urania meets in the woods want to know how they may choose the most suitable person for a lover, a subject matter that recalls certain *questioni* in the *Filocolo*.[131] However, Bigolina leaves the traditional subject matter of the prose romance behind when she allows her love debate to lead to an invective against the misogynistic attitudes of the five young men, since discussion of contemporary social issues does not typically intrude into the idealized, otherworldly romance realm.

Bigolina's defence of women begins when Urania addresses the ladies and is told by one of them that they find love to be their sole incitement to virtue, since the male-dominated society leaves them with so little else (116). Convinced that Urania is herself a man, the spokeswoman laments to her that men claim sole ownership of the glory of distinguishing themselves in letters and other intellectual fields:

> voi huomini acciò che la gloria tutta sia di voi soli ci impedite che nelle discipline delle lettere, et nelle belle et utili scienze si possiamo essercitare. Onde se Amor qualche poco in noi non desta lo ingegno, questa nostra, per lo vero, infelicissima vita passiamo ignude et prive d'ogni piacere, et sapere; et peggio è ancora, che le più volte la nostra troppa bontà, presso voi altri huomini nome di sciocche ci acquista. (116)

> [You men keep us from working in the field of literature and in the sciences, both aesthetic and practical, so that all the glory they bestow is yours alone; therefore we spend our lives, which are truly unhappy, deprived of all pleasure and knowledge, unless love awakens our wits to some extent. And what is worse, we are mostly thought of as foolish by you men, on account of our inherent great kindness. (117)]

Love, always the driving, animating force of the amatory prose romance tradition, takes on a new role here as a polemical tool calculated to show up the inequalities of society, as well as to appeal for women's educational advancement: it is presented as the only thing resembling a mental exercise that men have not denied to women. Bigolina has provided a sort of feminist commentary on the notion, expressed by Boccaccio in the proem to the *Decameron* (1: 7–8), that women suffer inordinately from unrequited love because they are confined to their homes and have no recourse to the strenuous physical and mental activities allowed to men. Although Boccaccio claims to provide a 'solution' to this problem by writing a book that will comfort and entertain his female readers, Bigolina herself offers no remedies, merely taking note of the cold social realities of her time. However, Urania's response reveals that Bigolina has not strayed far from some aspects of Boccaccio's perspective, since she acknowledges, like Boccaccio, that women must suffer more in love since they are weaker in spirit than men. Urania's male persona tells the women that his own sufferings in love must be exceeded by those of his female listeners, who are endowed with weaker souls ('di minor valore et forze havete gli animi vostri,' 120). Bigolina's feminist argument does not centre on notions of equality so much as notions of fairness: men take advantage of women's weakness and treat them in unjust ways, then accuse them of being the more evil sex. Urania holds forth at length concerning the differences between men and women in love, claiming that ancient histories confirm that women are far more likely to be treated poorly by their lovers than vice versa (122). Her argument says nothing about God or divine laws, centring instead on rational and naturalistic viewpoints, described in terms of astrological influences. Women are influenced by benign planets and 'gli elementi più molli' (the softer elements, 122), so that they tend to be nicer to their lovers.[132] Urania recommends that women avoid the evils of love as much as possible, but not because it is immoral; instead, she stresses that it works to their disadvantage and is not likely to contribute to their happiness (122). Having pronounced this preamble, she then proceeds to answer the ladies' *questione* concerning how to choose the best lover.

Bigolina's indictment of men for their unfair attitudes about women moves into its next phase when Urania meets the five young men the following day. The polemical tone of the debate is foreshadowed by the harsh reception Urania receives at the hands of the uncouth men, when she rides up to them dressed as a man, nearly out of her mind with grief over her lost love. The men shake her and pound her out of her reverie, which leads her to reproach them angrily for their lack of manners in terms that immediately evoke the conflict between the sexes (132–4).[133] No woman would ever act so discourteously, she tells them, and indeed she has just had proof of this in the woods where she met the five most courteous women. The men ask her forgiveness and invite her to their palace for a meal (136). Thus the subsequent debate on the value of women does not unfold in the natural setting of the *locus amoenus*, as the women's *questione d'amore* had, but rather in a banquet hall, which provides an atmosphere more evocative of Plato's dialogues and their numerous didactic Renaissance descendants. The debate revolves around a starkly polemical comparison between men and women: which sex has committed the worst crimes? Urania, still speaking in the guise of a man, asserts that although women are only a little less perfect than men (140, 146), the wickedest men are far more imperfect than the wickedest women, because they have consistently shown themselves capable of the most evil deeds:

> Ma per farvi conoscere ancora come le più triste donne di tanta imper-
> fettione et tristitia non sono, come i più tristi huomini si trovano esser;
> dicovi che molto bene dovete considerare da quale de' due sessi vengono
> il più delle volte le tante sceleragini et tristitie di che il mondo n'è pieno;
> gl'inganni, le usure, i tradimenti, gli furti, le rapine, et gli homicidij da cui
> vengono se non da gli huomini sempre? Poco huopo sarebbono le leggi
> cotanto tra gli humani hoggidì necessarie, se gli huomini, l'uno con l'altro
> con fede, et pace, come le donne fanno, vivessero. (144)

> [To show you even further that the wickedest women are not as imperfect
> and wicked as the most wicked men, I ask you to consider well from which
> of the two sexes come most often the many evils and villainies which fill
> the world. Who but men bring about deceits, usuries, betrayals, thefts,
> plunderings, and murders? The many laws which are necessary to the
> human race would serve little purpose, if men would only live together in
> good faith and peace, as women do. (145)]

Here Urania seems to give a subtle lie to her claim that women are somewhat less perfect than men, which is doubtless meant to be read ironically. Not only are men responsible for most violence and misery, they are presented as the sole reason for laws restricting human behaviour, whereas women, so much kinder, can provide a lesson to men on how to attain peaceful coexistence. Such an assertion on the part of a woman writer would doubtless have caused something of a stir among Bigolina's contemporaries, if it had ever managed to see print.

The defence of women had long been an established topic in a wide variety of didactic treatises, biographies, and dialogues before Bigolina's time, and it is clear that some of these works must have inspired her to add these elements to her eclectic and rather ambitious romance.[134] Bigolina's refutation of misogyny and her notion that men restrict women's opportunities for education both find parallels in *Della eccel-lenza et dignità della donna* by Galeazzo Flavio Capella, the first defence of women to be published in Italian (1525).[135] Capella's treatise provides a point-by-point refutation of the traditional accusations put forward by the enemies of women. He also claims that women have the same

intellectual capabilities as men, and indicates that they could successfully study law if they were allowed, even if he does not appeal for a
reformation of society along these lines.[136] However, it should be noted
that Bigolina herself avoids calling for absolute educational equality
for the sexes, since she specifies that women should only be knowledgeable in 'volgari lettere' (vernacular literature, 158), whereas both
of the male protagonists of her surviving works, Fabio and Thesibaldo
Vitaliani, are said to be skilled in Latin as well as vernacular letters,
with Thesibaldo an orator to boot (86, 302). Moreover, when the cross-
dressed Urania assumes the identity of Fabio at the beginning of her
conversation with the five women, she declares herself to be a student
of 'volgari lettere' (112–14), but says nothing about the Latin that Fabio
is said to have studied, doubtless because Urania herself does not have
this proficiency, as has already been specified at the beginning of the narrative: 'oltre che nelle volgari lettere fosse assai convenevolmente dotta'
(aside from the fact that she was quite properly skilled in vernacular literature, 84). It would seem that Bigolina did not think it appropriate for
women to know Latin, a language she was probably never permitted to
study herself: this is borne out by her writings, which are completely
devoid of even a single casual word or phrase in Latin.[137]

   Although Bigolina was doubtless familiar with the arguments of the
numerous treatises and biographical works concerning women, she
would have found her models for the refutation of a misogynist in a
dramatic conversational format within the popular dialogues that provided defences of women, such as Baldassare Castiglione's *Libro del
cortigiano (The Book of the Courtier, 1528)* and Lodovico Domenichi's
La nobiltà delle donne (1549).[138] However, it must be noted that in
Castiglione's case, his feminist approach lacks the polemical harshness
of Bigolina's, since it is scarcely his purpose to denigrate male behaviour
in the *Cortigiano;* moreover, Castiglione is not as inclined as Bigolina to
suggest that women should be accorded educational and social parity
with men. Moreover, when Castiglione's character Il Magnifico Iuliano
exalts women's capacity for perfection and claims that they are capable
of the same intellectual accomplishments as men (3.10–13), he does not
find it pertinent to refer to men's potential for wickedness, as Bigolina
continually does. Domenichi provides a much longer and more lavish defence than Castiglione, emphasizing an extended debate between various defenders of women and their detractor, Pier Francesco
Visconte, who declares himself 'procuratore e difensore de gli huomini'
(proxy and defender of men, 2, 57r), and throughout the dialogue tries

to prove that women are 'animali imperfetti' (imperfect animals, 4v).[139] Here Bigolina might have found a source for one of her more fervently stated points, that it was not Helen who was responsible for the destruction of Troy, as her male speaker claims, but rather the wily seducer Paris.[140] Domenichi's defence of women, unlike Castiglione's, is led by a woman interlocutor, Violante Bentivoglio, and thus might have provided a more sure inspiration to Bigolina in her creation of a similar debate in *Urania*.

Bigolina was not the first Italian woman to defend her sex in her writings; she was preceded in this regard by the Neapolitan poet Laura Terracina (1519–c. 1577), whose popular publications of the late 1540s could easily have been familiar to Bigolina as she was conceiving her own grand project. In her first collection of *Rime* (1548), Terracina exalts the deeds of ancient women in a series of octaves dedicated to Fabrizio Luna ('La prosa, e i vostri versi alti & sonori,' 19v–21r), claiming that these accomplishments would be better known were it not for the envy of male writers (octave 2, vv 1–4). Terracina's defence of women becomes more strident and sustained in her third collection of poems, *Discorso sopra il principio di tutti i canti di Orlando furioso* (1549): here she defends, exalts, or encourages women to express themselves in literature in seven of the work's forty-four cantos (5, 20, 24, 26, 27, 28, 38). Cantos 27 and 28 appear to be especially relevant, since they provide invectives against misogynistic attitudes that could have served as an inspiration to Bigolina. Moreover, Canto 27 is addressed to Isabella Villamarina, Princess of Salerno, a possible inspiration for Bigolina's character of the Savia Damigella, as will be discussed below in chapter 3. In the introductory octave to this canto, Terracina mocks men who are said to be 'dotti e savi' (learned and wise), and yet believe that the advice of women is useless (44r).

Other defences purported to be in women's voices had also appeared in *Lettere di molte valorose donne*, a collection of letters from women to other women, edited and perhaps at least partly authored by Ortensio Lando in 1548.[141] Here Bigolina might have seen Lucietta Soranza's letter encouraging women to write in order to escape 'la tirannia de gli huomini' (the tyranny of men, 31r–32r), or Countess Catharina Visconte Landessa's list of great women conjoined to an indictment of misogynists (95 r–v), as well as other rhetorically ornate defences of the worth of women.[142]

However, the pro-feminist work that appears to have had the greatest influence on *Urania* is the far older *Le livre de la cité des dames (The*

Book of the City of Ladies, 1405*)* by the medieval Frenchwoman Christine de Pizan (c. 1364–1430), a text which, as we have noted, should scarcely have been known in Italy in the sixteenth century. Christine's allegorical defence of women leaves various traces in *Urania,* certainly in the parallels between the descriptions of allegorical mirror images at the beginnings of both works (which will be discussed in the following chapter), but most evidently when Bigolina describes Judith, Esther, the Sabines, and Veturia in precisely the same order, and in the same terms, as Christine does in a sequence of four chapters in her own book; surely no coincidence.[143] Other similarities can be described: for instance, both Christine and Bigolina follow the same strategy of counterbalancing their exaltations of accomplished women with references to famous tyrannical men. Christine describes a series of Roman emperors who were distinguished not only for brutality but also for the stereotypically feminine fault of inconstancy, while Bigolina provides a list of ancient tyrants of her own as a means of refuting her opponent who has said that women are wickeder than men.[144] Moreover, both writers hold up the ancient sibyls as proof that men have not always had a monopoly on religious prophecy.[145] To be sure, Boccaccio also discusses certain sibyls in *De mulieribus claris* (21, 26), a work that served as a primary inspiration to Christine and could have been known to Bigolina either in the original form or in *volgarizzamenti* such as that of Betussi; nonetheless, he does not compare them to the male prophets of the biblical tradition, as Christine and Bigolina do. Bigolina also seems to have taken to heart this statement of Christine's, prominently placed at the opening of chapter 1.44 of *Cité des dames:* 'Qui trovera femme forte, c'est a dire, prudente, son mari n'ara pas faulte de tous biens' (Whoever finds a valiant woman, one of sound judgment, will be a husband who lacks for nothing).[146] This is echoed by Urania at the conclusion of her longest speech to the men, in which she has demonstrated that women, for all their faults, have never acted worse than the most evil of men: 'Et conchiudiamo ancora potersi beato chiamar quell'huomo al quale da' cieli fu dato in sorte, che valorosa donna gli fosse compagna' (And let us also conclude that any man may call himself blessed, if by chance the heavens have given him an excellent woman as a consort, 154–5). Both writers stress the benefits that men might derive from women if only they would recognize women's potential contributions to society and show them the respect that they deserve.

In the introduction to her translation of the *Cité des dames,* Rosalind Brown-Grant notes that misogynist writers were typically forced to cite their favourite authorities selectively, choosing to discuss only those women who could be presented as examples of wickedness in order to support their arguments (xxiv). On the other hand, feminist writers could employ the same tactic in refuting them, by citing only positive examples of famous women, as can be seen in Christine's work. Bigolina's approach is much the same: if the men will selectively mention only women known for shortcomings, Urania intends to cite the very same examples, but in order to turn the tables on the men she will stress only their positive aspects:

> Ma poscia che in dispregio loro adutti quegli essempi havete di crudeltà, di vendette, et di ruine per loro cagione, voglio con l'istesse vostr'armi difenderle, facendovi con quei medesimi da voi adutti essempi conoscere, come elle men de gli huomini sono crudeli, men vendicose, et meno d'alcuna ruina cagione. (148)

> [But inasmuch as you have brought forth examples of cruelty, revenge, and ruin caused by women, in order to condemn them, I wish to use the same weapons to speak in their defense, showing you through the very examples you have mentioned how women are less cruel than men, less vengeful, and less likely to cause any ruin. (149)]

For example, the male spokesman has already mentioned Circe as a wanton who seduced men before cruelly turning them into beasts (146), a view derived substantially from Boccaccio's in *De mulieribus claris* (38). Although Urania admits that Circe certainly appears to be cruel, and even that she was given to the vice of lasciviousness, she insists that Circe turned men into beasts primarily in self-defence, to prevent them from spreading stories abroad about her; thus she was not really cruel, since she refrained from killing the men (152). Bigolina could have found this same apology in the *Cité des dames,* wherein Christine, too, excuses Circe by saying she acted in self-defence because she was afraid of the men who had come to her island (1.32).

   Christine's defence of women, like Bigolina's, has as its very raison d'être the polemical refutation of misogynistic attitudes, since Christine's authorial persona receives instructions from her allegorical visitors to write the book precisely as a response to a male author's attack on women (1.1–2). Although Castiglione and Domenichi might have provided inspiration for the dramatized conversation between Urania and her male interlocutor, this could just as easily reflect the influence of Christine's sustained dialogue between her authorial 'I' and the personifications of Reason, Rectitude, and Justice. Moreover, Christine's emphasis on the role of Reason in constructing her defence of women is echoed in Urania's own heartfelt invocations of reason as her principal aid in refuting the opinions of the men (140, 146). Christine even provides an extended discussion of good judgment, along with several descriptions of famous women who exercised it, an example that might well have influenced Bigolina in her choice of an allegory (1.43–8).

However, there is one essential difference between Christine's episode of allegorical visitation and Bigolina's: Christine's three ladies are sent by God in response to the author's fervent prayer for advice, while Giudicio merely appears unbidden, a divine figure who makes only fleeting references to God and says he obeys a power that is only vaguely referred to as the 'dispositione de' cieli,' (the disposition of the heavens).[147] Christine implies that her misogynistic antagonists write from a place outside the word of God, so it is only right that God provide her with succour.[148] In fact, Christine's text is pervaded with religious references from beginning to end, whereas Bigolina consistently minimizes them. For instance, even though the names of the exemplary figures mentioned in Urania's extended passage defending women can all be found in the *Cité des dames*, Bigolina does not include any of the Catholic saints of whom Christine was so fond, save for one brief collective reference to unnamed virgins martyred for the faith (140). The only names that Bigolina actually provides are those of Christine's classical poets, mythological warrior women, sorceresses, seers, or queens, as well as dynamic heroines of the Old Testament or Roman history: all active, skilled, accomplished persons.[149] The numerous accounts of early Christian women who passively suffer horrendous torment and death in the name of the faith that fill the third book of the *Cité des dames* scarcely seem to interest Bigolina.

As we will have occasion to note in subsequent chapters, Bigolina consistently steers her text away from theological structures and religious solutions that frequently appear in allegorical or didactic literature, emphasizing instead the religiously neutral ground of the romance, in which the narrative is propelled more by adventurous happenstance and the decisions of characters than by providence. Bigolina's allegory has a personal dimension that seems to place it outside of the more universal realm of religious doctrine: in effect, Bigolina encounters a grotesque personification of her own erroneous notion of self-representation, the very embodiment of her private ethical crisis, for which (and by which) she must be reproached. As Alberto Ascoli reminds us in the context of certain characters' mistaken judgments in Ariosto's *Orlando furioso*, the Italian term *giudizio* was meant to render Greek words for 'crisis' or 'criticism,' and therefore implies individual awareness of the consequences of moral choices.[150] Seen thus, the stern rebuke of Bigolina's allegory of judgment brings with it an element of private moral tension that appears to owe little to the universal notions of divine justice that are so prominent in Christine's work.

By adapting Christine de Pizan's allegorical defence of women and shaping it to fit her unique vision of the established genre of the prose romance, Bigolina reveals an uncommon ambition as a writer who was remarkably unwilling to imitate any of her predecessors overtly, even as she strategically borrows and adapts elements from their works in order to put them to a quite original purpose. Thus it almost becomes an act of convenience to continue to characterize *Urania* as a romance, all the while recognizing its extensive debts to the novella, the dialogue or treatise defending women, as well as various other allegorical or didactic literary forms that will be discussed in subsequent chapters. The scope of her ambition will become more apparent as we explore her novel treatment of aesthetics and the visual arts in this work.

2 Writing a Portrait

Bigolina and Aretino

By the middle of the sixteenth century, Pietro Aretino was one of the most famous figures in Italian literary culture, renowned both in Italy and beyond the Alps. His genius and talent for promoting his own efforts had carried him from humble beginnings in Arezzo, where he had been born in 1492, to the courts of the papacy and Mantua, where he made a name for himself as a writer of satirical poems and epigrams, as well as a variety of other works. His tendency to compose artful critiques of powerful figures, as well as salacious poetry, got him in trouble on numerous occasions, and eventually led him to take up residence in Venice, the Italian republic with the greatest reputation for tolerance of nonconformists and literary gadflies.[1] This city, a flourishing centre of art, literature, and publishing, proved to be a perfect home for Aretino, and his house on the Grand Canal near the Rialto soon become a gathering place for some of the greatest personalities of the age, as well as for the publisher Francesco Marcolini and his circle.[2] Indeed, Mancini believes that Aretino's ideas and visions were an important influence on the artists associated with Marcolini, artists such as Sustris, who were soon to put their skills to work on the villas then undergoing renovation in or near Padua (*Lambert Sustris,* 14, 18). Aretino remained almost exclusively in Venice from 1527 until his death in 1556, basking in fame and the adulation of his contemporaries, quite active in the intellectual and cultural life of his new home, an honoured friend of great artists, writers, prelates, and rulers.

In many respects, Aretino's life and career reflect the birth of the modern age. At a time when the patronage of courts and wealthy individuals was still an essential component of most artistic production, Aretino showed a remarkable talent for creative independence, and he was enormously proud of his ability to make a living purely through the power of his pen. Indeed, his success depended to some extent on payoffs from the rich and famous who feared to see their names attached to one of his scathing published critiques; in this way he earned the epithet that Ariosto attached to him, 'flagello de' Principi' (the scourge of Princes).[3] He became quite well known as a publicist, ardently promoting the artistic and literary careers of his favourites through his writings. On the other hand, he showed equal enthusiasm for endeavouring to destroy the careers of his detractors and those who had fallen from his favour, such as Niccolò Franco, the author of *Filena*.[4]

Aretino's peculiar capacity to influence public opinion on a wide scale is most evident in the *Lettere*, his collection of more than three thousand vernacular letters published in six volumes over a period of twenty years, between 1537 and the posthumous final volume in 1557.[5] These letters, which Christopher Cairns has called 'the most successful image-projection of the sixteenth century' (*Pietro Aretino*, 35), were written to a dazzling array of correspondents of both high and low degree, and dealt with matters as lofty as the deeds of popes, emperors, and famous artists or as humble as gifts of food and the activities of servants. In Aretino's eyes, they functioned as the ultimate expression of the vast range of his opinions concerning society, politics, art, literature, and much else. Starting with the publication of the first volume, the *Lettere* instantly became quite popular, reflecting the new vogue for publication of works in Italian that Aretino himself, with his fascination for the power of the printing press, had done much to inspire.[6] In time, according to Aretino's example, the collection and dissemination of the private vernacular letters of other individuals became quite fashionable. Aretino's keen powers of observation and description, his fondness for expressing glowingly positive or scathingly negative opinions concerning almost anything and anyone, as well as his beguiling and innovative literary style, all served to ensure that the work would be quite influential and widely read, even outside of Italy. His many dozens of regular correspondents included such luminaries as the Holy Roman Emperor, Charles V; King Francis I of France; Pope Paul III; and his intimate friend Titian.

The year 1550 saw the publication of two volumes of the *Lettere*, the fourth and fifth, in quick succession. By this time, Aretino's world had

changed considerably, and many of the famous individuals who had
figured so prominently in the earlier volumes had faded from the scene,
among them Duke Federico Gonzaga of Mantua, the Spanish general Alfonso d'Avalos, and King Francis I, as well as the poets Vittoria
Colonna, Veronica Gambara, and Pietro Bembo. Nonetheless, the aging
writer was at the height of his fame, still immensely influential, still the
centre of attention. New names of correspondents begin to appear in
these later volumes, reflecting the appearance of a younger generation
of social, artistic, and literary contacts in Aretino's life. Among these
new names is that of Giulia Bigolina.

Book 5 includes three letters to Bigolina, written in the space of just
two months, September and October 1549. His first letter to her, numbered 338 in Procaccioli's edition of the *Lettere*, indicates that she initiated the brief correspondence with a letter of her own:

A MADONNA GIULIA BIG.
Se mai mi fur care lettere, carissima èmmi stata quella che di suo pugno
istesso mi ha datto in man propria la vostra cameriera gentile. Era meco,
quando ch'ella mi comparse inanzi, Tiziano; quel Pittor dico, che quanto
la fama è famoso; il cui soprano ispirito per esser tutt'uno col mio, nel
sentirmi leggere ciò che per mera cortesia mi scrivete ... (Aretino,
Lettere, 5:261)

[TO LADY GIULIA BIGOLINA
If ever letters were dear to me, most dear was the one that your kind cham-
bermaid delivered to me with her own hand. When she appeared to me,
Titian was with me; I mean that painter who is as famous as fame itself.
His most excellent soul was one with mine as he listened to me reading the
things which you write to me through simple courtesy ...][7]

It must be understood that at the time that Bigolina wrote to Aretino,
all evidence indicates that she had only recently emerged as a public
figure. Save for the possible mention of her by Masenetti in 1548, all
other written references to her during her lifetime date from the years
1553–60; moreover, it is quite likely that both of her surviving works
were also written after 1550.[8] Bigolina was doubtless familiar with the
earlier volumes of Aretino's correspondence, which had been published
steadily throughout her youth and early adulthood, to great acclaim.
She might also have had firsthand accounts of Aretino from Titian's
follower and former intimate Lambert Sustris, who at that time would

have recently finished the frescoes at the Villa Bigolin. Although it cannot be known exactly how Bigolina and Aretino became acquainted, it seems possible that Bigolina herself initiated this brief correspondence by sending Aretino a letter of praise. Anyone familiar with Aretino's earlier volumes of the *Lettere* would have known that Aretino was particularly fond of praise and often acknowledged laudatory letters or sonnets with grateful letters of his own, letters which he was all too happy to publish; therefore a letter to Aretino could easily serve to promote or publicize a budding career, and there is considerable evidence that Aretino's *Lettere* was regarded by many as a venue for such self-promotion.[9] In any event, as Aretino's third letter to Bigolina will make plain, the two had never had occasion to meet face to face. Bigolina's letter to Aretino has not survived, so we can only infer its contents from the things Aretino says to her in response. If she made any reference to her accomplishments on the Paduan literary scene, Aretino does not allude to it; in fact, he never indicates why he considers her a correspondent worthy of his attention, save to thank her for her kind gesture. Aretino's interest in the arts and in the doings of creative people – most often men, of course, but also occasionally women – was quite profound, as his myriad published letters attest; nonetheless, if Bigolina had hoped for some recognition on the part of the famous man for her literary abilities, she must have been disappointed.[10]

It would be easy to conclude from a superficial reading of this letter that Aretino, and Titian as well, were inclined to hold Bigolina in high regard. To be sure, Aretino begins by saying how pleased he is to receive Bigolina's letter, and how Titian was similarly moved by her kindness when the letter was read to him. Aretino also makes reference to the obligation that he owes to Bigolina for her expression of 'filial love' for him ('l'obligo ch'io tengo a l'amore filialmente portatomi da voi,' 5: 261). However, readers of Aretino's letters should always be careful not to accept at face value the words of a writer so famous for his subtlety, and so frequently inclined to malice. His tone becomes more ambiguous in the second half of the letter, where he muses on how he might be expected to regard his admirer's words. He clearly imagines that Bigolina is hoping that any attention that he pays her will help publicize her and make her name known 'in isquilla, sonante in gloria di se medesimo, ne i Templi di tutti i secoli' (as a trumpet peal, resounding in its own glory, in the temples of all the ages, 5: 261). Aretino had recently expressed a similar attitude towards women who wrote, including even the metaphor of the pealing fanfare, in a sonnet that appears at the end of Ortensio Lando's collection of letters attributed to various women, *Lettere di molte valorose donne* (1548):

> Donne in le squille de la fama ascritte,
> con gratie, & note reverende, & sole
> Hortensio lampa a le più dotte scole,
> et chiaro Heroe de le scienze invitte.
>
> Le carte illustri l'una a l'altra scritte,
> ha posto in luce del lor proprio sole;
> a ciò i gran sensi, & le gravi parole
> sieno al scrivere altrui norme diritte.
>
> Ma perche voi non sareste immortali
> se la nobil di lui pietosa cura
> non raccoglieva de i vostri sensi i sali;
> in dishonor de la sua stella dura,
> dateli loda a quel sapere equali
> con cui hor alza l'arte, hor la natura.   (162v)

[Women who are inscribed within peals of fame, with grace, and tones both reverent and unique: Ortensio, the splendor of the most learned schools, and shining hero of the deathless arts, has placed the illustrious letters written by one woman to another in the light of their own sun; therefore let their grand meanings and weighty words serve as proper examples to the writings of others. However, seeing that you would not be immortal if he had not, through his worthy and devoted efforts, gathered together the clever wit of your spirits, to the detriment of his hard misfortunes, give him praise equal to that wisdom with which he exalts both your art and your nature.]

This sonnet is one of a series of four by various Venetian writers that form an encomiastic conclusion to the volume. Aretino's ostensible purpose here is to praise the literary skills of the women who have written the letters, which would in fact echo the tone of the sonnet by Girolamo Parabosco that immediately precedes this one in the series (162r). However, in Aretino's sonnet we may readily detect more accolades for the compiler, Ortensio Lando, whose efforts have made the women immortal, than for the women themselves; as a consequence, Aretino insists that they must be grateful to him. In a similar way, in his letter to Bigolina, Aretino shows rather less interest in his addressee than he does in himself as a maker of resplendent names. It is important to emphasize that Aretino does not say why Bigolina should be made famous – he never mentions her accomplishments as a writer, nor what she might have actually done to deserve a name to resound through the ages.[11] He seems to dismiss her as one who seeks his attentions without having done much to deserve them. In fact, the conclusion of his letter very neatly 'puts her in her place' as a woman supposedly devoted to patriarchal notions of the activities suitable to her sex:

> Per il che l'umanità di che vediamvi composta, se ne congratula con la Natura, che tale vi ha fatta quale le sue caritadi vorrebbero che ci nascesse ciascuna. Che se ciò fusse, la vertú, e non il vizio; la moderanza, e non la superbia; l'onestà, e non la lascivia, predominaria il sesso che onorate con le gentilezze, adornate con i costumi, e alluminate con le osservanze. E per aprezzar piú il cielo che il mondo, la continenza vi è matrimonio, e la religione maestra. Sí che d'esservi in grazia mi vanto. Di Settembre in Vinezia. M.D.XLVIIII. Pietro Aretino. (5: 261–2)

> [On this account, the human kindness which we see you are made of rejoices with Nature; for Nature has fashioned you in just the way that she, in her benevolence, would wish to create every woman born. For if it were so, then virtue instead of vice, moderation instead of haughtiness, and chastity instead of lasciviousness would predominate in that sex which you honor with kindness, adorn with manners and illuminate with reverence. In order to appreciate heaven all the more instead of worldly things, you are married to continence, and religion is your teacher. Because of this, I am proud to be in your good graces. In Venice, September 1549. Pietro Aretino.]

She may be praised for her piety and chastity, but certainly not for her novellas and romances in prose. Even as he praises her, he makes a point of denying her any sort of literary, that is to say public, existence, or indeed any chance to make a name for herself outside of the domestic sphere. In so doing, Aretino participates in a process that was established by contemporary writers such as Baldassare Castiglione or Ludovico Ariosto, as Valeria Finucci has noted: each in his own way, these writers consistently promote 'the normalization and domestication' of women, even if superficially they appear to eschew misogynistic attitudes and promote a new appreciation of women's contributions to society.[12] From what we know of Bigolina, a writer inclined to take her ambitions very seriously, it is hard to imagine that she had hoped for nothing more than a generic response of this sort when she sent a letter to one of the most famous literary personages of Italy, especially one who was known as a publicist of the careers of others.

In any case, it seems that Bigolina remained all the more determined to attract Aretino's attention by sending him things. His next letter to her, which appears immediately after the first one in Book 5, and is dated the same month, indicates that Bigolina had heard of Aretino's perennial need for household servants and reliable governesses for his daughter (letter 339). Therefore, she had taken it upon herself to sponsor a young serving girl and send her, along with her mother, to be interviewed by Aretino in Venice. This time, Aretino's response is far less charitable:

A LA MEDESIMA

La Vilanella da la benignità vostra mandatami, è piú bisognosa che altri lei governi, che atta ella a governar altri. Certo la sua cera farebbe un torto grande al guardare Agnelle, caso che si mettesse a intertener bambine. Mi fece ridere sua madre dicendo che ha dodeci anni e va per undeci. Potria essere che M. Tiziano se la tirasse in casa a i servigetti de la figliola e de la sorella, che se cosí è, molto bene si loca e aconcia. Io ho de necessità, oltra tre ch'io ne tengo, d'una che insegni a l'altre, e non di chi ha bisogno d'imparare da loro. Dissi a la Reverenza del Padre Fra Giulio, che di quatordeci in sedici, e fino a diciotto, la desideravo, e di vista iscopariscente non troppo; imperoché dove è il bello, è quasi sempre il buono ancora. Dipoi quale è colui che compri, che non imponga al compratore, che comprando vegga d'avere verbi grazia una bella insalata, una bella zucca, e una bella anguria? 'O che belle pesche, o che belli meloni, o che bei fichi!' vocifera l'uno con l'altro in piazza; 'Che belle frutte, che bel istorione, e che belle menole sono in pescaria!' dice questo garzone a quel fante. In somma se nel vedersi diverse sorte di Donne, si grida: 'Che bella giovane, che bella sposa!', 'Che bella vedova!', o 'Che bella monica!', o 'Che bella massara!', è ben dovere. Sí che io, caso che il gran dipintore non la ritenga, rimandarovella, con il rendervi piú grazie che non avete fatto parole in cercarla, et ella passi nel venirsene a me, che ho compassione a fanciulla che ci nasce senza, disgraziata e sí povera. Di Settembre in Vinezia. M.D.XLVIIII. Pietro Aretino. (Aretino, *Lettere*, 5:262)

[TO THE SAME

The country girl whom, in your kindness, you have sent to me has more need of being looked after herself than she is capable of looking after others. Certainly her appearance would do great wrong to the herding of lambs, were she to begin spending time with little girls. Her mother made me laugh when she said that the girl is twelve years old, but she has not yet turned eleven. Perhaps Messer Titian will take her into his house to join the servants of his daughter and sister; if so, she will be well lodged and situated. In addition to the three I have already, I need a servant who can train them, not one who requires training from them. I told His Reverence Brother Giulio that I desired girls from fourteen to sixteen years of age, or up to eighteen; and not too unattractive, inasmuch as where beauty resides, good may almost always be found as well. And then, what man, wishing to buy something, fails to require his purchaser to see to it that he buys, for example, a beautiful head of lettuce, a beautiful squash, or a beautiful watermelon? 'O what beautiful peaches, what beautiful melons, what beautiful figs!' one calls to another in the market square. 'What beautiful seafood, what a beautiful sturgeon, and what beautiful *menole* {a small Mediterranean fish} they have in the fish market!' says this serving boy to that. After all, if upon seeing different kinds of women, one shouts out, 'What a beautiful maid, what a beautiful bride!' or 'What a beautiful widow!' or 'What a beautiful housewife!' it is all quite appropriate. Therefore, in the event that the great painter will not keep her, I will send her back to you, providing you with more words of thanks than the words you yourself employed in seeking the girl out. And she may stop by at my house on her way home, for I have compassion for a maid who is born without means, wretched and poor. In Venice, September 1549. Pietro Aretino.]

The attitudes towards women that Aretino reveals here should not have surprised anyone who was at all familiar with his work. It should also be remembered that Aretino had not made a secret of his habit of seducing his serving women in his earlier writings.[13] Here Aretino's comparison of attractive women to various fruits and fish reveals his allegiance to the more irreverent school of Renaissance Italian poetry, typified by the works of the anti-Petrarchist burlesque poet Francesco Berni.[14] He also satirizes certain Neoplatonic notions concerning the connection between beauty and the good, so commonly expressed in the vernacular culture of the time, by conjoining them to a lecherous comment about the potential usefulness of pretty serving girls.[15] In fact, in his use of anaphora to emphasize the comparison between the beauty of provender for sale in markets and the beauty of various categories of women that a man might ogle in public, it is even possible to discern a satirical echo of a specific passage in a very familiar Neoplatonic tract of the time, Pietro Bembo's oration on love in Book 4 of Castiglione's

Il libro del cortigiano (The Book of the Courtier).[16] Moreover, Castiglione's Bembo specifically associates beauty with goodness:

> Dassi adunque molta laude, non che ad altro, al mondo dicendo che gli è bello; laudasi dicendo: bel cielo, bella terra, bel mare, bei fiumi, bei paesi, belle selve, alberi, giardini; belle città, bei tempii, case, eserciti. In somma, ad ogni cosa dà supremo ornamento questa graziosa e sacra bellezza; e dir si po che 'l bono e 'l bello a qualche modo siano una medesima cosa, e massimamente nei corpi umani . . . (4.59, 321)

> [Therefore we give great praise to nothing less than the world, saying that it is beautiful. It is praised when we say beautiful sky, beautiful earth, beautiful sea, beautiful rivers, beautiful towns, beautiful woods, trees, gardens; beautiful cities, beautiful temples, houses, armies. In short, this charming and sacred beauty gives the highest adornment to everything; and one can say that the good and the beautiful are one and the same in a certain sort of way, and this is particularly true of human bodies . . .]

Aretino's second letter to Bigolina conveys something of the mocking tone of his earlier parodies of Renaissance dialogues on love, the *Ragionamento della Nanna e della Antonia* and the *Dialogo,* in which he had shown a similar tendency to disparage women according to their social categories. If addressed to a male acquaintance, this letter might have come across as nothing more than another reflection of its author's fondness for scurrilous jokes. But Aretino is not writing to a male acquaintance. Instead, he says these things to a respectable woman of a distinguished Paduan family whom he had not yet had occasion to meet, and who had tried to do him a favour. Moreover, there is no mistaking his arrogance and intent to insult when he tells her that his words of thanks to her are more substantial than the effort she made in attempting to ingratiate herself with him. The tone and purpose of this letter are complemented by the missive that immediately follows it in the volume, in this case addressed to an unknown woman of high degree (5.340). Here too Aretino scornfully rejects a serving woman whom the addressee has sent to him; he calls the servant 'una ruffianella, isporchetta e mariola' (a dirty, swindling little procuress, 5: 263), one who would be better suited to the lady's own household. Aretino has clearly put this letter beside the one to Bigolina to reinforce a specific point. Aretino's publication of his letter to the Paduan author, with the aim of having her see it disseminated across Italy and beyond, constitutes a veritable slap in the face.

We cannot know if Bigolina managed to see this letter before it was published, since Aretino sometimes composed letters purely for publication, not as actual missives to send to people.[17] Nonetheless, she must have remained undaunted. Shortly after the episode of the serving maid, she sent yet another item to Aretino, to which he refers in his third letter to her, dated the following month (letter 353). This time his thanks are more sincere, for once more she has sent him something he can truly appreciate, a sonnet praising him:

A MADONNA GIULIA.
Bigolina Graziosissima, egli è certo che chi vol farsi riputazione dove non
è, mandici in suo scambio la fama. Questo dico in proposito del parermi
d'averne qualche poco ancor io, poi che solo per conoscermi voi in bocca
di lei, vi sete mossa a scrivermi in laude un cosí vivo, un cosí nuovo, e
un cosí chiaro sonetto. Benché a ciò havvi spinto piú tosto la bontà che il
giudizio; e per non dilettarvi meno di ben dire che di ben fare, ciò avete
esseguito . . . (Aretino, *Lettere*, 5:276)

[TO LADY GIULIA
Most gracious Bigolina, it is certainly true that those who have not yet
made a name for themselves must send forth fame in the place of the
reputation they wish to gain. I say this because it seems I must still be a
little famous myself, for you only know me on account of my fame, and
yet you have taken it upon yourself to write so lively, original, and brilliant
a sonnet in praise of me. Kindness has moved you in this, rather than good
judgment; nonetheless, you have done it in order that you might take as
much delight in good words as you have in good deeds . . .]

In this letter, Aretino makes it plain that Bigolina only knew him through his reputation, another sign that he was inclined to regard her as yet another of his many publicity seekers. Although he is obviously quite pleased to receive a sonnet from her, he cannot resist slipping in yet another unpleasant reference to chambermaids: if the greeting of 'una minima serva' (a serving woman of no importance) is enough to guarantee his allegiance to her, then what is he to make of Bigolina's poetic creation? Aretino was a renowned master of the back-handed compliment, the superficial word of praise that masks an undertone of malice, as his letters constantly reveal. In this last letter, he manages to laud Bigolina with blandishments even while dismissing her as insignificant; she may be the author of a pleasant sonnet of praise for him, but she is not someone worthy of great respect.[18]

The publication of these three letters in 1550 must have been a truly remarkable moment in Bigolina's life. Her name had now appeared in print, in a book that was destined to be seen by a great many people in many lands; moreover, she had become known as a correspondent of Pietro Aretino, the man who wrote regularly to the Pope and the Holy Roman Emperor. He had even indicated that he had shared her letter with Titian, arguably the most famous painter of the time. Nonetheless, he had also published some rather unflattering comments about her, especially in his second letter, and he had gone so far as to employ a kind of parody of Neoplatonic attitudes towards beauty as a means of mocking her. In any event, this brief exchange of letters, a serving maid, and a sonnet mark both the beginning and the end of any known association between Aretino and Bigolina. Our author is not mentioned again in this volume, nor does her name appear in the subsequent and final volume of the *Lettere,* which was published after Aretino's death.

Not long after the printing of Aretino's letters to her, perhaps only two or three years later, the Paduan author produced her greatest work that has come down to us, the prose romance *Urania.* Although this book cannot necessarily be called an explicit response to Aretino's three letters to Bigolina, I believe it may be demonstrated that *Urania* does indeed provide a refutation of certain opinions about art and beauty which Aretino expresses throughout the *Lettere* as a whole. To a great extent, *Urania* must be seen as a polemical work: it is a polemic that sets out to refute several notions dear not only to Aretino but to most other theorists of the age, regarding the modes of perception of human beauty and how best that beauty might be depicted in literature and the visual arts.

Portraiture in *Urania*

To appreciate the audacity of what Bigolina says in *Urania,* first it is essential to take note of the revolution that Aretino's multivolume letter collection had long been fomenting in the realm of portraiture and the visual arts. In his several volumes of the *Lettere,* Aretino continually depicts a world awash in portraits, portraits of personages great and small, portraits by Titian or Giorgio Vasari or Leone Leoni, portraits that are sent from one person to another, portraits said to be so true to life that they inspire great admiration in the viewer not only for the subject but for the skill of the artist as well. Indeed, Aretino saw his epistolary collection itself as a kind of portraiture, as Raymond B. Waddington notes: 'So completely had Aretino defined the function of the book of letters as portraiture and so effectively had he stamped that invention with his own identity that the two became coterminous' (*Aretino's Satyr*, 58). Aretino imagined that he had invented a new way of capturing the identity of an individual, one that functioned in a realm forged from the confluence of words and visual images.

As Luba Freedman has shown, Aretino's persistent championing of the paintings of his good friend Titian led to a re-evaluation of the art of portraiture and the ways in which it might be evoked in both poetry and prose.[19] Before Aretino's time, sonnets inspired by painted portraits were not uncommon, and indeed they can trace their origin back most directly to the two poems that Petrarca wrote in praise of Simone Martini's portrait of Laura.[20] However, only with Aretino does one begin to see as much attention paid to the artist's skill and technique as to the painted subject, for in the older tradition of sonnets describing portraits the work of art served as little more than a point of departure for an exaltation of the painted subject itself.[21] In the *Lettere*, Aretino provided readers with nothing less than a new theory of the relationship between literature and art, as well as a whole new context for the age-old literary topos of ekphrasis, as will be discussed in the following chapter.[22]

Aretino's *Lettere* had a profound and immediate influence in Italy, first and foremost inspiring a new vogue for creating and distributing collections of letters in the vernacular. More subtle influences can be traced in the evolution of the discussion of the art of portraiture within the literary works of some of his contemporaries, who were most often disposed to follow his lead in the apotheosis of this form. Aretino's friend Lodovico Dolce, in his *Dialogo della pittura intitolato l'Aretino* (1557), made a deliberate attempt to establish Aretino as an authority on the subject of painting, and in so doing emphasized all the more the connection between art and literature, comparing Titian's artistic technique to that of poets such as Ariosto.[23]

In his letters, Aretino continually stresses the importance of the portraitist's skill at imitating nature, as well as the more subtle task of depicting the subject's *concetto*, or inner essence.[24] In Aretino's view, Titian excelled at portraying not only a person's appearance but also his or her character. As Freedman notes, Aretino appears to have been the first person to describe actual portraits in his letters and sonnets; he does not merely provide word portraits that may or may not have been inspired by real paintings.[25] For Aretino, the painting itself becomes a tangible, essential artifact, not just a fleeting excuse for a poem. Aretino also stresses the function of words in revealing the true intention of the artist, revelling in his own ability as a writer to give voice to Titian's portraits; for instance, in his letters there are references to the close association between the power of the pen (*penna*) and that of the paintbrush (*pennello*).[26] Clearly it pleased Aretino to imagine not only that he was as great an artist in his own right as Titian but also that his own skill with words could serve to enhance and even complete the aesthetic experience of looking at one of Titian's portraits. This notion of Aretino's was also disseminated in the writings of others, as is revealed in this passage in Sperone Speroni's *Dialogo di amore* (first published 1542). The two speakers are Tullia d'Aragona and Nicolò Grazia:

GRA. Certo Tiziano è oggidì una maraviglia di questa età, ma voi lo lodate in
    maniera che l'Aretino ne stupirebbe.
TUL. Lo Aretino non ritragge le cose men bene in parole che Tiziano in colori; e
    ho veduto de' suoi sonetti fatti da lui d'alcuni ritratti di Tiziano, e non è fac-
    ile il giudicare se li sonetti son nati dalli ritratti o li ritratti da loro; certo am-
    bidui insieme, cioè il sonetto e il ritratto, sono cosa perfetta: questo dà voce
    al ritratto, quello all'incontro di carne e d'ossa veste il sonetto. E credo che
    l'essere dipinto da Tiziano e lodato dall'Aretino sia una nuova regenerazi-
    one degli uomini, li quali non possono essere di così poco valore da sé che
    ne' colori e ne' versi di questi due non divenghino gentilissime e carissime
    cose. (2: 548)

[GRAZIA: Certainly Titian is the marvel of the age nowadays, but you praise
    him to such an extent that Aretino himself would be astonished.
TULLIA: Aretino does not portray things in words any less effectively than
    Titian does in colours. I have seen some of the sonnets he has written
    describing certain portraits of Titian, and it is not easy to judge if the son-
    nets were born from the portraits, or if the portraits were born from the
    sonnets. Certainly the two together, that is, the sonnet and the portrait, are
    a perfect thing: the former gives voice to the portrait, whereas the latter, on
    the other hand, dresses the sonnet in flesh and bones. I believe that to be
    painted by Titian and praised by Aretino constitutes a new regeneration of
    men: in and of themselves, men cannot be of such little value that they do
    not become the most noble and precious things in the colours and verses of
    these two.]

This passage was expurgated under the pressure of Counter-Reformation censors in later editions of Speroni's *Dialoghi* (Aretino's works had been placed on the Index of Forbidden Books shortly after his death).[27] However, during the 1540s it was innocuous enough to be reprinted often. It reveals not only the extent to which the artistic efforts of Titian and Aretino could be assimilated in the popular imagination but also the quasi-mystical power that these works, both painted and written, were thought to have over those who were portrayed within them: however mediocre these subjects might be, they would surely find themselves exalted, even 'regenerated,' by the creative abilities of these two men.

As we have noted, it was not long after 1550, when she must have seen Aretino's three letters to her in Book 5 of the *Lettere,* that Bigolina set about composing her prose romance, *Urania.* This work was to become Bigolina's vehicle for expressing her suspicions concerning the moral dangers of posing for portraits, as well as of the value of portraiture itself.

Bigolina establishes the rejection of portraiture as a central motif right from the beginning of the work, in the allegorical proem. Here Bigolina's authorial persona tells how she came to create this book: her idea was to leave a token of remembrance of herself to the young man Bartolomeo Salvatico, for whom she bears a deep and resolutely platonic love, and to whom she dedicates the work.[28] However, she did not arrive at the decision to write a book without first considering certain other art forms, and it is here that one of the great themes of *Urania* is introduced: the moral implications of the *paragone* between the arts. She tells us that at first she mused upon the possibility of having someone reproduce her likeness in a sculpture, only to realize quickly that this was the wrong art form for someone of her sex, degree, and humble accomplishments: sculptural depictions are appropriate for heroic men, not for a woman like her.[29] She then decides that it will not be improper to have her portrait painted so that she could give it to Salvatico (58–61). However, soon after deciding this she finds herself confronting the allegorical vision of 'Giudicio,' or Judgment, who explains that his appearance as a naked homunculus endowed with a huge head and a single great eye is symbolic of the various attributes of good judgment. As we have noted, Bigolina also sees herself reflected in his eye, but there she appears nude, with a stain on her left side representing the flaws of her character. This sight frightens and dismays her:

> Veduto c'hebbi quello così strano homiciuolo, che esser un horribile mostro credevami, tutta come io dissi, di spavento ripiena, et non sol di spavento, ma per vedermi così ignuda, di tal di me stessa vergogna, che harrei

voluto esser in quel punto sanza occhi, et perciò per uscir della camera forte tremando verso l'uscio mi volsi. (60)

[Once I had seen this strange little man, whom I took to be a horrible monster, I was, as I have said, filled with fear; and not only with fear, but also with so much shame at seeing myself naked that I would have preferred in that instant to be deprived of my eyes. Therefore I turned toward the door to escape, trembling hard. (61)]

However, the allegorical being manages to calm her and informs her of his identity. He also explains that her nude image is the natural result of staring into the eye of Judgment: anyone who troubled to look therein would appear in that fashion. Indeed, he says, there are a great many presumptuous people in the world who would benefit from such a sight of themselves (64). He goes on to describe, in a reproachful tone, the proliferation of bad judgment in the world, including the misogynistic attitudes of so many men who blame women for being wanton when they themselves so often indulge in that vice (66).

The little man then lectures Bigolina's authorial persona at length. Employing a Socratic mode of questioning, he helps her see that portraiture is the wrong art form for her purposes: she should never have imagined that a painted portrait could adequately communicate her heartfelt devotion for Salvatico, nor that it could serve as a suitable memorial to her after her demise.[30] The allegorical visitor informs her that posing for a portrait would be a mistake, a case of bad judgment in fact, for this would provide nothing more than a vain simulacrum of her external appearance. She is now made to understand that she must look within herself for a true memorial of her inner beauty to leave to Salvatico. Having declared this, the little man disappears abruptly, and soon thereafter the narrator tells us she has taken his advice to heart:

Et poi ch'egli così m'hebbe detto sanza che io lo potesse, come era il debito mio ringratiare, da gli occhi miei in un baleno si fu dileguato. Alla quale partita, come cosa, che è fuori di sè stessa io rimasi. Pur dopo poco spatio d'hora in me ritornando, et ripensando sopra la prima deliberatione che di mandarvi la imagine della mia faccia havea fatta, acciò ch'ella in voi la memoria di me viva tenesse, parvemi che assai sciocco fosse stato quel mio primo proponimento. Et perciò abbandonando il primo del tutto, al secondo mi venni accostando. Et così da quello aiutata, del mio basso intelletto una imagine trassi, la quale dalla volontà del mio cuore pigliando la effiggie et il colore da amendue insieme questa operetta ne è uscita, che *Urania* si chiama, pigliando il nome da quella sopra la quale tutta la istoria è fondata. (82)

[Just as he had finished saying this he disappeared from my eyes with a flash, without my having the opportunity to thank him, as I should have. When he was gone I was left stunned, but then regained my wits after a short space of time. I thought over my original plan to send you the image of my face, so that you would keep me alive in your memory; it now seemed to me to be very foolish. I therefore abandoned it entirely, and turned instead to the second proposal. Aided by this, I drew forth an image from my low intellect, an image which took its shapes and colors from the will of my heart. This little work, deriving thus from both my intellect and my heart, is called *Urania*, and it takes its name from that woman who is the whole subject of the story. (83)]

The shocking sight of her own image, her 'portrait' reflected in the mirror eye of Judgment, has led inexorably to the decision, at once both moral and aesthetic, to reject the glorification of portraiture and painting that was so prevalent during her time.[31]

We have already noted the remarkably innovative aspects of Bigolina's description of the genesis of her narrative concerning the adventures of Urania: she does not claim to recount real, lived experience, as was so often the case in the amatory prose romance tradition that she has adopted; nor does she say that she is repeating a story she has heard from others, as was so often done by writers of novellas. Instead, she explicitly declares that she has conjured up the story from her imagination, with a main character who, as we shall see, is meant to function as a sort of alter-ego for the author herself, since her actions and values clearly reflect Bigolina's own experiences as a character in the proem. However, it is important to note the task that the author has put upon this invented narrative: it is meant to stand in for a painted portrait that presumably would have captured the essence of the author as an individual. Bigolina has, in effect, set out to *write* the portrait that she has refused to allow another person to paint of her. Whereas a painter like Titian would have used the medium of colours on canvas to communicate the subject's *concetto,* which Luba Freedman has defined as 'the subject's essential characteristics as conveyed in the portrait' (26), Bigolina has pointedly refused such a recourse, and has declared her intention to write her own *concetto* into a work of literature. Thus *Urania* is meant to be seen as a sort of self-portrait, a distillation of the essence of who the author is, so that she may make a gift of herself to the young man she esteems.

At a stroke, Bigolina has rejected that pet notion of Aretino's concerning the relationship between literature and painting, so frequently trumpeted in the pages of the *Lettere*. As we have noted, Aretino was fond of believing that his own sonnets on Titian's paintings could serve to complete the viewer's experience by allowing the reader to effectively 'read' the portrait. 'His sonnet, Aretino suggests, discloses the portrait's message, as if the portrait were addressing itself through the sonnet to the living subject,' observes Freedman (*Titian's Portraits*, 26). But if Aretino's literature is supposed to help the viewer appreciate the true identity of the painted subject by giving a voice to the image, Bigolina is forthrightly saying quite the opposite – that literature must be seen as the truest portrait of the individual's identity, to the extent that it has no need of painted images at all. Literature is in itself the best portrait, as well as the best voice of the portrait.

Bigolina avoids any further recourse to allegory in her work, despite her allegorical beginning, and indeed the narrative that she creates is otherwise deprived of fantastic or supernatural elements.[32] Nor is she interested in legendary, remote, or exotic settings: instead, her story unfolds in the southern city of Salerno in a time close to Bigolina's own, under the peaceful rule of Prince Giufredi.[33] Bigolina leaves the allegory of Giudicio behind as she proceeds to her narrative, but not Giudicio's lesson, which receives its very embodiment in Bigolina's protagonist, a high-born maiden of Salerno named Urania who attracts the attentions of men more for her virtue than her beauty: 'Era costei per cagion di cotali sue virtudi, più che per gran bellezza che 'n lei si ritrovasse, da molti nobili giovani di Salerno amata, et desiderata' (This quality, more than any great beauty she may have had, caused her to be loved and desired by many noble youths of Salerno, 84–5). Urania personifies the message that the homunculus has just communicated to the narrator, Bigolina: a woman should be valued for what she does, not how she looks.[34] Urania at first resists the attentions of these men; but as we are told, Love has another fate in store for her (86). In time she falls in love with the very proper Fabio, who has been drawn to the reputation of Urania's virtue. He courts her in a discreet and honourable fashion, paying her visits and exchanging artfully composed letters and sonnets with her. Both Fabio and Urania are described as accomplished writers (86).

After Fabio has betrayed Urania by turning his attentions to Clorina, Urania composes her long letter of reproach to Fabio, admonishing him for his faithlessness (90–106). In this letter, Urania describes the cognitive processes whereby the soul comes to appreciate beauty, employing the Neoplatonic terminology typical of Cinquecento Italian treatises and dialogues on beauty and love. This in turn leads her to characterize the essence of Fabio's offence in terms of the age-old conflict between the relative merits of exterior and interior beauty:

Io so che altra donna, et più di me bella tu ami, chè se di me più bella non fosse, per così cieco non ti tengo, che per altra men di me bella io credessi che abbandonata m'havesti; quando certissima sono, ch'ella più di me virtuosa non sia. Hor dunque se di questa tua bella donna per la quale hai lasciato di amarmi, dovendoti da lei dilungare, un ritratto volesti portar teco, il quale la sua bellezza a gli occhi tuoi rappresentasse, come faresti quando ancora Apelle o Zeusi et altri eccellentissimi pittori fossero vivi, che più d'un ritratto potessero fare, overo facendone molti, che più d'una sola somiglianza della tua donna tenessero . . . Dimmi adunque, ti prego, quanti ritratti ti trovi haver teco i quali la bellezza mia ti rappresentano tutti? Et ecco il loro miracolo grande, che quello che dar non ti può la tua bella donna in eterno, nè tutti i più eccellenti pittori, nè ancora la gran maestro Natura lo ti potrebbe dare, io già te l'ho dato; che quante volte miri,et consideri le tante et varie sorti di rime et prose che da me composte tieni nelle tue mani, tanti ritratti vedrai esser quelle, quantunque diversi fossero, li quali ciascun da per sè et tutti insieme quanta sia in me bellezza ti manifestano. Hor vedi che già ti ho fatto conoscere come le bellezze, le quali ciascun giorno tu poi vedere, quando in me et in molti miei ritratti con lo intelletto tuo ti degnassi mirare, più meritano d'esser da te amate et tenute care, che qual'altra maggior corporale bellezza esser si voglia. (96–8)

[I know that you love another woman, one more beautiful than I. She must be more beautiful, for I know you are not blind, and you would not have abandoned me if she were less beautiful than I am. And yet I am absolutely certain she is not more virtuous than I. Therefore, if you were to have to go far away from this beautiful lady of yours, for whom you have ceased loving me, you would want to bring along a portrait that would still show her beauty to your eyes, just as you would have done in the days when Apelles, Zeuxis, and other most excellent painters were alive. These artists might produce more than one portrait, or perhaps they would make many of them and provide you with a variety of images of your lady . . . Tell me then, I pray you, how many portraits do you have with you that show my beauty? Here is their great miracle: I have already given you something which your pretty lady cannot give you for all eternity, nor all of the most excellent painters, nor indeed that great artist, Nature. Every time you look upon and contemplate in your hands the many and varied works which I composed, both poetry and prose, you will see they are all portraits, even if they are each different; and each of them by itself, as well as all of them taken together, show you how much beauty there is inside of me. Now you see what I have already made plain to you: that those beautiful things which you can see in me every day (that is, at such times as you might deign to use your intellect to regard me and my portraits), deserve more to be loved and held dear by you than any other greater physical beauty one could want to have. (97–9)]

As will be discussed in the next chapter, this passage reveals Bigolina's firm stand in one of the great intellectual debates of her time, the *paragone* between literature, especially poetry, and the visual arts. To some extent, Fabio's carrying an image of his beloved harks back to a famous analogy in Book 10 of Plato's *Republic,* wherein Socrates declares that painting is to be condemned because it reproduces nothing more than the external appearance of things, just as anyone might do simply by carrying a mirror everywhere.[35] However, it is not just painting that Bigolina is denigrating, but portraiture – more specifically, the use of portraiture not only as a reminder of the appearance of an absent lover but also as a means of portraying the essence of the self.[36] In these words there lies an implicit challenge to the contemporary apotheosis of portraiture, an apotheosis whose most strident spokesman was arguably Aretino himself, the man who once said he would happily carry around with him his own portrait by Titian to serve as a mirror (*Lettere,* 3.265).

Within the fictional frame of her prose romance, Bigolina now asserts that the sort of portraiture practised by artists is not only unnecessary, it is downright dangerous, for it provides no sure vehicle to convey the beauty of the soul, and might even lead to immoral choices, to bad judgments.[37] As the text shifts from the didactic mode to the mimetic (i.e., from the allegorical proem to the romance itself), Urania appears as a sort of mimetic stand-in to reinforce the lesson of Bigolina's reformed authorial persona, since she too is a woman who writes and has nothing but scorn for someone who must pose for a painting as a means of memorializing herself. Urania is wise enough to understand the lesson of the allegory of judgment, for she knows already what the authorial character has just learned: that a portrait painted by someone else cannot communicate heartfelt emotions or the inner beauty of the soul as surely as one's own work of literature. The letter to Fabio establishes Urania as Bigolina's wise and virtuous protagonist, a fictional embodiment of the principal message of the text.

Only literature, especially literature that is produced by the subject who wishes to be remembered, provides a true portrait of the beauty of the soul. Urania has proved this by writing sonnets to her beloved, just as Bigolina herself has proved it by writing the romance *Urania;* and the fact that Urania is not as attractive as other women, and thus would not leave as nice-looking a portrait, ought to be seen as irrelevant: what matters is the depiction of inner beauty. Bigolina, perhaps mindful of the usual terminology of the *paragone* debate, is careful to include both prose and verse in her exaltation of literature: other defenders of literature almost universally stress the epideictic value of works in verse, whereas Bigolina, whose chosen medium is prose fiction, must perforce mention both.[38]

The Caricature of Titian

This episode is clearly not Bigolina's last word on the subject of portraiture in *Urania,* since it also figures so prominently in the episode of the Duchess of Calabria. We are told that the duchess leaves the management of her affairs of state to her trusted counsellors, so that she may devote herself to a life of quiet solitude amid her substantial portrait collection, where she often goes to contemplate the images of other great lords and ladies (186). There were historical precedents for such behaviour: Bigolina might have had in mind the humanist Paolo Giovio, one of Aretino's frequent correspondents in fact, who collected portraits of celebrities and kept them in a personal gallery (his 'Musaeus') on Lake Como in the 1530s, or perhaps the famous private art collection of Isabella d'Este.[39] Moreover, a letter attributed to Pantasilea Lunarda Giordani, which Ortensio Lando includes in his *Lettere di molte valorose donne,* describes a gift of numerous portraits of distinguished women that are meant to edify the recipient (6r–v). But it is hard not to see the influence of Aretino here as well, with his continual praise of portraiture as a means of capturing the excellence of distinguished individuals. In fact, Aretino expresses a keen desire to have his own portrait added to Giovio's gallery, as he indicates in a pair of letters to Giovio (3.176, 4.49).

The duchess's troubles begin when her court painter, said to be the most famous of the time (186), brings her the portrait of Giufredi, the

Prince of Salerno, a man renowned for both his good looks and his fine manners. As the painter offers his work to the duchess, he tells her she now holds 'il ritratto di tutte le bellezze del mondo' (the image of all the beauty in the world, 188–9). When the duchess falls in love with the image, she prays to the goddess of love that she might receive the same miraculous gift as Pygmalion, that is, that the gods might make the image come to life (190).[40] She turns to her most trusted old counsellor for help, a man who has been a father figure to her, hoping for the best advice, but his recommendation is the very worst he could give, according to the ethical parameters of Bigolina's text. He convinces her that she must allow the painter to depict her as Venus in a version of the Judgment of Paris in a new painting designed to win the heart of the prince:

Perchè il buon vecchio, che sanza fine era desideroso di compiacerle, tolta c'hebbe da lei licenza molto tosto si ritrovò co'l pittore, et havendo la fede sua tolta in pegno, brevemente raccontolli il grande amore, che la lor signora al Prencipe di Salerno portava, et insieme quello, che egli havea deliberato di fare, per condure il suo desiderio a buon fine; il che fu ch'egli volle che lo accorto pittore con quella maggior diligenza ch'egli sapeva usare sopra uno nobilissimo quadro il giudicio di Paris pingesse; cioè le tre Dee, et seco Paris col pomo d'oro in mano, che fu di tanta ruina cagione. Et non sanza molta consideratione havervi volle che la Duchessa di Borbone, la quale era donna assai bella, ma di grandissima venustà ripiena; di maniera che a chiunque la mirava faceva nascer un gran desiderio di riverirla, anzi adorarla; ch'ella di Giunone il loco tenesse, et fosse co'l scettro in mano et la corona in capo, come Reina del Cielo. Et la figliuola del Re di Polonia, la quale in que' tempi era bellissima di persona, et di faccia, ma del tutto d'ogni amor vano rubella, per haver la verginità sua al grande Iddio consacrata, nè d'altra cosa che d'haver assai scienze pareva curarsi; volle egli che come Pallade tutta armata, et con la lancia in mano fosse dipinta. Et perchè havea più volte udito dire al Duca morto suo signore che non si poteva più bella cosa nel mondo vedere, come era l'ignudo corpo della Duchessa sua moglie; volle perciò, che la bella Signora nel loco di Venere con parte delle bellissime sue membra scoperte si pingesse. (194,196)

[Thus the fine old man, who desired so much to please her, took his leave of her and went to see the painter. Once the old man had sworn him to secrecy, he swiftly told him of the great love which their mistress bore for the

Prince of Salerno, and also of what he planned to do in order to bring about the thing she yearned for. This was his plan: the artist would use all of his skills to paint a very lofty image of the Judgment of Paris, showing the three goddesses together with Paris holding the golden apple, the cause of so much ruin. Without pondering long the old man decided that the Duchess of Bourbon, who was a beautiful woman filled with such charms that anyone who saw her felt a great desire to revere and even worship her, should stand in for Juno, holding her scepter and wearing the crown of the Queen of Heaven. And then he wished the daughter of the King of Poland should be depicted as Pallas, all armed and bearing a lance in her hand. She was at that time a very beautiful woman in face and body, yet opposed to any form of earthly love because she had sworn her virginity to God Almighty; indeed she seemed to care for nothing else but acquiring great knowledge. Finally, since the old man had often heard his lord, the late Duke, say that there was no sight more lovely on earth than the nude body of his wife the Duchess, he wished that his comely Lady be painted in the place of Venus, with a part of her gorgeous body uncovered. (195, 197)]

In short, the duchess's courtiers recommend that she do the very thing that Bigolina's authorial persona has rejected as improper, following the advice of the one-eyed allegory of judgment: not only must she pose in a painting, she must pose with her body partially uncovered. She has been asked to appear in one of the lush mythological paintings that had become quite fashionable, as well as controversial, by the mid-Cinquecento, and which were especially associated with Titian, the creator of so many of the best-known examples. It was, in fact, right around this time, in the early 1550s, that Titian began to refer to these paintings rather audaciously as *poesie* (poems), in a conscious effort to associate his mythological subject matter with the poetry of both the ancients and their contemporary humanist followers.[41]

The text goes on to describe the duchess's pose with considerable precision:

Chè facendole porre uno manto, overo bernia di carmesina seta, sopra l'ignude carni, la quale la manca spalla coprivale, et giù descendendo alla destra ascella tutta la destra spalla, il braccio, et la mammella scoperti restavano; et dalla parte sinistra il bel fianco, parte del ventre, la coscia con ambedue le gambe, et gli picciolini piedi tutta ignuda si dimostrava ... (196)

[He would have her place a mantle or cloak of crimson silk over her naked skin, covering her left shoulder, and descending down to her right armpit so that all of her right shoulder, arm and breast would be exposed. On the left side she would reveal in their nakedness her lovely flank, a part of her abdomen, her thigh and both legs, along with her tiny little feet. (197)]

At first it might seem strange that so much attention is paid to precisely which parts of the woman are covered or uncovered, since there is no indication of the position of her body as a whole – that is, whether she is standing or reclining – nor, indeed, how she relates to the other figures in the painting. To some extent that must have seemed unnecessary, because of the familiar subject matter of the painting. This pose cannot be the same as that of so many paintings of the period that showed reclining Venus figures, such as those of Lambert Sustris, Titian's *Venus of Urbino*, or his series of paintings of such figures with musicians, because the iconography of the Judgment of Paris always required the three goddesses to be standing before their judge, more or less in a row.[42] Otherwise, Bigolina quite evidently wishes her reader to be able to conjure up a precise vision of this painting; the reader becomes in effect a viewer who is invited to gaze at the spectacle of the lovely woman. We may observe that the flank that the duchess is said to expose is the left one, the same side where Bigolina's authorial persona saw a stain on herself in the mirror of Judgment's eye; in either case it would seem the ethical connotations are clear. Rona Goffen notes that it was generally believed that the right side of the body was 'superior' to the left (a notion evoked by the Latin term *sinister*), as well as warmer, for the presence of the liver.[43]

The Judgment of Paris was a popular subject for painters of mythological subjects throughout the Renaissance, doubtless to some extent for the sheer volume of naked female flesh it could put on display: in nearly all versions, including those of Lambert Sustris himself, three nude goddesses stand before the fascinated Paris, who gazes at them as he decides which is the most lovely and thus deserving of the golden apple that he holds (see figure 2.1).[44] His final choice could easily be viewed by many as something of a calamity, a supreme act of bad judgment, in fact, for it led to the fall and ruin of Troy.[45] The duchess is portrayed as a virtuous woman who wants to do what is right, but in her desperation she lets herself be swayed by the old counsellor, whom she trusts. We are told that she is fantastically beautiful, and when she poses semi-nude in the painting as Venus, both the artist and the old

Figure 2.1. Lambert Sustris, *The Judgment of Paris* (c. 1568). Galleria Sabauda, Turin

counsellor are nearly overcome by the sight of her. Bigolina's painting of a beauty pageant is all about looking and being looked at: we are told that the painter 'came close to committing some rash act' as he goes about his work, and even the old counsellor is aroused by the sight of his duchess, so that each man had to protect himself with a shield made of reason in order to resist temptation (196, 198). This may remind us yet again of Titian's emphasis on depicting sensual experience through sight, on his games of posing and gazing involving Venus figures.[46] The erotic quality of the gaze in so many of Titian's paintings, even those with a religious subject, has been noted in a recent study and was doubtless frequently remarked upon in Bigolina's time.[47] The artistic world of which Titian was the acknowledged master is the very one that Bigolina wishes to depict, albeit in an ironic fashion.

When the painting is finished, the painter carries it to Salerno and presents it to Giufredi (202). The prince's own portrait has been included in the painting, naturally enough in the role of Paris, his eyes fixed on Venus as he gives her the apple. Thus Giufredi finds himself involved in a sort of 'double gaze': he looks upon the naked limbs of the duchess as Venus both within the painting and without.[48] The painter now provides a lengthy and lavish ekphrasis of his work as a means of convincing the prince not only that he should accept the painting but also that he should come to desire the woman who is portrayed therein:

'Deh per cortesia mirate un poco Signore, come queste aurate crespe chiome paiono reti da allacciar mille indurati cuori . . . che la spatiosa, et lucida fronte; gli occhi, che a due stelle si assimigliano; quantunque la loro natural vivacità non vi si possa scorgere a pieno; le inarcate, et d'hebano ciglia; il ben proportionato naso, le gote di rose, la picciola bocca, le labra

della quale vincono di bellezza i coralli; nè d'altra cosa tanto mi doglio, quanto è del non haver potuto quelle orientali perle, ch'elle rinchiu-
dono, come io le vidi in lei, così pingerle ancora. Il mento di giustissima
misura, et che in parte alcuna non manca, o eccede, par che ciascuno dica
da per sè, "Qui, et non altrove tiene il suo regno Amore." Ma che diremo
poi noi di cotesta gola, et petto, che vincono di bianchezza le nevi? Et di
quel poco rilevato pomo, che non vi è chi mirandolo tutto d'amoroso desio
struggere il cuor non si senta. O Dio, che rotondo et ben formato braccio
è questo! Della mano non dico, perchè troppo ben si assomiglia a quella
che spesse volte l'arco, la faretra, et gli strali del fanciullo Cupido mod-
era et regge. Al bel ventre et rilevato fianco non credo già che la Invidia
alcun difetto vi ritrovasse. Ma mirate, Signore, più che ogn'altra cosa, con
somma attentione vi prego, la bellissima coscia della quale altra più bella
non credo che Fidia, o Policletto ne scolpissero mai. Et in fine chi da capo
a' piedi ben la mira, et considera, dirà che la gran Maestra Natura giamai
altro corpo più di questo d'ogni bellezza perfetto, nè creasse, nè potesse
creare.' (202, 204)

[Please see, my lord, how these golden curls resemble nets which could
entrap a thousand hard hearts . . . Notice her curved eyebrows, which are
the color of ebony, and her well-proportioned nose, as well as her rosy
cheeks and tiny mouth, whose lips in their beauty put corals to shame.
Regrettably I was not able to paint the oriental pearls which I saw enclosed
within those lips; nothing saddens me more. As far as her chin, which
is of most perfect proportions, is concerned, it has no shortcomings or
grossness whatever, and indeed it seems that each one who views it says
to himself, 'Here, and nowhere else, Love has established his realm.' But
then, what are we to say about this throat, and this bosom, both of which
are so much whiter than snow? And what of this slightly raised apple,
which no man can look upon without feeling his heart melt with amorous
desire? My God, how round and well formed is this arm! And I have said
nothing about the hand, which looks all too much like the one which is so
often seen to handle the bow, quiver and arrows of the youthful Cupid.
I do not believe Envy has found any defect in her lovely abdomen, nor in
her exposed side. But above all, my lord, pay the greatest attention to her
most lovely thigh, for I do not believe Phidias or Polykleitos ever sculpted
one more lovely. To sum up, whoever looks her over from head to toe,
and regards her closely, will conclude that the great Mother Nature never
created, nor ever could create, a body more perfect than this one in every
beautiful detail. (203, 205)]

As will be discussed more fully in the following chapter, this passage recalls the standard lyric and romance motif of the blazon or *descriptio mulieris* (description of a woman), ultimately derived from several commonplaces in Petrarca's poetry. However, an equally important model can be found in the hyperbolic descriptions of works of art, especially Titian's paintings, that Aretino included in so many of his letters. Bigolina might have derived the fragmentary description of the woman's individual parts from Petrarchism, as well as from contemporary dialogues on beauty, but the ekphrastic style, emphasizing the viewer's response to the sight of a work of art, is Aretino's. Here, for example, is Aretino's letter of 1531 to Count Massimiano Stampa (1.28), describing a painting by Titian of John the Baptist:[49]

E non dovete pregiare il dono, ma l'artificio che lo fa di pregio. Guardate la morbidezza de i capegli innanellati, e la vaga gioventú del san Giovanni. Guardate le carni sí ben colorite che, ne la freschezza loro, simigliano neve sparsa di vermiglio, mossa da i polsi e riscaldata da gli spiriti de la vita. Del cremisi de la veste, e del cerviero de la fodera, non parlo, perché, al paragone, il vero cremisi, e il vero cerviero, son dipinti, et essi son vivi . . .

[And you must not value the gift, but the artifice that makes it a thing of value. Look at the softness of the hair in ringlets, and the lovely youthfulness of Saint John. Look at his flesh, which in its freshness is colored so perfectly that it resembles snow sprinkled with red, moved by the pulses and warmed by the spirits of life. I do not speak of the crimson color of the garments, nor of the lynx fur of the lining, because, in comparison, true crimson and true lynx fur are painted, while these are alive . . .]

The same sort of language can be found in Aretino's often cited letter of 1537 to Veronica Gambara (1.222), wherein he describes Titian's painting of the Duke and Duchess of Urbino, lavishing praise on the beauty of the subject as well as on the art technique that brings it to life, and also in a letter describing Titian's *Annunciation*, addressed to Titian himself (1.223).[50] The hyperbolic gushing that Aretino makes fashionable here, replete with impassioned rhetorical questions and appeals to the viewer to notice this feature or that, finds a precise parallel in the words of Bigolina's painter.[51] At first glance it might seem that Bigolina is acknowledging Aretino's revolution in the traditional topos of ekphrasis, and striving to imitate it in the fashion of Aretino's many admirers.[52]

But by the conclusion of *Urania*, it becomes apparent that Bigolina is more inclined to satirize Aretino's method of art criticism than imitate it, since the act of posing and letting herself be painted, so that she can become the object of pleasure for the eyes of men, leads ultimately to the duchess's demise. Moreover, the character of the painter, who appropriates Aretino's language of ekphrasis, is meant to be seen as amoral, disreputable, and untrustworthy, for all his vaunted skill. In time, his gift will be rejected. The Prince of Salerno is indeed captivated by the painting, but not in the way that the counsellor, the painter, and the duchess intended:

> Mentre s'ingegnava il pittore di inalzar con somme lodi la eccellenza di quelle bellissime membra, il Prencipe, che fissamente il bel ritratto mirava, più di mille ardentissimi sospiri havea mandati dal cuore; della qual cosa essendosi accorto il pittore, et di certo credendo ch'egli di quelle singolari bellezze innamorato si fosse, et di ciò sentendone un'infinito contento, s'affaticava perciò più fortemente a lodargliele ogn'hora. Ma per dire il vero, il fatto in altro modo passava di quello ch'egli già divisato s'haveva; imperciò che essendo il buon Prencipe già più di due anni acceso nell'amor d'una assai bella donzella, la quale era figliuola d'un nobile conte suo vassallo; et che la savia damigella per compiacere al Prencipe veniva chiamata; mirando quelle estreme bellezze nelle membra di quella vaga Signora venne in consideratione, anzi in ferma credenza che tali, o forse anco più belle esser dovessero quelle della donzella, ch'egli amava cotanto. Per qual cosa d'un così novo, et intenso desiderio di vederle, et gustarle s'accese, che non solamente li cagionò quei focosi sospiri, ma fu etiandio cagione ch'egli ponendo in quel punto tutti que' rispetti da canto; i quali infiniti havea. Fece deliberatione subito ch'ella da Napoli fosse tornata dove da alcuni suoi assai nobili parenti era stata chiamata per nozze, di torlasi per moglie. (204, 206)

[While the artist strove to exalt with the highest praise the excellence of those gorgeous limbs, the Prince fixed his gaze upon the portrait and sent forth from his heart a thousand most ardent sighs. When the artist became aware of this, he was certain that the Prince had fallen in love with her singular beauty; and, feeling infinitely content, he made an effort to praise her even more. But to tell the truth, the situation was proceeding in another direction from that which he had planned. For the good Prince had, for the past two years, been in love with a very beautiful maiden who was the daughter of one of his vassals, a noble count, and she was called the wise maiden by everyone, in order to please the Prince. As he looked upon the extreme loveliness of the fair lady's body, the Prince came to imagine, and indeed he was convinced that the body of the maiden whom he loved so much must be the equal of the one in the painting; or perhaps it was even more lovely. For this reason he was seized by so strange and intense a desire to see the maiden's body, and to have a taste of it, that it made him heave hot sighs, and even caused him to set aside all of those scruples which he had once had in abundance. He immediately decided the maiden should return from Naples, where she had been called by certain of her noble relatives who wished to find her a husband, for now he would marry her himself. (205, 207)]

Thus the subtle and unseemly plot of the painter and the counsellor comes to nothing; all they have managed to do is inspire the prince to pursue a more proper and legitimate love affair. In the end the two courtiers leave Salerno in disgrace, and the hapless duchess, lamenting that she had put her body on display 'con poco suo utile' (with little advantage to herself), dies of grief when she hears the news (286).

A number of elements suggest that Titian served to a considerable extent as a model for Bigolina's painter. She never provides a name for this man, calling him simply the most famous painter of the time ('il più famoso pittore che in que' tempi vivesse,' 186). This certainly recalls the accolades for Titian that anyone living in the Veneto in the 1550s (and familiar with Aretino's *Lettere*) would have read or heard quite often; in fact, Titian's fame throughout Europe was extraordinary during his long life, and for a time he was the only artist allowed to paint the emperor Charles V.[53] Like Titian, Bigolina's painter prefers to associate himself with a ruler and to make a reputation for himself as the creator of portraits of great and powerful people. David Rosand has characterized Titian as having 'the courtly know-how of a Raphael and the almost arrogant self-confidence of a Michelangelo' ('Titian and the Critical Tradition' 5), qualities that certainly should remind us of Bigolina's artist, who moves confidently from one court to another, ingratiating himself with potentates and even having the audacity to execute portraits of one without his permission: his first portrait of the prince is done in secret (186), and subsequently he presents the *Judgment of Paris* to the prince without any prior announcement, to say nothing of a negotiated commission (198–202). In some ways, notes Rosand, Titian had become a sort of archetypical artist in his own lifetime: 'Titian's name was synonymous with the art of painting; acclaimed the highest representative of the art, he seemed its very embodiment, in effect, becoming himself

Figure 2.2. Titian, *Venus of Urbino* (1538). Uffizi Gallery, Florence

the personification of painting' (Ibid., 5). Hearing him exalted thus from every quarter, and possibly from Titian's associate Lambert Sustris himself as he decorated her family's villa, Bigolina might well have realized that she could find no better model than Titian, the very painter who was Aretino's close friend and inspiration, and who had moreover been a witness to Aretino's public humiliation of her, when she needed to create an artist as a character for her narrative. It is hard to imagine that her contemporary readers would not have noted the resemblance.

Moreover, Bigolina's artist proves quite adept as the creator of sensual images of women, a subject at which Titian had long excelled, and which had gained him great renown.[54] His *Venus of Urbino* is perhaps the best-known painting of the type (see figure 2.2), but it is worth noting that Titian was engaged in creating his provocative 'Venus with musicians' series during the years 1545–50, just as Bigolina was writing to Aretino and beginning to make a name for herself in Padua.[55] Bigolina even tells us that the duchess poses with a red mantle, employing what has been called 'Titian's signature color.'[56] Just as Titian himself was making his name resound throughout Europe as a maker of sensual Venus images,

Bigolina presents us with something of a caricature of him, a 'failed Titian' who triumphantly paints a half-naked Venus to please a prince, only to fall flat on his face, bringing ruin upon himself and his mistress.[57]

Titian was often called 'Apelles' during his career, the name of one of the most famous painters of ancient Greece, whom Titian consciously imitated, especially as a painter of nude Venus images. As Rona Goffen notes, the name 'Apelles' had become a standard appellation for an artist who was appreciated by Renaissance men of letters.[59] One of the best-known anecdotes about Apelles, which was often repeated in early modern writings on the arts, was that Alexander the Great gave his concubine Campaspe to the artist as a reward for painting her so well.[60] Goffen observes that Titian's fantastic career actually reflects a reversal of the old story of Alexander and Apelles, on account of the fact that Titian had become as distinguished a personage in his time as the potentates with whom he had continual dealings (*Titian's Women*, 126). Here Goffen discusses the likelihood that Titian's models were indeed his mistresses, or at least were regarded that way, in accordance with classical attitudes that had in fact been mythologized in the story of Pygmalion.[61] This perception, coupled with the fame and influence that accompanied Titian throughout his long life, allowed him to assume the role of Alexander, to be able to offer his own 'mistresses' to his powerful patrons instead of the other way around; the only difference is, he offers them in the form of paintings for their delectation. Titian's paintings were specifically designed to arouse male erotic fantasies, says Goffen (ibid., 126); and this is the very thing that Bigolina's own painter aspires to do when he uses the gift of a painting of his duchess as a means of giving her body to a princely patron. Elsewhere in *Titian's Women*, Goffen also cites Vasari's version of the story of Apelles and Campaspe, suggesting that 'the successful creation of the beautiful woman's image will be rewarded by possession of the woman herself, the incarnation of beauty. These intertwined themes of possession of the beautiful woman and the creation of her image permeated the Renaissance conception of the woman in art' (9). I would like to suggest that Bigolina boldly sets out to reveal the fallacy of this notion, which was so closely associated with Titian's artistic experience, when she creates her character of the painter.

Specific letters in Aretino's collection suggest further links between Titian and Bigolina's painter, especially those which describe how Titian provides people with portraits so that they may be revered in private chambers, much as the duchess does. An example can be found in a letter of 1541 (2.277), addressed to Ferrante Sanseverino, the real-life Prince of Salerno (a figure who, as has been noted, was quite evidently of great interest to Bigolina), which begins thus:

> Io ho dato in ricordo a M. Tiziano, il quale viene a la corte, che mi tolga col suo stile unico il contorno de la vostra imagine singulare, accioché io possa farmela dipignere in camera per riverirla come quelle de i Santi. (2: 308)

> [I have reminded Messer Titian, who is coming to court, to employ his unique style to capture for me the outlines of your singular appearance, so that I might have it painted in my room and revere it like an image of the saints.]

Later in that same volume (2.441, to Don Diego Mendoza) Aretino appends a sonnet to the letter describing Mendoza's joy at having Titian's portrait of his beloved lady in his room, where he may contemplate it like a holy relic.[62] Bigolina's painter does not merely remind us of Titian, he reminds us of Titian the way Aretino portrays him.

As for Aretino himself, his presence is felt throughout *Urania*. To some extent, as I have noted, the whole premise of the romance constitutes a rejection of so much of what Aretino champions in the *Lettere*. In the beginning of her proem Bigolina ponders how to leave a memorial of herself, and at first she decides to do the very thing that both Aretino and Titian might have counselled; that is, to have herself painted. After all, Aretino's letters frequently express the notion that a portrait should fulfil the subject's desire to be remembered by posterity.[63] In her proem Bigolina lets us know that she yearns to be remembered (58–60, 82), and that is probably at least part of the reason why she contacted Aretino in the first place; but the memorial that Aretino provided for her in his three published letters could scarcely have been satisfying. However, Bigolina was not to be thwarted, so shortly thereafter she set out to create a grand memorial of her own, the romance *Urania*. There her authorial persona learns the lesson of the allegory, that posing passively for a portrait painted by someone else is an inadequate means of communicating one's essence to the world. Her lesson in good judgment constitutes a rejection of Aretino's notion of how one should create a personal memorial.

Anyone who wanted to know how important portraiture was to Aretino had only to pick up a copy of one of the volumes of his *Lettere*, which would most typically bear the image of the author on the frontispiece.[64] Aretino loved to see himself portrayed and remembered in the visual arts, as several of his letters attest, and this is the very sort of vanity that Bigolina makes a point of rejecting in her proem to *Urania*.[65] Moreover, Bigolina's virtually unique creation of a female romance protagonist who is less beautiful than other women, yet who proves herself by far the most clever, capable, and virtuous, might be interpreted as a rancorous response to Aretino's comments on female beauty in his second letter to her. If Aretino says, in effect, that the only good chambermaid is a pretty chambermaid, Bigolina will show him what a less pretty woman is capable of, through her creation of the dynamic and resourceful fictional heroine Urania.

There is even a hint of Aretino's presence in the character of the duchess's counsellor, whose relationship with the duchess is said to be that of a father to a daughter; this recalls the reference in Aretino's first letter to Bigolina to the 'filial love' he says she has shown him. The counsellor and the painter stand as the very embodiment of bad judgment in the romance, and the episode in which they betray the trust of the desperate duchess, thereby bringing about her ruin and death, suggests a kind of allegory of Bigolina's failed relationship with Aretino and Titian. Instead of advice and encouragement in her efforts, Bigolina received nothing more from her illustrious correspondent than empty or equivocal compliments and a hint of mockery, with his ideological soulmate Titian looking on in the background. The full implications of her mistake, and the lessons she has learned from it, constitute the essence of *Urania's* moral message, that a woman should find within herself the ability to write her own portrait, instead of posing for one. By adopting the language of Aretino's lavish praise of portraiture as a means of rejecting the very validity of such praise, and by fictionally recreating in negative terms the same type of painting that had brought Titian so much glory and fame – a nude Venus – Bigolina declares the ultimate triumph of words over pictures, the complete validation of a woman who has learned to make the fullest use of her creative powers.

Of Mirrors, *Istoria*, and Women in the Arts

In some ways, there is nothing so remarkable in the meeting between Giudicio and Bigolina's authorial 'I'; after all, medieval and early modern literature is replete with narratives that begin with authors receiving allegorical or otherwise supernatural visitations, often in dreams, often as a prelude to a journey. This episode may also be seen as a variant of the typical medieval romance topos that Donald Maddox has called 'the specular encounter,' in which 'action becomes contingent upon a primary personage's receipt of crucial information pertaining to the self and various aspects of its identity' (*Fictions of Identity*, 11). In such a scene, romance protagonists often learn hidden truths from mysterious apparitions such as talking animals, who place the protagonist before a figurative mirror: 'This localized cognitive transfer creates an intersubjective enclave, in which the informant places the addressee before a *speculum* that mirrors its discovery of a modified self-image' (11). In Bigolina's case 'the modified self-image' is all the more dramatic and startling, since the mirror is more literal than figurative. However, it should be noted that Bigolina is drawn to a specific subcategory of the broad topos of allegorical or specular visitation in her own proem, a subcategory that is particularly associated with the ethical crises of authors who must choose proper modes of literary expression. A famous example of this type of allegorical vision may be found in Boethius's *Consolation of Philosophy*, in which a female figure representing Philosophy visits the author in his study in order to drive out the Muses of Poetry, who were providing the author with false inspiration (1.1). In works following Boethius's model, the supernatural visitor typically comes to reproach the author for some misguided notion, in order to set him or her on the correct creative path.[66] The most important of these texts for Bigolina is Christine de Pizan's *Le livre de la cité des dames*, which, as we have noted, has left various traces in both the proem and the main narrative of *Urania*. The authorial personas of both Christine and Bigolina are visited by allegorical figures who arrive in a critical moment, while each author ponders the ways in which women are, or ought to be, depicted in the arts; subsequently both of them receive lessons in how to write a proper book that will defend women. Glenda McLeod has noted how Christine's three visitors, the crowned ladies who are allegorically named Reason, Justice, and Rectitude ('Droitture'), are meant to represent 'the inner character of the narrator'(*Virtue and Venom*, 121n), and the same could be said for Bigolina's allegory of judgment: the author is having a conversation with her own conscience. Rectitude's declaration that Christine has a natural inclination for learning (2.36) may be compared to Giudicio's own validation of Bigolina's intellectual competence as an author: in a similar fashion, he tells her that the heavens have given her 'un desiderio infinito di sapere assai' (an infinite yearning for great knowledge, 80–1). Although Bigolina's grotesque Giudicio bears no physical resemblance to Christine's three visitors, Giudicio's mirror-like eye certainly seems to be derived from Reason's mirror in the *Cité des dames* (1.3), which allows those who look into it to know themselves completely, both their good qualities and bad.[67] It may be said that Bigolina's allegorical mirror serves much the same function as Christine's, even if Christine is not specifically interested in portraiture. Here is McLeod's analysis of Christine's mirror of Reason (*Raison*):

> Iconographically ... the mirror itself refutes other feminine allegories of sin, such as the figure of Vanitas, who often appears as a woman with a mirror. In Christine's catalog, Vanitas's association between women and exterior, physical, transient beauty gives way to Raison's quest for the internal, moral, eternal beauty of truth. (*Virtue and Venom*, 121)

In some ways, Bigolina has simply updated Christine de Pizan's defence of women in the *Cité des dames* in the context of the debate over the moral implications of Renaissance portraiture, with the art of portraiture standing in for the mirror of Vanitas, and Judgment's mirror standing in for that of Reason.[68] By adopting the topos of the allegorical visitation of the author in her proem, Bigolina establishes not only a parallel between her book and Christine's, but also a central theme for *Urania* as a whole: she will discuss women's search for appropriate methods for self-expression in the arts.

The explicit purpose of *Urania* is to provide a true self-portrait of its author. Bigolina's proem dramatizes the potential strategies of a woman endowed with artistic talent who wishes to take control of the way she is to be depicted in the arts, and who wishes to resist the prevailing tendency of contemporary male artists to depict women as generic – and therefore nameless – icons of beauty.[69] Bigolina was not alone among the talented women of her day in her search for a way to deal with this problem. Her experiences may be compared to those of the artist Sofonisba Anguissola (1532–1625), who was active in Cremona in the 1550s, while Bigolina was writing *Urania*. In a series of self-portraits, Anguissola made provocative efforts to take charge of how she was to be portrayed, ironically enough in painting, the very medium that Bigolina rejects as inadequate and inappropriate. One of Anguissola's paintings, *Bernardino Campi Painting Sofonisba Anguissola* (late 1550s), is particularly significant in this regard (see figure 2.3). Here we are shown Anguissola's teacher, Campi, in the act of painting his pupil on canvas; we see both the artist and the painted subject looking out to meet our gaze. A skilled man portraying a woman in a passive pose: this seems

Figure 2.3. Sofonisba Anguissola, *Bernardino Campi Painting Sofonisba Anguissola* (late 1550s). Siena, Pinacoteca Nazionale

to follow standard practice, until we realize that the true object in the painting is Campi himself, captured by Anguissola who paints him ostensibly in the act of painting her.[70] Anguissola manipulates our traditional notions of subject and object as a way of redefining the place of women in the arts and the reality of the objectification of women, much as Bigolina does in her tableau of the Judgment of Paris: the male artist purports to be the creative force, but instead he is spied upon, even mocked perhaps, by the artistic woman who has fashioned him out of her own imagination.[71] We observe Campi and the duchess's painter as they work, through the eyes of a woman artist. The aim of both Bigolina and Anguissola, kindred spirits who probably never met, is to avoid becoming the object of the male painter's gaze; as Mary Garrard notes, Anguissola 'claims artistic subjectivity through the mask of invisibility' by keeping herself 'on the unseen side of the picture plane.'[72] Bigolina, too, deliberately avoids the painter's gaze when she refuses to allow herself to be painted and retreats from her own 'portrait' in the eye of Giudicio; instead, she takes control of the situation as a literary artist and describes both a main character who rejects the value of portraiture as well as a failed fictional painting of her own, thereby asserting complete control over the effects of the gaze.

Bigolina uses two distinct terms to refer to *Urania* as a literary work, both in the same sentence: *operetta* and *istoria* (82). As a genre designation, *istoria* had considerable currency among her contemporary writers of prose romances, since it appears in the titles of both Corfino's *Phileto (Historia di Phileto veronese)* and Franco's *Filena (Historia amorosa ultimamente composta)*. As we have noted, Italians of this period did not use the term *romanzo* to describe these works; therefore, *istoria* is as close to a standard term in contemporary usage as may be identified for long prose narratives such as *Urania*.[73] However, in art circles the term had another meaning entirely; and given that Bigolina is quite interested in commenting on the visual arts in her book, it is worth inquiring into the possibility that she had another definition in mind.

In Book II of his treatise *Della pittura* (1435), Leon Battista Alberti had declared that *istoria*, by which he meant the dramatic, storytelling aspect of the subject that a painter chooses to create, was the element that truly bestowed greatness on a painting (56–7, 60). A painter had to know how to choose a proper *istoria* as a subject, and moreover depict it in an appropriate fashion; therefore Alberti recommended that painters associate with poets, who knew all the good stories (3, 94). For Alberti, who had a great influence on subsequent art theorists of the Renaissance, *istoria* was closely tied to *invenzione*, a classical rhetorical concept that he applied to the visual arts: in order to paint anything, an artist had to come up with a subject, an argument to be depicted, an *invenzione*.[74] All that is worthy in an *istoria* lies in its grounding in a clever and appropriate *invenzione*, asserts Alberti, so the painter has a moral duty to be particularly careful in conceiving of one (3, 92). During Bigolina's time, the art theorist Paolo Pino defined *invenzione* in specifically literary terms, even though he was talking of painting: 'questa s'intende nel trovar poesie, e istorie da sé' (this is understood to be the composition of poems and stories on one's own, 108). The process of conceiving of suitable subject matter was regarded as essentially the same for painters and writers both, as a result of the application of the terminology of rhetoric to painting, begun by Alberti and continued by Bigolina's contemporaries.

However, to a great extent women artists were not thought to be capable of fulfilling this function, since they were generally expected to be portraitists, and portraiture involved simply copying what one saw; thus a portrait was not said to require *invenzione*. Portraiture was merely *ritrarre* (reproduction, depiction), the lesser of the two modes of *disegno* (design), since it did not involve the superior function of *imitare* (imitation), in which the artist was expected to interpret, by means of *invenzione*, the subtle distortions that might be visible in the object.[75] Thus it was remarkable that Anguissola was acclaimed in her lifetime for her capacity to 'invent' in her paintings, for her ability to create a portrait that went beyond mere reproduction of external features, and therefore might reveal an actual *istoria*.[76] When Anguissola painted her family seated together in *The Chess Game,* a painting that particularly impressed Vasari, she showed that she aspired to create a domestic scene that was imbued with elements of narrative, 'una cosa storiata' (a thing with a story).[77] This is a work in which the arrangement of the subjects, along with the glances they cast at each other and towards the unseen artist who occupies the viewer's position outside of the painting (much as she does in the painting of Bernardino Campi), all serve to fulfil Alberti's dictum that a good *istoria* should communicate itself through the painted figures' gestures and glances.[78] It has also been demonstrated that Anguissola knew how to use the self-portraitist's principal aid, the mirror, to good effect in conceptualizing and fashioning herself in her paintings, so that the images she produced could tell a kind of story about who she was and how she saw herself.[79]

Just as Anguissola transcends her society's putative gender limitations by 'historiating' her self-portraits and her portrait of her family, Bigolina provides a grand conceit of her own: she refuses to pose for a painting, choosing instead to invent a story that includes a fictional male painter's failed invention for a woman's portrait. She cannot paint 'una cosa storiata,' but she can surely write a literal *istoria* and not only describe therein the *istoria* contained within her fictional painting of the Judgment of Paris but even tell of how the characters outside the painting react to it. She stresses elements of *istoria* in her account of the creation of the painting and the appearance of the figures within it, but these elements only attain their true meaning within the narrative when the experience of the Prince of Salerno as viewer is taken into consideration; thus the *istoria* of the painting becomes part of the wider *istoria* of the text itself. Bigolina demonstrates that she can provide those narrative elements that Alberti said a painting should contain, and more besides, since her chosen medium, prose fiction, allows her to describe all of the circumstances of the painting: how it was conceived, how it was made, how it was presented to its viewer, and how that viewer regarded it and came to be influenced by it. Bigolina means to show us how a romance *istoria* can outperform the *istoria* of any painting, and also how it can show the truth about the way women are so often depicted by male artists.

Bigolina systematically rejects all of the great claims for portraiture as it was championed by Alberti and Aretino: that it could effectively represent an absent person, that it could capture the essence of the subject's interior life; that it was more than mere superficial imitation; that dialogic interaction between portrait and viewer could only be a positive experience; that a portrait could take on the duties of friendship and provide an oratorical function.[80] (And in doing so she also rejects an entire culture that held such portraiture in awe.) Instead, she seeks to show how a work of literature, more specifically a work of fiction, the prose romance, can do all of these things more effectively. Alberti wanted an 'interlocutor' in every painting, a figure who would communicate the essence of the *istoria* directly to the viewer (*Della pittura,* 2, 72–4). Jodi Cranston has written of the 'transitive relationship between art and spectator' that prevailed in many Renaissance portraits as a result of Alberti's influence, wherein perspective, gestures, or glances serve to 'persuade the viewer to constitute the fiction' that the painting represents (*Poetics of Portraiture,* 73). In effect, the viewer is engaged as part of a dialogue, in Cranston's view (ibid., 74). In her dramatization of this process, Bigolina takes it a step farther: just as the fictional Prince of Salerno must interpret the moral implications of the 'transitive relationship' in order to see through the artist's deception in *The Judgment of Paris,* the astute reader of *Urania* is asked to evaluate the role of painting in society and be aware of its deceptive qualities.

In *Della pittura,* Alberti calls the mirror a 'buon giudice' (good judge) that the artist can use as a tool to correct imperfections in his work (2, 82). Aretino casts a satirical eye on this concept when, in the comedy *La Cortigiana* (4.18), he has his character Messer Maco, who has been taking lessons in how to be a courtier from the cynical painter Maestro Andrea, look at himself in a convex mirror and conclude absurdly that someone has stolen his true features.[81] Bigolina's Giudicio provides an uncanny parallel to both of these mirror-viewing episodes, since his eye is a mirror that shows up the imperfections of the person who is reflected there. Bigolina's mirror has two purposes: as a medieval-type *speculum* in the tradition of Christine, it guides and offers advice; however, it also serves to demonstrate to the authorial persona why the visual portrait is *not* an aid to good judgment, since it does not show the right things about a person. Thus Bigolina's allegory of Judgment may also be called an allegory of the failed function of the painted portrait. The 'portrait' Bigolina sees of herself is disturbing, and subsequently she comes to understand that the portrait she was planning to have made would have been just as disturbing, a betrayal of her integrity as an artist and a woman. In her reflection she is shown a distorted image of the truth; thus the image is both true and untrue in the same moment, rather like the distorted image of himself that the painter Parmigianino produced in his famous *Self-Portrait in a Convex Mirror*.[82] As Jodi Cranston notes, the mirror image in this work presents contradictory interpretive possibilities that emphasize 'the concept of the relationship between painting, portraiture and mirrors in the Renaissance, and how viewing in each situation involves neither pure perception nor judgment, but is located somewhere in between, each action interfering with the other' (*Poetics of Portraiture,* 141). Giudicio, whose mirror eye is rather like the circular convex mirror that Parmigianino used, offers this lesson: beware of the lies of portraiture. Bigolina's authorial persona learns this in the proem, just as the prince comes to learn it in the main narrative when he sees himself 'reflected' in the *Judgment of Paris*.

3   Ekphrasis and the *Paragone*

Ekphrasis in Western Literature

The Greek prose romance *Daphnis and Chloe,* written by Longus around the second century of the Christian era, opens with a scene of ekphrasis, the literary description of a work of visual art. The narrator tells how he once came upon a painting in a sacred grove in Lesbos and gazed upon it in fascination (17). The painting seemed to tell so remarkable a love story that the narrator finds himself compelled to seek out someone who knows which events inspired the images, so that they can be retold in words. The romance itself is the result: therefore, we never actually 'see' the painting, we only read the story that the painting inspired the narrator to create. Another Greek romance, *Leucippe and Clitophon* by Achilles Tatius, also written in the second century, opens in a similar way, with the narrator admiring a painting of the abduction of Europa in a temple in Sidon.[1] This sight prompts him to comment aloud about the phenomenal power of love, whereupon a man standing beside him, Clitophon, remarks that he knows more about this than anyone. This leads to Clitophon's first-person account of his tumultuous love affair with Leucippe, the very substance of the romance that follows. Not only is this narrative born of ekphrasis, it contains in turn several more episodes of ekphrasis, including even the conceit of ekphrasis within ekphrasis, since at one point the two lovers see a painting of Ovid's tale of Philomela and Procne, in which the tongue-cut and raped Procne must weave a tapestry to communicate the nature of the outrage that she has undergone to her sister Philomela (78–80). Just as the characters in the romance must attempt to interpret the significance of the pictures they have seen, within the picture itself are yet more pictures set forth for interpretation. As we have already had occasion to note, both *Daphnis and Chloe* and *Leucippe and Clitophon* were well known to the sixteenth-century Italian reading public and had considerable influence on European literature throughout the early modern period.[2] Their emphasis on ekphrasis as a mover and shaper of plot in the prose romance must have been quite familiar to the Italian authors who, like Bigolina, set out to write similar works.

Bigolina's innovative use of ekphrasis in *Urania*, as well as her rejection of Aretino's exaltation of the visual arts in his writings, can be best be understood in the context of a brief overview of the ways in which the topos manifests itself in Western literature.

The term 'ekphrasis' has been commonly used by literary critics to refer to literary descriptions of art objects only in recent years, even though it can be traced back to Hellenistic rhetoric, wherein it referred to the standardized technique of describing just about anything, including works of art; the word itself simply means 'description,' or 'recounting.'[3] The ancients imagined that poetry and painting had special affinities, a notion summed up in the phrase 'ut pictura poesis,' derived from Horace's *Ars poetica* and often repeated during the Renaissance.[4] The depiction of art objects in literary works has a very long and distinguished history, dating back, in the West at least, to Homer's elaborate description of the shield made by Hephaistos for Achilles in Book 18 of the *Iliad.* Many other memorable examples abound in ancient, medieval, and early modern literature, so that by the mid-sixteenth century it was a very familiar literary device, known from a host of epics, romances, and allegorical-didactic works in both verse and prose, as well as lyric poems. Early modern readers could have very precise expectations regarding this topos: they were accustomed to seeing it put to certain specific uses, in certain types of works, for it had been continually presented to them in circumscribed, even predictable ways.

In classical literature, ekphrasis might serve as an aesthetic device, an opportunity for the writer to show off his or her powers of description, or an excuse to retell a familiar story in a clever way. A principal example of this may be found in Homer's account of the shield of Achilles, a narrative tour de force designed to depict all human experience as a sort of visualized microcosm. As is typical of ekphrastic episodes occurring in a mythological context, the reactions of human observers to the divine artwork are absent in Homer's poem.[5] There is a similar lack of emphasis on the act of seeing in the episode of Arachne and Minerva in Book Six of Ovid's *Metamorphoses* (vv 1–145), even if the scenes depicted in Minerva's and Arachne's tapestries have more immediate bearing on the narrative, for they show the power of the gods to strike down impudent mortals, as well as the tricks the gods can play on them; all of this serves to foreshadow the swift and terrible fate of the boastfully defiant Arachne. This type of ekphrastic passage, retelling familiar myths without emphasis on the reactions of observing characters, will reappear during the Renaissance in the fifteenth-century Italian poem *Le Stanze* by Angelo Poliziano (also known as Politian), with its description of the artful intaglios on the doors of Venus's palace on Cyprus (1.97–119).

However, whenever the gods or figures of myth are not present in these ancient episodes of ekphrasis and the context strives for something closer to historical verisimilitude, we may generally note a much greater emphasis on the experience of the observer; moreover, in these works ekphrasis takes on a more significant role with regard to the substance and structure of the narrative. A prime example of this may be found in Book 1 of Virgil's *Aeneid,* when Aeneas is moved to tears by the sight of a fresco in Dido's palace in Carthage that shows the whole story of the Trojan War, from which he has just fled (vv 456–93).[6] In narrative terms, this scene sets the stage for Aeneas's own account of the fall of Troy and his escape, which he will soon describe to Dido; but it also has a more subtle, prophetic function, since it foreshadows the eventual destruction of Carthage itself, to be brought about by the Roman descendants of Aeneas. Thus the painting of Troy, viewed by a Trojan ancestor to the Romans, takes on a pivotal role within the poem, summing up what has gone before even while foreshadowing future events both in the narrative itself and in the history of Rome. Inasmuch as this scene also serves to 'humanize' the character of Aeneas, who cannot help but stare and weep when he sees the fate of his people worked in paint upon a foreign wall, we may note the extent to which a poet of the calibre of Virgil could exploit the expressive potential of an ekphrastic image.

In other ancient texts, especially the Greek prose romances of the first centuries of the Christian era, ekphrasis might play a similarly central role, linked to the very genesis of the narrative, as the examples of *Daphnis and Chloe* and *Leucippe and Clitophon* illustrate. Margaret Anne Doody, in her book *The True Story of the Novel,* has noted that while other authors of other literary forms have often taken up the task of describing works of visual art, 'prose fiction has always had special obligations to – and affiliations with – *ekphrasis*' (388). Only in the novel (the term she uses to designate the Greek tales as well) does ekphrasis so consistently work itself into the very fabric of narrative, and only in the novel does literature reveal such a conscious tendency to place itself in competition with the iconographic arts. Doody goes on to note that ekphrasis 'may always be considered a manifestation of the eternal war between poetry and painting. Literary artists in prose, as well as poets, are anxious to vindicate the verbal art, and to give it, finally, the higher position' (ibid., 398). Doody also points out another source of tension implicit in the novelistic application of the topos, since the presence of ekphrasis in a literary work immediately sets the task of interpretation before the reader; indeed, we cannot shake off the notion that descriptions of artwork in a text must *mean* something, something which the author is not always willing to make explicit (ibid., 388). Whoever is observing the images within the narrative must also be expected to derive some useful lesson from them, as the characters in *Leucippe and Clitophon* attempt to do quite overtly.

The didactic function is most apparent in another text of late antiquity, the *Imagines* of Philostratus the Elder (later his grandson, Philostratus the Younger, wrote a similar work by the same title). In this Greek work of the third century, which Norman E. Land has called the most important work on ekphrasis in antiquity, the author describes a stay at a villa that is decorated with a great many paintings.[7] When a boy asks him to interpret them, the author complies, providing a series of lectures on the mythological or nature scenes that appear in the paintings (3). Philostratus is primarily interested in providing a handbook for artists and therefore keeps his narrative to a minimum, even if his descriptions emphasize the stories and the actions of the figures that are depicted more than the techniques that artists might employ to reproduce them. The two texts of the *Imagines* had considerable influence on later applications of ekphrasis, and indeed Aretino follows their style and tone to some extent in his own descriptions of paintings in the *Lettere*, especially in his use of rhetorical questions addressed to the viewer, as well as in his emphasis on the viewer's experience and interaction with the scenes that are described, the very things that Bigolina satirizes in her painter's ekphrasis of the painting of the duchess.

In the later Middle Ages and early Renaissance, ekphrasis became a common feature in allegorical-didactic works, often serving as an elaborate device for presenting exemplary or allegorically significant figures. Instead of the Greek novelists' or Philostratus's supposedly real paintings, seen in realistic groves, temples, or villas, ekphrastic episodes are now suffused with an air of the supernatural, their figures often appearing in dream visions and sometimes endowed with the apparent ability to move or speak. Egregious examples of such works include Guillaume de Lorris's part of the *Roman de la rose* (vv 129–466), cantos 10 (vv 28–99) and 12 (vv 16–72) of Dante's *Purgatorio,* and, in a veritable tour de force, cantos 4 to 36 of Boccaccio's *Amorosa visione.*[8]

The didactic and exemplary nature of most medieval ekphraseis tended to preclude anything resembling the ironic treatment of the motif that Bigolina later was to adopt. By and large, the viewer is expected to respond to the messages communicated by the ekphrastic images in these works in a straightforward, unambiguous fashion, unlike Bigolina's prince, who must see through the painter's deception. However, an exception to this tendency may be found in *Guigemar,* one of the *lais* of the twelfth-century author Marie de France. In this work, a jealous husband keeps his wife locked up in a chamber beside a chapel decorated with paintings, which include an image of Venus throwing a copy of Ovid's *Remedia amoris* into a fire (vv 232–44). Ostensibly, the painting is intended to instruct the viewer, as well as the reader of the text, in the proper behaviour of lovers: Venus 'excommunicates' all those who would follow Ovid's precepts and seek a remedy for the sickness of love. However, the husband's choice of subject matter for a painting presumably meant to edify his imprisoned wife appears to be comically misguided, since the wife is destined to do the very thing the painted Venus would want: she will abandon her husband for her true love, Guigemar, as the narrative unfolds.

Descriptions of artworks, derived from both the classical and the medieval traditions, found a place in the Italian prose romance early on, starting with Boccaccio's contributions to the genre. There are several episodes of ekphrasis in the *Filocolo,* ranging from the somewhat gratuitous (some carved scenes of ancient historical events in Felice's palace in Marmorina, 2.32, meant to lend an air of sumptuousness to the setting) to the more overtly symbolic (a statue of a naked Cupid before Biancifiore's room in the tower of Alexandria, along with paintings of his deeds, 4.85).[9] However, the most significant instance of ekphrasis in the *Filocolo* may be found in the image of Christ in St John Lateran in Rome (5.52), which the fascinated pagan Filocolo gazes upon in a scene that suggests a link with the opening passages of the romances of Longus and Achilles Tatius. As in the case of *Leucippe and Clitophon,* the sight of a painting inspires an extended narrative from a bystander: a Greek named Ilario, also present in the church, recounts all of world history as well as the life and deeds of Christ, which brings about Filocolo's conversion to Christianity (5.53–7). There is also a striking display of a work of visual art in a more supernatural setting in Boccaccio's *Elegia di madonna Fiammetta:* when Venus appears in a vision to Fiammetta, she opens her mantle to reveal the painting of Fiammetta's future lover, Panfilo, that she holds between her breasts (24); this in turn brings about a love affair that will be almost as disastrous as the misguided obsession inspired in Bigolina's duchess by the painting of the prince.

When the Italian amatory prose romance was revived in the late fifteenth century, literary descriptions of artworks could for the first time be supplemented by woodcuts in printed editions. In 1499 Aldus Manutius prepared his famous edition of Francesco Colonna's prose romance *Hypnerotomachia Poliphili,* which included illustrations to enhance the main character's fantastic descriptions of numerous works of classical art and architecture in an extended dream vision. Reflecting another Quattrocento trend, the Renaissance exaltation of the artist as a distinguished individual begins to attach itself to descriptions of artwork in literature, as in the case of Book 11 of Sannazaro's *Arcadia,* wherein we are told that the renowned painter Andrea Mantegna had decorated a wooden vessel with a scene showing a goat-footed nymph nursing a baby satyr, to be given as a prize for some funeral games (101). The scene is modelled on a moment during the funeral games in Book 5 of Virgil's *Aeneid* wherein a craftsman named Didymaon is said to have made a shield given as a prize (vv 358–60). However, Sannazaro provides an autobiographical element that is not evident in his classical predecessor, since it is thought that Sannazaro actually owned such a vase made by Mantegna.[10] Even in the unreal setting of Sannazaro's pastoral romance, we may note a desire to enhance the validity and prestige of the artistic object by attributing it to a known artist. Such an effort also reveals a closer link to the world of the classical Greek romance authors, with their 'believable' scenes of ekphrasis, than to that of the late-medieval allegorical-didactic visionaries, even if neither the classical novelists nor the two Philostrati showed any interest in identifying the creators of the paintings that their characters see. Such scenes in the Greek romances are evoked by Sannazaro's descriptions of several paintings in a temple that are similarly deprived of allegorical or supernatural elements (*Arcadia,* 3, 18–20). These descriptions even include one of a *Judgment of Paris* that emphasizes its anonymous painter's process of choosing a suitable pose for Venus (ibid., 19–20), much like Bigolina's own version of this subject.

The authors of chivalric verse romances of the Quattrocento and Cinquecento made considerable use of ekphrasis, often bestowing upon it an encomiastic function or else employing it to summarize past or future historical episodes. These ekphraseis are most typically presented as fantastic supernatural marvels, in keeping with the tone of medieval romance that these works wish to evoke. Pavilions embroidered with scenes showing the future prowess of the houses of Aragon and Este, supernaturally created by such antique seers as the Sibyl of Cumae or Cassandra, appear in both Boiardo's *Orlando innamorato* (II, 27.52–61) and Ariosto's *Orlando furioso* (46.80–98). Book II of Boiardo's poem, first published in 1483, distinguishes between a 'realistic' ekphrastic scene, in which a group of Saracen kings views painted scenes of the life of Alexander the Great in Agramante's palace in Bizerte (II, 1.21–30), and the prophetic paintings of the enchanted loggia of the fairy Febosilla, in which a mysterious artist ('Chi fu il maestro, non saprebbi io dire') has somehow known how to depict the future deeds of the Este family, who will eventually become Boiardo's patrons (II, 25.43–56). In Ariosto's poem, characters encounter painted, carved, or woven scenes of prophetic import no fewer than four times throughout the narrative (26.30–6; 33.1–58; 42.73–8; 46.80–98).[11]

By the mid-sixteenth century, readers had numerous examples of such time-honoured, traditional ekphraseis before them, as well as one that was strikingly new. With the vogue for Petrarchism in the sixteenth century came various imitations of the two sonnets that Petrarca wrote in praise of Simone Martini's portrait of his beloved Laura.[12] Poets following this trend tended to minimize the importance of the work of art itself, using it primarily as a point of departure for lavish praise of the painted subject. This changed when Aretino began to write such sonnets of his own and include them in his *Lettere,* as we have noted in the preceding chapter. Here, as elsewhere, Aretino wrought something of a revolution, creating a new role for the description of artwork in literature.[13] Aretino introduced the notion of imaginary portraits in his published letters, descriptions of the way famous personages ought to look if an artist such as Titian had portrayed them.[14] For the first time in the history of ekphrasis, painting technique and the actual act of painting became as important as the subject that was painted. In time, Aretino's letters and sonnets on portraits came to be regarded as the true 'voices' of Titian's paintings, of both real and imaginary subjects. Aretino fancied that his sonnets were capable of uncovering Titian's true intentions and communicating them in a clear fashion to the person who had posed for the painting. As Freedman notes, Aretino 'was one of the first critics to draw special attention to portraiture as an important branch of painting. Aretino, then, inaugurated a trend that recognized literary description as the effective means for bringing out the message of the portrait, including one painted by such a master as Titian.'[15]

To some extent, Aretino can be said to have toyed with innovative methods of rendering visual images in literature throughout his career. His sonnets describing Giulio Romano's prints depicting sexual positions created both a scandal and a sensation back in the days when he still lived in Rome.[16] Later he satirized the established literary topos of describing characters who view images painted on a wall in his dialogue *Il ragionamento della Nanna e della Antonia* (21–4). Here, in an extended episode, Nanna recounts to Antonia all the details of the riotous sex acts she sees depicted on the walls of her rather unconventional convent, which naturally include images from Boccaccio's own story of illicit acts in a nunnery, the novella of Masetto da Lamporecchio.[17] Such satirical treatment of what had once been a solemn tool of allegorical and didactic literature shows that by the mid-Cinquecento the old classical and medieval topos of ekphrasis had reached a critical point. Having exhausted its old veins of meaning, it was now ripe for creative reinterpretations at the hands of writers of genius. If one of these was Pietro Aretino, another was surely Giulia Bigolina.

In several ways, Bigolina's *Urania* stands at the pinnacle of this long tradition of literary ekphrasis, providing a demonstration of how the various strands of the topos could be brought together in order to enhance meaning in a literary work. We have already noted how the ancient Greek love stories showed a tendency to attribute the genesis of their narratives to the authorial persona's observation of some fascinating painted image showing the power of love. Bigolina is likely to have been aware of this tendency, especially since Francesco Angelo Coccio's very popular Italian translation of Tatius's *Leucippe and Clitophon* had just been published in Venice in 1550. However, in *Urania* Bigolina turns that whole tradition around, for her narrative does not spring from the sight of a painting; rather, it springs from the *absence* of a painting that is merely proposed but never actually created. The narrative derives its origin from the rejection of a painted image as a vehicle for the expression of the power of love, since such expression ought to come from within, from one's own creative powers. Indeed, the only image that Bigolina's authorial persona sees is her own body, reflected in the huge eye of a fabulous naked Cyclops. The experience of that reproachful gaze is anything but pleasant: it is something she would rather flee from than embrace. In this way Bigolina rejects the old purposes of the amatory prose romance as it had existed since ancient times and makes a subtle declaration that here she will provide a new sort of love story, one in which deeds will matter more than physical appearances, one that will focus on the very nature and purpose of art.

Bigolina and the *Paragone*

Although marginalized, never published in her lifetime, and barely known as a writer outside of her native city, Bigolina was clearly a keen observer of the cultural trends of her moment in history, especially the fascination for the visual arts that was manifesting itself not only in intellectual circles but also among the literate public in general.[18] In the introduction to *Urania*, Bigolina shows that she intends to add her voice to the grand debates concerning the nature, purpose, and significance of the arts that characterized the middle years of sixteenth-century Italy. Certain elements of those debates are immediately apparent in the allegorical proem: as we have noted, Bigolina appears to describe her own personal crisis of *invenzione* or *inventio*, the rhetorical process whereby an artist or writer conceives of appropriate subject matter, while judgment (*giudizio* or *giudicio*) was itself a buzzword in many theoretical texts, referring to the visual artist's innate ability to evaluate the aesthetic potential of the work as it is about to be created, as well as the aesthetic qualities of the work after it has come to exist.[19] But the element that is most evident in the proem's conclusion, and that will have the greatest significance for Bigolina's text as a whole, is the *paragone*, the debate over which of the various arts has the most validity and nobility of expression.

The *paragone* was a persistent motif in Italian Renaissance culture, appearing especially in doctrinal dialogues and treatises on poetry, painting, and sculpture, but also, often in the most subtle ways, in the iconography of the visual arts.[20] In her proem, Bigolina has declared herself a partisan in one of the more typical manifestations of the *paragone*, the dispute over the relative merits of painting and poetry. Let us examine once more the most relevant passage at the conclusion of the proem:

Alla quale partita, come cosa, che è fuori di sè stessa rimasi. Pur dopo poco spatio d'hora in me ritornando, et ripensando sopra la prima deliberatione che di mandarvi la imagine della mia faccia havea fatta, acciò ch'ella in voi la memoria di me viva tenesse, parvemi che assai sciocco fosse stato quel mio primo proponimento. Et perciò abbandonando il primo del tutto, al

secondo mi venni accostando. Et così da quello aiutata, del mio basso intelletto una imagine trassi, la quale dalla volontà del mio cuore pigliando
la effiggie et il colore da amendue insieme questa operetta ne è uscita, che
Urania si chiama, pigliando il nome da quella sopra la quale tutta la istoria
è fondata. (82)

[When he was gone I was left stunned, but then regained my wits after
a short space of time. I thought over my original plan to send you the
image of my face, so that you would keep me alive in your memory; it
now seemed to me to be very foolish. I therefore abandoned it entirely,
and turned instead to the second proposal. Aided by this, I drew forth an
image from my low intellect, an image which took its shapes and colors
from the will of my heart. This little work, deriving thus from both my
intellect and my heart, is called *Urania*, and it takes its name from that
woman who is the whole subject of the story. (83)]

She has deliberately rejected portrait painting, an art form for which
she would have to rely on the skills and efforts of someone else, as a
valid artistic vehicle for communicating her deepest feelings. Instead,
she presents herself as the champion of individual self-expression, inventing a story that appears to have no source beyond her own imagination. To show her triumph over the art form that she has just rejected
as unworthy of her needs, Bigolina appropriates the very terminology
of painting ('le effiggie e il colore'), in order to describe the genesis of
her work of literary art. Moreover, she uses the term *imagine* ('image')
in two contrasting ways, with the clear intention of showing how the
traditional sort of image, a painted simulacrum of a person's physical
appearance, is inferior to a very different sort of image that she is able
to generate spontaneously within her mind, in her 'basso intelletto.'[21]
The first usage ('la imagine della mia faccia') would have made perfect
sense to the theorists of her age, since it plainly refers to the notion of
imitatio, the artistic reproduction of the external appearance of things
that both poets and painters were expected to strive to create.[22]

However, the second usage is quite deliberately provocative, for here
Bigolina claims to find an image within the recesses of her mind without having observed any external thing that might serve as a source
for it. She is not speaking of actual physical things but of inner notions
of things, what the Neoplatonic theorists of her age would have called
idea, or perhaps *concetto*, but not typically *imagine*.[23] Bigolina has issued a
forthright challenge to painters, who, at least in her view, are limited to

reproducing only the visual world around them. She has announced that she has no need of the images of the painters, since she carries her own superior images within herself. In the proem to *Urania,* Bigolina shows us her personal process of artistic maturation and self-realization in a sort of microcosmic *Bildungsroman,* as she progresses from thinking like a passive object, inclined to sit for a portrait done by a 'real artist,' to producing a work of art in her own right.

Inspired by the 'ut pictura poesis' dictum in Horace's *Ars poetica,* early modern theorists sometimes declared that painting and poetry had a special relationship, that they were 'sister arts' endowed with similar powers of description.[24] However, the old topos of ekphrasis often carried a hint of 'sibling rivalry,' a sense that one art must somehow outdo the other, and this partisan rivalry became more rancorous in the early modern era, when the arts of painting and sculpture began to free themselves from the taint of manual labour and assert themselves in the face of poetry's traditional primacy.[25] We have already noted how Titian made a conscious effort to compare his mythological paintings to poems by calling them *poesie,* thereby implying that painting was, in his hands at least, capable of attaining the higher status among the arts that had traditionally been reserved for poetry. Perhaps the most strident partisan of the superiority of painting to poetry was Leonardo da Vinci, who championed the painter's ability to reproduce natural images through direct observation (*Paragone,* 49–80). On the other hand, the importance of poetry as a handmaiden of rhetoric was affirmed by such writers as Sperone Speroni, who found painting inferior because it could only reproduce external images, not the essential character of the subject. While painting might delight the mind and the senses, rhetoric and poetry bring pleasure to the higher intellect, since they employ words, which Speroni calls 'strumenti dell'intelletto' (instruments of the intellect).[26]

Bigolina's *Urania* must be regarded as making a substantial contribution to this debate. However, Bigolina has rather audaciously set herself a special, even unique task: she will not simply describe the *paragone* in doctrinal or didactic terms in the fashion of many of her contemporaries, nor will she use pictorial imagery to describe a scene, showing off her skills in an effort to prove that literature has descriptive powers beyond those of painting. Instead, alone among the theorists of her day, she chooses prose fiction as a vehicle for expounding on the *paragone;* indeed, she makes the creation of a painting the very stuff of her narrative in the episode of the duchess and the painting of the Judgment of Paris.

The Judgment of Paris

Bigolina treats the *paragone* between painting and literature on three separate occasions within her book, and in three different ways. The first two ways employ literary styles that would have been quite familiar to the readers of her age, whereas the third, the tale of the painting of the Judgment of Paris, is much more innovative. The first appears in the discussion between Giudicio and Bigolina's authorial persona, in which a knowledgeable figure convinces a neophyte of the superiority of literature over painting by posing a series of probing questions; it is presented essentially as a dialogue, the format that was so popular in Bigolina's time as a vehicle for expounding on cultural or pseudo-philosophical topics. The second instance occurs early in the romance itself, when Urania sends her reproachful letter, expounding on the nature of love and the perception of beauty, to her fickle lover, Fabio. Here the reader easily recognizes the same lesson on the moral implications of portraiture and the greater value of literature that the allegory of Judgment provided to Bigolina's authorial persona in the proem.

By this point Bigolina has established the *paragone* between painting and literature as a central theme of her book, employing styles suggestive of both the dialogue (the allegorical proem) and the treatise (Urania's letter). Bigolina's readers would not have found these features out of place in a prose romance, the genre that so often included allegorical-didactic elements as well as dialogic and doctrinal *questioni d'amore*. But these two treatments lead us inevitably to a much more complex and innovative exploration of the topic, communicated solely through the actions and reactions of characters within the narrative: the episode of the painting *The Judgment of Paris*.

Why does Bigolina choose this particular subject for the duchess's painting? The most obvious reason, of course, is to provide a thematic link to the allegory of judgment at the beginning of the book, when the authorial persona learned how to avoid making a mistake in judgment with regard to her choice of a method of self-display.[27] The duchess is not said to be wicked or devious, just lovesick and misguided, so that in her wretched state she forgets her usual love of virtue and consents to a most unseemly revelation of her body not only to the eyes of her courtiers but by extension to the eyes of any viewer of the work of art. She participates in the forging of an entirely new image of herself as a sensual Venus figure, an act that would instantly serve to associate her in contemporary eyes with the world of the sixteenth-century Italian courtesan, the sort of woman who might pose as Venus in a painting, or indeed go so far as to call herself Venus on occasion.[28] In short, she commits an act of very bad judgment according to the ethical system around which Bigolina constructs her book.[29]

It is hard to see how Bigolina could have chosen a better standard art subject than the Judgment of Paris, a beauty contest in which the divine contestants brazenly bribe the judge, in order to make her point about the moral implications of good judgment. As Hubert Damisch notes, the Paris story, as well as the resulting Trojan War, lie at the origins of European consciousness, and thus Paris's choice is laden with many layers of significance: it tells of a kind of original sin, a first error of judgment in the context of European history.[30] Paris, like Adam (in a non-European context), is undone by an offer of fruit and gives in to temptation, with disastrous consequences. Here an entire civilization assigns itself a mythical origin grounded in error, says Damisch: the judgment is seen as a mistake because it contradicts the fundamental notion that sexual drives should be repressed for the good of society (*Judgment of Paris,* 191). As a voyeur, Paris is in a class by himself: he is allowed a privilege granted to almost no other mortal in mythological narratives, since he can gaze libidinously – and with impunity – on three goddesses who must perforce appear to him as they actually are, not in disguise, as would usually have been the case in other tales. The ethical implications are profound, as Damisch notes: 'what is at stake in the judgment of Paris is not so much a greater or lesser degree of beauty as it is the nature of beauty itself; thus it is not difficult to understand how philosophers, moralists, and theologians have repeatedly discerned ethical content in the story' (ibid., 210). The story deals with the very essence of beauty in its sexual context, as well as with the potential for social disaster if the wrong choice is made.

By having Giufredi take the role of Paris in the painting, the conspirators hope to make him commit a similar act of bad judgment, in fulfilment of the ancient legend: just as the original Paris chose Venus in the beauty contest, so must he. Indeed, how could he not? Not only is she so incredibly lovely in her state of partial undress that, as the wily painter suggests, Zeuxis would not have needed five different models to arrive at his composite image of Helen of Troy if he had had the duchess to look at (198–200), but she is, in all likelihood, the only one of the goddesses to appear semi-nude in the painting.[31] Neither the Duchess of Bourbon as Juno nor the Princess of Poland as Minerva are said to pose for this painting, so we are given to understand that the painter must have appropriated their images from portraits he had done of them earlier, as in fact he does in the case of the Prince of Salerno. Given that they are royal figures worthy of the highest respect, whose piety and propriety are stressed, one could hardly expect them to be shown with their bodies exposed, according to the mores of the day, and in any case we are told that Minerva appears 'tutta armata,' wearing the armour in which she was so often depicted in other artistic settings.[32] Her model, the Princess of Poland (a character almost certainly inspired by Katarzyna Jagiełłonka, the very pious daughter of Sigismund I, King of Poland at the time Bigolina was writing), is said to be distinguished for her virginity, piety, and love of knowledge, qualities that would seem to render a nude pose highly inappropriate.[33] As Carlo Caruso notes, Minerva was usually shown from behind in paintings of the Judgment, in deference to her prudishness as the only virgin goddess in the beauty contest; moreover, Ovid himself had said that Minerva looked more proper (*decentior*) with her armour on than without it, even as she participated nude in the Judgment.[34] It would appear that Bigolina has taken Ovid's view to heart, in defiance of myriad contemporary depictions.

Therefore we may conclude that the *invenzione* of Bigolina's painter constitutes a radical departure from the standard iconography of later Renaissance paintings of the Judgment of Paris, in which all three goddesses are generally shown to be nude; instead, in his attempt to skew things in favour of the lovesick duchess, he has endeavoured to make the decision as easy as possible for the prince who must make the choice by showing him only one nude goddess instead of three, and then expounding on the list of her physical charms to boot.[35]

As has been noted, *giudizio* had become an important concept in Cinquecento discussions of the arts, and this must also be taken into account in the context of Bigolina's theme of judgment. Robert Klein has traced the development of *giudizio* from its original role as an intermediary between the intellect and the senses, that is, between 'the intelligible universal' and 'the sensible particular,' to something closer to simple *discrezione* (discretion), a quality that could flourish within the mind of each inspired artist (*Form and Meaning*, 162–3). Once more, this is a revolution with which Aretino is closely associated, both in his own voice in the *Lettere* and posthumously, as a spokesman in Lodovico Dolce's *Dialogo della pittura*.[36] Although Dolce's dialogue, published in 1557, probably appeared too late to have influenced Bigolina in her writing of *Urania*, Dolce's reference to the Judgment of Paris in conjunction with his interlocutor Aretino's discussion of judgment in the arts shows that this notion was scarcely unique to *Urania:*

> Onde fu detto da Cicerone, che essendo cosi gran differenza da i dotti a gl'ignoranti, era pochissima nel giudicare. Et Apelle soleva metter le sue figure al giudicio comune. Potrei anco dire, che'l giudicio delle tre Dee fu rimesso a un Pastore.

> [That is why Cicero said that, great as the distinction might be between the learned and the ignorant, there was very little of it when it came to judging; and why Apelles would expose his figures to the judgment of all comers. I could also mention that the judging of the three goddesses was put into the hands of a shepherd.][37]

Here Dolce gives voice to an idea that Aretino also expresses in the *Lettere,* that even the humblest person might be capable of good judgment. In Aretino's way of thinking, *giudizio* and *discrezione* were essentially the same, and even a person ignorant of letters or academic training might well be able to judge the arts astutely.[38] Of course, it made sense for Aretino to promote this notion, since he himself had come from humble origins and had had a minimal education yet chose to involve himself in the doings of the greatest artists and intellectuals of the age. In his letter of 1537 to Gianfrancesco Pocopanno (1.246), Aretino attributed Michelangelo's greatness more to his innate sense of judgment than to any slavish adherence to the rules of art: 'Guardate dove ha posto la pittura Michelagnolo con lo smisurato de le sue figure, dipinto con la maestà del giudizio, non col meschino de l'arte' (See how high Michelangelo has raised painting with the immensity of his figures, which he depicts with the majesty of judgment, not with the pettiness of artistry, 1:343). In another letter of the same year, this time to Fausto Sebastiano da Longiano (1.297), Aretino makes an even clearer distinction between pedantic types who make a show of classical erudition and really talented people endowed with simple *giudizio* (here *giudicio*), a group in which he openly places himself.

Aretino had long been fascinated by the various applications of the term *giudizio,* as anyone who followed his career must have been aware. In addition to his references to it in the *Lettere,* he had also gained considerable fame earlier as a parodist of a popular literary form also known the *giudizio* or *pronostico* (prognostic), in which astrologers disseminated their predictions of events involving nations and great individuals for the coming year. Aretino parodied both the style and the content of the standard literary *giudizio,* using it as a forum for sly humour and satire at the expense of the great and powerful. His first *giudizio* of 1527 attracted a great deal of attention when he correctly predicted that Rome would suffer grave misfortune at the hands of invaders that year; subsequently he continued to provide yearly *giudizi* for the rest of the decade and for much of the first half of the 1530s.[39] Unfortunately only one of these *giudizi,* that of 1534, has survived in its complete form; evidently these works only saw limited publication as pamphlets, or else they only circulated in manuscript form.[40] In this work, Aretino shows how much he relished his new role as a seer, calling himself 'the fifth Evangelist' on the title page, as well as a prophet who could make more accurate predictions than any astrologer.[41] It is doubtless on account of the fame that he had gained as a writer of *giudizi* that Aretino at one point claimed that the gold chain he had received from King Francis I bore the inscription 'Lingua eius loquetur iudicium' (His tongue will pronounce judgment), even though elsewhere he would indicate that the last word of the inscription was actually 'mendacium' (a lie).[42] Aretino was clearly pleased to have it both ways.

In early modern painting, there were two common subjects that involved judgment, one Christian and one pagan: the Last Judgment and the Judgment of Paris. In the *Lettere,* Aretino has occasion to mention examples of both, and in each case he makes a pointed reference to the role of *giudizio* in the experience of either the artist or the observer. In the famous letter 4.189 to Alessandro Corvino (1547) concerning Michelangelo's *Last Judgment,* Aretino criticizes Michelangelo's poor judgment for including nudes in a religious painting for the Sistine Chapel:

> Adunque un Michelagnolo stupendo ne la fama, un Michelagnolo notabile ne la prudenzia, un Michelagnolo essemplare ne la bontade, ha voluto che la invidia dica ch'egli mostri in cotale opra non meno impietà d'inreligione, che perfezzione di pittura? (4:130)

> [So a Michelangelo who is stupendously famous, a Michelangelo who is noteworthy for his prudence, a Michelangelo who is of exemplary goodness, has seen fit to allow envy to advise him to display as much irreligious impiety as artistic perfection in such a work?]

For Aretino, who attributes Michelangelo's lapse to putative envy for Raphael's success, the 'poor judgment' of the *Last Judgment* lies not in imperfect technique but in a strange poverty of *invenzione* that is quite unworthy of a man normally known for his prudence.[43] This is close to Bigolina's concept of poor judgment in the arts – that is, a moral lapse on the part of a painter who is otherwise endowed with surpassing technical virtuosity. Aretino questions Michelangelo's motive in presenting a familiar subject in an unfamiliar way, since it might cause the viewer to react to the work in an inappropriate fashion, just as Bigolina's painter hopes the prince will do.

In this letter, Aretino goes on to say, somewhat outrageously, that he himself had used better *giudizio* in the words he had chosen for his *Ragionamento della Nanna e della Antonia*, a dialogue replete with scenes of orgies in a convent, among other scandalous things (4:130). His point, of course, is that the problem is all one of context: his own language was quite appropriate for a work of 'materia impudica e lasciva' (lewd and lascivious material), whereas Michelangelo's nudes were inappropriate for 'sí alta historia' (such lofty history), depicted in the Pope's own chapel (4: 130–1).

Later, Aretino describes *The Judgment of Paris* by the painter Girolamo Sermoneta in Letter 5.240 to Benedetto Cornaro (in the same volume in which Aretino included his letters to Bigolina):

Mi dice Tiziano, nel cui stile (come ho detto altre volte) vive occulta la idea d'una nuova natura, che non è unione che agiunga a la diligenza estrema che comprendano in cotali figure gli occhi di ciascun uom di giudizio ... (5:185)

[Titian, in whose style (as I have said on other occasions) lives hidden the idea of a new Nature, tells me that there is no harmony of colors (*unione*) that can add to the extreme precision that is perceived in such figures by the eyes of any man of judgment ...]

Here, an observer endowed with a sense of *giudizio* is the person who is best able to appreciate the painter's skill and artistic judgment, which in this case is not at all faulty.

In both of these letters concerning paintings, Aretino uses the thematic depiction of judgment in a work of art as an excuse to make a comment on the need for good judgment on the part of both the artist and the observer of the artwork, an idea that Bigolina will develop substantially in her turn. Bigolina was surely aware of the controversies surrounding the application of the term *'giudizio'* to the visual arts in the decades leading up to the composition of her narrative. Moreover, she must have known of the complex ethical, perceptual, and aesthetic connotations that *giudizio* had acquired in the writings of Aretino and others, as she went about adopting the notion of judgment as the central theme, as a kind of 'programmatic iconography' (a term Victoria Kirkham has applied to the recurring symbolism of the *Filocolo*, [*Fabulous Vernacular*, 9–10]), in her own grand commentary on the arts.

It was a common belief in both antiquity and the Renaissance that Paris had not made a wise choice when confronted with the three goddesses. In the long gloss on Venus that accompanies his verse romance *Teseida*, Boccaccio provides a description of paintings in the temple of Venus that includes an image of the goddess holding the apple she received from Paris, as well as an outright condemnation of people who choose as Paris did: 'Per lo pomo, il quale dice Venere avere in mano, vuole dimostrare la stolta elezione di quegli che così fatta vita ad ogni altra propongono' (By showing the apple, which he says Venus holds in her hand, [the author] wishes to demonstrate the foolish choice of those who prefer a life of that sort over any other).[44] For Neoplatonists such as Sallustius and Ficino, Paris represented the lowest sort of soul, the one that lives in accordance with sense perception; for the early Christian Fulgentius, Paris's choice of lust over wisdom or wealth made him as dull and stupid as a beast.[45] His inconstancy is also alluded to in at least one ekphrastic scene of the Judgment of Paris that Bigolina could have known, which appears in the series of temple paintings viewed by the narrator in the third chapter of Sannazaro's *Arcadia*.[46] Here Paris is seen to be distracted by the arrival of the three goddesses, all described as fantastically beautiful nudes according to custom, just as he is engaged in carving on a tree the name of his first wife, Oenone, whom he was soon to abandon cruelly in his pursuit of Helen. Sannazaro makes a point of stressing that Paris had not quite finished carving the name when he was interrupted. Renaissance readers would have known the story, especially from the fifth epistle of Ovid's *Heroides*, and they also would have been well aware of the grim lesson it taught concerning the wages of inconstancy: Oenone was a nymph skilled in the use of herbs, who later refused to succour Paris when he was dying from the arrow wound inflicted on him by Philoctetes. After his death, the repentant Oenone in turn hanged herself.

Christine de Pizan, who had considerable influence on Bigolina, is also known to have made the Judgment of Paris a sort of personal leitmotif throughout her career. In one of her *ballades*, Christine even places herself within the events and declares Minerva, the goddess who presides over her decision to become a writer, to be her own choice in the judging.[47] In the *Epistre Othea,* Christine is quite explicit in her condemnation of Paris's choice, not only because he let himself be swayed by his sensual desires, but also because his act led directly to the fall of Troy:[48]

> Comme Paris ne juges pas
> Car on reçoit maint dur repas
> Par male sentence ottroyer;
> Plusieurs en ont eu mal loyer.   (302)

> [Do not judge as Paris did, for one recovers with great difficulty from making bad judgments; many have had a bad reward.]

In the prose commentary that she appends to this poem, Christine is even more explicit about the dangers of bad judgment:

> Si est a entendre que, parce que Paris ne fu point chevaleureux ne moult de richece ne lui chalu, mais en amours furent toutes ses pensees, est entendu que a Venus donna la pomme d'or. Et pour ce dit au bon chevalier que semblablement ne doit faire. Et dit Pittagoras: 'Le juge qui ne juge justement dessert tout mal.' (303)

> [So it must be understood: Paris was not at all chivalrous, nor was he much interested in riches; instead all of his thoughts were on love, so it is understood that he gave the golden apple to Venus. Thus the good knight is told that he must not act in a similar fashion. And Pythagoras said: 'The judge who does not judge justly deserves every misfortune.']

The *Epistre Othea* tells of the advice that Othea, the goddess of prudence, gives to Prince Hector concerning how to be a proper knight. Not only does she tell him more than once to reject the sensuality that Venus represents (213–14), and to avoid following the example of Pygmalion (234–6), she also recommends that he not desire wealth, the gift that the goddess Juno offers him during the Judgment (269–70). Christine makes it clear that the only one of the three goddesses that Paris should have chosen is Minerva, the goddess of wisdom and, at least in Christine's text, chivalry (221–2). In fact, Bigolina has her own prince make virtually the same choice.[49] As he looks at the painting, Giufredi sees himself, as Paris, at the fateful moment of judgment: he is giving the apple to Venus. Clearly it is expected that he will act as judge outside of the painting as well as inside it: according to the scheme of the painter and the counsellor, he is supposed to judge as improperly as Paris did and choose the image of the incredibly lovely duchess.

But Giufredi passes Bigolina's test, for he selects someone besides the duchess, the 'wise damsel' (la Savia Damigella), the young woman on whom he has already set his sights. Of this character we are told very little: she has no other name, indeed no other description, than 'Savia Damigella,' but that appellation in itself suggests the two most emblematic characteristics of the goddess Minerva, or Pallas Athena: she is wise, and if we understand *'damigella'* in its archaic usage, meaning a young aristocratic woman who is not yet married, she is also virginal.[50] Ultimately, Giufredi does judge properly, according to Bigolina's system of ethics: he chooses the most appropriate woman. But he does so by rejecting the message of the painting and by rejecting the role of Paris that has been imposed upon him; he does not choose Venus but rather someone who has the attributes of Minerva. Bigolina was doubtless aware that the historical Prince of Salerno, Ferrante Sanseverino, had a celebrated marriage with the poet and scholar Isabella Villamarina, a woman remembered in numerous sources for the depth and breadth of her knowledge. Even though Bigolina's tale is hardly meant to be read as an accurate account of the historical prince's courtship and marriage, it is easy to see how Villamarina, whom Ortensio Lando called 'bella et savia' (beautiful and wise), and who was herself remembered as a poet, might have served as an inspiration for the creation of the character whom Bigolina calls the Savia Damigella.[51]

According to Hubert Damisch, Venus (or Aphrodite) never offers herself to Paris in all of the myriad retellings of the story, save in a few modern 'smutty' versions (*Judgment of Paris,* 141). The goddess is supposed to represent a model or standard of beauty but not be the actual prize herself; instead, she promises sexual pleasure in the form of another woman whom she can procure for the Trojan prince. Paris judges, but in turn is forced to rely on Venus's own judgment with regard to his reward. Bigolina may well be the first narrator to turn this notion around, for the duchess as Venus does indeed offer herself to the prince; if he imitates Paris and chooses as he is supposed to, his prize will be the veritable 'goddess' of beauty and love that he sees before him.

But even as Giufredi rejects the duchess in the role of the Carnal Venus, he does not reject the gift of sexual pleasure that she offers. Her ill-advised nudity only serves one purpose, to make Giufredi wonder about the look and feel of the Savia Damigella's limbs ('per la qual cosa d'un novo, et intenso desiderio di vederle, et gustarle s'accese,' 204). Instead of yearning to possess the duchess, he now yearns to marry the Savia Damigella and take her to bed as his wife. The duchess has made an improper display of herself, so the prince wisely rejects her in favour of a woman who is too wise to show such an inclination, one who has the attributes of Minerva, whose body is kept properly hidden (under armour, no less) in the painting. Since Giufredi has managed to transfer the image of the duchess's naked limbs onto the imagined image of the body of the Damigella, his act of good judgment lies in finding a proper channel for the lust the painting has inspired in him. He yearns for a nudity that is not visible, but merely imagined, interiorized, in a way that recalls Bigolina's conception of the story of Urania in her 'basso intelletto.'

As Patricia Simons has noted, 'The art of portraiture is selection, like most Renaissance art balancing archetype and experience, norm and nature, *imitatio* with *electio*. Any portrait of a woman is a representation of femininity imbued by social and poetic norms. Individualism, in its anachronistic and fixed sense, does not illuminate Renaissance portraiture of women' ('Portraiture, Portrayal, and Idealization,' 310). The actual physical subject was merely a point of departure, an initial concrete presence upon which the male viewer was expected to perform 'a phallocentric translation from the feminine surface back to the masculine creative process' (ibid., 311), so that he could make of her whatever he wanted. The painter's violation of the rules of decorous *invenzione* lies in his arrogant assumption that he could present the duchess, a highborn head of state as distinguished in her fictional environment as the historical Isabella d'Este was in her own time, as she actually appeared, with her flesh most indecorously exposed.[52] He even claims, in brazen defiance of the theoretical norms of the time, that he has no need to surpass nature by employing a selective composite such as Zeuxis created. Simons notes that Renaissance portrayals of women did indeed require some link with a historical personage, but 'filtered and mediated, to a point between portraiture and entire fantasy, reference and dream, experience and metaphor.' Simons speaks of 'a continuing state of unresolved desire or indecision before these portrayals' (ibid., 311). The unscrupulous painter does not allow for this, since he wants the prince to see the image exactly for what it is. However, the wise prince chooses to find ambiguity in the work even if the painter does not allow for it, performing thereby his 'phallocentric translation' of the image of the duchess by projecting it onto his fantasy of the Savia Damigella's body.

We have already noted how Bigolina's painter appropriates the style of ekphrasis that Aretino employs in his *Lettere*, only to put it to rather ironic purposes. In the *Lettere*, we have seen how Aretino expresses the notion that the power of his pen might serve to communicate Titian's true intentions to the person who appears in a portrait, so that he or she might properly appreciate the subtleties of the work of art. Bigolina's painter, a very intriguing literary creation, comes to represent every-thing Bigolina dislikes about the art of painting. Although he has characteristics in common with the sharp-witted and loquacious artists who appear in the novellas of Boccaccio, Sacchetti, and Bandello, or perhaps Maestro Andrea in Aretino's comedy *La Cortigiana*, compared to them he is morally bankrupt, especially as regards his attitudes towards the pursuit of his very profession. Perhaps the only contemporary fictional artist whom he may be said to resemble ethically is that of Bandello's novella 3.23, who steals his patron's woman when she poses for him; however, the transgression of Bandello's painter is that of a man consumed by lust, and thus it is only superficially related to his profession. The behaviour of Bigolina's painter violates a fundamental rule of decorum that may be traced back to Alberti's famous dictum that a painter ought to be 'un uomo buono' (a good man); in fact, Bigolina's creation of a fictional painter who is a smooth-talking villain, bent on deceiving his patron in terms of how he creates and presents his art-work, appears to be unique.[53] He may paint like Titian, but he talks like Aretino, slickly employing the ekphrastic style of Aretino's sonnets and letters in an effort to convince the prince not only to accept the painting but also to accept his role in the painting as well, as one who must give the apple to Venus.[54] The painter thinks his clever words should suffice to do this, just as Aretino fondly imagines his own clever words could cause patrons to truly appreciate the power and meaning of art. But Bigolina scorns and rejects her painter's bid and, by extension, Aretino's as well.

Robert Williams analyses early modern theoretical views of the art-ist's process of invention and judgment in order to demonstrate that artists of the age were seen to wield considerable power as manipu-lators of signs. It was commonly believed that an artist was capable, through knowledge of the principles of artistic decorum, of arranging iconic signs in order to compel a viewer to believe whatever he or she might want (*Art, Theory, and Culture*, 88–9). This is what Bigolina em-phasizes in her Judgment of Paris episode. There, the painter and the counsellor both violate the standing rules of decorum for artists, the notion that the mode of representation must be related to a larger understanding of purpose; ultimately their *invenzione* can be seen to be the result of a failure of *giudizio*.[55] The painter's effort to enhance the communicative power of his work through the spectacle of a sort of 'striptease,' dramatically pulling away the silken veil that covers the painting in the presence of the prince, only serves to cheapen his gesture (202).[56] Giufredi's own good judgment saves him, but the duchess lacks this power, and thus is doomed. She stands as a warning to readers to beware of the dangers of succumbing to the allure of false art forms.

The problem that Bigolina poses is in some ways unique to the literature of the arts in her time: how does a discerning viewer 'read' a painting that was created for an unethical purpose? In the event that the artist who created it has a faulty sense of artistic decorum, how is the observer to exercise good judgment and avoid being beguiled by the work of art? In raising these questions, Bigolina reflects some of the attitudes of early sixteenth-century polemics against the visual arts, such as those expressed by Erasmus in *Christiani matrimoni institutio* (1526), or by Ambrogio Catarino Politi in his *Disputatio de cultu et adoratione imaginum* (1542); it may also be said that she anticipates to some extent notions that would soon prevail among the art theorists of the Counter-Reformation.[57] However, it is interesting to note that unlike all of these, Bigolina provides an ethical context for her version of the polemic that is indifferent to matters of orthodoxy and faith; indeed, as has been noted, *Urania* is almost completely devoid of explicit references to religion.[58] Instead, the primary moral purpose of Bigolina's discussion of the arts lies in the defence of women from the traps and calumnies of the men who control the artistic voices of authority in her culture.

Rona Goffen observes that Titian displays 'an unabashed pagan ethos' in his sensual mythological paintings, and finds the lack of even a hint of Christian disapprobation in these works 'extraordinary.'[59] Likewise extraordinary, I would say, is Bigolina's bold effort to criticize such imagery in Titian's paintings: she declares her opposition to the great artist's cultural program, yet does so without any recourse to Christian disapprobation on her own part. She seems to have recognized that a criticism grounded in Christian ethics would have been too conventional for her purposes, which in the end are completely secular and not at all inclined to simplistic outbursts in the name of pious prudery. She attacks Titian's *all'antica* style and his neo-pagan sensuality not for any imagined affront to Christian morality but instead for their demeaning depictions of women as mere objects for visual gratification. In so doing, she anticipates the modern biform polemic against pornography, which provides arguments tailored for both the political right and left: instead of adhering to the more traditional 'right-wing' viewpoint that pornographic images offend religious principles, she opts for what we would call today the more 'progressive' secular notion that such images should be rejected as demeaning and offensive to women.

Descriptio Mulieris

By Bigolina's time, the description of the beautiful woman in terms that evoke painting had become a standard topos in lyric poetry (especially in the hands of Petrarchists), in romances in both prose and verse, in didactic dialogues on beauty, and in the ekphraseis of paintings in the letters of Aretino and his followers. Elizabeth Cropper has researched the literary sources of the topos in terms of its influence on Cinquecento painting, noting that such descriptions have late classical or medieval origins and were especially codified for later Italian writers by Petrarca and Boccaccio.[60] The romance and lyric traditions, awash in beautiful female characters, required such *amplificatio*, which soon became standardized and endlessly repeated. It typically included a catalogue of the charms of individual body parts and attributes, usually starting with the hair and other features of the head and ending at the feet.[61] Nancy J. Vickers sees the point of departure for this trend in Petrarca's strategies for describing his beloved Laura, which in turn derive from the poet's self-identification with Actaeon in Ovid's *Metamorphoses*. The fragmented description of the sight of a beautiful woman, the 'descriptive dismemberment' of her ('The Body Re-membered,' 109), mirrors the poet's fragmented emotional state and is presented as an endlessly fruitless attempt to produce a sort of painted portrait in words of a woman who can only be glimpsed incompletely through memory. Such descriptions of beautiful female parts, with their inevitable comparisons to natural objects and substances such as gold, milk, snow, pearls, roses, apples, and the like, become not only a standard topos in ekphrastic literature but also a fundamental element of the *paragone* between poetry and painting.[62] Moreover, the portrait of the woman, either in words or in colours, ultimately becomes the standard emblem of beauty in all its forms, as Elizabeth Cropper has noted: 'In the Renaissance *paragone* of painting and poetry, the portrayal of the beautiful woman ... is the test the poet sets for the painter, and the primary figure for the truthfulness of the representation of beauty itself.'[63]

   The Cinquecento romance tradition, to which Bigolina belongs, had perhaps inherited the *descriptio mulieris* most directly from certain famous scenes in Boccaccio's romances, such as Florio's encounter with two beautiful seductresses in a garden (*Filocolo,* 3.11), and the vision of Emilia on her way to her wedding with Palamone at the end of the *Teseida* (12.53–63).[64] In the first instance the sight of the women's beautiful parts is morally problematic for the protagonist, as it ultimately was for Petrarca, and will later be for Bigolina: Florio must recognize the women's charms as a threat and reject them. In the case of Emilia, it is not a first sighting of the woman by her lover that is described but rather a triumphant final sighting by the general public before the consummation of the marriage and the conclusion of the book. In Cinquecento romances, on the other hand, the topos is usually provided at the moment in which the lovely woman is first viewed by the man who will fall in love with her; thus, the reader is expected to see the woman's charms the way the lover sees them. Two famous scenes in Ariosto's *Orlando furioso* illustrate this: Ruggiero's first sight of Alcina, which leads to his beguilement and to their love affair (7.9–16), and Oberto's encounter with Olimpia, who is tied naked to a tree, as a result of which the two are soon married (11.65–71).[65]

   Cinquecento prose romances most often provide first-person narratives instead of the typical third-person style of the verse romance, with the male lover as the narrator describing his meeting with a woman whose beauty will soon overwhelm him. In these cases the *descriptio mulieris* acquires trappings of autobiography, closer to the lyrical experience of Petrarca; the best example can be found in the protagonist's first sight of his beloved in Niccolò Franco's *Filena.* Here the lover tells his own story, and the reader is expected to indulge in the beauty of the woman through his eyes, and through his experience of feasting his eyes on her (8r–9r).

   Such self-indulgent first-person descriptions, invariably presented as a kind of painting in words, were also an integral part of Cinquecento doctrinal dialogues on the beauty of women, such as those of Giangiorgio Trissino, Agnolo Firenzuola, and Federigo Luigini. Patrizia Bettella has shown how these dialogues, which purport to praise and even exalt women, have in reality a much more sinister aspect.[66] The piecemeal cataloguing of pretty parts reveals a desire on the part of the male observer to weaken the power of the phenomenally beautiful woman, who initially might take on a fearsome and monstrous aspect in his eyes, like Medusa in the case of Trissino's *I ritratti,* or a chimaera in Firenzuola's

Dialogo delle bellezze delle donne.[67] The description of parts in an imaginary painting becomes a 'processo di smontaggio' (a disassembling process; 'Corpi di parti,' 322) whereby the describing male establishes his desire to dominate and possess the monstrous woman, to make a sort of passive icon of her.

The idea that the appreciation of corporeal beauty involves a process of dismembering may be traced back to Neoplatonic theories of love, which tended to regard the material world with suspicion. A passage in Leone Ebreo's highly influential *Dialoghi d'amore,* published in 1535, may serve to illustrate this. Leone was quite learned and sought to write a syncretistic work in which the traditions of Moses, Plato, and Aristotle would all find reconciliation. There are only two speakers in the three sections that make up the *Dialoghi d'amore:* Filone ('great lover'), a character meant to be Leone's own spokesman, and Sofia, the object of his affections, who might be interpreted as both a real woman and an allegory of wisdom, as her name suggests. There is some irony in her identification, for however much her name might mean 'wisdom,' she must have everything explained to her by the all-knowing Filone; in fact, her main role in this dialogue, as is the case for so many other female interlocutors in early modern doctrinal works, is to ask questions or reach naive conclusions that in turn can give rise to a steady flow of erudite explanations on the part of the male speaker.[68]

At a certain point in Leone's third dialogue, during a discussion of beauty, Sofia asks Filone about the beauty of artificial things. Filone couches his response in Neoplatonic terms, declaring that it is all a question of the beauty of forms: just as natural beauty derives from 'le forme naturali' (natural forms), the beauty of artificial things derives from 'le forme artifiziali' (324). Filone provides an example: Sofia must imagine two pieces of wood, one bearing a carving of 'una bellissima Venere' (a most beautiful Venus), the other left in its natural state. The beauty of the Venus figure does not come from the wood but rather from the artificial form that has been imposed upon the material by the mind of the artist; in the same way, the beauty of the natural piece of wood derives from the divine intellect, wherein all forms exist already with more perfect beauty than they can ever acquire from being placed in material bodies (324). The idea of beauty is far more perfect in its integral state within the mind of the artificer than when it has been 'distribuita e smembrata' (distributed and dismembered) by having been placed in a corporeal form; thus the beauty of the concept of the beautiful Venus is reduced once it has been divided into parts and imposed upon a block of wood:

> le parti de la bellezza de la statua di Venere nel legno sono divise ciascuna per sé, onde fanno lenta e debile la sua bellezza in respetto di quella che è ne l'anima de l'artefice, però che in lei consiste l'idea de l'arte ... (324–5)

> [the parts of the beauty of the statue of Venus in wood are divided each unto itself, so that they make its beauty lazy and weak with respect to the beauty that is in the mind of the artificer, since therein lies the idea of artistry ...]

Conjoined with bodies, with physical forms, the idea of beauty must perforce lose some of its perfection. By the same token the material gains much when worked into art; 'il rozzo corpo' (the rough body) becomes more beautiful. The idea might be diminished, but the material itself is enhanced by the artist's efforts.

Niccolò Franco, the author of the prose romance *Filena*, also published one of the more intriguing dialogues on the subject of beauty, *Dialogo dove si ragiona delle bellezze*, in 1542. Franco had worked as Aretino's secretary in Venice for many years, where he had made a name for himself writing verses that mocked the Petrarchist style. However, in 1539 Franco had to flee Venice to avoid Aretino's wrath, after the two had a falling out.[69] Franco composed his lengthy dialogue, which is not often studied today, in Casale di Monferrato where he had taken refuge; there he was safe from physical threats, although Aretino continued to take his vengeance on him through printed attacks, many of which are evident in the *Lettere*. Franco sets his dialogue in the house of a woman named Buona Soarda, who is hosting a large group of distinguished erudite men. Her comments about beauty and the good lead to a long series of didactic refutations by her guests, who continually seek to put her in her place for presuming to know something about the true nature of beauty. Her name, meaning 'Good,' would appear to be emblematic, since she typically expresses notions about the nature of goodness that Franco regards as simplistic. Her putative naiveté resembles that of Leone's Sofia, although Filone is far more respectful of his beloved's opinions than these men are of Buona's; in the text her principal role is to express, in a rather pompous fashion, all of the ideas that Franco considers wrongheaded and in need of correction.[70]

In this work, Franco seems to want to set aside the irreverent tone of his earlier anti-Petrarchism and occasional scurrilous verse. In fact, the male speakers of the *Dialogo dove si ragiona delle bellezze* consistently aim to express the loftiest anti-materialistic tenets of Neoplatonism, to the extent that Franco's *descriptio mulieris,* or rather *descriptiones mulierum,* since there are so many, tend to be treated more ironically here than in any other work with which I am familiar, save Bigolina's *Urania.* Most remarkably, they are not pronounced by an amorous male but rather by Buona herself, who catalogues the beauties of all the women of Casale at the behest of Guglielmo da San Giorgio, 'il Signor Presidente,' the leader of the discussions. It seems evident that Franco is unwilling to ascribe such lowly observations to his men, whose task is to gainsay every one of Buona's pronouncements. Buona describes numerous women, many of them the wives of the men who are present, in meticulous detail (35v–41r). She compares their physical features (only those visible in public) to the usual things of nature, but generally takes pains to combine praise for the body with praise for the soul, as when she refers to a woman's teeth as 'chiare perle, verace testimonio de la chiarezza d'e suoi pensieri' (bright pearls, a true witness to the nobility of her thoughts, 36v); thus, one kind of beauty serves as a sign of the other. In fact, her praises touch on all manner of things besides the usual physical traits: nobility of family, eloquence, grace of manners, and so on. The fact that one of the men subsequently provides a few additional *descriptiones* for the women of Buona's household, with rather more emphasis on purely physical charms (43r–v), does not diminish the irony implicit in Franco's assigning the greater part of this text's descriptions of beautiful women to his only woman speaker, a person whom the reader is not expected to hold in high esteem.

Franco clearly owes a great debt to Leone Ebreo. When one of his characters, Cinisco, has to be 'called back to earth' by the others because his soul has been transported to the heavenly realm of Ideas (49v), we may note that the scene bears a resemblance to a similar episode at the end of Bembo's oration on Neoplatonic love in Castiglione's *Cortigiano* (4.71). However, Franco's version of this motif is modelled even more plainly on a moment in Leone's work, when Sofia has to shake Filone out of his reverie because his soul has become lost in contemplation of an interior image of her beauty (*Dialoghi,* 172). In heaven Cinisco claims his soul has beheld the very Idea of *Bellezza,* or Beauty, which is definitely of 'donnesca figura' (womanly shape, 50r); once more, we see that a woman must be the archetype of any representation of absolute beauty, although in this case Franco does not provide a description of her. Franco also borrows Leone's episode of the sculpted image of Venus: the listeners in his book are asked to imagine two pieces of marble, one of which bears 'una bellissima Venere' (a most beautiful Venus) rendered by Iacopo Sansovino, to illustrate how ideas of beauty pre-exist in the mind of the artificer (56v–57r).

Franco reserves his most interesting treatment of the *descriptio* motif for the end of the *Dialogo,* during an extended passage in which Il Signor Presidente exalts the Virgin Mary as a paragon of women. Here, praise of the Virgin becomes an occasion to vilify all other women for their vain attempts to enhance their beauty through cosmetics: 'la sola Bellezza' (the one true Beauty, 61r) never painted herself while she lived on earth in order to attract men. This idea leads to a remarkable treatment of the traditional *descriptio mulieris,* a description of the Madonna in which all of the standard physical attributes are listed only to be held up as examples of how their true beauty lay in transcendent things:

> Non era la limpidezza lucentissima, quella che la Fronte dela eterna Vergine facea gradire a i giudici che la miravano, ma lhonestate, et la Vergogna ... Non erano i sodi rilievi, quegli; che nel petto del alma Vergine faceano leggiadrissimo paragone, ma le tempre bellissime de la Temperanza, le quali a guisa di forte scudo le faceano usbergo e maglia ... Non era l'avorio, ne i cerchi ingemmati, onde la mano dela celeste Vergine, si mostrava vaghissima, ma la fede ... (61v)

> [It was not supremely lustrous limpidity that made the eternal Virgin's forehead so attractive to those judges who gazed upon it, but chastity, and shame ... Those things on the divine Virgin's bosom that made a most lovely paragon were not firm mounds, but rather the very beautiful tempered steel of Temperance, that served her as hauberk and chain mail, in the manner of a strong shield ... It was not ivory, nor bracelets of gems, that made the celestial Virgin's hand seem so very attractive, but rather faith ...]

Reading this, one can only wonder how it came about that Franco was hanged by the Inquisition in 1570 for the alleged impiety of his writings. Although his pious parody of the *descriptio* does not seem particularly scandalous, its true spirit might have been difficult to discern: this passage, like Bigolina's, is clearly in a more abstruse category than other more overt parodies of the *descriptio* (Shakespeare's sonnet 130, 'My mistress' eyes are nothing like the sun,' comes to mind, as well as the numerous anti-Petrarchan descriptions of unattractive women in rustic or *bernesca* Italian poetry).[71] In any case, it would seem that both Franco and Bigolina appreciated the potential for the subtlest sort of irony in this motif, even if the two authors stood at completely opposing ideological poles, one exalting his subject in order to malign average women, the other mocking her subject with the aim of defending them.

To return to the dialogues of Trissino and Firenzuola, in which supposedly monstrous women are rendered harmless and weak by descriptions that reduce them to the sum total of their parts, we do well to remember that each of these authors takes upon himself the role of artificer, since he creates a sort of literary painted portrait of the beautiful woman – he makes himself the controller, or tamer as it were, of her rough material, by pretending to create an artistic image of her. At this point it may be convenient to recall the words of Patricia Simons, cited above: Renaissance portraits of women are not meant to reflect the individual nature of the subject but rather the masculine creative process, the male's ability to control the feminine image. Nowhere is this more evident than in these doctrinal works on beauty.

To some extent, each of these dialogists must also confront the persistent problem of how to treat the subject of female beauty in a decorous fashion, especially since such descriptions inevitably involve some discussion of the nude or semi-nude female form. This issue, which will likewise consume Bigolina, is most compellingly addressed in Agnolo Firenzuola's *Delle bellezze delle donne,* published in 1548. As the art historian Mary Rogers has noted, with regard to the subject of the nude female body Firenzuola's dialogue maintains a skilful, if at times precarious, balance between the extremely chaste approach of Trissino and that of the more overtly voyeuristic Luigini ('Decorum of Women's Beauty,' 54). For this reason, it will be fruitful to examine Firenzuola's work in conjunction with Bigolina's own approach to the subject.

Firenzuola sets a difficult task for himself: he will discuss the beguiling aspects of the female form in a book meant to appeal to an audience of both sexes, even including women as participants in the dialogue, without alluding to those parts of the body that are normally hidden from public view.[72] How indeed does one discuss woman as erotic spectacle for the delight of male eyes, as Firenzuola so plainly aims to do, without violating the precepts of the Neoplatonic ethic, with its tendency to eschew the physical aspects of love? The work he creates is rife with moral tension and equivocation, yet in the end he would have the reader believe that he has cobbled together a solution of sorts, a compromise that allows for men and women to safely indulge in the age-old dichotomous game of male as spectator and female as specta-cle without risk of compromising the ethical values of the Neoplatonic perspective.

Firenzuola shows that he is aware of the implications of what he is trying to do from the very beginning. In his proem he says, following a tradition established by Boccaccio, that this work will not impugn the honour of any real person, even though he intends to describe the at-tractive qualities of certain ladies of contemporary Prato, because their actual identities will remain hidden (*Delle bellezze,* 526).[73] He goes on to describe how a young man named Celso, clearly meant to represent the author himself despite his coy protestations to the contrary, has come upon four women in a garden while they are engaged in debate over whether or not a certain lady of Prato is truly beautiful. One of the debaters declares that their discussion is purely a woman's affair, but Celso asserts the primacy of male authority by claiming that he has a definite opinion and that the judgment of males in this regard is not to be discounted. He then holds forth as an authority on the subject of female beauty for two days in two different settings, with a variety of listeners present. The parallels with Bigolina's romance need hardly be stressed: Urania too comes upon a group of women debating a *questione d'amore,* and remains with them for a time in order to enlighten them with her wise pronouncements (112–30). The irony is, of course, that Urania is only thought to have the authority of a man, on account of her disguise. Bigolina's rejection of Firenzuola's text is complete: whereas in the latter women are present but a man makes all the essential pro-nouncements, in *Urania* women do all the talking, with a 'man' who is really a woman acting as the final arbiter.[74]

Celso provides a definition of beauty: in essence, it lies in a harmoni-ous and properly proportioned union of diverse parts (*Delle bellezze,* 538). Such harmonious order lies beyond the scope of human reason; it is 'uno occulto ordine della natura' (a mysterious order in Nature, 14), which an arrow shot by the bow of human reason cannot reach ('non arriva saetta d'arco d'ingegno umano,' 539). Only the eye can judge it properly and find beauty where reason cannot. This emphasis on the primacy of sight in the process of appreciating beauty is common to nearly all the myriad discussions of the casuistry of love in this period, as we will see in the next chapter. In Firenzuola's case the emphasis on sight allows for the distancing from the lovely object that is essential to the values of Neoplatonism. Celso claims he loves a woman secretly and virtuously; he is happy just to see her, and does not desire what he knows he cannot have of her (544). Celso affirms that not only 'savi naturali' (those endowed with common sense) but theologians, too, believe that women's beauty is a simulacrum of the blessings of Paradise. Thus the dear women of Prato in Celso's audience should have no fear of his gaze: he is merely getting his sight accustomed to what he will see in heaven, and there can be no harm in it (546). Celso is quick to clear himself in advance of any charge of immorality, and in any case he has already declared that human reason, the faculty most concerned with distinguishing right from wrong, has no part to play in the appreciation of beauty.

References to painting abound in this dialogue, for ultimately its lesson will be how to depict women, as artists must so often do. Celso declares that he will follow the example of Zeuxis, in the familiar tale of the celebrated artist of Croton who had to conjoin the features of five different models in order to produce a composite image of Helen of Troy (538). In like fashion Celso sets out to describe the perfect woman by combining the varied pulchritudinous characteristics that each of the four women in his audience has, and he is not averse to ascribing one charm or another to them by name. Painting is the central metaphor for this process, as when Celso declares that he can scarcely describe the lovely throat of Selvaggia, one of the women present, by means of the 'rozzo pennello delle mie parole' (the rough paintbrush of my words),[75] or when he says he must grind all the necessary colours in order to produce his painting, not just the black and white that are suitable for writers (571). The process of describing female beauty has become essentially ekphrastic by Firenzuola's time – the painted woman is the ultimate icon, the ultimate embodiment of the very concept of beauty.

Firenzuola is careful to describe only those parts of the woman's body that can be normally seen in public, and he avoids overt discussion of the nude form, which Luigini will emphasize later in his *Libro della bella donna*. Nonetheless, Firenzuola declares a desire to see more of women's hidden features in public, such as freely flowing hair, a convention of Petrarchan poetry (560). With his emphasis on what wellborn women can or cannot display in the public environment, and his stated desire to avoid the discussion of the private spectacle of total nudity (even as he continually shows interest in the more intimate parts of the female body), Firenzuola maintains a singular degree of ethical tension, a consistent emphasis on problems of decorum, throughout his lecture.

In order to mitigate this, he often stresses intellectual content, providing diagrams of ideal proportions and exalting the utility of physical characteristics that might otherwise be reduced to their erotic potential. Breasts are nice to look at, says Celso, but they are also supremely useful for the nourishment of infants: whatever is attractive must have some more utilitarian function as well (559). In the same fashion, he declares that hair is not only lovely but also serves to diffuse the excess vapours of the brain (560). When discussing the body parts that fascinate him the most, Firenzuola sometimes employs peculiar ecclesiastical metaphors:

La latitudine del petto porge gran maestà a tutta la persona; dove sono le mammelle, come due colline di neve e di rose ripiene, con quelle due coroncine di fini robinuzzi nella loro cima, come cannelluzze del bello e util vaso: il quale oltre alla utilità di stillare il nutrimento a' piccioli fanciullini, dà un certo splendore, con sì nuova vaghezza, che forza ci è fermarvi su gli occhi a nostro dispetto, anzi con gran piacere; come fo io, che guardando il bianchissimo petto d'una di voi ... Eccoci a coprir li altari: se voi non racconciate quel velo come si stava, io non seguirò più oltre. (559)

[The breadth of the bosom lends great majesty to the entire body. The breasts are here, like two hills filled with snow and roses, with two little crowns of fine spouts at the top, like drinking straws for that beautiful and useful vessel. Besides their usefulness in distilling nourishment for little babies, the breasts have a certain splendor, with such a novel charm, that we are forced to rest our eyes upon them in spite of ourselves, rather, to our great pleasure, as I do, looking at the most candid breasts of one of you ... Here we go, covering up at the altars! If you do not rearrange that veil the way it was before, I will proceed no further. (31)]

Earthly beauty is juxtaposed, however jarringly, with the things of the church: this becomes a recurring motif, as when Selvaggia enjoins another of the women, Amorrorisca, to show her perfect teeth in the same way that holy objects are taken out and shown on feast days (557). Celso cannot stop looking at something as lovely as Selvaggia's bosom, and the coy game he plays, pretending to have seen too much, so that the lady in question has to cover up her 'altars,' raises the hint of an ethical crisis, albeit a slightly comical one, in what is otherwise an exaltation of Neoplatonic contemplation of beauty. Later on, Verdespina reproaches Celso for having forgotten to add arms and hands to his portrait, whereupon Celso claims that he has become so distracted by the sight of Selvaggia's bosom that he has become forgetful (593). Selvaggia, the woman Celso truly desires to possess, is a sharp-tongued, occasionally sarcastic character, whose attitudes and mannerisms suggest her emblematic name, which means 'wild.' Surely this was an appellation that Bigolina might have found suggestive as she went about creating her own book, in which a protagonist named after the Celestial Venus must confront and overcome the bestial Femina Salvatica, or wild woman.

In her study of these Cinquecento dialogues on beauty, Mary Rogers notes that the type of painting that Firenzuola would have in mind for his ideal woman would show a flirtatious, bantering, smiling lady, perhaps imaginary, perhaps recognizable: 'fully dressed and thus suitable for display in mixed company, but painted in a way that could stimulate the erotic imaginings of those male spectators so inclined.'[76] Rogers describes the sort of bodice that Selvaggia is supposed to be wearing, noting that this is a dress which encourages thoughts of undress on the part of the male spectator, perhaps with the collusion, or at least the temporary consent, of the woman involved. In fact it is Lampiada, another of the women, who urges Selvaggia at one point to let slip her veil again and expose her 'reliquie' (relics, *Delle bellezze,* 559); once more we see an overt link between hidden body parts and relics usually kept hidden by the church. The tension inherent in this text is summed up by Rogers: 'For all the insistence in Renaissance theory that seeing is, with hearing, the noblest of the senses, being able to perceive true harmony uncorrupted by matter or by animal passions, Celso's looking at women is evidently not a chaste Platonic matter of pure contemplation' ('Decorum,' 71). Yet at the conclusion of the dialogue, no moral crisis is alluded to, and indeed Celso's coy, flirtatious equivocations have left the reader with the impression that none truly exists. At one point Celso reveals the identity of a woman who, because of the beauty of her body, would serve as a perfect model if he had to paint a Venus (*Delle bellezze,* 562); in effect, Firenzuola sees nothing wrong with the very deed that serves as the basis of Bigolina's heartfelt polemic. Moreover, the 'painting' that Celso has produced in his two days of speaking is declared to be perfect by none other than Selvaggia herself: 'Or sì che mi pare che questa vostra dipintura stia come quelle che son di mano di buon maestro ...' 595 (now I believe your picture is like one of those wrought by the hands of a good master, 67). If she were a man, she claims, she would fall in love with Celso's image as Pygmalion did with his statue. This, we cannot fail to note, is precisely the myth that

Bigolina's duchess hopes to emulate, as she fixes her eyes uselessly on the Prince's portrait.

By the mid-Cinquecento, on the level of popular culture, male writers and artists such as Firenzuola, Aretino, and Titian were seeking to minimize the ethical risks of portraiture by creating a mode of expression that not only permitted but even encouraged women to make a spectacle of themselves for the delight of male eyes. In Firenzuola's case, the Neoplatonic perspective he chooses to adopt for his dialogue leads inevitably to ethical tensions, but he defuses these and ultimately trivializes them through pseudo-comic dramatizations of the acts of viewing bodies and covering them up. Like Firenzuola, Bigolina espouses certain Neoplatonic values; moreover, in her work of prose fiction she likewise chooses to dramatize the ethical tension implicit in the clash between the Neoplatonic ideal and the desire to view nude bodies. Nonetheless, her ideological perspective remains the very antithesis of Firenzuola's.

Only one thing is lacking in his portrait, concludes Celso, and that is the all-important Neoplatonic element of soul; however, he says he must leave that to a better artist:

> Lo 'ngegno, e le altre doti e virtù dell'animo non ci fanno mestieri, perciocchè aviamo tentato di dipignere la bellezza del corpo e non quella dell'animo, alla finzion della quale bisogna miglior dipintor di me, migliori colori, e miglior pennello che non è quello del mio debole ingegno ... (596)

> [Intelligence and the other gifts and virtues of the soul are not our business because I have tried to paint the beauty of the body, not that of the soul. For the latter, a better painter than I is needed, with better colors and better brushes than those of my feeble abilities ... 68]

Consciously or unconsciously, this is the challenge that Bigolina took up just a few years later, in her romance *Urania:* Bigolina will claim the mantle of the 'better painter' who can provide the portrait of the soul instead of that of the body. In doing so, she also provides a critical re-examination of the *descriptio mulieris* as it had been traditionally presented by poets, prose writers, and painters alike. She begins by banishing outright the whole notion of the sight of beauty in her account of the beginning of the love affair between Fabio and Urania. We are never told what either lover looks like, save that Urania is not as physically beautiful as she is virtuous (84), and in fact the two do not even meet through the chance sighting that is so typical of the old narratives of love. When boy meets girl, we are not given the usual description of the woman, with emphasis on the lovely appearance of each separate part of the body: Fabio simply hears the tale of Urania's consummate virtues, then calls on her at her house, eventually convincing her that his own virtues are worthy of hers. Bigolina's long-deferred blazon of body parts appears only in the context of the painting of the duchess, as is perhaps entirely appropriate in a work that functions more as a comment on the power of art (with Bigolina's own literary art triumphantly ascendant over the visual arts) than on the power of actual physical beauty.

The literary *descriptio mulieris* represents the extreme case of literature striving to attain the plane of the visual, to be more like painting. The emphasis is on colours, proportions, and the shapes and shades of body parts compared to natural objects: the reader is meant to 'see' the beautiful woman as an artist would render her. If this is hinted at more or less overtly in the lyric poets and romance writers, it becomes a full-blown conceit in the dialogues of Trissino, Firenzuola, and Luigini: for them, the description of the woman is indeed ekphrasis, the description of a work of visual art.

This process is taken quite seriously by every early modern author who engages in it, save one: Giulia Bigolina. In the name of the defence of women, she satirizes the old-school *descriptio mulieris*, and bends it to her own unique purposes.[77] She makes a point of not providing us with a catalogue of the lovely parts of her protagonist, Urania: we are never told the colour of her hair, the proportions of her body, or the appearance of her eyes, teeth, hands, and so on. Instead, we are given a catalogue of the parts of the miserable duchess, who loses her life for the rash act of posing as Venus, as an *exemplum* that stands in moral and iconographic contrast to Urania. Moreover, the catalogue is not provided by the narrating lover who seeks to control and possess her, nor is it provided by the third-person narrator who will soon see her in the arms of the deserving lover: instead it is provided by an unscrupulous, manipulating 'salesman,' the painter who fails in his efforts to 'sell' his painting to the wise prince. In fact, the prince never sees the lovely lady herself; instead, he sees only a cunning artifice of her, cunningly described by the very character who created it. Bigolina, clearly a keen observer of the art of portraiture in her time, takes pains to have her painter give us a painter's, not a poet's, description of the woman: whereas in nearly every purely literary *descriptio*, the woman's teeth are simply described as 'perle' (pearls), Bigolina's painter states regretfully that he was not able to paint the duchess's 'perle' because her mouth did not happen to be open (204).[78] Bigolina was doubtless quite aware that it was considered improper in her time to paint portraits of women with their mouths open, as Elizabeth Cropper notes.[79] If Bigolina were following the literary tradition of epideictic rhetoric, instead of creating one of the very first realistic descriptions of a painting within a work of prose fiction, the teeth would simply be *perle* and that would be the end of it. Instead, she has her painter describe the fictional painting as if it were a real painting, a real object occupying a narrative space meant to be seen as realistic; thus, the rhetoric employed to describe it must move beyond the old rhetorical devices of the poets. The description of it cannot help but acquire an ironic, even satirical tone, especially if one remembers Aretino's vogue for enthusiastically describing actual paintings in his *Lettere*.

The *descriptio mulieris* was meant to be a triumph of visual art, a literary motif that tried to do what a painting did, thereby paying a sort of homage to the power of painting. Bigolina, instead, makes of it a triumph of literature, a somewhat satirical plot element in a work of prose fiction, an ekphrasis placed in the mouth of a character in an imaginative narrative; nothing more. Visual art is completely subjugated by literature in *Urania:* here the painting of the beautiful woman only exists as a prop, a piece to be moved about on a stage and eventually to be discarded, when the protagonists of the work realize that its imagery is of no value to them.

Bigolina's Two Venuses

The philosophical notion, derived from Plato and the Neoplatonists, that there are two Venuses, one heavenly and chaste, the other vulgar and destructively sexual, is central to *Urania.* Urania herself, whose name ('the heavenly one') designates the celestial version of Aphrodite in Plato's *Symposium* (120–1), is clearly meant to be associated with the first, while the duchess goes so far as to personify the latter by posing as her in a painting.[80] The two characters, although ultimately antithetical, are in fact presented in similar terms at first: each is described as a solitary sort, disdainful of liaisons with men, so that Amore (Love in personified form) must reveal his power and cause them to fall in love as an act of cruel vengeance (86, 186). It is the way in which they respond to their newly imposed love desires that sets them apart.

Robert Hollander has identified the different aspects of Venus in her various representations from the classical to early modern periods, demonstrating that the dichotomy is not as simple as it first appears (*Boccaccio's Two Venuses*, 158–60, n44). Hollander catalogues three distinct aspects: Venus might represent perfect, intellectual, incorporeal love, or positive sexual love for procreation in matrimony, or else negative, destructive, antisocial lust. The medieval view, as exemplified by Boccaccio, tended to contrast the last two aspects, licit or illicit physical love, whereas ancient and Renaissance Neoplatonists, under the influence of Plato's *Symposium*, stressed the contrast between the first two.[81] The most important influence on Renaissance thought in this regard was Marsilio Ficino, who described the spiritual and procreative Venuses as complementary, each representing an essential aspect of human existence, each having something of the divine. Following Plato, Ficino declares that the heavenly Venus was born from the sea without a mother, the result of the castration of Uranus, whereas the more earthly, carnal Venus was the result of the union of Jupiter and Dione; seen in these terms, Botticelli's Venus, rising out of the sea, takes on celestial attributes.[82] Ficino associates the two Venuses with the two *demonii* (daemons) who are supposedly always present in our souls, one called Calodemon (good daemon) and the other Cacodemon (bad daemon), representing the twin loves of Venus (it is interesting to note how these two daemons survive in American popular culture as the tiny angel and devil who hover on either side of the heads of animated cartoon characters in moments of moral quandary, dispensing contradictory advice). Although the Cacodemon is putatively evil by virtue of its name, Ficino resolutely says that neither is truly evil: 'Invero amendui son buoni: imperocchè la procreazione de' figliuoli è necessaria e onesta, come la ricerca della verità' (truly both are good, since the procreation of children is necessary and right, like the search for truth; *Sopra lo amore*, 6.8, 102).[83] Giovanni Pico della Mirandola, Ficino's contemporary and another careful reader of Plato, likewise refused to denigrate the earthly Venus in his *Commentary on a Canzone of Beniveni*, although he does not go so far as to praise her for her generative powers (105–6; 152–5).[84] The good-versus-evil dichotomy between the two Venuses is more pronounced in Firenzuola's *Dialogo delle bellezze delle donne*, wherein we are told that 'le cose venuste' (beautiful things) derive only from the Venus who is the daughter of heaven, whereas 'le cose veneree' (lascivious things) can be traced to the Venus who is the daughter of the earth.[85]

On the surface, Bigolina appears to adhere more to Boccaccio's medieval view, perhaps sustained by the negative description of Venus in Christine de Pizan's *Epistre Othea:* the heavenly Venus is definitely to be preferred to the vulgar, and there does not seem to be anything redeemable in the Venus whom the duchess portrays. However, as we have seen, Bigolina does not make the experience of viewing the *Judgment of Paris* entirely negative, for it inspires a proper sort of lust in the prince, who is moved to speculate on the appearance of the nude body of the Savia Damigella. Thoughts of love should not be entirely deprived of the physical element, Bigolina tells us, for both the Prince and Urania ultimately find fulfilment in marriage (286).

But no one to my knowledge, from Plato on down, treats the topic in quite the fashion Bigolina does: only Bigolina associates the two Venuses with contrasting art forms and weaves their depiction into an ornate fiction of the *paragone*. In so doing, she defiantly rejects more than one predominant attitude of her time: not only does she modify Ficino's scheme of the heavenly and carnal Venuses by minimizing the morally acceptable attributes of the latter, but she even casts aside the Horatian doctrine of 'ut pictura poesis,' a painting is like a poem, that was so prevalent among early modern theorists of literature and the visual arts. For Bigolina, a painting is *not* like a poem, nor a prose narrative for that matter: there is a world of difference between them, especially regarding the portrayal of women. Urania, a fervent lover who is not the most attractive of women, as we are told early in the narrative (84, 86), has come to stand not only for the heavenly Venus (by virtue of her name) but for the art of literature as well, as a character who not only writes but is the very substance of the narrative that Bigolina, under the prodding of the homunculus named Judgment, has spontaneously conceived in her mind. The duchess, another fervent lover who is indeed presented as the most attractive of women, elects to play the 'carnal Venus card' as a means of winning the love of a man, buying into the cult of female beauty that constituted the standard for all beauty according to so many Cinquecento theorists, especially those who were writing about painting. In this regard, we may note a parallel between *Urania* and the only other early Italian prose romance to have a plot built around the experiences of a female protagonist: Boccaccio's *Elegia di madonna Fiammetta*. Here too, as Hollander has noted, a choice must be made between the Celestial Venus, who is described to Fiammetta by her righteous old nurse (1, 17), and the Carnal Venus, who subsequently appears to Fiammetta in a vision (1, 18). 'Between the words of the nurse,' says Hollander, 'which may be taken as they are delivered, and the words of Venus, which should be taken with more than a little cynicism, the entire moral climate of the *Elegia* is present in the form of a choice: Fiammetta may worship either Venus she chooses. She chooses the wrong one' (*Boccaccio's Two Venuses*, 45). Bigolina revisits this notion more than two hundred years later, providing her authorial persona with a similar choice between the Venuses. Instead of posing for a painting, which would put her in the category of the Carnal Venus (as the subsequent story of the duchess makes plain), the authorial persona spontaneously conceives the story of a romance protagonist who bears the very name of the Celestial Venus, thereby reversing Fiammetta's original ill-advised decision. However, with regard to characters' choices there is also one main difference between the two works: in *Urania*, the Venuses are now represented by rival art forms, and the choice to be made has been rendered considerably more complex by the involvement of proper and improper modes of artificial self-representation.

The contrast embedded within this fictional creation ultimately serves to illustrate the *paragone* between painting and literature. Bigolina creates a literary work expressly to show that she has learned the lesson of good judgment, and thus will avoid posing for a painting. Later she employs within her narrative the plot device of a character who, ill advisedly, poses in a painting that is meant not only to apotheosize the cult of female beauty that Bigolina scorns but also to illustrate a supreme act of mythological bad judgment – surely one of the cleverest conceits in all Renaissance literature. Bigolina wishes us to understand that the story she conceives *about* a painting, drawn from her own 'basso intelletto,' is far superior to any *actual* painting, in terms that are at once both aesthetic and moral. Alone among the writers of her time, she employs the vehicle of prose fiction to make her own point about the *paragone,* that a woman can indeed exercise good judgment and choose the art form best suited to represent the yearnings of her heart.

The Book as Object

There is a great irony implicit in most of the amatory prose romances that follow Boccaccio's model: they are novels of erotic love, yet their stated task is to emphasize the moral dangers of erotic love. An exception once more may be found in Corfino's *Phileto,* which is largely deprived of the admonitory elements of the *Peregrino* and the *Filena.* Robert

Hollander has noted Boccaccio's fascination with Dante's episode of Paolo and Francesca, who fall in love through reading an Arthurian romance (*Boccaccio's Two Venuses*, 102–7). Dante has Francesca describe the book as a 'galeotto,' named after Gallehault, the go-between for the love affair of Lancelot and Guinevere (*Inferno*, 5, 127–38). Boccaccio's most famous (and most controversial) reference to this episode appears in the subtitle of the *Decameron*, 'Prencipe Galeotto,' implying the book is to be regarded as a pander; in Hollander's view, this should also be seen as a warning against the dangers of the sort of erotic love so often described in the *Decameron* (*Boccaccio's Two Venuses*, 105–6).

However, before Boccaccio came up with that subtitle, he had already evoked the notion of the book as 'galeotto' in the *Filocolo*, written more than a decade earlier. Boccaccio had a tendency to refer to his literary creations as objects that can be dispatched or bestowed as gifts to their ideal readers; this is especially true in the case of his prose romances, inasmuch as the motif appears not only in the *Filocolo* (5.97) but also in the *Comedia delle ninfe fiorentine* (50) and the *Fiammetta*, wherein the first-person narrator reminds the reader more than once that she is writing her story down and that her book might one day be seen by sympathetic ladies or by her treacherous lover.[86] Much later, Corfino provides something similar in the *Phileto*, when he includes the author's address to his book as a personification (4–9). In the case of the *Filocolo*, the narrative is already a pre-existing entity in the form of the love story of Florio and Biancifiore, which had had a long life before Boccaccio ever adopted it for his own purposes. Therefore, in the opening chapter, we do not meet a narrator who recounts the story of his own experiences; instead, we hear of how the author came to create the book itself as a material thing, at the behest of his beloved Fiammetta.[87] In the concluding chapter, which has already been cited above in part, the author speaks directly to his creation, urging it to fulfil a role just like that of the romance that seduced Paolo and Francesca: he hopes the book will kindle love thoughts in the woman on whom he has bestowed it, in effect serving as his own 'galeotto' (5.97, 615–17). Moreover, Boccaccio has already inserted the motif within the narrative itself, in his description of the education of the children Florio and Biancifiore, who are being raised together in the palace of Biancifiore's parents, the king and queen of Spain. Their tutor has them read 'il santo libro d'Ovidio' (the holy book of Ovid), that is, the *Ars amatoria*, which, as the text makes plain, will contribute greatly to the love passion they will eventually feel for each other (1.45, 6). In fact, in Hollander's view, it will lead the two to worship the wrong Venus: 'Florio's and Biancifiore's reading of the *Ars amatoria* and their subsequent worship of Venus and her son are nearly fatal to the two lovers, who are united happily only after they correct their carnal affections under the sign of a better Venus' (*Boccaccio's Two Venuses*, 105). At first, the book leads them to venerate the Carnal Venus, but as Boccaccio demonstrates continually in his works, true happiness lies only in devotion to the Celestial Venus. The *Filocolo* has been called a 'teleology of desire,' in which all lower forms of desire are ultimately revealed to be false after a long digressive process fraught with ambiguities; in the end, they must be redirected by Providence towards God.[88] Boccaccio was clearly fascinated by the power of literature to move people to feel erotic desires, even if such desires are eventually shown to be immoral. To a certain extent, he bestows that role upon his first prose romance, stressing its existence as a physical object that can be given from one person to another and that has the potential to instil passion in the reader.

We have already noted the degree to which *Urania* differs from the *Filocolo*, and yet in this regard the two works have something in common. Bigolina, too, is interested in the genesis of her book, how it has come to exist as a narrative and even as a material object that might be given as a gift to a person, Bartolomeo Salvatico. She, too, writes her narrative in the third person, separating it from the realm of the first-person narrator of the proem. Nevertheless, she neatly avoids all of the irony that Boccaccio creates when he postulates that a book describing the dangers of erotic love might serve as a 'galeotto,' a pander, on behalf of its author. For Bigolina the 'galeotto' is not the book, nor indeed any other book; instead it is a painting. Bigolina implies that the real moral danger in the arts does not lie in literature but rather in portraiture, in the power of the visual arts to move a person to lust. And the 'errors' of her romance, such as they are, centre primarily on this: Bigolina's authorial persona at first proposes to have her portrait done as a means of memorializing herself and bestowing a token of her affection upon Salvatico. However, she is soon set straight, and thus creates a book instead, the most appropriate of all possible memorials, and one in which her heroic protagonist will personify the Celestial Venus and avoid committing errors of any sort. Bigolina does not create a work of art that can ever be suspected of playing the role of 'galeotto.' Instead, she leaves that role to the portrait that she never commissions for herself, and to the various portraits she describes within her narrative, such as the portraits that Fabio would require if he were to wish to keep a memento of Clorina's gorgeous appearance, or the portrait of the Prince that drives the duchess mad with desire, or the portrait of the duchess in the *Judgment of Paris*. This last is meant to be seen as the most brazen 'galeotto' of all, for it portrays the Carnal Venus, the great enemy of Urania's Celestial Venus, as well as the false idol of Boccaccio's Florio and Biancifiore.

Prose romance narrators who follow Boccaccio's tradition continually tell of their mistakes in love, to the extent that the problematic love affair becomes a veritable leitmotif of the genre. Bigolina, whose *Urania* is arguably the best early modern Italian prose romance after those of Boccaccio, gives us a narrator who speaks not of mistakes in love but rather of mistakes in art – her error of judgment leads her to choose the wrong medium as a display of her finer qualities. She does indeed follow the amatory romance tradition when she describes a supernatural visitation in her proem, akin to the sight of Amore in the lady's eyes at the beginning of the *Filocolo* (1.1, 6), or the vision of Venus in the *Fiammetta* (1.18), or the arrival of Peregrino's long-winded ghost in Caviceo's proem (4). She also follows the tradition when she places a love story, a story of love lost and ultimately regained after much suffering, at the centre of her narrative. But in terms of the central message she wishes to communicate, she leaves Boccaccio's tradition completely behind, and here we find the essential aspect of Bigolina's reformation of the amatory romance in prose: her topic is not limited to love, nor to the mistakes that those who are under the sway of love might make. Another of the principal purposes of her book is to provide a defence of women, a defence not only from the calumnies of men but more importantly from women's temptation to find their sense of self-worth in the mere depiction of their physical appearance. Love passion, if directed to its proper ends, is not the problem. The problem is essentially one of self-display, of women participating in the programs of men who never tire of looking at the *forms* of women, and who never tire of regarding women as mere icons, as spectacles for their amusement; in short, the way they appear in the dialogues on beauty. Bigolina takes up the amatory romance tradition that Boccaccio had bequeathed to Italian literature, reshapes and simplifies it in narrative terms by making it look and function more like the novella, then reworks its principal motifs according to her rather provocative ideological agenda, with the aim of transforming the genre's very raison d'être.

4 The Sight of the Beautiful

Beauty and the Senses in *Urania*

Although *Urania* often reflects the influence of the doctrinal debates on the nature of love and beauty that pervaded the culture of mid-Cinquecento Italy, it is still first and foremost a love story, not a didactic work of philosophy. Its protagonist, much like a hero of chivalric romance, is called to do great deeds and demonstrate her loyalty in the name of love. This emphasis on the need for action is evident right from the beginning of the proem, wherein Bigolina's authorial persona declares that true lovers are those who persevere in 'amorevoli operationi' (tasks of love), instead of giving up when the going gets difficult (56–7). The narrator says she has demonstrated this by writing letters and poems to the object of her affection, the young man Bartolomeo Salvatico (58); and as the proem progresses, she will learn from a persuasive allegorical being that she must write yet another work for Salvatico, a romance showing the greatest deeds of love, instead of passively posing for a painting.

Nonetheless, Bigolina quickly reveals her own fondness for pseudo-philosophical descriptions of the processes whereby the senses appreciate and respond to beauty, in the fashion of the theorists and dialogists on the subjects of beauty and love of her time.[1] There are two such doctrinal passages in *Urania*, the first in the speech of Giudicio in the proem, the second in Urania's letter to Fabio within the main narrative. The first arises in conjunction with Giudicio's oration on the problem of people who take it upon themselves to judge others, even though they themselves would appear to be stained with sin if they were to see themselves reflected in Giudicio's giant eye. The author has decided to offer a painting of herself to Salvatico, in spite of the fact that he is not the sort of person to appreciate such a gift, since he is sensitive, disinclined to judge others, and completely lacking in stains in the eye of Judgment (68). This leads Bigolina to address an old problem that had bedevilled the medieval scholastics: how can objects of the material world affect the intellect, which is essentially spirit and therefore not made of matter?[2] An image is a material thing, says Giudicio, which cannot act upon something that is contrary to its nature, such as a human soul, unless some agent were to act as go-between:

> Imperciò che essendo, come più volte ho detto, la imagine cosa materiale, et l'animo, over l'intelletto nel quale ella ha da operare, essendo essenza dello spirito, l'uno nell'altro non opererebbono mai, se un'altro mezzo, il quale dell'una, et dell'altra natura partecipasse, non vi si interponesse. Et questo mezzo il senso del vedere s'intende, il quale, rispetto all'essenza di sè medesimo, tende allo spirito, et rispetto all'operatione con la imagine, la quale è cosa materiale, s'accosta. (70, 72)

> [As I have said more than once, an image is material, whereas the soul or intellect upon which it would act is the very essence of spirit. Thus the one could not function with the other, unless some external means, participating in the nature of both, were to interpose itself; this means, we understand, is the sense of sight. In terms of its own essence, sight tends toward the spirit; in terms of its function, it tends toward the image, which is a material thing. (71, 73)]

Giudicio asserts that sight is in essence a spiritual sense, endowed with a special purpose as an agent linking the material and spiritual worlds. He goes on to describe the details of the role of sight in cognition:

> Non potendo adunque, la imagine altro che cose materiali, col mezzo però del vedere, all'intelletto rappresentare; le quali come due sono le essenze del senso, così due sono le cose, ch'egli dalla imagine trahendole, allo intelletto le rappresenta: ciò è il bello, et il buono, il qual buono per esser più che'l bello appropriato alla natura dello intelletto, per diritta linea in quello trapassa. Ma il bello, che è molto più a sua natura disgiunto, viene primieramente dalla imaginativa raccolto, la quale più che altra potenza dell'anima, con tutti i sensi tien parte. Et tanto ivi il bello si ferma, che viene a farsi habile a potere nello intelletto trascendere, il quale intelletto poi l'ha in sè stesso considerato, ne fa o piacendogli, o non piacendogli

quel concetto, che più gli pare. Perchè se la cosa considerata et conosciuta
gli piace, in conserva della memoria la manda, et se non gli piace disprez-
zandola da sè la discaccia. (72)

[And so, the image can reveal only material things to the intellect, and
it does this only by means of sight. Just as the sense of sight has two es-
sences, there are two things that sight is able to draw out of the image and
communicate to the intellect: these are the beautiful, and the good. The
good passes directly to the intellect, inasmuch as it is more appropriate
to the nature of the intellect than the beautiful. The beautiful, on the other
hand, stands at odds with the nature of the intellect and thus is taken in
primarily by the imagination, that part of the soul which, more than any
other, is the abode of the senses. The beautiful remains there so long that
in time it gains the ability to rise up into the intellect, where the intellect
takes it into consideration and forms whatever concept of it that seems
appropriate, either pleasing or displeasing. If the thing, now having been
known and given consideration, pleases the intellect, it is sent to be preserved in the memory; if on the other hand the intellect does not find it
pleasing, it disdains it and drives it back out. (73)]

This passage reflects the influence of the Aristotelian teachings of
Bigolina's day, which derived not only from the traditional debates of the
medieval scholastics but also from more recent studies of Aristotle's late-
classical Greek commentators, for which Bigolina's native Padua had
in fact long been renowned.[3] Medieval and early modern interpreters
of Aristotle were often drawn to expound upon the philosopher's pronouncements on psychology and cognition, as expressed in such works
as *De anima* and *Parva naturalia,* especially since it was thought by many
that Aristotle himself had not developed his theories on the nature and
workings of the soul sufficiently. Aristotle had described the soul or mind
as an immaterial entity, an essentially passive receptor of messages communicated to it by the sense organs, but he was rather vague concerning
both the origin of the soul and the details of the process. Later commentators proposed what Katharine Park has called 'the faculty approach'
('Organic Soul,' 467), in which the functions or faculties of the senses
and the intellect were meticulously expanded, categorized, and defined,
as can be seen in a very popular handbook of the late fifteenth century,
the *Margarita philosophica* of Gregorius Reisch (first published in 1503).
The early modern Aristotelians generally recognized that there had to be
two categories of sense, external (sight, hearing, touch, etc.), which were

associated with the sensitive soul, and internal (imagination, memory, cogitation, etc.), associated with the higher intellective soul.[4] The internal senses processed signals from the external ones and provided them with forms that allowed them to be appreciated by the loftier, less material intellect, even when the perceived object was no longer present. It was frequently postulated that there had to be a go-between for this process, an immaterial entity known as the *species sensibilis* (sensible form or sense image), which received the impression of the external material object as a seal is impressed in soft wax, thereby rendering it into a form that could be managed by the internal senses and, ultimately, by the intellect itself. The simile of the seal impression in the wax comes from Aristotle's *De anima,* but the notion of sensible forms, as found in the works of Reisch and Pietro Pomponazzi, was developed by later Aristotelians who found the master's original explanations inadequate.[5]

Bigolina has plainly absorbed many of these Aristotelian notions of psychology and sense perception; for instance, she stresses the great divide between the physicality of external objects of sense and the plainly non-physical intellect, which somehow must be made aware of the outside world. She also bestows precise functions upon the internal senses of imagination and memory and categorizes them according to something resembling Park's 'faculty approach.'[6] However, it must be noted that Bigolina adopts Aristotelian theories in her own peculiar fashion to suit the exigencies of her text, which in fact was a common practice in her time. There was no single accepted doctrine for all of these mechanisms; indeed, as Park has noted, the 'faculty approach' appealed to medieval and Renaissance philosophers precisely because it allowed them to describe intricate processes that might vary from one commentator to the next. 'This physiological orientation allowed Renaissance writers to elaborate a wide variety of practical applications for their psychological theories – applications that figure prominently in both the learned philosophy and the popular self-help literature of the period' ('Organic Soul,' 469). As in the case of certain pervasive Neoplatonic notions, Aristotelian psychology was scarcely the sole domain of intellectuals and academicians during the Renaissance. The 'democratization' brought about by a print culture that endeavoured to place books in the hands of an ever greater number of people during this period, especially in Italy, also allowed certain ideas derived from classical philosophy to flourish at the level of popular culture.[7] Bigolina's prose romance, a love story endowed with a pretence of classical erudition, may well be regarded as a sign of the times.

However, in adopting Aristotelian psychology to suit her narrative task, Bigolina does some rather remarkable things, which we must not fail to note. Although she recognizes the typically Aristotelian need for a faculty that might serve as a go-between to link the material world of sense objects with the immaterial intellect, she chooses to dispense with the traditional *species sensibilis*. Instead, Bigolina's scheme bestows this function upon the external sense of sight, which is somehow empowered to bring the perceived image directly to the internal senses of memory and imagination without any recourse to the *species sensibilis*. Here, in a rather haphazard fashion, Bigolina also allows Neoplatonic terminology and concepts to intrude upon her otherwise primarily Aristotelian psychological process: in claiming that sight communicates two aspects of a sense object to the intellect, the beautiful and the good, she employs terms that are suggestive of contemporary Neoplatonic treatises on beauty and love, as we have seen here in chapter 2. This allows her to make an observation not usually found in descriptions of the Aristotelian process of cognition: that the beautiful, so closely associated with physical bodies, is inherently incompatible with the purely spiritual intellect.[8] Thus sight, in Bigolina's estimation, is not as 'worthy' a sense as hearing, for the latter enjoys greater compatibility with the essential nature of the soul; this assertion will prove highly significant as the narrative continues to unfold.

Giudicio is interested in the sense of sight, but he does not say anything about the sight of actual physical bodies. Instead, he refers only to the sight of 'la imagine,' the image – specifically, a painting. He goes on to say that the author has not yet done anything worthy of a painting that might communicate those all-important elements, the beautiful and the good, to anyone; and in any case, people should never leave paintings of their physical beauty as gifts for others, since such an act would be 'vain and lascivious' (75). The emphasis is all on art, with the clear message that an art which is meant to communicate a person's physical beauty is simply not redeemable:

Et perciò io ti consiglio che non la imagine della tua faccia a quel gentilissimo giovine mandi, poi ch'ella per farlo di te raccordevole non è buona, ma più tosto quella della grande osservatione et amore che gli porti gli manderei, la quale nella sua memoria viva ti terrà di continovo. (74)

[Therefore I counsel you not to send the image of your face to that most gentle youth, for it is not a proper means to make him remember you.

Instead, you must send your great reverence for him, and your love; things which will keep you continuously alive in his memory. (75)]

As we know, the narrator soon realizes that the proper means to send her love and reverence to Salvatico must take the form of a literary creation that she conceives of herself.

Shortly after this, the proem concludes and the story of Urania and Fabio begins. Here Bigolina is quick to bring up once more the problem of sight, in order to provide a thematic link between the proem and the narrative. In her long, reproachful letter to Fabio, Urania makes many of the same doctrinal points that Giudicio had pronounced in the proem, and here, as before, sight is discussed primarily in the context of the painted image, with the same emphasis on the profound divide between matter and spirit. At first Urania does indeed acknowledge that a man admires two aspects in a woman, beauty of body and beauty of soul, and for a brief moment she shows an inclination to discuss the former: which parts of her body does Fabio now find displeasing, since he has chosen to abandon her for another woman?(92). However, she plainly prefers to stick to the beauty of the soul and to make Fabio see that she has so much more of it than her pretty rival, Clorina; and this she explains in terms of theories of sense and cognition:

Come tu poi sapere, due sono gli sensi nelli quali il virtuoso amante nell'amata sua si compiace, cioè nel vedere, et nell'udire; delle quali due parti mentre alla amata sua donna si trova l'amante presente, gli occhi et l'orecchi pasce et nodrisce. Et dopo che da colei che egli ama si è fatto assente, volendo pur ancora di quelle dolcezze gustare, le quali nel vederla et nell'udirla havea prima gustate, necessaria cosa è per esser il vedere, senso alle parti del corpo appertinente, ch'egli una imagine di quella bellezza nella Idea si formi, et col mezzo di quella la desiata bellezza miri et consideri; chè sanza un tale interposito mezzo, non potrebbe in assentia di quella bellezza gioire. Imperciò che le attioni materiali et quelle dello spirito sono due estremi che giamai da loro stessi si unirebbono, se per opera d'alcun mezzo non venissero a unirsi. (94)

[As you know, the virtuous lover takes pleasure in his beloved through two senses, sight and hearing: thus he feeds and nourishes two parts of his body, the eyes and the ears, while the beloved is in his presence. When he is away from her, yet still wishes to partake of the sweet pleasures which he first tasted through the sight and sound of her, it is necessary for sight to form an image of her beauty within the Idea, inasmuch as sight is a sense which appreciates the physical body. By means of that image the lover can gaze upon and contemplate the beauty he yearns for, since without such an image as intermediary, he could not enjoy that beauty in the beloved's absence. The workings of matter and spirit are two extremes which, on their own, would never be able to come together unless some intermediary strove to unite them. (95)]

As was typical among the theorists of the age, Bigolina focuses entirely on the ways in which males appreciate the beauty of females, not vice versa. However, she has her own reasons for doing this. In the works of most writers, this viewpoint can be attributed to the usual bias of a male-dominated society towards the experiences of men, whereas in Bigolina's case, men are clearly not the 'more perfect' sex; instead she declares them to be the essence of the problem, and proposes to re-examine their modes of behaviour.[9] Bigolina has very little to say about how the lover appreciates his beloved while in her presence, save to reaffirm that sight and hearing are the two senses that allow him to do this. She reserves most of her attention for how he might appreciate her when she is not in his presence, in those moments when some sort of image must preserve her appearance in the lover's Idea, the term often employed by contemporary art theorists to designate the concept of reality that is formed within the mind out of received sense perceptions.[10] Bigolina says that a painting must serve as an intermediary between soul and physical beauty – in effect, as a sort of *species sensibilis*. In describing this, she provides once more a system of faculties and functions that evokes neo-Aristotelian concepts of the process of cognition:

Ma così dell'udir non aviene, chè essendo egli parte all'anima pertinente, subito che le parole escono di bocca a quel che le dice sanza ritrovare impedimento che l'arrestino, passano all'intelletto dello ascoltante, il quale intelletto poscia che quella dilettatione che gli pare ne ha presa alla Memoria le raccomanda, et ivi si fermano. Onde ciascuna volta che lo intelletto vuol delle già udite parole compiacersi ancora, sanza adoprare alcun mezzo a sua natura disgiunto, dalla Memoria riducendosi quelle medesime, et non l'imagini di quelle vi trova, et in quelle considerando, quella dolcezza ne sente che prima udendole havea sentita. Hor se dunque non può lo amante in assenza, nella corporal bellezza della amata sua donna mirare se gl'interpositi mezzi non vi intervengono, et lo intelletto della sua che son le parole udite, le quali la bellezza dell'anima gli scuoprono, può

molto ben sanz'altri mezzi da sè stesso mirarla, et intenderla. Manifesta
cosa è adunque che assai più nobile la bellezza dell'anima sia da tenere,
et tanto maggior la bellezza nell'una che nell'altra anima s'intende essere,
quanto è più atta a riempir de' sue varie bellezze gl'intelletti, et le memorie
di quei che la mirano, et delle bellezze sue varij ritratti può fare. (94, 96)

[But hearing cannot work in this same fashion, inasmuch as it is the sense
appropriate to the soul. As soon as words exit the mouth of the person
who pronounces them, they pass into the intellect of the hearer without
encountering any impediment. The intellect, upon finding something delightful in these words, consigns them to the Memory, and there they remain. Whereupon each time the intellect wishes to take pleasure yet again
in what it has heard, it goes into the Memory without using any means
foreign to its nature; there it finds not an image, but the very words themselves. Contemplating these, the intellect feels once more the sweetness it
knew when it first heard them. Thus, even if the absent lover cannot gaze
upon the corporeal beauty of his beloved lady without some means which
function as a go-between, the intellect can still regard and appreciate the
words it has heard, which reveal the beauty of the woman's soul, without
any intermediary at all. It is therefore quite obvious that the beauty of
the soul must be regarded as the nobler of the two by far. One can see
that a given soul may be so much more beautiful than another if it has a
greater capacity to instill its varied beauty into the intellects and memories of those who look upon it, and if it can create diverse portraits of that
beauty. (95, 97)]

There is nothing radical about Bigolina's assertion that the beauty of
the soul is nobler than the beauty of the body, since it was common currency in the popular Neoplatonism of the day. Sources may be found
for a good many of her notions, as we shall see in the next subchapter;
indeed, Aristotle himself had said that hearing was a more important
sense for the mind than sight, although without any special emphasis
on the sight of beauty.[11] Nonetheless, Bigolina carries this line of rea-
soning to a novel, even revolutionary conclusion, with respect to the earlier doctrinal works that must have influenced her. Ultimately, the sight
of physical beauty reveals itself to be an inherently invalid feature of
Bigolina's process of falling in love, for the simple reason that a lover
like Fabio, who is inordinately moved by the physical appearance of a
woman, would have to carry around a simulacrum of his beloved – a
painted portrait – and contemplate it often, if he were to satisfy the

desires of his sense of sight while his beloved is away (98). This suspicion of the ethical implications of the sense of sight is reinforced later in the text, when Urania meets the five wrongheaded young men in the woods, and hears one of them say,

> Imperciò che da noi per lo innanzi non fu mai considerato che in altra cosa eccetto nel compiacimento de' sensi nello innamorarsi s'havesse ad esercitare, et credevamo che pur che gli occhi nella lor vista sodisfatti fossero, che ogn'altra parte di noi dovesse star queta, et contenta. (138)

> [For in our case, up to now we imagined that nothing but the pleasure of the senses mattered in affairs of love; and moreover we thought that as long as the eyes were content with what they beheld, every other part of us could remain tranquil and contented. (139)]

Bigolina makes it plain in the following passage that this way of regarding women, as beautiful objects designed to appeal to the male sense of sight, cannot be separated from the misogynistic notion that women are inherently imperfect, and thus inferior to men (140). Therefore, Urania's sustained oration concerning the essential injustice of this view of women takes as its point of departure the rejection of the notion that the appreciation of true beauty begins with indulgence in the sight of a physically beautiful woman.

As we have noted, Bigolina's views regarding the validity of the role of sight in the cognition of beauty will lead her to an outright condemnation of certain widely accepted notions concerning the ethical implications of portraiture, as well as the portraitist's way of looking at beautiful objects, particularly women. To appreciate the extent of Bigolina's challenge to contemporary points of view on this topic, it will be necessary to trace the origins of her ideas among the writings of the most influential Renaissance theorists of love and beauty who preceded her.

Sight in the Doctrines of Love

By Bigolina's time, sight had long played an important role in Italian descriptions of the process of falling in love, especially among the poets of the *dolce stil novo* school in the thirteenth and fourteenth centuries, for whom the poet's sight of the beloved woman was an essential point of departure in a love experience that was completely deprived of indulgence in the lower, more 'sensual' senses. This emphasis on the importance of sight was continued by Petrarca, whose poems typically dwelt on memories of the sight of the absent beloved, as well as by the Renaissance Neoplatonists. The first great expounder of Neoplatonism in the context of love in early modern Italy was Marsilio Ficino, whose *Sopra lo amore,* a commentary on Plato's *Symposium,* was published in Italian in Florence in 1544. Throughout much of the second half of the Quattrocento, *Sopra lo amore* had circulated in manuscript form both in Italian and in Latin, under the title *Commentarium in convivium Platonis de amore.* Many of the Neoplatonic notions that pervade Italian erudite culture throughout the sixteenth century, and that appear in *Urania,* ultimately derive from Ficino's interpretations of Plato. Indeed, we have already had occasion to examine a part of this work in chapter 3, in conjunction with Bigolina's treatment of the two Venuses.

Bigolina's basic premise is consonant with Ficino's notion that true beauty cannot be corporeal if it is to appeal to the soul.[12] When Bigolina stresses the materiality of bodies as opposed to the essential immateriality of the soul, we may be reminded of the assertion in *Sopra lo amore* that the soul appreciates only what is incorporeal in bodies, and that true beauty must be more than mere shapes, proportions, and colours (5.3, 72). Therefore, it follows that images of corporeal things transmitted through sense organs cannot be imprinted directly upon the incorporeal soul, according to Ficino's interpretation of Plato (6.6, 97). The soul receives images of external things through the action of a go-between known as the spirit (*spirito*), which the soul informs; as the soul regards the images, it conceives superior images of its own within the Imagination, and conserves these within the Memory (6.6, 98).

Bigolina follows all of this to some extent, although she is a bit fuzzy on the details; in the end, she provides no real coherent Neoplatonic system but rather adopts and modifies the standard notions whenever it suits her narrative or doctrinal purposes. As we have noted in the context of Bigolina's Aristotelianism, she is by no means alone among the writers of her time in doing this. Bigolina agrees that a lover must form an image of the beloved within the Idea, so that the beloved may be contemplated whenever he or she is absent. But from here she goes off in a direction that Ficino never follows: if the lover has failed to create this 'portrait' within the Idea, he or she is forced to look upon more physical mementos, such as actual painted portraits. Mere physical beauty is not in itself sufficient for the creation of such an inner portrait, says Bigolina; therefore, Fabio cannot possibly form such an image in

his mind of the lovely but unvirtuous Clorina. For Bigolina, the important distinction is between what the soul contemplates through sight as
opposed to hearing, something Ficino does not discuss. Since Bigolina
is ultimately interested in adapting theories of cognition to illustrate her
views on the *paragone* between the arts, she modifies the Neoplatonic
scheme to suit her ideology, which diminishes the importance of sight
(painting) in favour of hearing (literature).[13]

Bigolina's deep mistrust of the sight of physical beauty finds some
parallel in Ficino's treatise, but only to a limited extent. True beauty may
be incorporeal, says Ficino, but physical beauty still has an important
role to play.[14] In the Fifth Oration, Ficino has his speaker Marsuppini assert that the cognition of our intellect takes its origin from the senses, so
that we would never know of or desire the goodness hidden in things
if we were not attracted to it by the visible signs of external beauty.
Physical beauty is essential for showing the good, and thus is quite
useful (5.1, 67–8). Marsuppini recognizes three nobler, more spiritual
senses: reason, sight, and hearing, which are to be distinguished from
the more material senses of smell, taste, and touch; however, he does
not allow that hearing has a special link to the soul, as Bigolina does
(5.2, 69–70). In fact, he claims that 'Colori, Figure, Voci' (colours, figures,
voices), the things communicated by the higher senses, do not move the
body at all, but rather aid the spirit in its search for truth (5.2, 70). Thus
sight and hearing exist on the same plane, and there is nothing inherently suspicious in the sight of beauty.[15] Later on, Ficino asserts rather
baldly that every love begins with the sight of earthly beauty ('adunque
ogni Amore, comincia dal vedere,' 6.8, 103); sight thus becomes an essential first step in the journey towards a wholly spiritual love. This
view was shared by another Quattrocento Neoplatonist, Giovanni Pico
della Mirandola, even though Pico is known to have objected to many of
Ficino's beliefs concerning the nature of love: in his *Commento sopra una
canzone d'amore*, Pico states that the sight of sensible beauty may lead to
desire either for bestial coitus or for union with the divine, depending
on whether or not the viewer is inclined to associate that visible beauty
with the body in which it is found (3.2). Thus Bigolina's forthright declaration that an image of herself would be 'troppo vana, et lasciva' (too
vain and lascivious, 74), as well as her apparent belief that the love process does not require any visual stimulus at all, stands at odds with one
of the most fundamental and often expressed Neoplatonic beliefs.

Ficino's ideas were sustained by a contemporary humanist who also
wrote primarily in Latin and was active in Florence: Francesco Cattani

da Diacceto (1466–1522). Two of his works appeared after his death in Italian editions, *I tre libri d'amore* and *Panegirico all'amore*. For the erudite and rather scientific Cattani, the appreciation of beauty most certainly began with the sight of a material object, which allowed the mind to form its image (*effingere*, literally 'to mould'):

> Quando adunque per lo aspetto ci s'appresenta nella fantasia qualche spettacolo, il quale noi approviamo, come bello & pieno di gratia; subito l'anima eccitata nella cognitione della sua bellezza interiore, desidera non solo fruirla, ma effingerla. Et perche tale espressione ha dibisogno della materia, & del subietto, atto a quella ricettione; per questo desidera esprimerla in quello, che essa ha provato, & da cui è stata eccitata a tale espressione . . . (*I tre libri d'amore*, 116–17)

> [Thus when a certain spectacle presents itself to our imagination by means of sight, and we find it pleasing as a beautiful and graceful thing, right away the soul, stirred by the awareness of the object's inner beauty, desires not only to enjoy it, but also to form an image of it. Since such an expression has need of physical material as well as the subject which is suitable for its reception, the soul wishes to express it in the same way that it has experienced it, and in the same way in which it has been inspired to give it form . . .]

Cattani, citing Plato, the Neoplatonists, and the Pythagoreans, observes that the soul is quite disposed to find worth in any object of beauty; moreover, he is quite untroubled by the notion that the sight of physical beauty has the potential to stimulate the generative force ('la virtù generativa,' 118), from which comes sexual desire. Cattani, perhaps following Ficino, likewise discusses the two Venuses quite matter-of-factly, without attempting to impute to the Carnal one any threat to a person's moral integrity: each has an essential part to play in the workings of the world, with the Celestial one representing 'bellezza divina' (divine beauty), while the Vulgar one represents 'bellezza sensibile' (sensible or tangible beauty, 108–9).[16]

Bigolina seems to have found more of a kindred spirit in Pietro Bembo, whose *Asolani*, a dialogue on love first published in 1505, communicated Neoplatonic ideals of love in terms appealing to a broader, less erudite audience.[17] Although there are no passages in *Urania* that establish a firm and undeniable link with the *Asolani*, some of Bembo's ideas still seem to have filtered down to Bigolina's text, albeit in altered form. Given Bigolina's literary inclinations, it is safe to say that she must have known this monumental work, which had a pervasive influence on those who wrote on the subject of love throughout her century.

In this dialogue, six young people, three men and three women, converse about love in a garden setting over a period of three days. The *Asolani* was to become something of a work in progress, since Bembo found it necessary to publish a somewhat revised version of it in 1530, to reflect his evolving views on the subject. In either edition, Bigolina could have found inspiration both for her disdain for the depiction of female beauty in painting and for some of her notions regarding the role of the senses in the love experience. Bembo places his exaltation of the sight of the beautiful woman in the mouth of Gismondo, his defender of the joys of love and the principal speaker of the second book. In a significant chapter (2.22), Gismondo asserts that beautiful women are the nicest things one might look upon, and uses the three women present as cases in point. His description of the physical charms of the perfect female, beginning with the hair and face and ending with the sight of one of his companion's breasts pushing against her light garments, is expressly referred to as if it were a painting, presaging the treatment of women's beauty in the context of painting that will become fashionable in later dialogues on beauty (2.22, 292). When another of the women objects to this, Gismondo retorts that women may try to hide their bodies from the eyes of men, but their lovers will always succeed in seeing what they wish (2.22, 292–3). Gismondo then carries his painting metaphor even farther, exalting Love as an artist who provides a lover with a painted image of his beloved that he may carry within his mind:

> O amore, benedette sieno le tue mani sempre da me, con le quali tante cose m'hai dipinte nell'anima, tante scritte, tante segnate della mia dolce donna, che io una lunga tela porto meco ad ogni hora d'infiniti suoi ritratti in vece d'un solo viso, et uno alto libro leggo sempre et rileggo pieno delle sue parole, pieno de' suoi accenti, pieno delle sue voci, et in brieve mille forme vaghissime riconosco di lei et del suo valore . . . (2.27, 298–9)

> [O Love, may your hands be ever blessed by me, those hands with which you have painted, written, and marked so many things in my mind that portray my sweet lady; so that at all times I carry with me a long canvas that holds an infinite number of her portraits, instead of but a single face. Moreover I forever read and read again a thick book full of her words, full of her tones, full of her sounds; in short, I am aware of a thousand most lovely forms both of her and her virtues . . .]

This passage provides a remarkable contrast with Urania's letter to Fabio, in which we are told that no painted portrait could ever convey the deepest feelings of love in the same way as poems or books. Gismondo, expressing notions that are quite typical of late-medieval and early modern love lyrics, declares that the power of Love personified is more than capable of duplicating not only the effects of portraits of the beloved within the lover's mind, but also the effects of her voice as if recorded in a book. This cannot help but remind us of Bigolina's treatment of the *paragone* between letters and the visual arts as portrayed in Urania's letter to Fabio, save that in Bembo's straightforwardly sentimental case, there is no hint of rivalry between the two art forms, no indication of which of them might be superior to the other.

Gismondo's emphasis on love as a joyful experience is meant to refute the views of the speaker of the first day, the melancholy Perottino, who had stressed the sufferings of lovers. In Book III the visions of both Perottino and Gismondo are tempered by Lavinello, Bembo's spokesman for the Neoplatonic view of love. Here we find a specific rejection of Gismondo's sensual 'painting' of the ideal lovely woman, as well as some words of caution regarding the role of the senses in the process of love. Borrowing from Plato's *Symposium*, Lavinello defines love as a desire for beauty, but not the sort of beauty Gismondo has championed, as he tells Gismondo in no uncertain terms:

La qual bellezza che cosa è se tu con tanta diligenza per lo adietro havessi d'intendere procacciato, con quanta ci hai le parti della tua bella donna voluto hieri dipignere sottilmente, né come fai ameresti tu già, né quello, che ti cerchi amando, haresti a gli altri lodato come hai. (3.6, 320)

[If you had previously sought to understand what this beauty is with as much diligence as you employed yesterday when you wanted to paint for us so precisely the parts of your beautiful lady, you would not love now in the way that you do, nor would you have commended to the others that which you seek by loving, as indeed you have.]

Lavinello specifically rejects the sort of beauty that one might paint in favour of a beauty that cannot be painted, and in this regard he serves as something of a precursor to Bigolina's Giudicio. Lavinello goes on to say that the proper sort of love yearns for both the beauty of the body and that of the soul, and flies to them through two 'windows': that of hearing, which is oriented towards the soul, and that of sight, which inclines towards the body. Thus our eyes recognize the beauty of forms while our ears recognize that of voices, which reveal the beauty of the soul: 'Né ad altro fine ci fu il parlare dalla natura dato, che perché esso fusse tra noi de gli nostri animi segno et dimostramento' (Nor for any other reason were we given speech by nature, except that it might be a sign and a revelation of our souls, the one to the other, 3.6, 320). Bigolina echoes this notion in her assertion that hearing is the sense that communicates most directly to the soul, and this, as we know, becomes the basis for her claim that poetry is a better art than painting. Bembo does not bring up the *paragone* here, nor does he explicitly condemn the role that sight plays in the appreciation of beauty; nonetheless, his rejection of the attitudes behind Gismondo's sensual 'painting' might easily have spoken volumes to Bigolina as she went about adopting the prevailing theories of her time to her own literary needs.

Once more Bembo addresses the issue that will be central to Urania's letter to Fabio: how can the lover enjoy the beauty of the beloved object when it is no longer present? The difference between the two writers lies in Bigolina's application of the motif to a discussion of the moral implication of the *paragone* between the arts, a problem that does not interest Bembo. For Bembo, the beloved can always be visited in thought or reflection (*pensiero*) even when he or she is beyond the reach of the lover's eyes or ears. We can enjoy the beautiful aspects of our beloveds whenever we like, says Bembo, through the agency of thought, which must be considered a form of memory in this context (3.6, 321). As she does with the ideas of so many of her contemporaries, Bigolina discerns a moral crisis where another writer finds none: in this case, Lavinello is even in agreement with the sensual Gismondo, and no differentiation between the powers of sight and hearing is implied. According to Lavinello, love is simply the desire for beauty, and the senses that allow us to appreciate that beauty are the higher, more spiritual ones of the eye, the ear, and *pensiero*. Following Ficino and ultimately Plato himself, Bembo declares that moral danger lies in loving with the lower senses of touch, taste, and smell, which can only lead one to love 'sozze cose' (filthy things, 3.6, 321); he does not make an ethical distinction between the modes of reception of the eye and the ear.

Lavinello concludes this chapter by sternly reproaching Gismondo for his failings, but chooses a most intriguing ancient legend to illustrate this: he compares Gismondo to the poet Stesichorus, who was struck blind for lampooning Helen as the cause of the Trojan War in his verses.[18] Only after Stesichorus had composed a recantation was his sight restored. Lavinello hopes Gismondo will likewise rethink what he has said, thereby regaining the light of good judgment that he has plainly lost ('et sì rihaverai tu la luce del diritto giudicio, che hai perduta,' 3.6, 322). There is some irony in this conclusion, since Stesichorus was blinded for maligning the world's most beautiful woman. It is therefore implied that a poet who said such things not only showed bad judgment but deserved to lose his eyesight as well, the means whereby he could best appreciate such beauty; and yet Gismondo is to be blamed for being too fond of gazing at lovely women. All the tensions inherent in the Neoplatonic attitude towards sight are encompassed in this one legend: the sight of beauty, especially that of a woman, is both essential to the love process and yet at the same time inherently suspect for its implied indulgence in sensual yearnings. Bembo, like any other good Neoplatonist, ultimately finds he cannot do without the agency of sight in the appreciation of beauty, even as he makes a considerable effort to minimize its importance.

As is well remembered, the *Asolani* ends with something of a palinode. Lavinello relates a conversation he has just had with a wise and holy hermit, who refutes the opinions on love of all three of the speakers, Lavinello included (3.19, 341). The hermit enjoins Lavinello to leave off all yearnings for earthly love; instead, he must desire only true beauty, which is divine, immortal, and unfailing. However, like many another literary palinode, this does not necessarily serve to invalidate completely all that had been said in the previous pages. Renaissance dialogues generally followed the Ciceronian concept of balanced debate *in utramque partem,* which allowed for some authority to be ascribed to all of the participants.[19] Bigolina, in the fashion of other readers of her time, might well see wisdom both in what Lavinello says to refute Gismondo and in what the hermit says to refute them both, without fear of doing Bembo's work an injustice.

The first half of the sixteenth century saw numerous dialogues and treatises that treated the topic of love. Many of these were very popular and had considerable influence; however, in none of these would Bigolina have found much support for her ideas regarding the role of the senses and the arts in the love experience. An eminent example of these is Castiglione's hugely influential *Il libro del cortigiano (The Book of the Courtier),* published in 1528. An eclectic work, it contains much that might have appealed to Bigolina, including a discussion of the *paragone* between the arts. Castiglione also describes the process whereby one falls in love, ending with a transcendent account of the Neoplatonic love experience pronounced by Bembo himself.

The *Cortigiano* begins with an intriguing image, one that finds something of a parallel in the proem to *Urania*. We have seen how Bigolina conceived her book as a sort of portrait, the portrait one should write in order to avoid posing for a painting. Castiglione, too, presents his *Cortigiano* as a metaphorical painted portrait, meant to depict a lost generation of discussants who used to meet at the ducal palace of Urbino.[20] Castiglione wants his book to serve as a memento of those who have passed on, as portraits were so often meant to do; however, unlike Bigolina, he sees nothing amiss in the comparison between the art forms of portraiture and literature.[21] For Bigolina, the painted portrait is something to reject on ethical grounds in the context of literature, whereas for Castiglione it is an ideal to be imitated, imperfectly in his case:

> mandovi questo libro come un ritratto di pittura della corte d'Urbino, non di mano di Rafaello o Michel Angelo, ma di pittor ignobile e che solamente sappia tirare le linee principali, senza adornar la verità de vaghi colori o far parer per arte di prospettiva quello che non è. (1.1, 50)

> [I send you this book as a painted portrait of the court of Urbino; not one by Raphael or Michelangelo, but rather by a mediocre painter who only knows how to draw the fundamental outlines, without the ability to adorn the truth with pretty colours, or make something seem to be what it is not by means of the art of perspective.]

Such diametrically opposed views of the book as a portrait can only lead to a more definitive parting of the ways. In fact, Castiglione goes on to provide not only a heartfelt exaltation of painting as a means of memorializing beauty but also an unequivocal declaration of the primacy of sight in the love process. Count Ludovico da Canossa, Castiglione's principal speaker in Book I of the *Cortigiano*, declares the superiority of painting over sculpture as a decorative art; of the two principal orientations of the *paragone*, painting versus poetry and painting versus sculpture, Castiglione is clearly mostly interested in the latter. He then declares that his ideal courtier should know the art of painting, which is both 'onesta e utile' (honest and useful, 1.52, 111), and which was so much lauded by ancient writers. Moreover, it is a source of pleasure, especially as a means of capturing the beauty of women:

> E questo pensino quei che tanto godono contemplando le bellezze d'una donna che par lor essere in paradiso, e pur non sanno dipingere; il che

se sapessero, arian molto maggior contento, perché più perfettamente
conosceriano quella bellezza, che nel cor genera lor tanta satisfazione.
(1.52, 111)

[Let this be on the minds of those who find so much enjoyment in the contemplation of the beauties of a woman that they feel they are in paradise,
and yet who do not know how to paint; for if they knew how to do this,
they would have even greater contentment, since they would know even
more perfectly that beauty which gives rise to so much satisfaction in their
hearts.]

Castiglione, like Bembo, follows the precepts of *in utramque partem* in
his dialogue; therefore, a statement made by one of his interlocutors
should not necessarily be taken as reflecting the author's own belief.
However, none of Ludovico's hearers raises any fundamental objection to his views that the ideal courtier should indulge in the sight of a
beautiful woman, and that no man knows and appreciates the beauty
of women more than a painter. Ludovico goes on to speculate that
Alexander must have given his concubine Campaspe to Apelles, who
had fallen in love with her while painting her, because he knew that
painters were more capable of appreciating a woman's beauty than
other men (1.53, 112).[22] In effect, the ability to paint women is seen as
a great virtue, not a source of moral anguish, in this text. Bigolina specifically defies this notion by giving us a painter of women who is a
complete charlatan, and who scarcely knows the nature of true beauty,
at least as she perceives it.

As for love arising from the sight of beauty, Castiglione appropriately
allows his interlocutor, Bembo, who had demonstrated his knowledge
of such things in the *Asolani,* to wax eloquent about this in the fourth
and final book of the *Cortigiano.* Here, in no uncertain terms, the process
of falling in love is said to proceed from the sight of corporeal beauty:
love is first and foremost a desire for beauty, and therefore cognition
must precede desire (4.51, 315). Desire naturally yearns for the good
but is in itself blind and cannot know the good but through the senses.
Bembo specifies that he is talking about 'bellezza ... che appar nei corpi
e massimamente nei volti umani e move questo ardente desiderio che
noi chiamiamo amore ...' (beauty ... that appears in bodies and especially in human faces, and gives rise to this ardent desire that we call
love, 4.52, 316). This beauty is due to 'un influsso della bontà divina' (an
influx of divine goodness). This *influsso* flows down over all creation,

but when it finds a perfectly proportioned face, with certain colours and shadows and lines (he could be describing a painting here), it infuses itself therein and shows itself to be most beautiful (4.52, 316). This draws the eyes of others to itself; the eyes penetrate the lovely object so that it is impressed upon the soul, causing delight and a desire to have the lovely object. However, from this can arise a problem of *giudicio* – if the soul lets itself be wholly guided by sense, it falls into grave error and imagines the lovely body to be the thing it actually desires; it wants to join itself to that body, 'il che è falso' (which is false, 4.52, 316). In this portrait of the carnal lover who is deceived by the 'falso giudicio del senso,' Bigolina could have found a paradigm for her grand drama of good versus bad judgment, with the duchess personifying the carnal lover who allows herself to be deceived by sensual desire.

However, there is much in Bembo's speech that Bigolina will reject outright. For instance, he is keen to associate physical beauty with goodness, a bit of standard Neoplatonism that Aretino satirized so cruelly in his second letter to Bigolina, and that Bigolina banishes from the pages of *Urania*. Beauty, says Bembo in the *Cortigiano*, is born of God and is like a circle, with *bontà* or goodness at its centre. Just as no circle is deprived of a centre, no beauty is without goodness. Bad souls only rarely dwell in attractive bodies; thus, 'la bellezza estrinseca è vero segno della bontà intrinseca' (external beauty is the true sign of internal goodness, 4.57, 320). In bodies we see the impression of the grace of character, which is also evident in nature: a tree bearing lovely flowers is the harbinger of fine fruits. Good and useful things have a certain 'grazia di bellezza' (grace of beauty, 4.58, 320). He concludes that the body is not of such 'vil materia' (vile material) that it cannot be impressed with the qualities of the soul, which rules over material nature and conquers the 'tenebre del corpo' (the darkness of the body) by means of divine virtue (4.59, 322). Bigolina defies all of this with her revolutionary creation of a romance heroine who is not supremely beautiful yet who is more virtuous and wise than such dazzling beauties as Clorina and the duchess.

When Bembo discusses the senses in Castiglione's text, he stresses the absolute primacy of sight in terms that are more explicit than those of the *Asolani*; moreover, in the *Cortigiano* there is no holy hermit waiting in the wings to tell the speaker when he has dared to praise physical beauty too much. Here Castiglione, with Bembo's voice, presents a neat and tidy process whereby one begins to love: in the presence of beauty, the eyes snatch the image and bear it to the heart, where it is contemplated by the soul. The soul is warmed, while the 'vivi spiriti' (living spirits) that flash out of the eyes add fuel to the fire. The soul seeks a remedy, and thus arms the fortress of reason, closing thereby the pathways of sense and appetite (4.62, 324). Guided by reason, the ideal courtier recognizes that the body is not the true source of beauty. True beauty is incorporeal, 'un raggio divino' (a divine ray) that has lost much of its dignity by conjoining itself to something that is ultimately vile and corruptible: thus beauty is perfect only when separated from the body (4.62, 324).

Touch is rejected here as the lowest of the senses, but sight is exalted as supreme: just as one cannot hear with the palate, nor smell with the ears, one cannot enjoy beauty ('fruir la bellezza'), nor satisfy the desire that beauty stirs up in our souls with touch. Instead, one must employ 'la virtù visiva' (the visual faculty), the sense of sight that is so affected by that beauty (4.62, 324). As in the case of Ficino, hearing is also exalted, but not more than sight: together, the two senses are 'ministri della ragione' (ministers of reason), and neither is said to have a more direct line to the soul than the other (4.62, 324). Castiglione's Bembo mentions only one of the arts in conjunction with his oration on the senses; but, significantly, it is one that does not interest Bigolina at all: music, which would have to play so large a part in the life of the perfect courtier. Naturally it is specifically associated with hearing, the sense which for Bigolina will become the ideal conduit for literature rather than music.[23]

For Ficino, Bembo, and Castiglione, the greatest moral danger lies not in looking at physical beauty but in desiring to possess it carnally. There is nothing inherently wrong with gazing at a beautiful object as long as one does it wisely, that is to say, rationally. Other theorists might emphasize different aspects of this process, but by and large they do not depart substantially from its fundamental premises. For example, Mario Equicola (1470–1525), whose *Libro de natura de amore* was first published in 1525, claims Plato's authority in neatly dividing sight and hearing from the lower senses, and in regarding as equally valid all the things that these two higher senses might contemplate, works of art as well as human bodies:

Dicamo dunque, con Platone, quel essere il bello che ne delecta non in qualunque voluptà, ma per il viso et audito, delectandoci apparati, orna-menti, picture, belli homini et bruti, edificii, sculpture, canti, diverse voci, ragionamenti et fabulationi. La suave voluptà del'odorato, la dolceza del

gusto, il iucundissimo moto venereo non dicemo bello, per essere più corporei, et più il corpo che l'animo delectare. (341)

[Then let us say, along with Plato, that the beauty which delights us does
not lie in any voluptuous pleasure, but rather in sight and hearing: decorative displays, ornaments, paintings, handsome and ugly men, buildings,
sculptures, songs, different voices, rational discussions and storytelling all
delight us. We do not call the delicate pleasure of smell, the sweetness of
taste, and the most pleasant motion of Venus beautiful, because they are
more corporeal, and give delight more to the body than to the soul.]

For Equicola, anything that brings delight to the higher senses may be
called beautiful, and there can be no harm in merely looking at things.
On the other hand, sexuality ('the most pleasant motion of Venus') requires a descent into the lower sense of touch, where only pleasure can
reside, not true beauty, which is perforce less corporeal. Thus we may
gather that the essential corporeality of the objects that one contemplates through sight does not in itself constitute a source of ethical crisis
for Equicola, as it will for Bigolina.[24]

As the century progressed, more dialogues and treatises on the subject of love were produced. Another possible influence on Bigolina,
especially if the dialogist Mario Melechini can be believed, was the
Dialoghi d'amore of Leone Ebreo, a work we have already had occasion
to discuss in chapter 3, in the context of ekphrasis. This highly popular
work, reprinted five times in Italy between 1541 and 1552, was likely
known to Bigolina, even if she shows no inclination to borrow phrases
from it verbatim in *Urania,* as Melechini has her do as a speaker in his
unpublished dialogue *A ragionar d'amore.*[25]

As we have noted, there are only two interlocutors in Leone's dialogue: Filone (who is the author's spokesman), and Sofia, who may be
seen both as the woman whom Filone loves and as an allegory of wisdom, albeit a rather naive one.[26] The presence of Sofia as an interlocutor
allows Filone to use her as the principal 'exhibit' in his description of
the love process, which appears primarily in the third dialogue. When
she asks him why he appears to be lost in thought, he explains that her
beauty has entered his eyes and penetrated his *fantasia,* his imaginative
faculty, wherein his mind, or *intelletto,* has been contemplating a sort
of effigy of that beauty. The scheme here, with its dichotomy between
the exterior and the interior sense functions, is largely Aristotelian: in
his *De anima* Aristotle had described role of the Imagination as a sort

of clearing house for messages from the sense organs, primarily sight, since Aristotle traced the etymology of the Greek word for imagination back to the word for light: 'Since sight is the chief sense, the name φαντασία (imagination) is derived from φάος (light), because without light it is impossible to see' (*De anima* 3.3, 163). As we have noted, Bigolina adopts this notion as well, for she specifically mentions the *imaginativa* as the place of the senses, wherein the sight of something beautiful is received (*Urania* 72).

Leone's process of cognition gives absolute primacy to sight, much as the speaker Bembo does in Castiglione's *Cortigiano*. Like Ficino, he divides the senses into two groups, the spiritual (sight and hearing) and the material (touch, taste, smell). In Leone's scheme, sight is in itself of two kinds, *sensibile* and *intelligibile*: the first is oriented towards the corporeal world; the second, 'il vedere intellettuale' (the sight of the intellect), renders the incorporeal world intelligible to the intellect (*Dialoghi*, 179). Both types of sight, corporeal and incorporeal, require illumination: one type of light comes from the sun, the other from the divine intellect (180). Hearing is most certainly subordinate to sight, for it derives its cognition from the action of the tongue, which reports what has already been seen by the eye. Thus the antecedent of hearing is sight; the ear is subordinate to the eye, 'come origine principale a l'intellettual cognizione' (as the principal origin of cognition of the intellect, 180). For his part, Ficino does not speak of a special connection between hearing and the intellect; indeed, in his case such a connection seems rather to be accorded to sight, which can be both physical and intellectual. In a subsequent passage Leone exalts sight above all of the other senses because only sight can appreciate the entire physical universe, both earthbound and celestial; moreover, it has for an intermediary 'aere illuminato da la celestial luce' (the air illuminated by celestial light), which exceeds all other parts of the world in beauty just as the eye is superior to all other parts of the body (183–4). Therefore sight is the more excellent sense not only for what it can comprehend, but also for its mode of functioning, which links it to heavenly things.[27]

In Leone's text, as elsewhere, we see relatively little concern for the moral consequences of feasting one's eyes on physical beauty, the thing that will become Bigolina's great bugbear. Leone says the soul's love is biform (*gemino*), 'non solamente inclinato a la bellezza de l'intelletto ma ancora a la bellezza ritratta nel corpo' (inclined not only toward the beauty of the intellect but also toward that beauty which is portrayed in the body, 196). A man (as usual we hear only of the experiences of men) might be drawn to one or the other of these, to a greater or lesser degree; there is nothing particularly wrong with the more earthly sort of love (which is the less excellent and perfect of the two) as long as it is not indulged in overmuch. Leone says this of people who have clear eyes of the mind, who are capable of rising above 'li vulgari,' the vulgar crowd:

> conoscono che quella bellezza che si truova ne' corpi è bassa, piccola e superficiale a rispetto di quella che si truova ne l'incorporei; anzi conoscono che la bellezza corporea è ombra e immagine de la spirituale, e participata da quella, e non è altro che il risplender che il mondo spirituale dà al mondo corporeo; e veggono che la bellezza de li corpi non procede de la corporeità o materia loro ... (318)

> [they know that the beauty which is found in bodies is low, small, and superficial in comparison to that which is found in incorporeal things; indeed they know that corporeal beauty is but a shadow and an image of spiritual beauty, and that it shares in spiritual beauty, and that it is nothing more than the resplendence that the spiritual world gives to the corporeal world; moreover, they see that the beauty of bodies proceeds neither from their corporeality nor from their substance ...]

Leone does not allude to a potential ethical crisis in all of this. Of course physical beauty is inferior to the spiritual, he tells us, but as long as discerning minds are aware of it and do not overindulge in the former at the expense of the latter, there is little to worry about. The material world does not present a danger to Leone; indeed, it can be redeemed by participation in the spiritual, as Filone tells Sofia: 'Sappi che la materia, fondamento di tutti li corpi inferiori, è da sé deforme e madre d'ogni deformità in quelli; ma informata in tutte sue parti per partecipazione del mondo spirituale, si renda bella ...' (Be aware that material, which is the basis of all inferior bodies, is in itself deformed and the mother of every deformity in those bodies; however, if it is given form in all of its parts by participation in the spiritual world, it may make itself beautiful, 320). Bigolina might have derived her mistrust of the material world from reading Leone but not her notion of the moral crisis that it clearly represents to her.

Niccolò Franco treats this subject as well, in his *Dialogo dove si ragiona delle Bellezze*. Like Leone, Franco declares vision and hearing to be the higher, spiritual senses, as opposed to the corporeal senses of smell, taste, and touch. Only the former can grasp beauty (11r). Later, when Franco returns to the subject, he associates the perception of beauty through sight, which involves light, with the intellect's perception of beauty, while the perception of beauty through hearing is associated with the appreciation of the beauty of the world soul, which consists of concordance and harmony (57v). In this scheme it is clear that neither sense is superior to the other. However, the eyes have their usual exalted place in the process of falling in love with beautiful people: Franco calls them 'Capitani d'Amore' (captains of love, 22r). Love derives from the soul but must perceive beauty through the higher senses, whereupon it is then retained in the memory; however, Franco is not interested in Bigolina's favourite problem – that is, how to continue to appreciate the beauty of the beloved even when he or she is absent (22v).

As in his series of *descriptiones mulierum* in this same dialogue, Franco tends to mention beauty of the body in the same breath with beauty of the soul, so that they are sometimes hard to separate. He claims that even lovers burning with desire are capable of perceiving angelic beauty in the sight of the beloved (52r). As usual in the Neoplatonic scheme, the lover must turn away from contemplation of the lovely body as soon as possible, in order to follow human beauty up the ladder towards 'la vera bellezza,' or true beauty (52r). Love is seen as an artist, who paints 'la leggiadria d'un bel volto' (the gracefulness of a pretty face) within our senses and our hearts; this sort of painting, directed towards a very proper end, gives the soul something to contemplate, so that it can remember the divine things it once knew in heaven (53r). Sight is essential to this process, since what we see in physical objects is a gift from the spiritual world; however, average, common people ('il volgo') cannot appreciate what the 'occhi corporei' (eyes of the body) are capable of, and remain indifferent to the beauty that is perceived by the intellect (54v). If beauty only resided in bodies, the speaker Vallaro asserts, then we would never know how to detect beauty in objects that lack perfect proportion; but there are many kinds of beauty, in many things (55r). Franco claims that the soul has two faces, one that looks towards the intellect, which is superior to it, and one that looks towards the senses, which are inferior: the two work in coordination (58v–59r). The face of reason makes the corporeal incorporeal, whereas the face of sense makes the incorporeal corporeal; thus corporeal beauties are recognized by the soul by means of both faces, and love for both kinds of beauties, body and intellect, may be engendered. As we have already had occasion to note, Franco borrows much from Leone Ebreo, who similarly described the soul as having two faces in the third of his *Dialoghi d'amore* (331).

As we move closer to the time of *Urania*, we may note the evident lack in these doctrinal works of a codified system for the process of perceiving beauty and falling in love. Although there is much common ground among them, each writer tends to emphasize different aspects of the process, for different reasons, in a rather haphazard fashion. Sperone Speroni's *Dialogo d'amore* (1542) may stand as a case in point, for here we see a process for falling in love that differs in many respects from its predecessors, even if it employs the same basic notions. The speaker Nicolò Grazia says that when a man sees a beautiful woman, the sight enters through the eyes and goes first to the heart (2: 538). Subsequently, reason, which dwells in the head, takes note of this charming novelty and gathers it into itself, where it forms an image of the beloved woman. The love that the image fosters feeds on the image, and since it is 'in cima dell'anima, non lontana dalla sua nutrice ragione' (at the top of the soul, not far from reason, its nurse, 2: 538), it awakens every part of the body to its purpose, just as the sun causes the humours of the earth to bring forth fruits. Speroni extends this rather alimentary description of the process of love and the sight of beauty to encompass a complete definition of man: just as a bear licks a formless lump of flesh into a bear cub (an anecdote derived from Pliny, and adopted as a personal emblem by Titian), so does love, rooting itself in the parts we share with brutes, take a higher form when 'cleaned' by reason.[28] Man is like a centaur, brute below, human above, licked by reason; we need only add two wings, like Pegasus, to allow man to move in a flash, and the picture is complete (2: 539). Grazia's point in all this is to show Tullia d'Aragona, the person for whom he is pronouncing this lecture, that love and reason are not opposites in conflict with each other, as she has asserted.

As has been noted, Speroni was the most illustrious Paduan intellectual of Bigolina's time, so it is quite likely she was familiar with his works.[29] Just before Speroni's account of the aesthetic affinities between Titian and Aretino in the *Dialogo d'amore*, which has already been discussed in chapter 3, we encounter this exaltation of the special ability of painters such as Titian to reproduce the sight of physical beauty through portraiture, pronounced by Tullia d'Aragona for the benefit of Bernardo Tasso:

TULLIA: Or che altro è il mondo fuor che una bella e grande adunanza de ritratti della natura? La quale, avendo animo di dipingere la gloria di Dio e

quella in uno luogo solo ricogliere non potendo, produsse infinite specie di
cose, le quali, ciascheduna a suo modo, in qualche parte l'assomigliassero.
Il mondo adunque è tutto insieme un ritratto di Dio, fatto per mano della
natura. Ritratto è l'amante, ritragge lo specchio e ritragge l'artefice; ma el
ritratto del dipintore (il quale solo è dal volgo appellato ritratto) è il men
buono di tutti gli altri, come quello che della vita dell'uomo solamente il
color della pelle ne rappresenta, e non più oltra.

TASSO: Voi fate torto a Tiziano, le cui imagini sono tali e sì fatte che egli è meg-
lio l'essere dipinto da lui che generato dalla natura.

TULLIA: Tiziano non è dipintore e non è arte la virtù sua ma miracolo; e ho
opinione che i suoi colori sieno composti di quella erba maravigliosa, la
quale, gustata da Glauco, d'uomo in dio lo trasformò. E veramente li suoi
ritratti hanno in loro un non so che di divinità che, come in cielo è il paradiso dell'anime, così pare che ne' suoi colori Dio abbia riposto il paradiso d'i
nostri corpi: non dipinti ma fatti santi e glorificati dalle sue mani. (2:547–8)

[TULLIA: Now what else is the world but a lovely great collection of portraits
of nature? Since nature desired to paint the glory of God but could not
gather all of it in a single place, it produced infinite species of things, which,
each in its own way, might resemble some part of this glory. Therefore the
world, all taken together, is a portrait of God, executed by the hand of nature. The lover is a portrait, portrayed in turn by both the mirror and the
artist; however, the portrait made by a painter (which is the only thing the
common crowd calls a portrait) is the most inferior of all, since all it shows
of a man's life is the colour of his skin, nothing more.

TASSO: You do wrong to Titian, whose images are made in such a way that it is
better to be painted by him than to be generated by nature.

TULLIA: Titian is not just a painter and his skill is not art, but rather a miracle;
moreover I am of the opinion that his colours are composed of that marvellous herb that transformed Glaucus from a man to a god as soon as he had
tasted it. Truly his portraits have something of the divine in them, so that
just as heaven is the paradise of souls, it would seem that God has placed
the paradise of our bodies in his colours: they are not merely painted, but
made holy and glorified by Titian's hands.]

This passage, like the one that follows it concerning Aretino and
Titian, was much altered in subsequent editions under the pressure of
Counter-Reformation censors, who took exception to Speroni's claims
that Titian's paintings were miraculous and that God had made them
into a sort of paradise of bodies. However, it is quite likely that Bigolina

had occasion to see the passage in its original form, with its praise of a certain painter's ability to reproduce the truest portraits of all – those of God – on canvas, merely by employing his sense of sight to observe the physical beauties of nature. Bigolina consistently rejects this view in *Urania.*[30]

The lack of a coherent system for all of these theories of love and the senses was acknowledged by Giuseppe Betussi, who was born in Bassano near Padua around 1512, and died circa 1573. His influential dialogue *Il Raverta,* subtitled *Dialogo di messer Giuseppe Betussi nel quale si ragiona d'Amore e degli effetti suoi,* was first published in Venice in 1544, with two more editions appearing before 1550. The speakers are Raverta, who is clearly a mouthpiece for Betussi himself, Betussi's lover, Franceschina Baffa, and Lodovico Domenichi, who makes a point of criticizing the opinions of the single female interlocutor, much as the male speakers in Franco's dialogue do.

Betussi's narrative opens with Raverta approaching Baffa while she is reading Leone Ebreo's book (4). Since she cannot find therein a single coherent definition of love, she asks Raverta for further explanation, which he is happy to provide. As is typical in these dialogues, the female interlocutor is presented as needing instruction from an erudite man, even though the historical Baffa is known to have been a poet herself, as Aretino attests.[31] Raverta provides a definition of love that does not stray far from standard Neoplatonic precepts: love is a desire to participate in something judged by the soul to be both beautiful and good (8–11). Raverta outlines the senses involved in this process. Once more, sight and hearing are presented as the spiritual senses, along with the intellect or reason, a triad that can be traced back to Ficino and Bembo. According to Raverta, there are three types of beauty: that of the soul, appreciated by the mind; that of the body, appreciated by the eye; and that of the voice, appreciated by the ear (11). When Baffa asks about the beauty of bodies, Raverta defers to Trissino's description of such beauty as if it were a painting, since such descriptions are 'ufficio di pittore' (the task of a painter, 11). Raverta goes on to describe the classic Neoplatonic scheme for the appreciation of the beauty of bodies: these must not be seen solely by the corporeal eye but also by the eye of the intellect that can know a higher beauty than the merely physical (13).

When Baffa wonders aloud why God gave man eyes and ears if they are not sufficient in themselves for appreciating true beauty,

Raverta rebukes her in language that recalls Bigolina's stern allegory of judgment: 'Oh, in quanto grande error sète a imaginarvi non che a dir ciò!' (Oh, how great is your error, not just for imagining such a thing, but for expressing it, 13–14). The eyes and ears are essential organs for contemplating physical beauty, so that the soul can come to know the true beauty of the spirit. The eyes are the first organs to be aware of beauty, before the ears can come to appreciate its harmony. Bigolina might well have taken to heart Raverta's observation that hearing is the more purely spiritual sense ('l'udito è vie più spirituale'); he asserts that the beautiful harmonies we hear pass most quickly into the mind (16). However, Betussi does not proceed from this to a denigration of sight, nor does he really make much of this point; he merely notes it in passing.[32] Instead, he concentrates more on a phase of cognition that does not appear to interest Bigolina at all: the creation in the mind of spiritual eyes and ears, so that corporeal beauty perceived by actual eyes and ears can be communicated to the soul in a manner that it can appreciate.

Baffa's confusion concerning the role of the eyes and ears leads to a highly significant passage that might well have influenced Bigolina. Raverta declares that we cannot love something that has no physical essence, 'una cosa che non abbia essere' (a thing that has no being, 17). We must first stand before visible and corporeal things, which then cause invisible and incorporeal things to take shape within our imagination. To illustrate this, he describes how painters create works of art:

> Il pittore, se naturalmente vuol formare una imagine a sembianza d'un'altra, se non ha la vera e viva forma dinanzi che gli rappresenti quella ch'egli vuole, potrebbe farla così simile? Certo no. Ma da quella visiva forma quella che ha in mente. Ma che più? Gli astanti, che contemplaranno quella imagine, nel primo incontro non la raffigureranno per una pittura? Certo sì. Nondimeno con gli occhi dell'intelletto, invisibilmente, subito, formeranno nell'anime loro la vera e perfetta idea, a simiglianza della quale quella è stata formata. Sì che da quello oggetto visibile passano al contemplativo, e da quella colorita imagine considereranno quale si sia la viva. Onde, stando in tale imaginazione, ameranno più la vera, la quale tosto che vedranno, se sarà simile a quella formata a sua similitudine, molto loderanno quel ritratto, ma più il vero. Se anco troveranno quella imagine non esser conforme alla sua idea, ma che la viva sia più difforme, poco uno e meno l'altro cureranno. (17–18)

[If the painter wishes to form an image that truly resembles another image, could he duplicate it so exactly without having the true and living form before him, the thing that shows him what he wants to depict? Certainly not. He forms what is in his mind from what he sees. Need I say more? As for the viewers who will contemplate that image, will they not take it for a painting at first glance? Of course they will. Nonetheless, invisibly and immediately, by means of the eyes of the intellect they will form within their souls the true and perfect idea that the work of art was made to resemble. In such a way they pass from the visible object to the contemplative, and from the image in pigments they will come to consider the nature of the living image. Therefore, absorbed in such imagining, they will have greater love for the actual subject; and as soon as they see that true subject, if it is similar to the image that was formed to resemble it, they will praise the portrait a great deal, but they will praise the actual subject even more. However if they find that the image does not conform to its idea, and that the living subject is even more dissimilar, they will care little for the one and less for the other.]

Betussi, like Michelangelo in his poetry, finds a way to exalt the artist's creative process by associating it with the Neoplatonists' methods of contemplating the world of ideal forms.[33] The painted portrait might not exceed the actual subject in perfection, but it serves a very useful purpose nonetheless by allowing the viewer to form an image of the subject within the soul. Thus a painting can lead us to true and proper love for an absent subject, since first we grow to love the image that resembles it.[34] This is precisely the role that Bigolina rejects for the painter's art: in *Urania* a painting can never provide a worthy simulacrum of someone who is absent, just as it cannot communicate true beauty, nor indeed induce a person to love the object it is meant to resemble.

However much these descriptions of the role that the senses and reason play in the love process might differ from one another, in one respect they are all in agreement: the whole sublime process begins with sight, usually the sight of a beautiful woman, which is generally not regarded as a bad thing. This primacy of sight, although not necessarily the sight of a beautiful woman, is also promoted by the poet Tullia d'Aragona (c. 1510–56), one of the speakers in Speroni's *Dialogo d'amore*. Her own dialogue on love, *Dialogo della infinità d'amore*, was published in 1547.

This dialogue, one of the liveliest and most entertaining of the corpus, centres primarily on a conversation between d'Aragona and her ideological opponent, the Aristotelian intellectual Benedetto Varchi. D'Aragona gives herself a prominent role in the work both as a speaker and as an expounder of doctrine, surely a polemical response to the ways in which women, even women who had made a name for themselves as writers, were typically portrayed in dialogues written by men.[35] Here d'Aragona is as interested in the method of the debate as in the subject matter to be discussed, in recognition of the fact that early modern women could only rarely obtain the rhetorical training needed to hold their own with an erudite speaker like Varchi: throughout much of this work, d'Aragona must continually try to make Varchi debate on her terms, not on his. She belittles him, often quite comically, for his efforts to steer the conversation back to the sort of abstruse Aristotelian logic-chopping at which he so evidently excels.

In the midst of all this, some attention is paid to the sight of beauty, which d'Aragona prefers to discuss in Neoplatonic terms: she reproaches those who give themselves 'in preda agli appetiti carnali, sottoponendo la ragione, la quale doverebbe esser la reina, al senso ...' (as prey to the carnal appetites, placing reason, which should be queen, beneath sense, 227). She also claims to derive great pleasure from reading the words of Bembo's holy hermit in the *Asolani*. She refutes Varchi's argument that the irrational, more physical sort of love is redeemable because it is natural and generative, a point of view that recalls Ficino's description of the vulgar Venus. Inspired by Bembo, d'Aragona asserts that man can only reach divine heights through divine love (226–7). It is interesting to note that when she and Varchi speak of the origin of love in the sight of a beautiful person, they do not make the usual references to a man gazing upon a woman. Instead, in keeping with their focus on the works of Plato and Aristotle, they discuss the ethical implications of men who are attracted to young men and boys (228–9). D'Aragona also wishes to know if women, who are supposed to have less 'anima intellettiva' (intellective soul) than men, are equally worthy of being loved; Varchi insists that they can and should be the objects of honest and virtuous love (229). D'Aragona has a few hard questions for Varchi: for instance, if the ancients felt only virtuous and non-carnal love for males, why did they tend to fall in love with younger, more attractive ones? This leads to the text's only discussion of the sense of sight: Varchi replies that no one can know anything but through the senses, and of these the noblest and most perfect is sight, and with this d'Aragona agrees (230). However, in her typical down-to-earth fashion, she disputes Varchi's subsequent assertion that 'il bello e il buono sono un medesimo' (the beautiful and the good are the same, 230), since, as she claims, she has known a good many attractive reprobates.

D'Aragona's assertion that sight is the noblest and most perfect sense would surely be in keeping with her professed fondness for Neoplatonism, and for the ideas of Bembo: she, like almost all of her contemporaries, wants to locate the start of the love process in the sight of something physically beautiful. Her description of the functioning of cognition follows Leone Ebreo's, as Varchi acknowledges: love that is generated by reason employs the 'sentimenti spirituali,' or spiritual senses: sight, hearing, and *fantasia*. Those who desire corporeal union in order to become one with their beloveds must inevitably fail, because bodies cannot interpenetrate the way souls can (223).

Such transcendent, non-corporeal notions were not likely to impress the irreverent Aretino, for whom Neoplatonism constituted the sort of pedantry that he was inclined to mock throughout his career. His second letter to Bigolina surely illustrates this, but she might also have taken note of his supremely ironic burlesque of the casuistry of the senses in a letter to Abbot Vassallo (5.463) that appeared in the same volume as his letters to her. Here Aretino writes of a musical performance by the lutenist and courtesan Franceschina Bellamano:

> Non è dubbio, Signore Abate, che i piaceri sono ruffiani de la voluptà. E che sia il vero, le cose che nel Liuto cantò ieri la Franceschina Signora, mi penetravano con sì dolce sorte di musical maniera nel core che sarà forza venire al quia del congiungimento amoroso. Certamente, che tutte tre le sorti de le bellezze sono, in lei, più che in altra quella del corpo, quella de l'animo, e quella de la voce. Onde chi più sa ricoglie la prima con gli occhi, la seconda con la mente, e la terza con gli orecchi. Tal che in vertù de i prefati sensi, si ricreano in modo gli spiriti di qualunche l'ascolta, la comprende, e la vede, che in cielo, e non in terra, si dimora, in quel mentre ch'ella nel suo mestiero si essercita. Sì che a lei me ne vado di volo. Di Maggio in Venezia, M.D.L. Pietro Aretino

> [There is no doubt, Lord Abbott, that pleasures are the pimps of desire. To tell truth, the things that Lady Franceschina sang yesterday with the lute entered my heart in such a sweet musical manner that it must surely constitute the essence of amorous union. Certainly the three kinds of beauty are present in her, more than in any other woman: beauty of the body, beauty of the soul, and beauty of the voice. Therefore he who is most

discerning takes in the first with the eyes, the second with the mind, and the third with the ears. In this way, by grace of the aforementioned senses, the spirits of whoever hears, comprehends and sees her are restored; and he dwells in heaven, not on earth, while she practices her profession. As a result, I fly to be in her presence. May, in Venice, 1550.]

Aretino is probably following the pronouncements of his friend Betussi in this description of how the senses appreciate beauty, since in *Raverta* we find the same distinction between the roles of the eyes, the ears, and the mind, which appreciate respectively the body, the voice, and the soul (*Raverta*, 1). However, it is also clear that Aretino is poking fun at the sententious wisdom of all the dialogists and essayists who have been examined above, and indeed he is mocking the dominant discourse of an entire culture when he calls the pleasures of the senses pimps in the service of desire, and tells of dwelling in heaven while he yearns to be with a courtesan whose music may be compared to sexual intercourse. Despite their antithetical motivations and antagonistic points of view, Bigolina and Aretino have this much in common: both have found the means, albeit divergent and conflicting means, to present a challenge to the dominant voices of the age.

The Body and the Gaze in the Arts

This apotheosis of the sight of beauty as the essential first step in the process of falling in love must have appeared all but universal by the time Bigolina set out to write *Urania* in the 1550s. From works as lofty and rarefied as Ficino's *Sopra lo amore* to more practical, even occasionally 'raunchy,' examinations of the love experience, such as Bartolomeo Gottifredi's *Specchio d'amore* (1547), in which a worldly nursemaid lectures the unmarried daughter of a respectable family on the ways to attract a man, the emphasis is first and foremost on the sight of an attractive face or body.[36] In the face of all of this doctrinal solidarity, Bigolina, who does not appear to have belonged to any illustrious academies, or to have attracted the attention of very many of the great cultural lights of her time, quietly launched her one-woman polemic in the form of a romance on the topic of love, a romance that defies an imposing tradition by greatly diminishing, and even regarding with suspicion, the role of the sense of sight in the love process.

Bigolina departs from all the principal theorists of her time in concentrating her discussion of the *image* of beauty and how such an image affects the intellect. She treats the sight of beauty in metaphorical, even abstract terms: she is not interested in actual corporeal beauty so much as in the sight of its material simulacrum.[37] She stresses the materiality, and ultimately the very artificiality, of beauty by describing paintings that are meant to make people fall in love with real people in a morally inappropriate fashion.[38] Thus, when the senses are discussed in *Urania,* the emphasis is on the arts, either on painted images of physical beauty or on literary works that communicate the essence of the soul and the heart. Bigolina makes a point of evoking the standard comparison between the sight of physical beauty and the sight of artistic beauty, as exemplified by the passages from the works of Castiglione, Franco, and Betussi cited above, only to employ it for a strikingly new ideological purpose.[39] In *Urania* the visual arts are consistently denigrated as an inadequate and ineffectual medium, as a metaphor for the inadequacy of sight as a means to appreciate true beauty.

At the beginning of the book, Bigolina's authorial persona makes a great show of rejecting the sight of her nude body in Giudicio's eye because it fills her with shame. This rejection of the sight of nudity serves to dramatize the central message of the proem, that women who seek to gain renown through mere display of their physical appearance show poor judgment and ultimately will fail in their endeavours. This rejection of the validity of corporeal display finds a parallel, as well as further confirmation, in the story of the duchess. However, as we have noted, Bigolina is careful not to reject the validity of the sight of the body per se. For instance, in her view it is entirely proper for the prince to speculate about the nude appearance of the Savia Damigella, the woman he hopes to marry, because he imagines that she is too wise ever to make such a vulgar display of herself. Thus his vision of her body can remain, for the time being at least, validated by its very interiority.

In *Urania,* the apparent rejection of the body should be seen in far more subtle terms: it stands as a metaphor for a failed effort to perpetuate oneself in the arts. Those who seek to memorialize themselves by posing for paintings, by relying entirely on a sort of passive, iconic visual display of their physical essence, will surely fail to make a lasting or worthy impression. Seen thus, the shame Bigolina feels at the sight of herself takes on a more complex dimension. It is not just shame that she is seen nude, but shame that she ever sold herself short by imagining that all she needed to do was sit for a portrait in order to give the best gift of herself to her beloved Salvatico. Bigolina succeeds in communicating this message by stressing the rejection of the artistic simulation of outward physical beauty in favour of a different sort of art that women should be able to produce on their own. It is not the body that she rejects but the artistic rendering of the body for the sole purpose of giving pleasure to the sense of sight. So many women in Bigolina's potential audience might have imagined no other means of achieving public renown; however, as her authorial persona learns, and then seeks to teach, there is a much better way.

Urania is pervaded with a sense of crisis, a crisis that wise characters (and, by extension, wise readers) must learn to overcome. It is a crisis born from the moral implications of seeing and being seen; or, in Lacanian terms, of gazing and being gazed upon, of how one is to regard an object of desire. Here is a central question that the text sets out to answer: how are we to interpret things that are presented for the sole purpose of being looked at?

In his study of how Lacan's psychoanalytical concepts may be applied to early modern portraiture, Harry Berger, Jr, declares that people sitting for portraits always reveal that they are conscious of the act of posing, of 'giving themselves to be seen'; therefore a painting 'represents the three-way diachronic transaction between painter, sitter and observer in a purely fictional field' ('Fictions of the Pose,' 99). He calls this 'the fiction of the pose.' This in turn is precisely what Bigolina fictionalizes in her romance: in effect she gives us a 'fiction of the fiction of the pose,' and in so doing, casts doubt on the very thing that, as Berger tells us, Renaissance portraiture always pretended to offer – an 'orthopsychic image,' a 'correct' portrayal of the psyche or personality of the sitter (94). Berger calls the gaze the scopic dimension of Lacan's *donné-à-voir* (given-to-be-seen), the visual aspect of 'the dominant discourses by which a culture constructs its subjects to imagine and represent themselves, *to give themselves to be seen,* and to model themselves on the exemplary or orthopsychic norms of the group' (94–5). The viewer has a 'scopic encounter' when he or she looks upon a portrait, and thus is compelled to interpret the intricacies of the 'fiction of the pose,' that is to say, what was actually going on when the painting was being created. Seen in these terms, we may readily identify three such 'scopic encounters' in *Urania:* the authorial persona's sight of herself in the eye of Giudicio, the duchess's first sight of the portrait of the prince, and the prince's first sight of the portrait that includes both himself and the duchess (the *Judgment of Paris*).

In the first encounter, Urania is astonished and dismayed to see herself reflected nude in Giudicio's eye. This reminds us of the gaze that

Lacan imputes to Sartre – 'the gaze by which I am surprised,' the gaze that reduces the subject to shame because it causes all perspectives to be reordered.[40] In the eye of Judgment, she is shown a shocking parody of the portrait that she has just planned to have made of herself, the very artifact that would have to have been produced by the gaze of another, or in Lacan's terms, the Other, *objet A*. She imagines one appearance for herself, the way she thinks she actually looks in that instant ('orthopsychically' fully clothed); however, the allegory forces her to regard another appearance that she finds shameful and terrifying: she is naked, with flesh as white as snow, save for a stain on her left side that indicates her shortcomings. Although Bigolina does not make a point of stressing it, we are forced to assume that her authorial persona continues to observe herself in Giudicio's eye the whole time he is talking to her – indeed, what else could she be looking at? Thus the reader is made to realize, perhaps with a bit of a shock, that the author sees herself in this bizarre fashion, in this strange nude monster's eye, throughout the whole eleven pages of her conversation with him, which is nonetheless conducted in a calm and rational fashion.

Perhaps it is not always wise to attempt to imagine literary allegories as if they were real, even if medieval and early modern illustrators frequently found it expedient to depict them in such a fashion. However, Bigolina presents this encounter in quite realistic terms: she makes no effort to suffuse it with fuzzy, dream-vision abstractions. The scene takes place while the authorial persona is awake, and walking around her room. She feels a tug on her dress, then turns to see a little naked man with a huge head and single huge eye standing before her. The reader is asked to visualize much: the persona sees herself nude in her interlocutor's eye, and moreover we must imagine that the allegorical figure is seeing her in the same fashion throughout their long conversation – after all, he is Judgment, who sees everything as it truly is. He may be benevolent and wise, a supernatural being who only appears on earth according to the disposition of 'the heavens' (78), but he is nonetheless male, nude, and moreover privileged to get a very long and thorough look at the author's body. (This is like a Renaissance equivalent of the psychotherapeutic 'nude encounter groups' of the 1960s, with questions and answers on abstruse topics being exchanged as if nothing were out of the ordinary, while everyone is naked.)

Nonetheless, Bigolina's point is plain. Giudicio employs a shock effect with the stated aim of reordering the writer's priorities so that she will re-examine her judgment to have herself portrayed as a visible object.

He causes her to dwell on the shameful sight of her body in the eye of
a masculine Other, so that she will perforce renounce any ambition to
make a further spectacle of herself and thereby choose a wiser mode of
self-display. She must, as Anne Christine Junkerman has noted in her
study of Giorgione's portrait known as *Laura,* learn how to control 'the
degree of access of the viewer's gaze' if she is to flourish as an artist herself.[41] As a consequence, she is made to realize that she must renounce
the role of sight in any future efforts at self-portrayal.

At this point, it will be useful to return once more to the artist whose
presence looms largest in *Urania:* Titian. In 1555, around the same time
that Bigolina was writing, Titian made a painting, *Venus with a Mirror,* in
which he was to take so special an interest that he carried it around with
him all of his life (see figure 4.1).[42] Here we see a seated nude woman,
partly draped in a red mantle just like Bigolina's duchess, contemplating herself in a mirror. As Rona Goffen notes, Venus's pose with the
mirror 'authorizes' the viewer to gaze upon her, just as she gazes upon
herself: *Venus with a Mirror* is all about seeing and being seen, 'about
the exaltation of beauty that is embodied in the goddess and knowable
through sight' (*Titian's Women,* 136). This Venus is the ideological enemy
of Bigolina's authorial persona and Urania both, for she does not care
if we look at her; indeed, she is there for that very purpose, beguiling
both herself and us with her musings upon her reflected image. Titian
was, in fact, just as inclined to exalt and apotheosize sight in his paintings as the writers whom we examined at the beginning of this chapter.
Goffen describes the depiction of synaesthesia – the simultaneous appeal to more than one sense – in Titian's *Worship of Venus,* a painting
inspired by one of the ekphraseis in Philostratus's *Imagines,* noting that
here sight emerges clearly as 'the victor of this paragone of the senses.'[43]
So often Titian's women stare boldly and perhaps even shamelessly out
at the viewer, who is thereby made all the more conscious of his or her
own role as voyeur; examples may be found in such paintings as *Sacred
and Profane Love, Venus of Urbino, La Schiavona,* and *Flora.*[44]

Berger provides this observation: 'Commentators have always sin-
gled out Titian's ability to compress character and action in the sitter's
eyes, the look, the scopic encounter with observers' ('Fictions of the
Pose,' 113). Bigolina too imputes such power to the eyes of a portrait,
the one that the duchess's painter creates of the Prince of Salerno:

> Ma come si fermò a riguardare il ritratto, parvele alhora che un mare di
> foco et un monte di ghiaccio tutto in un medesimo punto adosso le se

Figure 4.1. Titian, *Venus with a Mirror* (c. 1555). National Gallery of Art, Washington, DC

riversassero. Imperciò che Amore, il quale sino a quell'hora havea tardato a farle il suo grande valor manifesto, et non volendo più differire s'havea ne' begli occhi di quel ritratto nascoso.

Chè quantunque fossero sanza obietto et inanimati, essendovisi Amore entro riposto, fecero nondimeno quel medesimo, anzi maggiore effetto in lei, che gli vivi et animati del prencipe non harrebbono fatto; ch'ella in quelli mirando parvele, che da due folgori, anzi da due accutissime saette il suo cuore trapassato le fosse. (188)

[Then, when she stood before the painting and looked at it, it seemed to her that both a sea of fire and a mountain of ice poured down upon her in the same instant. For Love, who had until then delayed in revealing to her the extent of his power, was now no longer willing to put things off, and had hidden himself in the beautiful eyes of the portrait.

These eyes were formless and inanimate; yet once Love had come to rest in them they had the same effect on the Duchess as the living, animate eyes of the Prince would have had, or perhaps their effect was even greater. Looking at them, it seemed to her that her heart was pierced through by two lightning bolts, indeed by two very sharp arrows. (189)]

Lacan spoke of the power of a picture – specifically Holbein's *The Ambassadors*, with its artfully created image of an anamorphic skull – to draw in the viewer's gaze and trap it, thereby 'annihilating' the viewing subject (*Psycho-Analysis*, 89). Recent art historians have evoked Lacan's imagery to describe the technical skills that a painter might employ to effectively trap the viewer's gaze within a web of illusions arrayed on a flat surface.[45] In the passage cited above, Bigolina lends dramatic life to this process in her work of fiction, describing a painting that the reader cannot see, and thus must only imagine; nonetheless, her aim is scarcely to laud the painter for his illusionistic skills: instead, she intends to show the dangers of the hypnotic power of art. Up to the moment she fixes her eyes on the prince's eyes within the portrait, the widowed duchess has led a blameless, exemplary life, showing no inclination to irrational or morally questionable behaviour. After this moment, she will commit nothing but errors. In this scheme, sight, specifically the sight of two painted eyes that seem to hold the viewer under their sway, becomes the catalyst for disaster. The duchess has allowed herself to be seduced by the painting's 'fiction of the pose,' the pretence that the real-life prince must embody all the idealized virtues that the work of art seems to portray. Bigolina has dramatized this process, but with one essential difference with respect to Berger's scheme: the prince has not actually been part of the conspiracy, because he is not 'aware' that he is being looked at. Berger's 'fiction of the pose' always implies that the sitter is consciously striking the pose, as in the example of Titian's portrait of the Duke of Urbino, who, according to Berger's interpretation, 'is gravely, thoughtfully, attentive to the task of sustaining a complicated pose that delivers the prearranged symbolic message' ('Fictions of the Pose,' 114). This might be true of any of the myriad real portraits that were created during the Cinquecento, which were supposed to include the sitter's conscious effort to put himself or herself on display, but this is not the case in Bigolina's fictional painting of the prince. As she takes pains to tell us, the devious painter managed to capture the prince's image in secret, without consulting him, during a visit to the court in Salerno (186). Since Bigolina wants us to think well of her prince, she deliberately excludes him from any complicity in the 'three-way diachronic transaction' that would normally be necessary for the creation of a portrait. In fact, the prince gets painted twice in this book without his consent.

Moreover, the prince is further absolved of all blame by Bigolina's resolute efforts to diminish the apotheosis of the mystical powers of painting, the apotheosis that had been made cultural currency in Bigolina's day by such voices of authority as Aretino, Speroni, and Dolce. Painting, as a failed art form, holds no special place for Bigolina; instead, she stresses how formless and inanimate the painted eyes of the prince actually were, and even resorts to the metaphorical gimmick of pretending that the personification of Love had come to rest in the eyes of the portrait with the nefarious intention of trapping the duchess in the bonds of destructive passion. In and of itself, Bigolina seems to be saying, a painting has no real power and no real function. This orthopsychic illusion is entirely the creation of the painter, a cunning artifice of dubious ethical intent, wholly deprived of redeeming aesthetic value.

On the other hand, the duchess is entirely complicit in her own portrait, and the carefully contrived 'fiction' of her pose in the *Judgment of Paris* becomes a central element of Bigolina's plot. She perfectly illustrates Berger's definition of the gaze in the context of portraiture as the 'given-to-be-seen' when she participates in the flawed *invenzione* of the painter and the counsellor, who construct a false orthopsychic norm for her to embody, quite literally, in her gift to the prince. In this painting, as we have noted, the duchess indulges in a veritable orgy of 'giving herself to be seen': not only does she reveal herself to two of her servants while posing, but she also ends up showing her body to the prince's gaze, not just once but twice, in two very separate yet simultaneous contexts, both within the painting (where he looks upon her in the guise of Paris) and without (as he looks upon the painting itself). Nor can it be an accident that Bigolina chooses a supremely voyeuristic art subject for the duchess's pose, in order to dramatize the fate of women who are made to submit to improper displays of themselves. In a later generation, the painter Artemisia Gentileschi will similarly choose an overtly voyeuristic topic as a means of calling attention to the fates of vulnerable women who are gazed upon by clothed, controlling men, in her version of *Susanna and the Elders* (1610). As Mary D. Garrard has shown, Gentileschi reworks an established theme in order to emphasize the psychological distress of Susanna, who is more clearly victimized by her two potential rapists in this version than in any other.[46] In both Bigolina's fictional painting and Gentileschi's actual one, male voyeurism (as only a woman can depict it) serves to emphasize the vulnerability of women who are displayed for the titillation of men, as well as the possible grim consequences of such display, whether willing or unwilling.

In her fictionalized account of 'the fiction of the pose,' Bigolina shows us how all is not necessarily well behind the triumphant facade of the contemporary exaltation of portraiture. Not only might orthopsychic fictions have dubious origins, she seems to be saying; they might also lead to dubious ends, if the whole story be known. Bigolina has given us an extended, dramatized version of all the intrigues that might lie behind a Titian-style portrait, intrigues which the casual viewer of such artworks could scarcely be expected to discern. She is reminding us that when we look upon one of Titian's Venuses, we are really seeing the end result of some long and intricate process, one that has involved an actual woman setting herself up to be gazed upon by actual men and then dealing with the inevitable consequences. A painting might give us a pretty picture to entertain briefly our sense of sight, but in the end it is a patently flawed vehicle, one that can scarcely provide anything useful for the intellect. Only literature, the plainly superior art form, can give us the whole beginning, middle, and end of 'the fiction of the pose,' thereby causing us to question in potentially useful ways the implications of the so-called orthopsychic image. In *Urania*, literature triumphs over painting, and therefore over sight itself, because here the sight of beauty is refracted diachronically through the lens of narrative. When painted portraits are reduced to mere literary descriptions, the real stuff of them lies in how and by whom they are made, and for what purpose: things that only a book can fully tell us. Here we see nothing less than a literary burlesque of the 'trap of the gaze,' with an elaborate account of all the things that can happen when we look upon a beguiling work of art.

Regrettably, Bigolina's *Urania* was probably read by no more than a tiny handful of people during her time, and by even fewer for a long time afterwards. Despite all of her fondness for traditional social virtues and moral propriety, and despite her clear preference for the beauties of the soul over those of the body, Bigolina never loses herself for long in lofty discourse, never aspires to the Neoplatonic transports of Castiglione's Bembo, for whom the sight of a pretty face may become a signpost for the contemplation of the divine. Instead, she stays on earth and worries about the practical problems of women in love, and the ways in which women may resist misogynistic male attitudes and safely create public personas for themselves. Ultimately her love, in true romance fashion, is oriented towards happy marriage, unlike Bembo's in either the *Asolani* or the *Cortigiano*. Bigolina poses the question that no dialogist, no essayist, nor indeed any other romance writer appears to show the slightest interest in: how might an excellent, accomplished, virtuous woman, one who does not happen to be endowed with the prettiest face, make herself loved? The experiences of Urania are meant to provide the answer.

The Woman's Portrait as Gift

Bigolina's ethical crisis of portraiture begins with her flight from the notion that she herself, in the form of her authorial persona, might pose for a painting. She was not alone among Italian women writers of the time, especially those in the Venetian orbit, in showing such fascination with the potential significance of a painting of herself. This is an understandable response, given the fixation for painted images of women in the treatises on ideal beauty of Trissino, Niccolò Franco, Firenzuola, and Luigini, as well as the risks of societal disapproval inherent in any Cinquecento woman's ambition to put herself on public display. The motif also appears in the poetry of Bigolina's contemporary, the Venetian Gaspara Stampa (1523–54), who provides two sonnets within her volume of *Rime* (1554) that describe a sort of diptych of imaginary paintings, supposedly to be displayed side by side.[47] In the first of these sonnets the poet calls upon all the best artists in every medium, urging them to combine their skills in order to create a painting of her faithless lover, Collaltino del Collalto, who must be shown with two hearts, since he holds both his own and the poet's (55 vv 12–14). In the second sonnet the poet calls upon the artists to create an equally imaginary painting of herself that must somehow capture the paradox of her existence: she lives, and yet she has neither soul nor heart left in her body (56, vv 1–4). The artists are also charged with the extraordinary task of simultaneously depicting both extremes of the poet's emotional state within her features, the left side 'afflitto e mesto' (suffering and sad, v. 10) and the right 'allegro e trionfante' (joyful and triumphant, v. 11), recalling

Bigolina's own contrast between the appearance of her left and right sides in the reflection of Judgment's eye. These two sonnets are part of a cluster of four that deal with the visual arts, since two more sonnets (57, 58) on the topic of portraiture follow these. Stampa stresses the miraculous nature of these fantastic portraits, and in this sense her poetic treatment of portraiture is closer to the unreal episodes of ekphrasis that characterize certain chivalric romances and allegorical-didactic works: her paintings, showing people with either two hearts or none at all, could only exist in some imaginary poetic landscape. Unlike Bigolina in her episode of the duchess, Stampa does not provide us with a painting that is meant to resemble the real ones her readers could easily see around them.

However, a much more real portrait, ostensibly a tangible, transferable object like Bigolina's *Judgment of Paris*, appears in the two sonnets that the Venetian poet Veronica Franco (1546–91) addressed to King Henri III of France and that she appended to her dedication to the king in her *Lettere familiari*, published in 1580. Whether or not the painting actually existed, the event that Franco describes, her reception of King Henri at her house during his state visit to Venice in 1574, perhaps in her professional capacity as courtesan, seems to have been real enough.[48] According to Franco's dedicatory letter, the king took her portrait with him when he left, as she puts it, 'in cambio di quella viva imagine che nel mezo del mio cuore Ella ha lasciato delle sue virtú eroiche e del suo divino valore' (in exchange for the living image of your heroic virtues and divine valor that you left deep in my heart).[49] It is easy to read this description of an exchange of images, a literal one for a figurative one, as a sort of high-flown sublimation of the rather more utilitarian exchange that might have taken place. What should not be spoken of openly in a book dedication might be alluded to, even allegorized perhaps, in exalted, poetic terms. In her first sonnet, Franco compares Henri's visit to a famous mythological act of seduction, Jove descending upon Danae in her house; as Gabriel Niccoli notes, this bit of personal mythography serves to make the historical event of the visit more 'artistically palatable' to her refined audience, who would naturally expect such circumlocutions ('Veronica Franco's Epistolary Narrative,' 133).

But it is likewise easy to read this literary episode as an absolute antithesis of what Bigolina had done with the motif of the painted portrait as gift, even as a sexually charged gift, a generation before Franco was writing. As we have noted, Bigolina's attitude towards portraiture stands in polemical contrast to the cult of portrait worship that had been instituted in the first half of the Cinquecento, especially in Aretino's letters. Whereas Bigolina explicitly refuses to have herself painted, and chooses instead to write a work of literature in which she dramatizes the dangers of portrait painting for women, Franco shows herself at first glance to be much more in tune with Aretino's attitudes. Moreover, Franco's letter of gratitude and praise to Tintoretto for his portrait of her is well known, and even though she acknowledges therein that the portrait is so beautiful that it might represent some sort of 'diabolico inganno' (trickery of the devil), she quickly discounts any danger that it might pose to the viewer.[50] In any case, it made perfect sense that a courtesan, whose very livelihood thrived on publicity and the promotion of a public persona, would not share Bigolina's suspicion of portraiture. Franco's reference to the painting that she proudly gave to King Henri as a token of gratitude and affection reflects precisely the tone of Aretino's *Lettere,* which shows a world replete with portraits that are endlessly described, compared, solicited, praised, and passed back and forth as gifts. In this, Franco would seem to place herself squarely in the mainstream of prevailing cultural attitudes, while Bigolina remains, as usual, a voice in the wilderness.

Nonetheless, in terms of the *paragone* between the arts, especially as it is manifested in the literary woman's exaltation of her own creative abilities, Bigolina and Franco have much more in common than at first appears. Let us look at Franco's second sonnet to the king, wherein the painting reveals its symbolic importance:

Prendi, re per virtú sommo et perfetto,
quel che la mano a porgerti si stende:
questo scolpito e colorato aspetto,
in cui 'l mio vivo e natural s'intende.

   E s'a essempio sí basso e sí imperfetto
la tua vista beata non s'attende,
risguarda a la cagion, non a l'effetto.
Poca favilla ancor gran fiamma accende.

   E come 'l tuo immortal divin valore,
in armi e in pace a mille prove esperto,
m'empío l'alma di nobile stupore,

   cosí 'l desio, di donna in cor sofferto,
d'alzarti sopra 'l ciel dal mondo fore,
mira in quel mio sembiante espresso e certo.

[Take, king, sum of virtue and perfection, what my hand reaches out to give you: this carved and colored countenance, in which my living, real self is represented. And if such a lowly and imperfect image is not what your blessed gaze expects, consider my motive rather than the result. A small spark can still kindle a great flame. And because your undying, celestial valor, tested by a thousand trials in war and peace, filled my soul with noble wonder, So the desire felt in a woman's heart to raise you above heaven, beyond this world, see, expressed and proved, in this likeness of me.][51]

As Margaret Rosenthal has noted, Franco places the greatest emphasis on the notion of transaction in these two sonnets, all the while muting or mythologizing, through her borrowings from the story of Jove and Danae in the first poem, any reference to the sexual union (*Honest Courtesan*, 109–10). Franco makes it plain that the gifts that each provides to the other are quite different. From him she has derived a benefit that is intangible, internalized, and personal: he has filled her soul with his 'immortal divin valore,' something that cannot be objectified or easily made evident to anyone else. On the other hand, his benefit from her manifests itself in a work of art, in an external, tangible, real-world thing that is moreover endowed with a public function, since it can be put on display. He takes away her portrait as a sort of objective correlative for the pleasures of their night together; but as Franco makes plain, the painting may also serve to symbolize the renown that she will bestow upon him in the form of public praise, praise that will quite naturally take the form of written poetic words, as the sonnet itself attests. The painting, a work of one sort of art, becomes a tangible symbol for another form of artistry, one that is clearly meant to be seen as superior – that is, literature, the form at which Franco herself excels. The sonnets, not the painting, are her true gift. In effect, Franco brings about a subtle reversal of traditional gender roles in much the same fashion as the character Urania: she takes on the traditional guise of a man, doing things, accomplishing things in the external world, whereas the king's gift to her is nothing more than a passive state of being, his 'valore' filling her soul, which cannot be put on display.

Gabriel Niccoli has noted that Franco's personal mythopoesis serves to place the writer herself 'at the centre, as opposed to the margins, of her own text' ('Veronica Franco's Epistolary Narrative,' 133). I would add that one of the ways in which this process occurs here is through evocation of the *paragone* between portraiture and letters filtered through feminist exigencies. The portrait itself bears only Franco's 'sembiante,' her features, which were taken from her when she posed passively for a portraitist who would naturally be expected by the average Cinquecento reader to be male, the efforts of Sofonisba Anguissola and other woman portraitists notwithstanding. However, in the context of the *querelle* between the arts, the painting has a similarly passive role as a mere object as well: it only serves to communicate Franco's desire to exalt Henri's greatness, 'alzarti sopra 'l ciel dal mondo fore,' in quite another art form, one in which Franco herself is understood to flourish. Although Franco's appropriation of the motif of the author's portrait as a gift does not reflect Bigolina's moralizing stance or her forthright disdain for the art of portraiture, the conclusion that both writers reach is ultimately the same: it is not enough for women who know how to write to merely sit for a portrait that will capture their looks for the pleasure of the male sense of sight. They must, in effect, occupy the centre, what Niccoli calls 'man's privileged spacing,' and thereby abandon the roles of spectator and, indeed, spectacle, that had been for so long nearly their sole lot and that are so perfectly symbolized by the gorgeous painted portrait. Instead, say both Bigolina and Franco, such women must write their own self-portraits, by means of their own skill. A generation before Franco, and from a very different cultural perspective, as a married scion of the Paduan nobility, Bigolina had already revealed her willingness to accomplish the very task that Niccoli attributes to Franco – that is, she 'breaks new ground in the domain of culture and gender specifics in that she systematically, and significantly, slows down the cycle of women watching men watch themselves' ('Veronica Franco's Epistolary Narrative,' 131). This, as both women plainly indicate, must be done through the diminution of their society's continual glorification of the sight of a woman's physical beauty, a process that must in turn be accompanied by a newfound emphasis on women's ability to create their own works of literary art.

Wildness in *Urania*

The character Urania is the fictional counterpart to Bigolina's authorial persona in the proem. This is confirmed not only by the lesson on the moral implications of portraiture, which Bigolina learns and Urania already knows, but also by the two characters' experiences on the edge of 'wildness.' When Bigolina's persona looks within the eye of Judgment she sees not only her sensual aspect and her vanity but also the sort of wild otherness that lurks beneath the surface of humanity and that has the potential to make her – and all of us – unfit to live in civil society.[1] In short, she sees characteristics that she must learn to overcome if she is to give a proper gift to the young man Salvatico, whose very name means 'wild.' The book that she writes will be her gift for the 'Wild One,' so part of her literary task will be the depiction of wildness, a mode of behaviour that the protagonist, Urania, must know how to recognize and avoid, even as she exploits it on occasion in order to further her own goals. Perhaps not strangely, wild behaviour and wild people are recurring motifs in her book. Viewed on a grand scale, *Urania* is Bigolina's commentary on the conflict between reason and unreason, two forces that are constantly at odds within her text and that stand as its central dichotomy. Bigolina's affection for a man named Salvatico inspires a book-long exploration of what wildness truly means – a pun on a name leads to a serious and intricate literary creation.

Scholars of the persistent phenomenon of the wild man in Western culture have noted its self-reflexive, mirror-like role. Sharon W. Tiffany and Kathleen J. Adams make the following observation in their book *The Wild Woman:* 'Contrasts between the known and the unfamiliar invite self-reflection. Uncivilized or primitive others – their "peculiar appearance" and "strange customs and beliefs" provide a mirror in which we perceive ourselves' (6). Roger Bartra, in his *Wild Men in the Looking Glass*, also notes that wild imagery is really about ourselves, our own image in the looking glass: 'The wild man was created to answer the questions of civilized man; to reveal to him the meaninglessness of life in the name of cosmic unity, thereby sensitizing him to the tragic and terrible compromise brought on by his individuality and loneliness' (204). The savage mind 'marks the presence of a mental universe ruled by *mythos* and opposed to *logos*' (206). Wildness represents unreason, and yet we are strangely moved to contemplate it, to gaze upon our wilder side as if in a mirror, confronting it with a combination of horror and fascination. Bigolina lends life to this metaphor by having her authorial persona contemplate her 'wild side' in Judgment's mirror-like eye.

The classical, medieval, and early modern West was replete with images of wild figures, in folklore, literature, and the visual arts. A profusion of wild men and women turn up in romance plots, folktales, legends, and manuscript illustrations, as well as in paintings, church carvings, and sculptures guarding doorways or holding up lintels. For convenience, these wild folk may be divided into two basic types: the permanent and the temporary. Permanent wild people, who are born wild and stay wild, are an integral part of medieval legend and folklore.[2] They trace much of their origin back to Graeco-Roman woodland deities, and were essentially regarded as natural denizens of wild places such as mountains or forests, although they were sometimes endowed with supernatural attributes and might even be associated with demons or witches.[3] By Bigolina's time they were often presented as noble savages who dwelt in an uncorrupted state of rustic simplicity, and ultimately depictions of this type of wild person were to become mainstays in heraldry and folk festivals, where they may still be seen today.[4]

Temporary wildness, on the other hand, was a condition that a rational human, often a male romance protagonist, might be said to acquire as a result of a psychological crisis or a run of bad luck. In medieval and early modern narratives such figures as St John Chrysostom, Merlin, Yvain, Tristan, Lancelot, Partonopeu of Blois, Boccaccio's Beritola, and Ariosto's Orlando all pass through temporary phases of wildness and alienation from civilized society before being rescued and restored in some fashion to a comfortable state. Wildness in all of its forms, notes Richard Bernheimer, was always associated with irrationality and loss of mind: 'We find ... that to the Middle Ages wildness and insanity were almost interchangeable terms' (*Wild Men in the Middle Ages*, 12).

Thus wild people, whether permanent or temporary, stand in stark contrast to civilized society and are frequently at odds with it.

After establishing the theme of wildness in *Urania* by dedicating it to a man named Salvatico, Bigolina goes on to provide her protagonist with certain traits that recall the temporary wild men of romance. Urania, rejected by her lover, Fabio, at the beginning of the narrative, finds herself resisting the kind of madness that clearly derives from the topos of the grief-stricken male romance hero, the one who goes completely mad for a time and lives the life of a wild man in nature. Exiling herself from her native Salerno and from the company of others, she suppresses her true identity and rides around Italy disguised as a man; that is, the 'wilder' of the two sexes, as Bigolina's text makes plain more than once, especially in the scene in which Urania is subjected to physical abuse at the hands of the men in the forest, as a means of awakening her from her dazed condition (132–4).[5] She deliberately seeks desolate natural places in order to give vent to her sadness undisturbed, and even though she maintains her civilized aspect, the link between her and earlier romance protagonists who combine the need for solitude with explicit wildness is quite evident. Later on, when she has returned to Salerno to attempt to reclaim her beloved Fabio, Urania encounters a wild woman of the permanent type, the Femina Salvatica, who is kept in shackles in the Prince's palace, and upon whom Urania must bestow a kiss if she is to free the imprisoned Fabio and thereby bring her wanderings to a triumphant conclusion. We also are told the story of the Huomo Salvatico, the wild woman's bestial consort, who has likewise been confined in the palace and who has already suffered a terrible death before Urania's arrival (232–4). Yet another wild figure, the unscrupulous character Menandro in the guise of a faun, appears in Fabio's allegorical dream (240–4).

Urania is permeated by the theme of wildness more completely, and in more varied ways, than any other romance I have seen. Although it can be demonstrated that Bigolina derives these episodes from various literary sources, her treatment of them is highly original, if not unique; moreover, her application of the theme provides a key for understanding the purpose of the work as a whole.

Urania's (Nearly) Mad Flight

Urania's problems begin when she first discovers that Fabio has forsaken her for another woman. She becomes so despondent that she is certain she will die, and her state of mind leads her to contemplate departing from her native city in order to avoid the company of others:

> Et perciò per non incorrere in così gran scandalo, com'era di dover così vilmente lasciarsi condure a morte, et per non far del suo male allegra colei, per la quale d'ogni suo contento et d'ogni sua gioia era priva, deliberossi che che incontrar di ciò le ne potesse di volere sanza indugio vestito da huomo et sola fuor di Salerno partirsi, et andar pe' 'l mondo errando sin tanto che il lungo patire et molti disagi che per lo camino harrebbe sofferti, il soverchio amor che a Fabio portava, anzi più tosto la insania le levasser del cuore, et di sè stessa la facesser pietosa. Imperciò che di là dove amor scolpito nel cuor le lo haveva, per accidente che incontrar le potesse, non conosceva di poterlosi altrimente levare. (88)

> [Yet she desired to avoid the great scandal that would arise if she allowed herself to die in such a vile fashion; moreover, she did not wish to give her rival, the one who had deprived her of all her joy and happiness, any cause to rejoice at her demise. Therefore she resolved, no matter what might come of this course of action, to flee Salerno without delay, dressed as a man, and wander the world until such a time as the great suffering and considerable discomfort that she would undergo along the way might free her heart from its excessive, indeed insane, love for Fabio; only thus could she prove merciful to herself. She could think of no other way to remove love from her heart, once it had become engraved therein, unless it be by some accident. (89)]

On the brink of madness, Urania must gather her wits and make a rational choice. Bigolina has appropriated an established topos in medieval chivalric romance: protagonists, usually male, who suffer from extreme despondency of love often seek solitude in the hope of avoiding madness, and also in order to give vent to their sorrow out of the sight of others.[6] This corresponds to one of Cesare Segre's models for the depiction of madness in medieval literature, 'la follia cavalleresca' (chivalric madness), which is quite amply represented in various texts; one of the earliest of these is the verse romance *Yvain* of Chrétien de Troyes.[7] In this poem, the protagonist hears that his wife no longer wishes to see him because he has violated her trust. Overcome by feelings of guilt and shame, Yvain decides to wander off alone for fear that he will go insane if he stays in the company of other knights.[8] A vain hope, for once he is alone he does indeed go insane, living naked in the forest and tearing his flesh, until rescued by a woman who rubs his nude body with a special balm while he is asleep, banishing his melancholic fury and restoring him to his place in society by means of 'a magical erotic act,' as Bartra characterizes it.[9] The celebrated episode of Orlando's madness in Ariosto's *Orlando furioso* likewise begins with the distraught lover seeking solitude in order to express his sorrow unobserved, although the text does not indicate that he does so in order to avoid madness. Instead, he marvels at the state to which his condition has reduced him, convinced that he has become someone other than himself, until he finally slips into a state of insanity that is much like Yvain's, tearing off his clothes and uprooting a prodigious variety of trees (23.124–35).

For his part, Tristan is a character much associated with love madness, either feigned, as recounted in the two anonymous poems that bear the title *La Folie Tristan*, or entirely real, as can be seen in an episode in the thirteenth-century *Roman de Tristan en prose*, which portrays the insane hero leading a wild existence in the woods, as well as in an early fourteenth-century Italian prose version, *Tristano Panciatichiano*.[10] In the *Folie Tristan de Berne*, Tristan is depressed over his inability to see his beloved Yseut because she is so closely guarded by her husband, King Mark, and fears he will go insane if he does not see her ('qant ne la voi a po ne derve'; if I do not see her I will easily become insane, v. 93).[11] However, his solution, like Urania's, is practical, and thus allows him to avoid Yvain's fate: instead of actually becoming crazy, he only disguises himself as a crazy man, so that he can penetrate the king's court and speak to Yseut without suspicion.

This romance topos begins with insanity, or at least the fear of insanity, which then leads to a complete alteration of the character's normal behaviour and appearance, as well as his or her self-imposed exile from society. In the case of the standard male romance protagonist, the flight to the woods to avoid being seen and recognized in a state of grief leads to the protagonist's complete loss of identity: he does not want others to witness his condition, so he makes an effort to avoid being seen, and in time his savage appearance makes him unrecognizable anyhow. In the *Roman de Tristan*, this occurs not only to Tristan, but also to Lancelot, who goes insane from grief when his beloved Queen Guinevere, in a jealous rage because she has found him with another woman, banishes him from her presence:

En tel maniere erra par le forest.III. jours et.III. nuis sans boire et sans mengier, es plus sauvages liex qu'il savoit, conme cil qui ne voloit pas estre conneüs ne encontrés par home qui l'arestast ... (6.155)

[In such a manner he wandered through the forest three days and three nights without drinking or eating, in the wildest parts that he knew of, like one who did not wish to be recognized or encountered by someone who might stop him ...]

In time Lancelot becomes completely mad and lives like a wild man for an extended period, while various knights go on quests to seek him out. The passage cited above suggests a link with the lyric poetry of Petrarca, who describes his own efforts to find the wildest places, 'i più deserti campi,' in which to vent his grief beyond the sight of others.[12] As the lover teeters on the edge of madness, his fervent wish is to find solitude, to suppress his true identity, to avoid being recognized. The state of wildness may be more or less voluntary on the part of the protagonist, and more or less explicitly bestial, but the result is the same: anonymity, solitude, and alienation from normal civilized life.[13]

Segre has studied the ways in which these characters are depicted in their various texts, and has created a typology for them based on a series of semantic dichotomies. Beneath the wider oppositional scheme *natura/cultura* (nature/culture), which applies equally to all of the characters, Segre arranges a variety of other descriptive pairs that might be emphasized more in one text than in another: *nudo/vestito* (naked/dressed), *armato/disarmato* (armed/disarmed), *silvestre/cortigiano* (savage/courtly), *grido/discorso* (shouting/discourse, i.e., mindless speech as opposed to rational conversation), and *cibo crudo/cibo cotto* (raw food/cooked food), describing the protagonist's fundamental change in eating habits that leads him to eat only uncooked things.[14] As Segre suggests, it will not do to consider these dichotomies with modern eyes, which might be inclined to regard nature in positive terms: in the medieval view, the state of nature subtracts rather than adds, depriving the formerly courtly character of certain fundamental elements that define his place in society, such as clothing, weapons, cooked food, and even the ability to speak rationally (*Fuori del mondo*, 92). Segre's dichotomies always imply a process of degeneration from a positive to a negative state, and in this scheme nature is very much the opposite of civilization, since it does not impart any benefits to the knight who finds himself living in it, and who ultimately must be rescued from it.

The lovesick aristocratic lover who retreats from society in order to take up a wild existence survived in the narrative consciousness of Bigolina's time, as the episode of Orlando attests. It is also evident in Bandello's novella 1.27, which we have already examined in chapter 1 since it resembles a short romance (thirty pages in length in Francesco Flora's edition).[15] This story of the love affair of Don Diego and Ginevra la bionda ('the blonde,' the romance-style epithet by which she is known throughout the text), reveals certain parallels with Urania's experiences. Bandello's narrative also contains elements that presage the modern novel: there is considerable ambiguity of motive on the part of the characters, and even after Diego and Ginevra have fallen in love with each other nothing happens for a considerable time because neither can decide how to act, a state of affairs that would be peculiar, to say the least, in both the romance and the typical early modern novella.[16] While the two are dithering, another woman makes an effort to win Diego's love, and when a false story is spread that he has acquiesced, the jealous Ginevra withdraws her favours, such as they have been, and leaves Diego distraught. His efforts to prove his innocence come to nothing, since Ginevra has the idea fixed in her mind that he is faithless. After this, the plot proceeds in a manner that must appear familiar to the reader of *Urania:*

> Don Diego, poi che vide invano aver tentato tutti quei rimedii e mezzi che gli potevano recar profitto, avendo il viver in dispregio e per se stesso non si volendo uccidere, deliberò tentar un'altra via, cioè allontanarsi da la cagione del suo male e andar qualche dí vagabondo in qua e in lá, sperando che questo gli devesse scemar tanta sua fiera doglia. (1: 346)

> [When Don Diego saw that it had been useless to attempt all of those remedies and means that could have worked to his advantage, he disdained his existence, yet did not wish to kill himself through his own efforts. He decided to try another way, that is, to distance himself from the cause of his distress and go wandering here and there as a vagabond for a few days, hoping that this might reduce his ferocious grief.]

His next decision also has certain parallels in Bigolina's romance: he makes preparations for departure in disguise (although not as a member of the opposite sex, but rather as a hermit, and not alone, since he takes a servant with him); subsequently he also composes a letter of explanation to be delivered to his beloved, in the same fashion as Urania (1: 346). His servant attempts to dissuade him from this course of action, much as one of Urania's servants does (88), but ultimately the two men ride off until they arrive in wild and uninhabited area. At this point, the plot moves in a different direction from Bigolina's, adhering more closely to the medieval romance prototype of the hero reduced to wildness by his state of grief. Diego and his servant take up residence in a cave, where they sleep on leaves and live on whatever the servant can hunt with his crossbow, as well as roots, fruits, acorns, and the like (1: 347). The servant tries continually to convince his master that Ginevra is not worth these privations, but Diego simply grieves and looks worse and worse, losing weight and his natural colour, and growing a big beard, so that 'più a uomo selvaggio che ad altro rassembrava' (he resembled more a wild man than anything else, 1: 348). Although he is never called insane and does not undergo his wild experience in complete isolation, Bandello clearly means to follow the principal conventions of the medieval romances that we have seen, as outlined in Segre's scheme. Diego remains in this state for about fifteen months, until he is rescued by another knight, named Roderico, who recognizes him in his altered state by a birthmark covered with six or seven blond hairs.[17] The rescue and recognition scene are, as we have noted, standard features in tales of this type, as are the wild existence, the bestial appearance, and the attention to details of diet.

For Bigolina, the *follia cavalleresca* topos is quite evidently present, but only as a point of departure for what will become a very different depiction of character. At first, Urania's love distress does lead her to display the incipient markers of the behavioural pattern: she fears she is going insane and therefore seeks to flee from society and adopt an appearance that will allow her not to be recognized. However, after this none of Segre's degenerative dichotomies can be applied to her, for she does not become fully insane, nor does she really go wild. Of course, she has no weapons to cast aside, nor any knightly duties to neglect. She does not lose her clothing; she only changes it for that of the opposite sex. She dispenses with neither her courtliness nor her eloquence, and indeed we are not given any indication of her eating habits after she leaves Salerno, save that at one point she attempts suicide by refusing to eat for an entire day (162).

Bigolina continually sees fit to modify the *follia cavalleresca* topos to suit her own purposes, by commingling it with a variety of other elements. At the beginning of the episode, after Urania has written her long reproachful letter to Fabio, she mounts her horse and departs from Salerno in secret:

> et verso Napoli prese il camino dove qualche giorno avea deliberato fermarsi. Ma come vi fu giunta, il che fu co'l maggior affanno che alcun'altro

cuore amoroso sentisse giamai, sì dal patir cagionato, che ne' viaggi non
si può fuggire, massimamente essendo avezza ad haver tutti e' suoi com-
modi sempre, et sì ancora per cagion dell'amoroso strale il quale fuor di
misura la pungeva, che vedendo come ogn'hora più s'andava dilongando
da quell il quale mal grado di lei stessa, era suo cuore et sua vita, et sanza
il quale parevale che sanza spirto s'andasse. Così poco riposo parevale di
ritrovare in quel loco, che non fermandovisi più di un sol giorno, il seguente matino salita a cavallo di Napoli si partì, facendo disegno di andar
primieramente a Roma, et poscia di parte in parte tutta la Italia cercare et
vedere; così pensandosi, et con tal pensiero ingannando sè stessa, che per
molte et varie cose vedere et per lo assai patire dovesse venir a sciemarsi
quella accerba passione della quale Amor con sue proprie mani il suo cuor
le havea colmo, non sovenendole (quantunque molte isperienze havesse
vedute) come egli ne' gentili cuori con maggior forza et valore, ne' più
grandi affanni si facesse sentire. (108)

[She took the road to Naples, where she had planned to stay a few days.
But she arrived there having suffered the greatest woe that any amorous
heart had ever experienced; and this was partly due to the discomforts
which one cannot avoid while traveling, especially in her case, since she
had always been used to having her amenities. But it was also due to
the arrow of Love, which pierced her very deeply even though she saw
she was continually getting farther away from him who was the cause
of it. In spite of herself, he was her heart and her very life: without him,
it seemed to her that she was wandering about deprived of her spirit.
And so she found little rest in Naples, and stopped there for only one
day. The next morning she got on her horse and left Naples, planning
first to go to Rome, and after that seek out and visit all the places in Italy.
Thinking in these terms she deceived herself into believing that by seeing much, and suffering much, she could reduce the bitter passion that
Love had poured into her heart with his own hands. Despite the many
experiences she had witnessed, she did not remember that Love makes
himself felt with greater force and valor, and greater suffering, in gentle
hearts. (109)]

Urania begins her 'mad flight' not by heading straight for the woods
(although she will end up there) but rather with a sightseeing tour of
the great cities of Italy. This merging of *la follia cavalleresca* with a sort
of stress-relieving vacation tour recalls a similar episode in Boccaccio's
Filocolo, when the lovesick and fearful Fileno flees Verona to avoid Florio's

vengeance, riding across Italy from one lavishly described locale to the next (3.33, 244–5). However, by the time Fileno is discovered on the hilltop where Boccaccio's birthplace, Certaldo, will one day stand, his weeping and recriminations have left him with some of the traits of the typical romance wild man, with a great beard, brown skin, and tangled hair (3.36, 252). Boccaccio's romance, unlike Bigolina's, is filled with the stuff of myths and marvels: eventually, we are told, the gods take pity on Fileno's grief and turn him into a spring endowed with the power to speak and even predict the future birth of the author (4.2–5); this condition prevails until Florio comes much later to break his enchantment and restore him to human form (5.34–7). Although Bigolina spares her protagonist such a hard fate, and indeed has no interest in involving her character in supernatural adventures, Urania's experience cannot be entirely pleasant, in keeping with the requirements of the old *follia cavalleresca* topos. As in the case of Segre's dichotomies, the protagonist is expected to undergo a sort of process of subtraction, in the form of a loss of comforts due to the difficulties of the journey. Urania's 'therapy' for the grief of love is supposed to work on two somewhat contrasting levels: it will require her to see much but also to suffer much.

Urania's potential for suffering is emphasized by a reference to a commonplace of medieval Italian love poetry that serves to remind us that the character is herself a poet: lovers who have gentle hearts can expect to suffer more acutely from the power of love.[18] In terms of literary precedents, Urania's retreat into solitude does not evoke the experiences of Orlando so much as those of Petrarca. This orientation becomes all the more apparent when Urania finally does reach a nature setting, soon after her departure from Naples:

> et havendo per più di sei hore sempre cavalcato sanza mai accorgersi quello si facesse, o in qual parte s'andasse, nè accorta se ne sarebbe ancora, se non che all'entrar di un piacevol boschetto dove era una bellissima fonte, la quale da verdi et diritti alberi che la circondavano era da meridionali raggi del sole difesa. (110, 112)

> [She rode on for more than six hours ever unaware of what she was doing or where she was going; nor would she ever have known, if she had not entered a pretty little wood. A very lovely spring was there, protected from the rays of the noonday sun by the straight green trees which surrounded it. (111, 113)]

This nature setting, with trees set around water in a manner suggestive of the *locus amoenus* of the Petrarchan love lyric, takes the reader far from the expectations of the *follia cavalleresca* topos, with its unpleasant woodland experiences. Moreover, a second type of *locus amoenus*, the garden settings of Boccaccio's *Filocolo* and *Decameron*, as well as those of Bembo's *Asolani*, will soon be evoked, when Urania finds that the spring is a place where young aristocratic women have gathered to converse during the hot hours of the day (112).[19] Thus Urania's journey has become something of a journey for the reader as well, for we have ended up in a place that defies initial expectations, and without even the ironic treatment of Ariosto, who brings his grief-stricken Orlando to a similar Petrarchan nature setting only to have him lay waste to it with his sword in a fit of wrath after he has come to realize it was the love bower of Angelica and Medoro (23.100–36). For Orlando, the pretty place in nature becomes the very thing to precipitate him into his descent into madness, which will leave him a naked savage in the woods, whereas for Urania it serves the same purpose as it had for Boccaccio and Bembo: a perfect forum for a very civilized discussion of love and society. Not that Bigolina's text is deprived of an irony of its own, however, since Urania adopts the identity of Fabio, the very man who rejected her, even as she pretends to give the women a man's point of view on how best they may choose a man to love.

The wild figures of the romances that inspire Bigolina are almost invariably male; however, Ariosto does provide an episode with elements of *follia cavalleresca* involving a female character that seems to have influenced Bigolina somewhat. In Canto 32 of *Orlando furioso*, the warrior maid Bradamante is overwhelmed with grief when she is led to believe that her beloved Ruggiero has abandoned her for Marfisa, the other fighting woman of the poem.[20] Like Urania, she tries to prevent her condition from being generally known, although her method differs from Urania's in a quite comical fashion: she stuffs a sheet in her mouth to muffle her cries (32.36). At the end of an extended lament that resembles one of Urania's repeated outbursts, she resolves to kill herself, again comically, since the sword that she thrusts against herself is hindered by her armour (32.44). Subsequently, she decides to ride off and die in battle in Ruggiero's presence, perhaps even by his hand (32.45–6). Insanity is never mentioned here, and even though some of Bradamante's actions are doubtless meant to suggest the mad deeds of other similar characters, she still prepares for her flight with a rational deliberation that cannot help remind us of Urania. Bigolina's debt to this episode becomes even more apparent when Bradamante is later seen to ride aimlessly in the throes of her mental distress, allowing her horse Rabicano to choose the path, just as Urania does on two occasions:[21]

Come nave, che vento da la riva,
o qualch'altro accidente abbia disciolta,
va di nochiero e di governo priva
ove la porti o meni il fiume in volta;
così l'amante giovane veniva,
tutta a pensare al suo Ruggier rivolta,
ove vuol Rabican; che molte miglia
lontano è il cor che de' girar la briglia.   (32.62)

[And as a ship, which an off-shore wind or some other cause has detached from her berth, goes without a helmsman or steerage wherever the river might leave it spinning, so went the young lady in love, all absorbed in thoughts for her Ruggiero, wherever Rabicano wished; for many miles away is the heart that should guide the reins.]

Moreover, both Bradamante and Urania end their aimless rides with attempts to seek lodging in desolate regions as night comes on.[22] In the case of Bigolina's episode, the inhospitableness of a nature setting is emphasized for the first time in the text ('una solitaria et gran campagna'; a wide and deserted region, 162), and this, coupled with a first reference to the desperate Urania's need for food (she decides to starve herself to death to end her grief, 162) suggests at least a tenuous link with scenes of wildness in other romances.

We see, therefore, that Bigolina's creation of the lovesick wanderer Urania makes an essential departure from the example set by romance characters such as Yvain, Tristan, Lancelot, and Orlando, since Urania's rational deliberations ultimately lead her to avoid their descent into the total 'wildness' of insanity. As I have noted elsewhere, such behaviour would not be permitted to a female romance protagonist who is meant to be taken seriously.[23] In her study of the prevalence of love-melancholy in romance characters, Marion A. Wells takes note of 'the implicit gendering of romance as a feminine genre' due to the frequent appearance in romance of male warriors who have succumbed to the disease of love-melancholy, a condition typically associated with women (especially under the name 'hysteria').[24] In the throes of love madness, Wells remarks that romance warriors such as Orlando or Tasso's Tancredi

are left weak and ineffective, both mentally and physically: the masculine soul has become subjugated to a feminine love-object, which
results in 'the feminization or infantilization of the melancholic lover
as a result of his obsession' (*Secret Wound*, 23). Bigolina has, in effect,
completely turned this notion around by casting a female protagonist
instead of a male in the role of the jilted lover who risks succumbing
to love madness. Thus, Bigolina presents the reader with something of
a paradox: a romance (an 'implicitly feminized genre') that has a de-
cidedly 'unfeminized' female character in the role usually reserved for
a 'feminized' male. Whereas male characters are said to be feminized
by their sufferings for love because they give way to madness and are
prevented from doing their heroic and manly duties, Urania finds so-
lace and, as the plot progresses, her true purpose, by adopting manlike
characteristics. The disguise that at first merely allows her to ride alone
unmolested in time allows her to expound on the nature of love and
deliver a heartfelt defence of women to the two groups of young aris-
tocrats whom she encounters in the woods near Naples, who take her
pronouncements seriously precisely because they think she is a man.
Paradoxically, Bigolina creates a romance heroine who almost gives
way to a 'feminine' hysterical madness over lost love, in the fashion of
the male romance heroes upon whom she is modelled, but then resists
the pattern. Thus Bigolina's romance is still 'gendered as feminine' because it is built around the experiences of a woman protagonist, but not
quite in the same fashion as a work in which a male protagonist 'femi-
nizes' himself by succumbing to hysterical madness and betraying his
masculine virtues. Instead of losing control of herself and engaging in
the empty behaviour of wildness, Urania is made to serve a more useful
and exemplary role as the author's doctrinal mouthpiece in this decid-
edly unmelancholic example of the romance genre.

In some ways Urania also resembles another type of character, the
one who deliberately chooses to wander far from home in order to avoid
committing suicide for grief, as in the case of Bandello's Don Diego.
Among Italian prose romances, this type finds a distinguished antecedent in Sincero, the first-person narrator of Jacopo Sannazaro's *Arcadia*.
Denied the object of his affections, Sincero resolves to die, and ponders
the best methods, until fear of death causes him to change his mind:

> Tal che rivolto il fiero proponimento in più regolato consiglio, presi per
> partito di abandonare Napoli e le paterne case, credendo forse di lasciare
> amore e i pensieri inseme con quelle. (49)

[So that, having converted the cruel proposal into more temperate counsel, I decided to abandon Naples and my father's household, believing
that I would also leave behind love and worries.]

Sincero's choice, like Urania's, is ultimately somewhat therapeutic: the
aim is to avoid the insanity that depression caused by love might bring.
This 'therapy' may be traced as far back as Ovid's *Remedia amoris*, a
text that provided counsels for lovesick men who might otherwise be
tempted to kill themselves:

Tu tantum quamvis firmis retinebere vinclis,
I procul, et longas carpere perge vias;
Flebis, et occurret desertae nomen amicae,
Stabit et in media pes tibi saepe via:
Sed quanto minus ire voles, magis ire memento,
Perfer, et invitos currere coge pedes.   (vv 213–18)

[Only go away, though strong be the bonds that hold you, go far, and
make a lengthy voyage; you will weep, and the name of your deserted
mistress will haunt your mind; and oft will your foot halt in mid-journey:
yet the less you wish to go, the more be sure of going; persist, and compel
your unwilling feet to run.][25]

Ovid, like Bigolina, even stresses the need for suffering as a cure for
lovesickness, although the two writers differ in the type of suffering
they have in mind. For Ovid, the suffering comes from separation
from the beloved, whereas Bigolina, ever mindful of the ways in which
women's experiences differ from those of men, refers specifically to the
hardships and privations that must be endured by travellers (108). Her
readers were doubtless expected to imagine that such hardships would
be especially acute for an unescorted woman, however disguised she
might be.

Following Ovid and Sannazaro, and perhaps Ariosto's Bradamante,
Bigolina gives us a more 'refined' experience of wildness in her account
of the flight of a lovesick protagonist who makes careful choices in an
effort to avoid inappropriate behaviour. Urania seeks wild places, but
does not give herself over to overtly wild behaviour. In the chivalric romances that inspire Bigolina, the topos of the wild protagonist typically
involves a complete transformation of bodily appearance: clothing is
replaced by nudity, filth, and sometimes body hair.[26] This 'before and
after' contrast is laden with irony, especially in an age when clothing

and accoutrements served as primary visual indicators of social class, for the chivalric hero is routinely depicted as the finest of all men before his downfall, attractive and elegantly attired. For these men, the transformation is essentially one of degree: the highest and most refined man is reduced to the appearance of the lowest and most bestial. Bigolina follows this aspect of the topos in that she knows that her character must likewise transform her appearance in terms of the covering of her body, but she clearly realizes that she cannot do so in the fashion of the older romance characters. Instead of the usual nudity, filth, or hairiness, Bigolina has Urania indulge quite rationally in cross-dressing, a very different sort of transformation of appearance. Bigolina's protagonist adopts not only the appearance of the man who has wronged her but even his very identity when she calls herself Fabio (112, 166). In short, Urania's transformation is one not of degree but of kind: Bigolina's heroine completely alters her appearance in terms of gender, even as she selects clothing that maintains her dignity by preserving her identity with the aristocratic class. Once more, Bigolina has revealed her intention to create a unique work by adapting established literary topoi to suit her own purposes, and by studiously avoiding slavish imitation of them.

In terms of therapy for love madness, cross-dressing was something that never had to be considered in the *Remedia amoris,* since Ovid's advice was entirely directed at men, who could wander freely wherever they willed. Urania yearns for the freedom to give vent to her grief in the solitude of nature, in the fashion of Petrarca and so many male romance characters, but to do so she knows she must completely suppress her true identity and resort to the expedient of looking and acting like a man. Only thus, of course, can she have the luxury of riding alone and undisturbed over much of the Italian peninsula for days on end; but the choice of this course of action also has a more subtle dimension. As Bigolina's plot unfolds, we will come to understand that a woman who impersonates a man is indeed flirting with a kind of wildness, even if her appearance and manners convey the height of civility.

Literary wild men of the temporary sort sometimes display rare, even supernatural abilities. In his temporary wild state, as described in Geoffrey of Monmouth's *Vita Merlini,* Merlin discovers his gift for prophecy. Wildness might also confer unexpected benefits, as in the case of the wild man of the hagiographic tradition, St John Chrysostom. He lives for many years as a hairy savage in remorse for having murdered a princess who had tempted him to lust; later he discovers that his act of penance has actually brought the dead woman back to life.[27] To some extent, Yvain's wild exile likewise serves a penitential purpose, expiating his guilt for having offended his wife. In keeping with this tradition, Urania's ride in disguise allows her to discover her own rare abilities, although as we have come to expect in Bigolina's text, her benefits are neither supernatural nor penitential. Instead, she finds that her disguise allows her to flourish as a teacher when she comes upon the two groups of young people in a wood, and indeed, as I have already noted, her pronouncements in defence of women are particularly effective precisely because she is thought to be a high-born man of great refinement.[28]

Urania may be descended from a typically male type of romance protagonist, but she also bears some resemblance to Madonna Beritola, one of the very few wild women protagonists of the romance tradition, who appears in one of the *novelle-romanzi* of Boccaccio's *Decameron* (2.6). Beritola, fleeing political unrest that has led to the imprisonment of her husband, finds herself stranded on the island of Ponza when pirates make off with the ship that carries her two young sons, one of them a newborn infant. Ironically, she herself escaped capture because of her habit of retiring to a remote part of the island during the sojourn to grieve in solitude for her lost husband; thus a self-imposed temporary exile from society leads to a complete abandonment that she would not have chosen willingly. At first, she is utterly desperate, perhaps even 'hysterical' (to borrow Marion Wells's term), calling out uselessly for her sons and fainting on the beach. Subsequently, she gains control of herself and plans a more rational course of action:

> Ma poi che la sua fatica conobbe vana e vide la notte sopravenire, sperando e non sappiendo che, di se medesima alquanto divenne sollecita, e dal lito partitasi in quella caverna, dove di piagnere e di dolersi era usa, si ritornò. (1: 204)

> [But when she realized that her efforts were in vain and that night was approaching, she began to think of her own needs, and hoping she knew not what, she left the shore and returned to the cave where she was accustomed to cry and lament.][29]

Here we may recognize a situation similar to Urania's, even if there is no explicit reference to insanity. Beritola's deliberate choice to leave off pointless behaviour and see to her own needs resembles Urania's decision to undergo the rigours of a journey as a means of looking after herself. Beritola then takes to eating grass and nursing a pair of fawns with her own milk, consciously adopting a wild mode of existence after careful examination of her options:

> Per che, parendo alla gentil donna avere nel diserto luogo alcuna com-
> pagnia trovata, l'erbe pascendo e bevendo l'acqua e tante volte piagnendo
> quante del marito e de' figliuoli e della sua preterita vita si ricordava, quivi
> e a vivere e a morire s'era disposta, non meno dimestica della cavriuola
> divenuta che de' figliuola. (1: 205)

> [Thus the gentle lady felt that she had found some company in that de-
> serted place, and then having become as familiar with the doe as with
> her two offspring, she resolved to spend the rest of her life there feeding
> on the grass, drinking the water, and weeping whenever she recalled her
> husband, her children, and her past life.][30]

After many months of this existence, in which she maintains control over her emotions to some extent by adopting baby deer as substitutes for her lost children, Beritola is reduced to a truly wild aspect, lean, dark, and hairy, even wielding a club to protect her deer from the dogs of the landing party that eventually rescues her (1: 206).[31] Beritola is forced to be wild by her circumstances, but her actions resist many of the stereotypes for wild male romance characters, and indeed literary and folkloristic wild folk in general. If wild men are commonly preda-tory, aggressive, menacing, and insane, Beritola shows us another side of the wild existence, electing instead to be herbivorous, maternal, nur-turing, and rational.[32] Beritola, like Urania, indulges in the wild life of exile on her own terms, terms that reflect her own particular needs. Both women find that they must continue to express their grief for what they have lost, but each takes pains, after careful deliberation, to pro-vide herself with a secure, comfortable, and even comforting arrange-ment for pursuing such action.

Bigolina revisits the established topos of the exiled, lovesick, wild romance protagonist in her own way, adopting it to suit her own pur-poses. Ultimately we find that in *Urania* the topos scarcely plays its traditional role of emphasizing the helplessness and uselessness of the protagonist gone mad for love, who continually must be rescued and redeemed by the actions of others, as Merlin, Yvain, Tristan, and Orlando all illustrate. Instead, the ever-resourceful Urania essentially rescues herself. When she is wooed by Emilia, who like everyone else is convinced that Urania is a man, she decides that the only wise choice she can make is to return to Salerno and resolve the crisis that originally led to her exile by means of her own actions (170–80). She does this by encountering and outwitting the Femina Salvatica, the other great wild woman of Bigolina's tale.

Femina Salvatica

When Bigolina's Prince of Salerno decides he must condemn Fabio and Menandro for the crime of attempting to steal his marvellous rose garland, he finds himself in a very difficult position (222–4). Both men are equally guilty, yet Fabio is his favourite – indeed, the favourite of all the populace. The prince yearns to appear just and impartial, but he also would like to find a way to save Fabio. The two men were caught fighting over the garland because each wished to bestow it upon Clorina, beloved by both; therefore the prince decrees that he will free whichever man Clorina chooses as a husband (224–6). He imagines that she will choose the very popular local boy Fabio, instead of the foreigner Menandro.[33] Whichever man she does not choose, declares the prince, will be put to death in the space of three days, unless some maid succeeds in passing a most fearsome test: she must get a kiss from the prince's captive Wild Woman, who hates other women so much that she tries to kill them on sight. The maid who achieves this feat will free the man and have him for a husband.[34]

When Clorina chooses Menandro, the prince can only hope that someone will succeed in the ordeal he has ordained, to allow Fabio to be spared. Fabio's popularity guarantees that there is no shortage of young women who make the attempt to kiss the terrifying Wild Woman and claim Fabio for a husband; however, at the moment of truth each one loses her resolve and retreats in terror. At this point in the text Bigolina digresses, in order to explain who the Wild Woman is:

> Et per farvi la cagion manifesta per la quale quella Salvatica Femina così spaventevole era, dico che essendo già due anni innanzi stati donati al Prencipe quella femina, et con lei un'huomo salvatico, il quale era tanto sdegnoso et spiacevole, che harrebbe spesse volte per poco, et per niente ucciso un'huomo; et veniva perciò co'gravissimi ceppi a' piedi tenuto sempre. Ma non così era la Femina, la quale essendo quasi come dimestica divenuta qua, et là per tutto il palagio con le donne della madre del Prencipe

n'andava dimesticamente. Ma tanto era smisurato l'amore ch' ella al suo Salvatico Huomo portava, che non lasciava mai un'hora passare che non lo ritornasse a vedere; et con grandissima affettione mille et più volte non lo basciasse. (232)

[Now I will make plain to you the reason why the Wild Woman was so fearsome. Two years before, the woman had been given to the Prince as a gift, along with a wild man who was so irascible and repugnant that he would have killed a man for little or no reason. Because of this, his feet were always restrained by the heaviest shackles. But the female was not restrained thus, for she was almost like one of the household, wandering here and there about the palace in the company of the ladies who attended the Prince's mother. But so great was the love she bore her Wild Man that she never let an hour pass without going back to see him and kiss him more than a thousand times, with the greatest affection. (233)]

This ideal arrangement comes to an end one day when an inquisitive boy goads the Wild Man into a rage by poking him with a stick. The Wild Man is so frustrated that he eats his own hands, in a sort of bestial parody of Dante's Count Ugolino in *Inferno* 33, who likewise bites his own hands in a fit of helplessness.[35] When a woman of the palace retinue tries to get the Wild Man to stop doing this by beating him with a club, the Wild Woman suddenly appears, attracted by all the shrieks and noise. Since the Wild Woman imagines that all of the Wild Man's injuries are due to the beating that she sees he is receiving, she launches herself on the woman and mauls her to the point that she later dies, along with the traumatized Wild Man (234). From this point on the Wild Woman hates all females, and will try to kill any woman who approaches her, so that she must be kept shackled just as her wild consort formerly was.

Bigolina is deliberately vague about the origin of her wild folk. She never says that they formerly dwelt in the woods or mountains, although readers of her time would surely have expected this to have been the case.[36] She says nothing about the circumstances of their capture, which ordinarily received great emphasis in literary or artistic accounts of wild men. Nor does she ascribe any prophetic or supernatural abilities to them, as can be seen in so many other tales of wild men, such as those that will be discussed here later. Instead, she presents them as if they were part of the natural order of things, a bestial human type that has no special origin, no ability to speak, nor any miraculous gift to bestow upon the civilized people who capture them.[37] The malevolent, murderous Huomo Salvatico, who is already dead before the main action of the romance begins, appears as a sort of stock wild male character, one-dimensional, monumentally irrational, and completely subject to his instincts. The Femina is, on the other hand, a little more complex, as one might expect in a work that emphasizes the motivations and experiences of women. She is presented at first as an amiable simpleton who is happy to follow the ladies-in-waiting about the palace, utterly harmless until the sight of her lover's death brings out all of her latent ferocity. Through a tragic misunderstanding, exacerbated by her inability to think rationally or grasp the ways of civilized folk, the Wild Woman has become consumed by an irreconcilable hatred of all womankind.

Urania and Emilia, both dressed as men and with the former having adopted the identity of her erstwhile lover, Fabio, ride into Salerno on the last day before the real Fabio is to be executed (246). Emilia stoutly declares that she herself will dare to kiss the Wild Woman in order to save the young man who means so much to her beloved (250). However, when Emilia sees the terrifying Wild Woman, she loses her resolve, which allows Bigolina to make an extended pronouncement (through her mouthpiece Urania) on the need for true lovers to demonstrate the depths of their passion through acts of bravery and self-sacrifice (252, 254), a motif that has clear parallels with the opening lines of the proem to *Urania* (56).[38]

Meanwhile, Urania has laid her own plans for kissing the Wild Woman and passing the Prince's test:

> La Urania a cui maggior cura premea il cuore, che non facevano le parole, che costei le diceva; sanza darle altra risposta ritrossi con l'hoste, et fece tanto, ch'egli le ritrovò una certa veste come di masnadiere, la quale unta, et bisunta, per molto sudore stranamente putiva; et pigliata che l'hebbe, con quella parte più unta si fregò d'avantaggio il collo, la faccia, et le mani, di maniera che sè, e di sè stessa stomacata si stava. Et indi ritrovato similmente un vil capellaccio, che a similitudine della veste era bene unto, et che quasi tutta la faccia coprivale, in capo se lo pose; et similmente la unta veste si mise intorno. (252)

> [Urania, whose heart was heavy with greater worries than those caused by Emilia's words, went off with the innkeeper without saying anything else to her. From the innkeeper she was able to get a suit of clothes such as a brigand would wear, which was very greasy and smelled oddly from

the great quantity of sweat it held. Once she had it, she rubbed the greasy parts on her neck, her face, and her hands to such an extent that she found herself sickening. After that she likewise found a ragged hat, which was greasy like the outfit and covered almost her entire face. She put this on her head, and put the filthy outfit on as well. (253)]

By means of this stratagem, Urania succeeds where so many other women, even those who made the effort to dress as men, have failed. She approaches the Wild Woman very cautiously, saying calming words, and as soon as the smell of her clothing becomes apparent to the Wild Woman, her plan has the desired effect:

ma quando che le fu più vicina sì che la Femina puote quel gran puzzo della bisunta veste, ch'ella havea in dosso sentire, parendo a quella, che quel fosse il proprio e naturale odore dell'huomo, del quale ella così forte-mente si dilettava, incominciò quella sua ferina faccia quanto più poteva a rasserenare, et a cennare la Urania, che più vicina le si facesse; la qual cosa ella vedendo un grandissimo conforto, et speranza ne prese; et con-fidandosi nella sviscerata fede, et amore, con i quali ella si movea per dar aiuto al suo Fabio, sanza più alcuna cosa temere, fattasi a lei più vicina, sopra una di quelle sue pilose gotaccie un gran bascio le diede. Ma lei, che cagion dell'odor della veste credevasi che la Urania fosse huomo; nè restando sodisfatta per un sol bascio, anzi essendo per quello desto in lei l'appetito, con ambe le braccia, et con tal furor la si strinse al suo petto, che poco vi mancò che quel ferino furore, facendola per la gran stretta scop-piare, non privasse Salerno di una, la quale doveva da gli habitatori di quello esser non poco prezzata. Et tanti, et tanti salvatichi, anzi ferini basci le dava, che più volte la Urania si ritrovò in strano pensiero di non dover viva uscirle di mano. (256)

[When she got close the Wild Woman could smell the great stench of the filthy outfit that Urania was wearing, which seemed to her to be exactly like the natural odor of the wild man who had once delighted her so much. Her bestial face became as calm as could be, and she gestured to Urania to come nearer. At this, Urania was much comforted, and she felt hopeful. Trusting to the boundless faith and love which had moved her to bring aid to her Fabio, all her fear left her and she came right up to the Wild Woman, planting a big kiss on one of her hideous hairy cheeks. But the Wild Woman was convinced that Urania was a man, from the smell of her clothing. She was not satisfied with a single kiss; indeed, it merely kindled a desire within her for more. Using both arms, she crushed Urania against her bosom with great force, so that her savage passion squeezed her until she nearly burst; and thus Salerno came close to losing a woman whom its citizens had cause to regard with the highest esteem. The Wild Woman then gave her so many savage, even bestial kisses, that more than once the bizarre notion came over Urania that she would never get out of her arms alive. (257)]

Bigolina provides a moment of comic irony: Urania now fears she will be kissed to death for being taken for a man, instead of being dismembered because she is a woman. But she has passed the test, with many people there to witness it; in time she escapes from the woman's arms without injury. At the conclusion of the romance, with all of her myriad deceptions having served their purposes, she at last reveals her true identity and claims Fabio as her rightful husband, her prize for having been the only one to kiss the Wild Woman.

As the studies of Bernheimer and Bartra make plain, malevolent wild women abound in medieval and early modern literature. Bartra describes the fear of medieval travellers in the Alps, where wild folk legends were especially persistent, and where it was thought a man might be tempted to approach a seductive young woman only to have her spontaneously turn into an evil hag (*Wild Men in the Looking Glass*, 101). Bernheimer notes that there are more wild women than wild men in the folktales he has studied, and if there is one motif that may be typically ascribed to them, it is their craving for the love of non-wild men. 'Indeed, so universally are they charged with this instinctive immodesty,' says Bernheimer, 'that this trait may well be the key to their origin psychologically' (*Wild Men in the Middle Ages*, 34). As Bernheimer observes, sometimes personifications of the sin of Luxuria were depicted with the standard wild attributes of nudity and body hair.[39] In fact, all wild folk, male and female, were generally seen as unable to control their sexual passions.[40] Bigolina acknowledges this tradition in her own work, but, significantly, is indifferent to the sexual proclivities of her Wild Man. Instead, she focuses all of her attention on the unrestrained yearnings of the Femina Salvatica, who is willing to shower affection indiscriminately upon anything she takes to be a man.[41]

I know of no narrative preceding Bigolina's that includes her motif of a woman disguised as a man who must kiss or otherwise tame a ferocious wild woman.[42] However, there is indeed a tradition of cross-dressed women who succeed in rebuffing or capturing wild men, and it seems likely that *Urania* can claim descent from such tales. A germ of the motif may be traced back as far as Ovid's *Fasti*, in which the wild deity Faunus attempts to rape Omphale, the lover of Hercules, only to be undone because the two lovers have switched clothing in preparation for a rite in honour of Bacchus. Faunus infiltrates the lovers' cave but is deceived by their cross-dressing, so that he climbs into Hercules' bed by mistake and quickly finds himself hurled to the floor by the enraged hero. Ultimately, Ovid's story is meant to explain how the bestial Faunus, and later his worshippers, came to disdain clothing (2. 303–58).

A more immediate source for this motif in *Urania* may be found in certain medieval tales of the renowned prophet (and occasional wild man) Merlin. *Lestoire de Merlin*, an anonymous Old French prose romance of the thirteenth century, contains an episode in which a woman named Avenable, disguised as the squire Grisandoles, comes to the court of a Roman emperor named Julius Caesar. Cross-dressed ironies abound in this text, as in Bigolina's: we are told that the emperor's wife is 'luxurieuse' (unchaste, 281) and that she keeps a retinue of twelve young men disguised as her ladies-in-waiting, so that she may constantly satisfy her lust in secret; thus the episode begins with a woman disguised as a man infiltrating a court filled with men disguised as women.

Merlin, not yet a wild man, rides through the forest to visit the emperor, who is greatly troubled by a dream he has just had, of a huge sow wearing a circlet of gold (282–3). Merlin changes himself into a stag and enters the streets of Rome, going right up to the emperor in his palace and saying to him, 'Iulius cesar a coi penses tu' (Julius Caesar, what are you thinking?', 283). The stag announces that no one will be able to explain the emperor's dream save a certain wild man, then abruptly departs. The emperor now decrees a quest for his bravest knights: whoever can catch the wild man will receive his daughter's hand and half of his kingdom as a reward. A test involving a wild man decreed by a potentate, with lofty marriage as a prize: this motif clearly percolates down to Bigolina's own romance, although albeit in 'feminized' form, for her test is ordained for women instead of men, and the wild creature in question is likewise female.

Caesar's knights ride off to seek the wild man, but to no avail, for Merlin has other plans. Still in the guise of a stag, he approaches Grisandoles in a wood and tells him (the text consistently identifies the disguised Avenable as male) how to set a trap of delightful food as a means to catch the wild man, who turns out to be, in fact, the shape-shifting Merlin himself (284). With the help of four men, Grisandoles chains up the sleeping wild man and transports him back to the city. On the way the wild man sees many strange sights and laughs enigmatically at each of them; the last time he laughs is in the emperor's presence when he sees the empress and her twelve 'ladies.' Only now will the wild man speak, when bidden by the emperor: he reveals the empress's trick, whereupon Caesar has her and her twelve lovers burned alive (288). The wild man also explains that Grisandoles is really a female, the most beautiful in the land and a virgin ('& sest pucele,' 289); moreover, she has succeeded in passing the emperor's test when so many men could not. The emperor has Grisandoles undress before the whole court, just as the empress's lovers were made to do, to prove her true sex. The wild Merlin goes on to pronounce many prophecies for the empire and to advise the emperor that he should now marry Avenable, which he does forthwith (292).

This story served as a source for the later French verse romance *Le roman de Silence* by an author identified only as Master Heldris of Cornwall. With this work the motif of the wild man who can only be tamed by a woman disguised as a man is developed much more fully. Whereas the motif was only a brief interlude in the long and complex narrative of *Lestoire de Merlin*, in *Silence* it becomes the culmination of the work's central plot. The girl Silence is born in England at a time when females have been denied any right to inherit their parents' land and wealth, so her parents decide to secretly raise her as a male, with a name that symbolizes her concealed nature (96–8); indeed, throughout most of the text the character is referred to as male. In time Silence enjoys great renown as a courtier for King Evan of England, but he creates trouble for himself when he twice rejects the advances of the queen (190–2, 264–8). The angry queen now ardently desires to bring about Silence's death, and to this end she causes the king to send him on what appears to be a hopeless task: he must catch Merlin, who is living in the woods as a wild man (270–2). Merlin himself has prophesied that only a woman will be able to catch him, so by all appearances Silence seems bound to fail in the quest that has been imposed upon him. When Silence laments what he has been commanded to do, he notes how difficult it is to get close enough even *to kiss* the wild man, which seems to prefigure Urania's own situation with the Femina Salvatica:

Coment prendroie jo celui
C'ainc ne se lassça a nului

Baisier, ne prendre, ne tenir,
N'a cui nus hom puist avenir?   (274)

[How could I capture the one who has never let anyone kiss, catch, hold or
come anywhere near him?[43]

Silence wanders disconsolate for a long time, until he meets a man who
tells him what Merlin looks like these days: as hairy as a bear, and as
fast as a deer (278). The old man is very likely Merlin himself in disguise, arranging his own capture just as he did in the ancestral *Lestoire de
Merlin*.[44] The old man gives Silence advice about how to catch the wild
man by using milk, honey, wine, and meat as bait (280). By these means
Silence catches the wild Merlin and takes him back to King Evan, who
curses Merlin for a false prophet since he had once said that he could
only be caught by a woman (288). As Merlin is taken to the court he
laughs at several things he sees, including a nun in the queen's entou-
rage. When pressed to explain himself, Merlin reveals all sorts of hidden secrets, just as he does in Geoffrey of Monmouth's *Vita Merlini* and
Lestoire de Merlin; as a result, both Silence and the nun are undressed
before everyone, so that the former is revealed to be a woman and the
latter a man who has served as the wicked queen's secret lover.[45] Still
standing there nude, Silence recounts the whole story of her upbringing. The romance ends with the queen and the false nun being put to
death, while Silence is dressed as a woman (now called Silentia) and
accepted by the king as his new wife (313).

Although it is hard to say if Bigolina was directly familiar with
these medieval French romances, she surely seems to have known the
Italian novella collection of her own time that contains a version of the
Roman de Silence, albeit one that lacks the character of Merlin. Giovan
Francesco Straparola provides the story of an Egyptian princess named
Costanza who, not satisfied with the womanly arts she has learned, becomes accomplished in the manly arts as well, including skill at arms.[46]
Her parents, having already divided the patrimony among Costanza's
three older sisters, can only offer her a husband beneath her station
for lack of a dowry. Scornfully disdaining this union, she rides off to
seek her fortune in a more masculine fashion (1: 250–1). Although no
explicit disguise is mentioned, she calls herself Costanzo and clearly
is able to pass as a man, seemingly by sheer force of will; in any event
the text consistently refers to her as a male. When Costanzo arrives
in Bithynia he places himself at the service of King Cacco; however,

eventually he finds that his position is compromised by the amorous attentions of the queen, which, like Silence, he rejects. The queen's love turns to hate, as in *Silence*, so she vengefully contrives to have Costanzo sent into the woods wherein there lives a population of satyrs, hoping to get him killed (1: 255–6). The king, who has long wished to capture one of these wild creatures, dispatches Costanzo to fulfil this task, at the suggestion of the queen. The redoubtable Costanzo lulls a group of satyrs to sleep with wine and bread, then ties one up and rides home with the creature slung over his horse (1: 256; and it is worth noting that he does this without any aid or counsel from anyone). On the way home the satyr wakes up and laughs at various things he sees, following the well-established motif in the Merlin stories. The king locks his wild man up, gives him the name Chiappino, and tries continually to get him to speak (1: 257). The queen, hoping to compromise Costanzo's situation further, suggests that perhaps he can get Chiappino to speak; this Costanzo does by promising the wild man he will have him freed (1: 258). At one point in the interrogation process, Chiappino will not wake up from a deep sleep until Costanzo has poked him several times with an arrow, a narrative moment that appears to have provided some inspiration to Bigolina, since she too has her Wild Man goaded with a stick.[47] Eventually Chiappino reveals a series of prophetic secrets that are very like those of the Merlin stories, including the fact that the queen has a number of male lovers disguised as women among her ladies-in-waiting, as well as Costanzo's own true identity as a woman (1: 259–60). The king has the queen and her lovers burned, then marries his former champion, now renamed Costanza.

Straparola, like Bigolina, dispenses with one traditional element of this type of tale, as exemplified by the experiences of Avenable and Silence: he does not make his heroine strip naked in public in order to reveal her true sex. Such dramatic revelation of the body as proof of a cross-dressed female character's true sex is actually quite pervasive in stories of women who do great deeds while disguised as men.[48] In so many stories of this type, public nudity has a symbolic value, representing the need to uncover long-hidden injustices and iniquities so that wrongs may be set right and the social order restored: thus adulterous queens and their accomplices may be done away with, or cross-dressed heroines may be revealed to their rightful husbands so that they can rejoin society in their proper guise. Although this motif might not have appeared appropriate or dignified to the creators of the characters Costanza and Urania, it has been noted in the previous chapter that Bigolina does indeed make similar use of the shock value of nudity in the allegorical proem of her book. Here the nude appearance of the authorial persona in the eye of Giudicio likewise serves the purpose of revealing hidden secrets, with the aim of setting the narrative on its proper course: the author must be informed of her true, 'uncovered' nature if she is ever to conceive of the story of Urania.

The story of Costanza is not the only tale of a wild man included in Book I of Straparola's *Le piacevoli notti*. In *favola* 5.1 we encounter a young prince named Guerrino who liberates a wild man imprisoned in his father's palace; later Guerrino benefits from the grateful wild man's supernatural knowledge. Although both of these tales have left traces in *Urania,* neither of them can be said to serve as a direct source for the essence of her plot.[49] Bigolina is only superficially drawn, as we have noted, to the ancient motif of the capture and imprisonment of wild folk by rulers in their palaces: she says nothing about where her wild people were taken, nor how; only that they had been given to the prince at some earlier time (232). The motif of the pursuit and capture of wild men can be traced all the way back to classical tales of the Sileni, who were occasionally seized for the wisdom that they could impart while in captivity.[50] As the various Merlin stories and Straparola's two tales show, it was commonly imagined that captured wild men were endowed with supernatural powers or prophetic knowledge and could generally be counted on to speak when the necessity arose. In Straparola's case, this is true both of permanent, 'natural' wild men, as in the story of Costanza, and of the temporary variety, since eventually we are told that Rubinetto, the wild character in Guerrino's story, was formerly a normal man who only became wild when he was rejected by the woman he loved (1: 327–8). Bigolina sees fit to break completely with this established tradition: her wild people have no supernatural abilities, no gifts to bestow in gratitude for having been set free. They are simply bestial versions of normal human beings, repositories of all the wild tendencies that lurk beneath the civilized veneer of humanity. Since they function as emblems of wildness pure and simple, without redeeming characteristics as far as civilized people are concerned, no one in Bigolina's tale even tries to get them to speak.

As the studies of Bernheimer and Bartra have shown, civilized humans were routinely depicted to be at odds with feral human denizens of the woods in certain standardized ways. Civilized men are sometimes seen fighting with wild men in order to protect damsels in distress, as in the case of Brandimarte in Boiardo's *Orlando innamorato*

(1.23. 5–18).[51] Grand hunts for wild men appear in the arts, or are re-enacted in folk festivals or pageantry. Civilized women might be shown leading captive wild men, if they are not otherwise fleeing their lustful advances.[52] When wild women appear in literature or the arts, their voracious, even demonic, sexual appetite is invariably presented as a threat to the civilized men who encounter them.

But what of the relationship between civilized women and their wild female counterparts? This never seems to have been depicted in any art form – to the best of my knowledge, it appears nowhere else but in *Urania*, where Bigolina fully exploits the ironic potential of such an encounter. Her disguised female protagonist, clearly descended from such antecedents as Avenable, Silence, and Costanza, is able to pass a test involving a wild creature precisely because she is a woman disguised as a man: as in the case of Silence, she even accomplishes something that no one but a woman is expected to do. However, Urania does not outwit, defeat, and tame a wild *man* but rather a wild *woman;* and in creating such a character, Bigolina takes the symbolic connotations of the old motif in a very new direction. If Bigolina had merely wanted to pay homage to the old wild man motifs as a simplistic way of exploiting the pun on Bartolomeo Salvatico's name, she could easily have imitated her romance sources by having the cross-dressed Urania capture a wild man in some standardized fashion, as a kind of transparent allegory of her affection for Salvatico. But Bigolina is too clever a writer for this, and in any case she has other points to make. Instead of the usual wild man, she overturns the old motif by having her protagonist defeat and tame a wild woman, seemingly with the aim of showing how women must learn to dominate themselves and overcome their own less civilized impulses. Urania has to 'come to grips' with the Wild Woman in much the same fashion that Dante has to grapple with the hairy Lucifer at the bottom of his Hell in order to learn the true nature of sin (*Inferno*, 34 vv 73–5). In this context, a civilized, disguised woman conquering a wild woman stands not only as a more original plot device than the old motif of a civilized, disguised woman conquering a wild man but also serves to communicate a more original and uniquely conceived vision.

The Game of the Senses

Urania spends most of Bigolina's narrative disguised as a gentleman of the aristocracy, while she plays the part of the temporarily mad lover,

the romance protagonist who must live in exile in order to avoid lapsing into total insanity. This disguise serves her well as long as she moves
among other people of the same social class, who consistently take her
for an exceedingly refined young man. Later, when she reaches Salerno,
she finds that the aristocratic costume is no longer adequate. It will not
suffice to fool the Wild Woman, who will not let any woman come
near her, not even those who put on men's clothing, since the creature
has an exceedingly refined sense of smell ('perchè perfettissimo havea
l'odorato, perciò che quella era donna subitamente conobbe,' 236). The
clever Urania knows that the simple disguise that has served her so
well thus far is not good enough for this task, for it is designed merely
to trick the eye, the noblest, most 'aristocratic,' of all the senses. To deceive the Wild Woman, she must find a way to fool the Wild Woman's
baser senses as well, especially her sense of smell.[53] She accomplishes
this not just by disguising herself as a lower sort of man but by daringly
donning filthy, foul-smelling man's clothing in order to impersonate the
Wild Woman's dead lover, the Huomo Salvatico. In the didactic portion
of her letter to Fabio (94–6), Urania has already demonstrated her familiarity with the hierarchy of the senses, which, as we have noted, was so
much discussed in the theoretical works of the time in conjunction with
the *paragone* between the arts, as well as in the context of the perception
of beauty. Now she finds a very practical application for that knowledge, for it allows her to fool the basest sensual instincts of a woman by
assuming the basest sensual aspects of a man.[54] Urania's resourcefulness allows her to become nothing less than a true wild man, at least
as far as the Wild Woman's nose is concerned: 'When she got close the
Wild Woman could smell the great stench of the filthy outfit that Urania
was wearing, which seemed to her to be exactly like the natural odor of
the wild man who had once delighted her so much' (257). Urania's trick
of the senses has the desired effect: it causes the Wild Woman to forget her murderous wrath and instead arouses her lust. By these means
Urania steals the kiss that frees Fabio from the sentence of death.

There is a biblical antecedent for this episode involving Esau, the hairy
wild man of the Old Testament, which might possibly have served as
another source for the author. When Jacob tricks his half-blind father,
Isaac, into bestowing upon him a blessing meant for Esau, his hirsute
twin brother, he does so by a cunning trick of the senses: with the help
of Rebekah, his mother, he impersonates his brother's wilder aspects,
applying hairy garments to his hands and neck and wearing clothes that
smell of the fields where Esau is accustomed to hunt.[55] As in the case of

Bigolina's episode, two senses must be tricked in order to pull off the ruse, but the sense of smell is again the clincher: when Isaac kisses Jacob, the wild smell of Esau is what convinces him he has given his blessing to the son whom he intended (Genesis 27: 26–7). Bigolina seems to have absorbed a central lesson from this passage: if one is to impersonate wild folk in order to win 'the game of the senses,' smell becomes the most important sense of all, especially if kissing is involved.[56]

Throughout this text, Urania flirts with different kinds of wildness, always for some rational purpose, always with the aim of manipulating the motif to her advantage. She only 'goes wild' within carefully defined boundaries. She allows herself an interlude of wild exile in order to deal with depression over the loss of her lover, but without indulging in the unseemly, completely bestial madness of her romance predecessors. Subsequently, Urania encounters the Wild Woman, who has indeed become completely crazy over the loss of her own lover, a loss that has transformed her from a docile companion to a murderous beast who must be confined in shackles. Urania now finds it necessary to adopt a very different sort of wild persona. She impersonates the Wild Man not only to overcome the obstacle created by the Wild Woman's madness but to exploit it to her own advantage and thereby cure her own state of depression. The ironic implications here are clear: one case of depression caused by lost love can be cured by the exploitation of another, similar case. In this narrative, Urania makes a habit of impersonating missing lovers to her advantage. She had already impersonated her own lost lover when she presented herself as Fabio to the five women in the woods and to Emilia; now she cunningly impersonates the Wild Woman's deceased consort in order to win the prize she has always sought: the undying love of Fabio himself. By these means, Urania breaks the pattern of so many love-mad romance heroes who precede her, who must be rescued from their situation by the efforts of others.

Roger Bartra, in his commentary on the studies of Bernheimer, asserts that the wild man legends serve to give external expression 'to the impulses of imprudent physical self-assertion latent within each one of us,' the very thing that Freud was moved to call the id (*Wild Men in the Looking Glass,* 136). According to this interpretation, the myth of the wild man responds to a persistent psychological need in human beings, a need to explore a hidden, disturbing aspect of ourselves. The wild man, whose very state of wildness is, in Bartra's words, 'a consequence of the loss (physical or affective) of the loved object,' represents 'all the symptomatology of mania and melancholy' (136). This idea is particularly pertinent to Bigolina's text, wherein no fewer than four characters – Urania, Emilia, the duchess and the Wild Woman – are seen to suffer inordinately from the frustrations of love; moreover, Urania is brought to the brink of wildness by the loss of her lover, while her wild antagonist goes completely insane over her lover's death. At the risk of invoking Freud yet again, we may identify Urania as a sort of alter ego of the author Bigolina, since Urania's conquest of the Femina Salvatica must represent Bigolina's own conquest of irrationality within herself – Urania outwits a beast who is nothing but passion, whose very name suggests Bartolomeo Salvatico's; and this is the young man whom Bigolina, speaking as author in the proem, insists that she loves in a completely rational way. At first Urania flirts with wildness as a means of banishing her own mania and melancholy; subsequently she triumphs over the incarnation of feminine wildness by impersonating the dead Wild Man.

Bigolina elevates an inchoate medieval romance myth to new artistic heights by weaving it into the structure of her subtle and sophisticated narrative. Her persistent depiction of wildness in its various forms ultimately serves an exalted purpose – that is, the revelation of the greatness of the human spirit, which takes the form of Urania's triumph. Bigolina recognizes the essential role played by artistic portrayals of wildness as summarized by Bartra: 'The medieval wild man lives in a state of incivility, misfortune in love, and misery, and through contrast has permitted the figure of the civilized man to shine intensely. It could be said that the wild man – uncultured, unloved, disgraced – has for a long time been preparing modern man for modernity' (144–5). Bigolina has, in effect, built an entire romance around this notion.

Bartra concludes his study with a lengthy analysis of Miguel de Cervantes' story of the wild man Cardenio in *Don Quixote* (1.25). Cardenio's account of his wild existence inspires Don Quixote himself to drop out of society as a madman, but not, as he is careful to explain, in the fashion of Ariosto's Orlando:

'¿Ya no te he dicho,' respondió don Quixote, 'que quiero imitar a Amadís, haciendo aquí del desesperado, del sandio y del furioso, por imitar juntamente al valiente don Roldán, cuando halló en una fuente las señales de que Angélica la Bella había cometido vileza con Medoro, de cuya pesadumbre se volvió loco, y arrancó árboles, enturbió las aguas de las claras fuentes, mató pastores, destruyó ganados, abrasó chozas, derribó casas,

arrastró yeguas y hizo otras cien mil insolencias dignas de eterno nom-
bre y escritura? Y, puesto que yo no pienso imitar a Roldán, o Orlando, o
Rotolando (que todos estos tres nombres tenía), parte por parte, en todas
las locuras que hizo, dijo y pensó, haré el bosquejo como mejor pudiere
en las que me pareciere ser más esenciales. Y podrá ser que viniese a
contentarme con sola la imitación de Amadís, que sin hacer locuras de
daño, sino de lloros y sentimientos, alcanzó tanta fama como el que más.'
(1.25, 275–6)

['Have I not already told you,' replied Don Quixote, 'that I intend to imitate Amadís, and to act the desperate, foolish, furious lover so as also to
imitate the valiant Orlando, when he found signs by a spring that the fair
Angelica had disgraced herself with Medoro, and the grief turned him
mad, and he uprooted trees, sullied the waters and the clear springs, slew
shepherds, destroyed flocks, burned cottages, tore down houses, dragged
away mares and performed a hundred other excesses, worthy to be recorded on the tablets of eternal fame? And although I do not intend to imitate Orlando, or Roland, or Rotolando (for he had all these three names)
step by step in each and every one of the mad things he did, said and
thought, I shall act out a résumé, as best I can, of those that seem most
relevant. And it could even be that I might settle for imitating Amadís
alone, because his madness did not involve doing any damage, but just
weeping and being heartbroken, and he achieved as much fame as the
best of them.][57]

Bartra calls this episode 'the best and subtlest portrayal of the wild man
during the Renaissance' (*Wild Men in the Looking Glass*, 195), but of course
he reckons without Bigolina, whose work was still almost completely
forgotten at the time he was writing. Bartra notes that Cervantes' character must choose between the types of madness that had been established by two of his illustrious predecessors in the romance tradition,
Garci Ordóñez de Montalvo, the author of *Amadís de Gaula* (1508), and
Ariosto: 'When Don Quixote decides to become a wild man, he has two
options from which to choose: Orlando's furious rage or Amadís' sad
melancholy. But, Cardenio's wild delirium wavered between the two
extremes of a symptomatology recognized today as that of a man-
ic-depressive.'[58] Since Quixote has neither Orlando's strength nor
Amadís's black humour, he must find some other way to ritualize his
anguish for Dulcinea, who is of course a mere figment of his imagination. Ultimately, Bartra concludes that the creation of the complex wild

character Cardenio represents a kind of literary revolution: 'In the face of the challenges laid down by the European Renaissance, Cardenio represents the inadequacy of the epic delirium of the medieval knight and the inutility of crafting the civilized man's soul with the passion of lovesickness' (201).

Well before *Don Quixote,* Bigolina's Urania provides her own commentary on the old topos of the madness of the romance lover, although without recourse to Cervantes' irony and comic touch. Like Cervantes, Bigolina re-examines a stock situation from a new perspective, with the aim of communicating an entirely new concept. Inevitably, her solution is unique. Instead of the usual hero mad for love, Bigolina gives us a heroine disguised as a hero mad for love, a trick she will exploit to the full in a series of episodes. Urania is a romance heroine who must find a novel way to imitate the great romance heroes, rather like Quixote; moreover, she too finds the circumstances of her choosing bound up with her experiences with wildness and wild characters. However, she has no august female predecessors whom she can deliberately imitate, unless we consider Beritola, whose relative passivity can only provide her with a partial model, or Bradamante, whose circumstances coincide with Urania's in only a few details. Instead, she starts out rather like Amadís, following an established male paradigm; however, soon enough Bigolina imparts a kind of dynamism to her that leaves the old topos far behind. By the tale's end, Urania has become a character like no other in the tradition.

Quixote must do more than simply choose between the experiences of Orlando or Amadís; he must *find another way;* and in his choice of a method for madness we find the essence of Cervantes' greatness as a writer. Cardenio is a failure, says Bartra, because he represents the inadequacy of the epic delirium of the medieval knight (201). To this Quixote offers a sort of 'artificial wildness,' according to Bartra:

> The languid power of Cardenio's wild madness is retaken by Don Quixote's mimicry, and with it emerges the potent, new figure of a redeemed wild man. This wild man is redeemed not because he proposes a journey to the past, to a lost golden age, but because he consciously employs a primitiveness to transform the world around him into a modern reality. (201–2)

Urania too must find her own way to deal with romance madness, and her way is arguably no less significant and fascinating than that of Quixote: in fact, she gives us not just one form of 'artificial wildness' but two. First she indulges in a sort of constructive, even instructive, madness in the service of both society and herself, by pretending to embody the type of the male romance hero who loses himself in nature in order to assuage his grief. Thus disguised, she is able to serve as a didactic mouthpiece for Bigolina's notions of love and the role of women in society, through her preaching to the young people in the wood, as well as to Emilia. Then, when this guise is no longer sufficient for her purposes, she triumphantly reveals her ability to exploit 'the game of the senses' to her advantage by successfully impersonating a wild man as a means of fooling and defeating a wild woman, thereby restoring herself to her lost happy state. Throughout this process she deftly handles an additional onerous task, one that would not trouble a male character in quite the same way: she successfully safeguards her honour and good name.

Urania's kissing of the Wild Woman emerges as more than a fleeting homage to older romance motifs. It stands as a central metaphor in a text whose primary function is to communicate the need for women to make audacious choices if they wish to advance their causes in a hostile world. Such audacity on the part of women is a consistent motif in Bigolina's surviving works: not only does it characterize the experiences of Urania, who must employ resourcefulness and subterfuge to bring about the resolution of her crisis; it also applies to Bigolina's authorial persona in the proem, who must dare to defy convention in order to give artistic form to her deepest feelings. Moreover, this parallel between the motivations of both the narrator and the principal character is also a feature of Bigolina's only other surviving work, the 'Novella of Giulia Camposanpiero and Thesibaldo Vitaliani,' wherein the narrator's audacity in recounting a tale that is thought to be beyond her powers is matched by the audacity of the female protagonist who dares to woo, then rescue, the man she loves. In the end, Bigolina provides no greater message in her oeuvre than this: she is saying that women, both fictional and real, must consistently dare to display a combination of courage and cleverness if they are to flourish and attain their desires. In effect, they all must learn to kiss the Wild Woman if they are to know themselves, and know all that they may achieve.

Conclusion

Bigolina's reformation of the often neglected and overlooked genre of the Italian prose romance ultimately appears to be quite substantial. Although her masterpiece resembles the standard prose romance as established by Boccaccio and his followers in its superficial features, upon closer inspection it reveals traits that set it in a class by itself. Bigolina reaffirms the value of erotic love, which had been viewed with suspicion in the works that follow Boccaccio's model, thereby restoring to *Urania* one of the salient traits of the ancient romance. She greatly enhances the didactic function of the genre, which heretofore tended to confine itself to the extraneous interlude of the *questione d'amore:* in Bigolina's hands, it is now expanded to reach all parts of the narrative, and to embody the central meaning of the text. She has also completely reconceived the role of ekphrasis, formerly a gratuitous indulgence in imagery or a fantastic piece of stage scenery, in works of the romance type. Her paintings are realistic objects set within the narrative, described as the sort of art that one might actually see on a wall somewhere in real life, and the ways she has her characters interact with them serve to illustrate her cultural polemic against both the prevailing views of the beautiful woman and the *paragone* between the arts. Bigolina took a genre of literature that had produced few grand exemplars in Italy, indeed relatively few works of any sort, one that was, moreover, often ignored – at times even scorned – by the literary theorists of her time, and transformed it into a vehicle capable of communicating the sort of social and aesthetic concepts that had previously been reserved for other, more purely didactic, forms.

In *Urania*, Bigolina repeatedly (and artfully) challenges some of the most cherished beliefs of late Renaissance popular culture: that a poem is just like a painting; that painters are ideal communicators of the beauty of women; that physical beauty has intrinsic value as an external sign of inner, spiritual goodness. Along with her original treatments of the painting/literature *paragone* and the cult of feminine beauty as revealed by the sense of sight, Bigolina also seeks to renew the expressive potential of the prose romance by inventing startlingly new purposes for such time-honoured romance and epic motifs as ekphrasis, the exile of the grieving lover, and episodes of wildness: all of these ultimately reveal themselves to be auxiliaries in her grand campaign to remind women that they can leave a far greater mark on civilization through their own creative acts than by merely posing for a painting.

There emerges from the pages of *Urania* a portrait of the artist (the *literary* artist) as a unique and powerful individual, one who must find the moral courage to set right the misconceptions of her society. The one trait that unites all of Bigolina's surviving writings, including not only her two narratives but also her will and single known letter, is a sort of didactic audacity, a willingness on the part of the female protagonist, who is either the author herself or somehow identified with her, to take risks in order to teach certain truths or attain the things that she believes are hers by right.[1] As the allegory of Judgment tells her in the proem to *Urania,* the heavens have bestowed upon her a great burden: they made her a humble woman, with all the limitations to education and experience that this might imply, yet at the same time they gave her an almost infinite desire to gain knowledge.[2] Here is Giudicio's description of the author:

> Ma si sa che sei donna, et solamente tanta virtude et sapere possedi quanto parvero a i cieli che all'humile tuo essere bastevole fosse; quantunque (et forse fu per tua grandissima penitenza) un desiderio infinito di sapere assai, ti donassero. (80)

> [Instead you are a woman, possessing only as much virtue and wisdom as it seemed fit to the heavens to bestow upon your humble being. The heavens did, however, bestow upon you an infinite yearning for knowledge, and perhaps this has been a very great cross for you to bear. (81)]

Bigolina clearly perceives that it is her duty to strive to exceed the limitations placed upon her because of her sex, even as she lays out the standard formulaic assertions of humility that were expected of early modern women writers.[3] In this spirit, she dares to write a provocative book, one in which her doctrinal mouthpiece, a writing woman named Urania, is given several set-piece didactic speeches on love, beauty, the arts, and the rights of women: examples include her letter to Fabio, her lessons to the young people in the forest, and her reproach of the feckless Emilia's refusal to attempt to kiss the Wild Woman.

Bigolina stands at odds with her culture in a variety of ways. Although on the surface she appears to embrace the distrust of the art of painting that was already being expressed in some Counter-Reformation circles, she does so on her own terms, and her solutions are hardly theological.[4] She may be following the spirit of the Counter-Reformation to some extent, but not the substance. I have already noted the absence of religious references in *Urania*. One might ascribe this to the general lack of conventional piety in the mimetic genres of the early modern romance and novella, especially the latter, wherein anticlericalism typically flourishes and pious attitudes are often viewed in ironic terms. More telling is Bigolina's minimizing of theological influences and inspirations in her one supernatural moment, the allegorical proem. Here her authorial persona is visited by a righteous, even preachy allegorical figure, whose origins are nonetheless rather mysterious: Giudicio seems to come from a heaven of some sort, but his account of himself, such as it is, is largely deprived of elements of Christian theology. We have noted how this episode may be compared to the allegorical visitation at the beginning of Christine de Pizan's *Book of the City of Ladies:* when facing her own moral quandary, Christine prays for help and receives it in the form of three allegorical ladies sent to her by God. On the other hand, no one ever prays to God in *Urania,* neither in the proem nor in the main narrative. Bigolina's Giudicio is said to occupy only the vaguest of supernatural niches in some kind of non-doctrinal pantheon; we are never told precisely where this is, nor to whom Giudicio owes ultimate allegiance. As a result, the religious orientation of Bigolina's authorial persona, who must benefit from his lesson, remains similarly vague.

At the same time, Bigolina also resists the usual cultural alternative for Renaissance writers who wish to downplay the presence of Christian theological elements in their works – an emphasis on classical trappings and imagery. We have already noted how classical elements abound, at times anachronistically, in the prose romances of Boccaccio, Caviceo, and Corfino, which still make a superficial display of their links to the novels of antiquity. On the other hand, Bigolina avoids such classical elements almost completely; for instance, her characters do not muse upon Roman ruins or the ancient origins of places as they ride around

Italy. Gratuitous mythological allusions are so common in Renaissance narratives that more irreverent writers often saw fit to parody them, as in the case of Aretino's burlesque of the story of Tithonus and Aurora in the opening of the Second Day of his *Ragionamento della Nanna e della Antonia* (157); yet there are no such allusions to be found in *Urania*. Indeed, it is quite significant that the only classical deities to appear in Bigolina's book, apart from rhetorical references to the god of love, are figures in a painting that is specifically meant to make an ironic comment on the moral messages implicit in contemporary mythological artworks. Urania does cite both legendary and historical figures from the classical tradition as exempla in her impassioned defence of women, just as her model Christine does, but she also mentions biblical and medieval personalities in a mélange that is clearly meant to represent the totality of sources available to anyone who would undertake such a defence (142–52). She mentions these classical figures almost in passing, when they suit her overall purpose, but she would evidently not have the reader believe that she owes any overtly humanistic allegiance to the culture from which they derive.

Bigolina scrupulously avoids grounding her story exclusively in either Christianity or classicism: she does not merely reject one in order to replace it with the other. When the lovesick duchess prays that Venus will grant her the same boon as Pygmalion so that she may consummate her yearnings for the prince as he appears in his portrait (190), Bigolina's text betrays no sign of Christian outrage at a pagan invocation. If the duchess's prayers violate an ethical system, it is scarcely a system endowed with anagogical overtones. Instead, the duchess will ultimately suffer scorn and even death for having chosen the wrong art form for the expression of her deepest yearnings, and for having decided that her true 'talent' lay in the objectification of her physical form in the courtesan-like 'impersonation' of the goddess of love in a painting. In effect, she has offended not the Christian God but rather the author's grand scheme for defending and exalting the feminine sex in aesthetic terms.

Ideologically, *Urania* lies in a camp of Bigolina's own making, at odds with the predominant cultural orientations of its age. Whereas the contemporary male-dominated aesthetic culture, besotted with humanism, revelled endlessly in the virtues of voyeurism and the objectification of women in tales of ancient artists, Bigolina provides a solitary and audacious refutation that she quite evidently thought up on her own, since no precedent exists for it in literature. Beside a hundred references to male fantasies of the artistic pose as embodied in the tales of Pygmalion and Galatea, of Campaspe and Apelles, or of Zeuxis and the lovely ladies of Croton, to say nothing of the often lewd visions of authors such as Aretino, Firenzuola, and Luigini, Bigolina sets a bold exception, as well as a challenge, in the form of the episode of her duchess and painter. In so doing, she provides her own peculiar 'fiction of the pose,' a means to communicate a unique message about the ethical and sociological implications of the arts. She also inaugurates a veritable revolution in the portrayal of the visual arts in works of fiction, thereby providing an entirely new ethical orientation and ideological purpose for such portrayals. When she discards the old narrative models of ekphrasis that dated back more than a millennium before her time, she helps set the prose romance on a new course, one that points to certain morally ironic applications of ekphrasis that are familiar to us today in the modern novel, such as the fire and cooking pot painted on the wall of Geppetto's wretched room in Carlo Collodi's *Pinocchio,* or the grotesque fantasy portrait of Oscar Wilde's *Picture of Dorian Gray.*[5]

So little of this woman's oeuvre seems to have survived, yet she furnishes us with a series of tiny glimpses that reveal a rather grandiose and ambitious personality. Surely such a glimpse emerges in her daring gambit of introducing herself to so great and famous a personage as Aretino in 1549, when she had scarcely had the opportunity to make a name for herself as a writer. Bigolina also shows that she is aware of the greatest gift that literature may bestow upon those who undertake to create it: personal immortality. Like Ovid in his epilogue to the *Metamorphoses,* who knows that he will live on forever in his poem, Bigolina ends her preamble with the fervent hope that she will live on in the memory of Bartolomeo Salvatico, the young man for whom she has written her book.[6] Thus, as she says, she aspires to attain a 'double life' in death, just as she has had one in life through her efforts to emulate – indeed mirror herself in – Salvatico's remarkable qualities (80). Her assurance that she will live on in Salvatico's memory, and by extension in the collective memory of all mankind, lies in the work of art that she has created and bequeathed to the ages. It was simply her hard luck that the artfully prepared manuscript that she provided to Salvatico was to languish unpublished and virtually unread for nearly half a millennium.[7]

Surely the most tangible sign of Bigolina's somewhat grandiose vision of herself can be seen in the one document that survives in her own handwriting, her testament in the State Archive of Padua, dated 27 June 1563.[8] Only here may we knowingly hold in our hands an object that Bigolina created completely by herself, and it tells us that even in a simple legal document she was willing to reveal a keen sense of her own importance, as well as an inclination to express the deeper work- ings of her mind. Alone among all the legal documents I have seen in this or any other archive, Bigolina's will aspires to be a sort of work of art all on its own: its elegant handwriting and precise structure fly in the face of the sea of notarial scribbles that surround it in the extensive collection of legal papers that the notary Antonio Villani left to the ar- chive in a bound volume, now known as AN 829. Bigolina's didactic and introspective preamble almost makes the reader think that what follows will be another work of literature instead of a mere apportion- ing of wealth and goods. Moreover, it might even be said that its author aims for a visual as well as a conceptual effect, since she appears to have provided a sort of colour coding of its two sections: the didactic preamble and the initial paragraphs pertaining to the disposition of her body and the conduct of her funeral are in golden-brown ink, whereas the nine paragraphs describing the actual distribution of her goods to her heirs and servant are in black ink. At the end, with her signature 'Io Giulia Bigolina figliuola del quondam M. Girolamo Bigolino' (I Giulia Bigolina, daughter of the late Mr Girolamo Bigolino), the golden-brown ink, quite apparently reserved for any description of herself, returns and thus in effect neatly frames the more 'businesslike' paragraphs in black (66r). Of course, it is not impossible that the author composed the different parts of the will at different times, and in the presence of different ink pots; nonetheless, the overall affect is somewhat striking, with golden-brown references to herself framing a long black passage referring to her heirs, of whom moreover she does not always have en- tirely nice things to say (such as when she stipulates that they must pay fifty ducats to the orphans if they fail to heed her instructions regard- ing the disposition of her body, 65r). Bigolina, it would seem, was ever inclined to strive for effect, even in the humble legal document that she drew up in her own hand. This testament, the last known product of her mind to be discovered and published, provides an unconventional artefact that may serve to flesh out our scanty portrait of a woman who had no qualms about defining herself as a unique individual. In it we glimpse the personality of a writer who could create a book that strives not only to defy but even to modify a number of prevailing cultural conventions.

Bigolina was a woman who dared to say what no other woman of her time was saying, and she likewise created two fictional women, Urania and Giulia Camposanpiero, who are like alter egos to her, equally daring and equally accomplished. What Urania dares, Bigolina also dares – in effect, she kisses her own Wild Woman, when she takes on the greatest authorities and most pervasive opinions of her time concerning art, beauty, and literature. The result is a discussion of the arts that is itself a unique work of art, a book quite unlike any that had existed before it.

Appendix

Bigolina's Will in the State Archive of Padua (Archivio di Stato di Padova, Archivio Notarile 829)

In nomine Patris + et Filii + Spiritus sancti + amen
1563 adi 27 Giunio   65r

Conoscendo io Giulia Bigolina quanto questa nostra humana vita è fragile, et caduca, et come spesse volte aviene che un' ilquale un giorno vive sano, et allegro, l'altro sequente vien tratto alla sepoltura, ne si truova maggior' insania ne'l mondo quanto è quella di tale che a cio spesse volte non pensa, ne si puo dir che vi pensino quelli, iquali nella matura etade si lasciano a non pensata Morte cogliere senza haver di se', et de l'haver suo doppo di sè ordinato, et disposto, ond'io per non cadere in tale errore, et per lasciar pace, et concordia doppo me tra quelli ch'hanno ad esser miei heredi, o che aspetino da me gratitudine alcuna, o percio deliberato mentre io son per la Iddio gratia sana dell inteletto quantunque non molto de'l corpo di ordinare, et disporre l'ultima mia volonta qui sopra questa carta de mia man propria

Et prima l'Anima mia peccatrice, et indegna raccomando al Creator che lha generata pregandolo nelle viscere della sua misericordia che si degni liberandola in tutto da le pene infernali farla partecipe de gli meriti de la sua sacratissima passione

It.[1] Voglio, et ordino che'l mio corpo doppo che appara morto sia lavato, et vestito con l'habito berettino di Santa Chiara, cioe delle Rever:de Monache di San Bernardino da Padoa, et se sarà d'inverno o veramente nell'una delle due stagioni o da l'un capo o dall'altro congiunte a quello siano ubligati gli miei heredi a tener detto mio corpo hore. 40. in casa facendo[li] tener compagnia o da Monache, o da altre buone perso,[ne] et se sarà d'Estate lo tenghino senon hore 30, et sia[no] ubligati a questo sotto pena contrafacendo di pagar duccati 50 alli poveri orfani

It. voglio doppo il termine de l'hore 30, over 40, senza alcuna funeral pompa con duoi soli Preti della Parrochia, con 4 torze di peso d'una lira l'una, portate da 4 Monache di San Bernardino sia condotto detto mio corpo nella Chiesa di detto San Bernardino, et ivi in una delle Sepolture delle Monache sia sepolto, però prima avisando le mie fraglie, cioè il IHS,[2] et San Giovanni dalla Morte, et altre, se in altre in quel tempo mi ritrovasse, et sia sodisfato ogni mio debito qual con esse in quel tempo io mi ritrovassi havere, et sia da dette mie fraglie com'è usanza accompagnata alla [65v] Sepoltura, et harrei piacere se cio piacere se cio piacera al mio herede d'esser similmente accompagnata alla sepoltura da gli orfani cantanti le letanie, ma a cio non lo stringo. et se per caso il R:[do] Padre Maestro Ottavio mio Figliuolo (come ha piu volte detto) fatte pur disposto di volere il mio corpo nella sua Chiesa de gli heremitani non gli sia da'l mio herede quanto a questo interdetto, ma nel resto sia adimpita tutta la mia volonta

It. lascio per ragion di legato al R.[do] Padre maestro Ottavio mio diletto figliuolo l'usufrutto della metà d'otto campi posti nella villa di Mestrino da goder per indiviso con Silvio suo fratello si il cortivo essendogliene, come gli campi et similmente siano comuni a pagare il livello de gli stara sette, et mezzo for.[to 3] et a pagar le dadie, et sussidii, et s'intendi che detti campi gl'habbi solamente ad usufruttuare in vita e dopo la morte di detto Maestro Ottavio ritornino al mio herede essendo in vita, et non essendo in vita, a chi havera ragion da lui

It. sia dato nel detto tempo della mia Morte al predetto mio figliuolo Maestro Ottavio le due casse bianche d'Albero lavorate, un paro di lenzuoli, un paro d'intemele,[4] un Mantile, et sei sonaglioli d'esser tolti a sua ellettione

It. lascio per segno d'amorevolezza alla R:[da] Monacca Suor Gabriela nel convento di Santo Bernardino da Padoa mia cara Figliuola, che le sia datto la mia cappa che io porto in capo, una mia vestidura la miglior che io mi ritrovi havere in quel tempo, et sei delle miglior mie camise, et facci vender dette robbe facendossene de'l tratto un'habito, o quello piu le piacera

It. lascio a Vendramina mia fedel Serva se sarà in casa nel tempo della mia morte, che le sia datto per mercede di sua servitu duccati dodeci per una volta sola a lire sei, et soldi quatro per duccato, et habbi a darglieli il mio herede co'l comodo d'anni duoi, cioè duccati sei all'anno

It. sia datto ancora a detta Vendramina per segno di mia amorevolezza, et per gratitudine il letto sopra il quale ella dorme cioè, non li duoi migliori ma il terzo [66r] migliore, et le sia datto una cattena da fuoco, et tutti gli miei vestimenti di dosso si di lino, come di lana, et non ritrovandosi star in casa meco nel tempo della mia morte non habbia cosa alcuna de'l mio, ma solamente non essendo stata sodisfata de'l suo salario habbia attione di dimandar al mio herede d'esser sodisfata di mio

It. che non sia negato a detta Vendramina se sarà in casa in quel tempo alcune sue robbe che si tengono ad uso di casa cioè una coltre di tella turchina, un pezzo di spaliera vecchia alla divisa, un capecciale di penna, et un piumazzo

It. d'ogn'altro mio havere stabile, et mobile, presente, et ch'ha da venire lascio mio unico, et legittimo herede il car:mo Figliuolo Silvio Vimerca,[5] alquale concedo piena liberta che ne possa disponere in vita, et in morte ad ogni suo piacere, et dopo lui a suoi heredi

It. s'il predetto mio figliuolo Silvio per alcun caso venisse a morte senza haverne ordinato cosa alcuna, non vi si ritrovando però figliuoli legitimi, vadi detta mia faculta al R:do Padre Maestro Ottavio mio Figliuolo mentre che vive, et dopo la morte sua vadi a M. Socrate Bigolin mio Fratello overo a suoi heredi et essendo viva Suor Gabriela mia figliuola siano obligati a darle duccati dodeci all'anno mentre che vive

It. ch'el detto mio herede sia ubligato a pagar mezzo staro all'anno For:to alla Maria[6] mia sorella mentre che ella vive come sono ubligata ancor io per lo testamento di mia Madre. Et questa sia l'ultima mia volonta da non poter esser contrafatta da legatarii, ne da heredi, sotto pena di perder ogni beneficio che gli concede questo mio Testamento. Et priego l'Eccellente Dottor di medicina il Mag:co Girolamo di Negri, et l'Eccellente Dottor di Legge il Mag:co M. Diomede Soncino, ambi miei honorat:^{mi} parenti che siano insieme contenti d'esser miei comissarii nell'esecutione di quest'ultima mia volonta

Io Giulia Bigolina Figliuola de'l quondam
M. Girolamo Bigolino

Bigolina's will, translation:

> In the name of the Father, the Son, and the Holy Spirit, amen.
> 1563, on the 27th of June

I, Giulia Bigolina, am aware of how frail and transitory is this human life of ours, and how often it happens that a person might one day live in health and joy, yet the next be taken to the grave. There is no greater insanity in the world than that of the person who does not often think about this; nor can it be said that those who are advanced in years, yet allow themselves to be taken by death all unawares, without having arranged for the disposition of themselves and of their goods, are thinking about this. Therefore, in order not to fall into this error, and in order to leave peace and concord after my demise among those who will have to be my heirs, or those who expect any sign of gratitude from me, I have decided, while I am by the grace of God of sound mind, even if not so healthy in body, to draw up my final will here on this paper, in my own hand.

First, I commend my sinful and unworthy soul to the Creator who made it, and I pray that He, from the depths of his mercy, will deign to allow my soul to participate in the benefits of His most holy passion, thereby freeing it entirely from the punishments of hell.

Once my body appears to be dead, it is my wish and command that it be washed and dressed in the grey habit of Saint Clare, by which I mean the habit of the reverend sisters of Saint Bernardino of Padua. If it is winter, or even in one of the two seasons that precede or follow winter, let my heirs be obliged to keep my aforementioned body in the house for forty hours, in the company of nuns or other good persons. Otherwise, if it is summer let them keep it for thirty hours, and let my heirs be held to this on pain of payment to the poor orphans of fifty ducats, should they disobey me.

I wish, at the end of the thirty or forty hours, that my aforementioned body be borne to the church of the aforementioned Saint Bernardino without any funeral pomp, accompanied only by two parish priests with four candles of one *lira* weight each, carried by four nuns of San Bernardino; there I wish it to be placed in one of the tombs of the nuns. However, first I wish that my confraternities, that is, IHS [Jesus] and San Giovanni della Morte, as well as any others that I might have joined by that time, be informed, and that all the debts that I might have to them be paid. As is customary, I wish to be accompanied to my burial site by these confraternities, and I would also like it if my heir will allow some orphans to sing litanies as they follow me to my grave, but I will not compel him to do this. And if by chance my son the reverend father Ottavio is still willing (as he has often said) to allow my body to be placed in his church of the Eremitani, let my heir have no objection to it; but in all else let things be done according to my will.

To my beloved son the reverend father Ottavio, I leave as a bequest the usufruct of half of the eight fields situated in the town of Mestrino, to be enjoyed in common with his brother Silvio whether untilled or cultivated, and let them also share payment at the level of seven and a half bushels of wheat, and share payment of the taxes and subsidies. Let it be understood that he may have use of these fields only during his lifetime, and after the death of the aforementioned Master Ottavio the fields will once more be the property of my heir, should he still be alive. In the case that he is no longer alive, they will be the property of whomever he shall name as his heir.

At the time of my death, let my aforementioned dear son Maestro Ottavio be given the two white chests of worked wood, a pair of sheets, a pair of pillowcases, a tablecloth, and six bells which he may select at will.

As a sign of my loving affection, it is my wish that my dear daughter the reverend Sister Gabriela, a nun in the convent of Saint Bernardino of Padua, be given the hooded cloak that I wear on my head, one of the best dresses that I might have at that time, and six of my best chemises, and let her sell these things and use the profit to have a habit made for herself, or whatever else may please her.

I wish that my faithful servant Vendramina, if she is still in my house at the time of my death, be given a single payment of twelve ducats, at six *lire* and four *soldi* per ducat, and that my heir have the leisure of paying her over the space of two years, that is, six ducats a year.

As a sign of my loving affection and gratitude, let the aforementioned Vendramina be given the bed on which she sleeps, that is, not one of the two best ones, but the third best; and let her be given a chain for hanging kettles, and all of my undergarments, be they of linen or wool; but if she is not beside me in my house at the time of my death let her not have a single thing of mine, and only in the event that she has not received her salary may she have the right to demand that my heir give her anything of mine.

Let Vendramina not be denied, if she is in the house at that time, those things of hers which have been kept for use in the house, such as a bed-cover of dark blue cloth, an old piece of headboard, a feather bolster, and a feather cushion.

I leave every other possession of mine, whether fixed or mobile, whether currently mine or a future possession, to my sole and legitimate heir, my dear son Silvio Vimerca, to whom I grant full rights of disposition while in life or in death in whatever way may please him; and after him, to his heirs.

And if my aforementioned son Silvio should by chance come to his demise without having made any arrangements, and without leaving any legitimate heirs, let all my goods go to my son the Reverend Father Maestro Ottavio as long as he may live, and after his death let them go to Socrate Bigolin my brother, or to his heirs; and if my daughter Sister Gabriela is alive, let his heirs be obliged to give her twelve ducats a year as long as she may live.

Let my aforementioned heir be obliged to pay a half bushel of wheat a year to my sister Maria as long as she lives, just as I am obliged to do by my mother's will. Let this be my final wish, which may not be infringed by legatees or heirs, under pain of loss of every benefit granted by this testament. I pray that the excellent and magnificent Doctor of Medicine Girolamo di Negri, as well as the excellent and magnificent Doctor of Law Diomede Soncino, both my most honoured relatives, be content to join together as executors of this, my final will.

I, Giulia Bigolina, daughter of the
late Girolamo Bigolino

In nomine Patris + et Filii + et Spiritus sancti + amen
1563 adi 23 Giugno

Conoscendo io Giulia Bigolina quanto questa nostra humana vita è fragile, et caduca, et come spesse volte aviene che un' il quale un giorno siamo sano, et allegro, l'altro seguente men siamo alla sepoltura, ne si ritroua maggior insania nel mondo quanto è quella di tale che a cio spesse volte non pensa, ne si puo dir che vi pensino quelli, i quali nella matura etade si lasciano a non pensata Morte cogliere senza haver di sè, et di l' haver suo doppo di sè ordinato, et disposto; ond' io per non cadere in tale errore, et per lasciar pace, et concordia doppo me tra quelli ch'hanno ad esser miei heredi, o che aspettino da me gratiimono alcuna, o percio deliberato mentre io son per la Iddio gratia sana di intelletto quantunque non molto del Corpo di ordinare, et dispor ne l' ultima mia volonta qui sopra questa carta di mia man propria

E prima l'Anima mia peccatrice, et indegna raccomando al Creator che l'hà generata pregandolo nelle viscere della sua misericordia chi si degni farla partecipe de gli meriti de la sua sacratissima passione

Voglio, et ordino che'l mio Corpo doppo che appara morto sia lavato, et vestito con l' habito beremino di Santa Chiara, cioè delle Reuer. Monache di san Bernardino da Padoa, et se sarà d'inverno o veramente nell' una delle due stagioni o da l' un capo o dall' altro conguinti, a quello siano obligati gli miei heredi a tener detto mio Corpo hore q o in casa facendo tener compagnia o da Monache, o da altri buoni persò, et se sarà d' Estate lo tenghino se non hore 30, et sia obligati a questo sotto pena di contrafacendo di pagar ducati 50 alli poveri orfani

Et voglio doppo il termine de l' hore 30, over q o, senza alcuna funeral pompa con duoi soli Preti della Parochia, con q torze di peso d' una lira l' una, portata da q Monache di san Bernardino sia condotto detto mio Corpo nella Chiesa di detto san Bernardino, et ivi in una delle Sepolture delle Monache sia sepolto, però prima auisando le mie fragie, cioè il IHS, et san Giovanni dalla Morte, et altre, se in altre in quel tempo mi ritrouasse, et sia sodisfatto ogni mio debito qual con esse in quel tem po io mi ritrouasse havere, et sia da dette mie fragie com' è usanza accompagnata alle

Sepoltura, et haverò piacere se ciò piacerà se ciò piacerà al mio herede di esser sole-
nnemente accompagnata alla sepoltura da gl'Orfani havendo le levarne, ma a ciò non lo
stringo. et se per caso il R.do padre Maestro Ottavio mio figliuolo (come ha più
volte detto) fosse pur disposto di voler~~~~ il mio corpo nella sua Chiesa de gli
heronimiani non già sia dal mio herede quanto a questo interdetto, ma nel resto sia
adimpita tutta la mia volontà

¶ Lascio per ragion di legato al R.do padre maestro Ottavio mio diletto figliuolo l'usufrutto della mità di otto campi posti nella villa di Meffrino da goder
per indiviso con Silvio suo fratello si il fortune essendogliemi, come gli campi
et similmente siamo comuni a pagare il Livello de gli Frara sette et mezzo per
et a pagar le dadie et suspidei, et s'intendi che detti campi gli habbi solamente ad
usufruttuarii in vita et dopo la morte di detto Maestro Ottavio ritorni al mio
herede essendo in vita et non essendo in vita, a chi haverà ragion di lui

¶ sia dato nel detto tempo della mia Morte al predetto mio figliuolo Maestro Ottavio le due Casse bianche d'Albero inchiodate, un paro di lenzuoli, un paro d'invo-
coli, un Mantile, et sei tovaglioli di esser solti a sua discretione

¶ Lascio per segno d'amorevolezza alla R.da Monaca Suor Gabriela nel convento di Santo Bernardino da Padoa mia cara Figliuola, che le sia dato la
mia Cappa, che io porto in capo, una mia veftadura la miglior che io~~~~
et sei delle miglior mie camiscie, et facci vender dette robbe facendossene del na~
un habito, o quello più le piacerà

haversi in
quel tempo

¶ Lascio a Vendramina mia fidel Serva si sarà in casa nel tempo della mia
mia morte, che li sia dato per mercede di sua servitù ducati dodicci, a lei
sei, et soldi quatro per ducato, et habbi a darglieli il mio herede col comodo d'un
duoi, cioè ducati sei all'anno

per una volta
sola

¶ sia dato ancora a detta Vendramina per segno di mia amorevolezza, et per gran~
sudore il Letto sopra ilquale ella dorme cioè non li duoi migliori ma il terzo

migliori, et le sia dasto una camisa da fuoco, et tutti gli miei vestimenti di dosso
sì di lino, come di lana, et non ritrovandosi star in casa meco nel tempo della mia
morte non habbia cosa alcuna del mio, ma solamente non essendo fatta sodisfatta
del suo salario habbia attione di dimandar di mio herede à esser sodisfatta di
mio

Item che non sia negato a ditta Vendramina se sarà in casa in quel tempo alcune sue
robbe che si vengono ad uso di casa cioè una colcra di tela turchina, un
pezzo di spaliera vecchia alla divisa, un capedale di pena, et un piumazzo

Item di ogni altro mio havere stabile, et mobile, presente, et ch'ha da venire lascio mio
unico, et legitimo herede il mio car.mo figliuolo Silvio Vimerca, al quale concedo
piena libertà che ne possa disporre in vita, et in morte ad ogni suo piacere,
et dopo lui a suoi heredi

Item s'il presente mio figliuolo Silvio per alcun caso venisse a morte senza haver
mi ordinato cosa alcuna, non si ritrovando però figliuoli legitimi nadi dona
mia facultà al R.do Padre Mathio Ottavio mio figliuolo mentre che vive, et
dope la morte sua nadi a M.r Socrate Bigolin mio Fradello ovver a suoi heredi
et essendo viva Sior Gabriela mia figliuola siano obligati a darli ducati doi
et alli anno mentre che vive

Item ch'il detto mio herede sia obligato a pagar mezzo stare all'anno Fori.o alla
Maria mia sorella mentre che ella vive come sono obligata ancor io per lo
testamento di mia Madre. Et questa sia l'ultima mia volonta da non po
ver esser contrafatta da legatarii, ne da heredi, sotto pena di perder ogni
beneficio che gli concedo questo mio Testamento. Et prego l'Eccellente Dottor
di medicina il Mag.co M.r Girolamo di Negri, et l'Eccellente Dottor di Legge
il Mag.co M.r Diomede Severino, ambi miei honorati parenti che siano insie
me contenti d'esser miei comissarii nell'escecuzione di quest'ultima mia volonta

Io Giulia Bigolina figliuola del quondam M.r Girolamo Bigolino

Notes

Introduction

1 On the production of prose works by sixteenth-century Italian women, and Bigolina's place therein, see Cox, *Women's Writing in Italy*, 112–14 and 149–50. Hélisenne de Crenne's contribution to the genre in French, *Les angoysses douloureuses qui procédent l'amours*, appeared in 1538, predating Bigolina's.

2 On romance as a mode, see Parker, *Inescapable Romance*, 4–5.

3 For Gamba's description of *Urania* as 'la lunga e nojosa novella' (the long and boring novella) see Bassano del Grappa, Biblioteca Civica, *Novellieri, materiali bibliografici* 4:73–4, and Bigolina, *Urania*, ed. Nissen, 25 and n (hereafter Bigolina, ed. Nissen). On the topic of descriptions of *Urania* before the publication of its recent editions, see Finucci, 'Introduction,' to *Urania*, 2002, 26–9, 33 (hereafter Finucci, 2002) and Bigolina, ed. Nissen, 22–5, 50.

4 See Corfino, *Phileto*, ix and n, for Giuseppe Biadego's rediscovery of this romance in Verona.

5 On the commingling of romance and novella traits in *Urania*, see Bigolina, ed. Nissen, 30–6, 39–40.

6 Finucci, 2002, 57–63.

7 For the episode of Urania's defence of women, see Bigolina, ed. Nissen, 138–60. All subsequent citations of *Urania* will be from this edition.

8 On the appropriation of these modes by males, see Finucci, *The Lady Vanishes*, 13.

9 Gino Raya emphasizes the indifference of early modern literary theorists to the prose romance: 'I trattatisti del Cinquecento, che si affaticano a disciplinare lirica ed epica, commedia e tragedia, non fanno quasi parola del romanzo in prosa, che rimane effettivamente – specie nella prima metà

del secolo – in un cantuccio da Cenerentola' (Sixteenth-century treatise writers, who labour hard to codify lyric and epic poetry, comedy and tragedy, scarcely utter a word about the prose romance, which effectively remains – especially in the first half of the century – like Cinderella, in a corner; *Storia dei generi letterari*, 91). The translation is mine, as are all translations from Italian, Latin, and Old French that follow, unless otherwise indicated.

1 The Reformation of the Prose Romance

1 Bigolina's great-grandfather Battista acquired Petrarca's house in 1470 through a long-term lease (*enfiteusi*), which lasted until 1518; see Mancini, *Lambert Sustris a Padova*, 54. Finucci's date for Bigolina's birth, which differs somewhat from mine, is based on her interpretation of a notarial document in the State Archives of Padua (Archivio notarile [AN] 4830), which supposedly confirms that Bigolina's husband, Bartolomeo Vicomercato (or Vilmercato), received her dowry in 1534. Since girls in the Venetian Republic typically married at around sixteen, this would suggest the years 1518–19 for her birth (Finucci, 2002, 17nn). However, the document AN 4830 only indicates that Bartolomeo was already the son-in-law of Giulia's mother, Alvisa, by that year, since Finucci misreads the word 'dicte' (aforementioned) as 'dotis' (dowry). The phrase in question actually reads as follows: 'dominus Bartholomeus Vilmercato filius domini Baptiste interveniens nomine dicte domine Aluisie eius socrus' (Lord Bartolomeo Vicomercato, son of Lord Battista, presenting himself in the name of the aforementioned Lady Alvisa his mother-in-law), 827v, lines 8–9. Since there is no reference in this document to a dowry, the year of Bigolina's birth cannot be conjectured with such certainty. According to Mancini, Bigolina's parents might already have been married in 1515 (*Lambert Sustris*,132, n20); in any case Bigolina's father, Gerolamo, is known to have received Alvisa's dowry in March 1516, so Bigolina herself could have been born as early as 1516, for all that is known. For Alvisa's dowry, see AN 4839, f. 697r, and Bigolina, ed. Nissen, 4.

2 For biographical information on Bigolina see Finucci, 2002, 13–22; Bigolina, ed. Nissen, 1–20; Finucci, 2005, 2–5; and Nissen, 'Giulia Bigolina la prima romanziera italiana,' 51–2. On the history of the Bigolin family, see Mancini, *Lambert Sustris*, 53–84, and Geremia, *Leggenda ritrovata*, 45–73.

3 See Bigolina, ed. Nissen, 1–4 (which includes an English translation of Scardeone's paragraph); as well as Finucci, 2002, 23 and n, and Cox, *Women's Writing in Italy*, 136.

4 On Borromeo's editions see Finucci, 2002, 27–31; Bigolina, ed. Nissen, 23–5; Finucci, 2005, 9–10.

5 Finucci has produced two editions, the first with Bulzoni Editore in 2002, which provides *Urania* in Italian, and the second with the University of Chicago Press in 2005, containing an English translation of *Urania* and both the Italian and English texts of 'Giulia Camposanpiero.' My edition, published by Medieval and Renaissance Texts and Studies, appeared in 2004 and includes both *Urania* and 'Giulia Camposanpiero' in Italian, with English translations.

6 Cesare Malfatti, always careful to note the financial conditions of the Paduan families that he describes in his *Cronichetta*, refers to the Bigolin as possessing little wealth ('con pocche facoltà in loro havere'): Padua, Biblioteca Civica MS 1239 XV, 5v.

7 For Vicomercato see Finucci, 2002, 17, 19–20; Bigolina, ed. Nissen, 4–5; and Finucci, 2005, 3–4. Finucci cites Mario Melechini's unpublished dialogue *A ragionar d'amore* as proof that Vicomercato was still alive when that work was written, c. 1554–5, but the use of the past absolute in the passage she cites does not appear to demonstrate that fact; see Finucci, 2002, 19, and Besançon, Bibliothéque Municipale MS 597, ff 58v–59r. Moreover, since the passage in question in Melechini's dialogue is actually paraphrased from the influential *Dialoghi d'amore* by Leone Ebreo, its biographical veracity may be further called into question; see my discussion of Melechini here in chapter 4 (n25), and Leone, *Dialoghi*, 6. For evidence that Vicomercato was in fact already dead by 1554, see Bigolina, ed. Nissen, 5.

8 For the possible date of *Urania*, see Finucci, 2002, 49–50; Nissen, 'Motif of the Woman in Male Disguise,' 207–8; and Bigolina, ed. Nissen, 19–20. The work refers to the dedicatee Bartolomeo Salvatico as 'dottor di leggi' (doctor of law), so the year in which Salvatico took his law degree provides an indication of the earliest possible year for the dedication. Finucci claims 1554 for this, the year Salvatico began teaching at the University of Padua, whereas I prefer 1552, when it is known that Salvatico received his degree (Veronese and Francesca, *Acta Graduum Academicorum*, 79). Finucci also states that *Urania* could not have been written after 1558, since that was both the year of Salvatico's marriage and the year that appears beside Bigolina's name in della Chiesa's list of women writers, published in 1620 (della Chiesa, *Theatro delle donne letterate*, 171–2; Finucci, 2002, 25–6). Although the year of Salvatico's marriage might possibly mark a valid *terminus ante quem*, it should be noted that della Chiesa's inclusion of the year 1558 is not likely to have anything specific to do with *Urania*, because this author quite clearly did not do any research of his own: everything he writes is paraphrased from Scardeone's Latin biography of Bigolina, and Scardeone does not provide names or dates for any of her specific works. For the record, Apostolo

Zeno's manuscript transcription of della Chiesa's list includes the abbreviation *f.* (probably meaning *floruit,* 'flourished') beside the years associated
with della Chiesa's various subjects; as far as Zeno was concerned, the year
1558 was not likely to have had a more precise significance in Bigolina's
case (Venice, Biblioteca Marciana, Zeno, *Zibaldoni,* vol. 1, 218r). It might
only have indicated the approximate year that della Chiesa's sole source,
the historian Scardeone, was writing. For the date of 'The Novella of Giulia
Camposanpiero,' see Bigolina, ed. Nissen, 42–4, and Finucci, 2005, 10 and n.

9 Mancini, *Lambert Sustris,* 54.

10 For the Bigolin in Santa Croce, see Geremia, *Leggenda ritrovata,* 45–73.
Mancini describes the condition of the Villa Bigolin, as well as the frescoes
that survive within it, throughout *Lambert Sustris.* The villa has long been
closed to the public.

11 On the social gatherings at Rota's villa, and Bigolina's possible participation in them, see Forin, *La bottega dei fratelli Mazzoleni,* 91–2.

12 Padua, Archivio di Stato, AN 829, 65r (full text provided here in
Appendix). See also Bigolina, ed. Nissen, 7–8.

13 Scardeone, *Historiae de urbis Patavii,* 418. For Bigolina's lost 'Fabula de
Pamphilo Etrusco,' see Finucci, 2002, 26, and Bigolina, ed. Nissen, 21, 29.

14 For Petrarca's influence, see Finucci, 2002, 100n, 148n, 182n; and Bigolina,
ed. Nissen, 39, 205n, 273n. For Christine's influence, see Bigolina, ed.
Nissen, 35–6 and n, 65n, 143nn, 149n, 151nn, 153n. For Caviceo's influence
see Bigolina, ed. Nissen, 39n and 83n. For Ariosto, see Finucci, 2002, 44, 47
and n, 55, 63 and n, 101n, 112n, 127–8n, 136n, 148n, 151n, 172n, 176n; and
Bigolina, ed. Nissen, 39, 40n, 143n, 299n. For Straparola's influence, see note
106 below.

15 For a comprehensive list of early editions of Christine's text, see Yenal,
Christine de Pizan, 50–2.

16 Aretino, *Lettere,* 338 and 339 (5: 261–2).

17 For this marriage, and evidence for Speroni's familiarity with Dioclide, see
Mancini, *Lambert Sustris,* 60. Mancini's family tree of the Bigolin includes
both Giulia and Dioclide (148).

18 On the cultural interests of Dioclide Bigolin, and his probable knowledge
of Titian's portrait, see Mancini, ibid., 58–62.

19 For Sustris's extensive Padua period, during which he maintained a work-
shop, see Ballarin, 'Profilo di Lamberto d'Amsterdam,' 68–73.

20 See Mancini, *Lambert Sustris,* 57–62, 78–9.

21 For Venus and Cupid, see Mancini, ibid., plate 58. The satyrs are on the
cover of Mancini's book and on plate 74. See also Bigolina, ed. Nissen, 41n.
For Plato's use of the name Urania, see *Symposium,* 120–1.

22 Mancini, *Lambert Sustris*, 2–3.

23 On these paintings by Sustris, see Ballarin, 'Profilo,' 63; Formiciova, 'Nuove attribuzioni,' 184; and Arasse, 'The *Venus of Urbino*,' 97. For Titian's influence on Sustris, see also Ballarin, 62–4 and 76–7, and Arasse, 96.

24 For the attribution of the *Judgment of Paris* in the Galleria Sabauda of Turin to Sustris, see Francis Richardson, *Schiavone*, 201, and Reid, *Oxford Guide to Classical Mythology in the Arts*, 2: 824. Another work by Sustris on this subject can be seen at mutualart.com/artists/lambertsustris: Lambert Sustris, *The Judgment of Paris*, sold by Sotheby's, New York, 24 January 2008, lot 357.

25 Masenetti, *Il divino oracolo*, 23r. See also Bigolina, ed. Nissen, 8–9, and Finucci, 2002, 19 and n.

26 Bigolina, ed. Nissen, 16–18.

27 For a description of the history and members of the Infiammati, see Samuels, 'Benedetto Varchi, the Accademia degli Infiammati, and the Origins of the Italian Academic Movement.' Speroni himself provides a contemporary account of a debate on the roles and the status of married women that was purported to have been held by various learned individuals in Pia degli Obizzi's villa in his *Dialogo della dignità delle donne* (1542); for another reference to Pia's salon, see also Betussi, *Libro . . . delle donne illustri*, 200r–201v.

28 On Speroni's and Tomitano's contributions to the language debate, see Vitale, *La questione della lingua*, 67–70, and Brian Richardson, 'The Cinquecento,' 186.

29 On the significance of Ruzante's use of *pavano*, see Padoan, *La commedia rinascimentale veneta*, 63–5.

30 On the popularity of Beolco's dialect comedies during Bigolina's time, see Scardeone, *Historiae*, 288–9, and Lovarini, *Studi sul Ruzzante*, 109–12. On the pervasive influence of *pavano* as a literary language adapted by various authors for rustic themes, see Viola, *Due saggi di letteratura pavana*, 32–5, and Padoan, *La commedia rinascimentale veneta*, 68–74.

31 See Bigolina, ed. Nissen, 53–4.

32 Elsewhere I have noted a possible parallel between the plots of *Urania* and Beolco's comedy *L'Anconitana*, as well as Lovarini's assertion that Bigolina was a precursor to Beolco in the production of fiction on rustic themes, even though she lived a generation later and showed no interest in rustic themes (Bigolina, ed. Nissen, 26, 40n; Lovarini, *Studi sul Ruzzante*, 225n). Lovarini's claim seems all the more absurd in light of his evident familiarity with Scardeone's *Historiae de urbis Patavii*, wherein Bigolina is plainly described as still alive at the time Scardeone was writing (late 1550s).

33 On the surge in interest in publishing works by women following the death of Vittoria Colonna in 1547, see Cox, *Women's Writing in Italy*, 80–4.

34 Scardeone, *Historiae*, 418. For Scardeone's text, and the use of the term *comoedias*, see Bigolina, ed. Nissen, 1–2 and n.

35 The first attempt to codify and define the novella genre was undertaken only after Bigolina's time, by Francesco Bonciani in 1574. He discusses the novella in conjunction with the Latin term *fabula* (140–1), and also with Aristotle's definition of comedy (145, 147–8, 151–2). In the early seventeenth century, della Chiesa paraphrased Scardeone's description of Bigolina, translating the term *fabula* into Italian as *novella (Theatro, 171)*. On the use of the terms *fabula* and *comedia* in the context of the humanistic Latin novella, see Albanese, 'Di Petrarca a Piccolomini,' 262–3. See also *Merriam Webster's Encyclopedia of Literature* s.v. 'comedy,' 'fabula.' On the tendency of critics across the centuries to avoid defining the novella, see Segre, 'La novella e i generi letterari,' 47–8, and Quondam, ' "Limatura di rame," ' 553–4.

36 Bigolina, ed. Nissen, 3–4. For a contemporary assessment of the problem of immoral subject matter in the novella, see Bonciani, *Lezione sopra il comporre delle novelle*, 163. Smarr notes that Italian women tended to avoid the topic of love in their dialogues as well, with the exception of Tullia d'Aragona (*Joining the Conversation*, 241).

37 Zumthor, *Toward a Medieval Poetics*, 293. In his study of the *Paradiso degli Alberti* of Giovanni Gherardi da Prato, a novella collection that includes some romance elements, Garilli associates Gherardi's apparent disdain for harmony and formal unity with the ideals of Gothic architecture ('Cultura e pubblico,' 33–4). This fragmentary aspect of romance has been extensively studied by Vinaver, *The Rise of Romance* (68–98). For an association between romance fragmentariness and the madness of Ariosto's Orlando, see Giamatti, *Exile and Change in Renaissance Literature*, 67–75.

38 Meneghetti notes that the lack of a clear definition of the prose romance as genre led many authors to adopt the style of the *novellatore;* that is, since Italians were not sure how to write a romance in prose, they tended to produce romances that had traits of the novella collections with which they had traditionally been more familiar ('Il romanzo,' 135).

39 For summaries of these problems of definition see Stevens, *Medieval Romances*, 15–28; Parker, *Inescapable Romance*, 3–15; Brownlee and Scordilis Brownlee, *Romance*, 1–22; and Fuchs, *Romance*, 1–11, 33–6. Zumthor reminds us that *roman* had only a vague meaning throughout the Middle Ages (*Towards a Medieval Poetics*, 285).

40 On the conversion of medieval Italian epics and romances from verse to prose, see Vitullo, *Chivalric Epic*, 93–5, 99–113.

41 Wellek and Warren, *Theory of Literature*, 216. These authors provide a suc-
cinct distinction: 'The two types, which are polar, indicate the double
descent of prose narrative: the novel develops from the lineage of non-
fictitious narrative forms – the letter, the journal, the memoir or biography,
the chronicle or history; it develops, so to speak, out of documents; stylisti-
cally, it stresses representative detail, "mimesis" in its narrow sense. The
romance, on the other hand, the continuator of the epic and the medieval
romance, may neglect verisimilitude of detail (the reproduction of individ-
uated speech in dialogue, for example), addressing itself to a higher reality,
a deeper psychology' (216).

42 On the remarkable coincidence that the first Italian and English prose romances to be written by women both bear the name *Urania* and deal with
a protagonist by that name, see Finucci, 2002, 51 and n, 66n; and Bigolina,
ed. Nissen, 37n. Wroth's romance, which does not reveal signs of Bigolina's
influence, was published in London in 1621.

43 See Doody, *True Story of the Novel*, 1–2. Doody is inclined to call any long
prose work of imaginative fiction a novel, from classical to modern times,
in defiance of the convention of most critics writing in English (1–4, 15–16).
On the terms *romance* and *novel*, see also Fuchs, *Romance*, 33–6.

44 For examples of such usage, see the studies by Albertazzi *(Romanzieri e
romanzi)* and Raya *(Storia dei generi letterari)*, and Meneghetti, 'Il romanzo',
173–7. In her Italian edition of *Urania*, Finucci prefers the more precise
term *romanzo in prosa*.

45 Panizza, 'The Quattrocento,' 158–9; Brian Richardson, 'The Cinquecento,'
231–2. For these problems of terminology, see also Swennen Ruthenberg,
'Coming Full Circle,' 147–9 and *passim*.

46 In verse: *Caccia di Diana, Filostrato* (except proem), *Teseida* (except proem),
Amorosa visione, Ninfale fiesolano. In prose: *Filocolo, Fiammetta, Corbaccio*. In
prose with some verse: *Comedia delle ninfe fiorentine, Decameron*.

47 For the influence of the French *romans*, so prominent in the court of Robert
of Anjou, on Boccaccio's early works, see Branca, *Boccaccio*, 38.

48 On Boccaccio's inclination to create novellas with elements of romance
see Guglielmi, 'Una novella non esemplare,' 33; Baratto, 'Realtà e stile,'
129–54; Segre, 'La novella e i generi letterari,' 54–5; Wetzel, 'Premesse per
una storia del genere della novella,' 274–5; and Zatti, 'Il mercante sulla
ruota,' 80–1.

49 On this topic, see Segre, 'La novella e i generi letterari,' 49, and Branca,
Boccaccio, 68.

50 Stevens, *Medieval Romances*, 15.

51 Fuchs, *Romance*, 10.

52 See Reardon, 'Introduction' to *Ancient Greek Novels*, 12–13; Doody,
    True Story, 21–2; and Fuchs, *Romance*, 12. On Chariton's use of the term
    'ερωτικά παθήματα (sufferings of love) for his own romance and its
    eventual application to the ancient genre as a whole, see Heiserman, *Novel
    before the Novel*, 3–10.

53 Bakhtin notes that the novel is always at odds with 'the great organics
    of the past,' i.e., with totalizing critical visions such as those of Aristotle,
    which stress the harmonious interaction of genres; such visions have
    always tended to ignore the novel, or, in its day, the ancient prose romance
    (*Dialogic Imagination*, 5).

54 See Meneghetti, 'Romanzo,' 127–8.

55 For descriptions of these Italian versions of Greek romances see Raya,
    Storia, 91–3. On Coccio's rendering of Tatius, see also Doody, *True Story*,
    246–7. Auzzas notes that the renewed interest in the ancient Greek ro-
    mances in sixteenth-century Italy contributed to a rise in the production of
    'il romanzo erotico,' or amatory romance ('Narrativa veneta,' 134).

56 For the designation 'romanzo morale' and descriptions of such works, see
    Albertazzi, *Romanzieri*, 71–112.

57 For a list of these, see Albertazzi, ibid., 134, and Raya, *Storia*, 103–4.

58 On the categories of medieval romance, including the amatory, see
    Meneghetti, 'Romanzo,' 141–2, 149.

59 Meneghetti, ibid., 147, 149–50. See Kirkham, *Fabulous Vernacular*, 202–4 and
    n, for these narratives as sources for Boccaccio.

60 Segre, *Le strutture e il tempo*, 148–9.

61 On the relationship between the genres of *cantare* and romance, includ-
    ing a discussion of *Ottinello e Giulia*, see Bendinelli Predelli, 'Dal cantare
    romanzesco al cantare novellistico,' 176, 184–5.

62 Borromeo, *Notizia de' novellieri italiani*, 6, and Gamba in Bassano del
    Grappa, Biblioteca Civica, MS *Novellieri, materiali biografici*, 4: 73–4. See also
    Bigolina, ed. Nissen, 23–5 and n.

63 Dante, *Paradiso*, 1, 100–2, and Bigolina, ed. Nissen, 74, 76, 78.

64 Bigolina, ed. Nissen, 82. On the occasional use of the term *operetta* to des-
    ignate long prose works in early modern Italy, see Nissen, 'Motif of the
    Woman in Male Disguise,' 217n.

65 Bigolina, ed. Nissen, 85n.

66 On the significance of Odysseus's persistent lying, see Fuchs, *Romance*, 21.

67 For this aspect of chivalric romance, see Fuchs, ibid., 39.

68 For a study comparing all of these cross-dressed characters to those in
    Bigolina's works, see Nissen, 'Motif of the Woman in Male Disguise,'
    202–5. Graziella Pagliano provides an extensive list of cross-dressed Italian

novella and theatre characters in 'Il motivo del travestimento di genere nella novellistica e nel teatro italiano del rinascimento.'

69 Bandello, *Novelle*, 2.36. On the implications of cross-dressing in this novella, which has a plot similar to that of the anonymous comedy *Gli ingannati*, see Pagliano, 'Il motivo del travestimento,' 41–2.

70 This motif also appears, outside of a romance setting, in Betussi's accounts of 'Buona lombarda valorosa in armi' and 'Margherita Regina d'Inghilterra,' in *Libro . . . delle donne illustri*, 157v and 162v–63r.

71 Albertazzi, *Romanzieri*, 3–6. On the history of the early modern Italian prose romance, see also Raya, *Storia*, 57–105; Porcelli, *La novella del Cinquecento*, 96–103; and Auzzas, 'Narrativa veneta,' 134–8. For the medieval origins of the prose romance see Meneghetti, 'Romanzo,' 173–7.

72 These difficulties in characterization may be exemplified by Passano's catalogue *I novellieri italiani*, which lists romances such as *Il libro del Peregrino* and *Hypnerotomachia Poliphili* (referred to as *romanzi*) among its novella collections and single novellas (211–15, 511–14).

73 On the influence of the *Filocolo*, *Fiammetta*, and *Comedia delle ninfe fiorentine*, in particular, on later Italian prose romances, see Auzzas, 'Narrativa veneta,' 134. With regard to the *Filocolo's* influence, see Kirkham, *Fabulous Vernacular*, 17–18.

74 Even as he acknowledges the *Filocolo* as the first great original Italian novel ('questo primo grande romanzo originale della nostra letteratura,' 45), Branca nonetheless provides a warning not to read the work as a modern novel, on account of its pervasive medieval elements and structure (*Boccaccio*, 46). Battaglia characterizes the *Filocolo* simply as the first work of Italian prose fiction (*Boccaccio e la riforma della narrativa*, 155). For Antonio Enzo Quaglio's definition of the *Filocolo* as a sort of medieval cento or miscellany ('un centone di tipo medievale') that cannot be read as a modern novel, see Boccaccio, *Filocolo*, viii.

75 'Certo grande ingiuria riceve la memoria degli amorosi giovani . . . a non essere con debita ricordanza la loro fama essaltata da' versi d'alcun poeta, ma lasciata solamente ne' fabulosi parlari degli ignoranti' (Certainly the memory of these loving youths receives great injury . . . when their fame is not exalted with due remembrance by the verses of any poet, but rather consigned only to the false speech of the ignorant, 1.1, 7). See also Chrétien de Troyes, *Oeuvres*, 3, vv 20–2.

76 For Sapegno's characterization, see his introduction to Boccaccio, *Elegia di Madonna Fiammetta*, 171.

77 Branca, *Boccaccio*, 44, 68. On this topic see also Scordilis Brownlee, 'Cervantes as Reader of Ariosto,' 110.

78 On the prayers of the *Fiammetta,* see Hollander, *Boccaccio's Two Venuses,* 47–8; for his discussion of the entire work see ibid., 40–9.
79 For the *Fiammetta's* links to Ovid's Phyllis, see Porcelli, *Dante maggiore,* 147–8n. On the presence of the *Heroides* in *Fiammetta,* see also Scordilis Brownlee, 'Cervantes,' 111–13. For the parallels between Seneca's nurse and Boccaccio's, see Salinari's and Sapegno's notes to this edition of the *Fiammetta,* 14–17nn.
80 On the medieval applications of the term elegy and Boccaccio's adoption of it for this work, see Segre, *Le strutture e il tempo,* 88–92.
81 On Boccaccio's debt to Dante for his concept of the elegy, see Branca, *Boccaccio,* 68, and Muscetta, *Boccaccio,* 137.
82 Segre, *La struttura e il tempo,* 91.
83 Muscetta calls the *Filocolo* a poem in prose, and claims that Boccaccio was trying to write both history and epic at once (*Boccaccio,* 24). According to Doody, this passage shows how Boccaccio would like to equate poetic narrative and prose narrative in a jocular fashion, and create thereby a new literary style (*True Story,* 194).
84 Battaglia notes that the *Fiammetta* is the first work of Western literature to focus exclusively on a female protagonist (*Boccaccio e la riforma narrativa,* 173).
85 Tonelli refers to the *Paradiso* as 'una specie di romanzo' (a kind of romance, *L'amore nella poesia,* 172). Garilli uses several terms for it: *libro, opera,* and finally *romanzo,* both with quotation marks and without ('Cultura e pubblico,' 8, 37, 40). See also Raya, *Storia,* 78.
86 On the characterization of this work as both romance and novella collection see Salwa, ' "Il Paradiso degli Alberti," ' 755–8.
87 For the *Paradiso's* links to the *Filocolo* see Lanza's introduction (Gherardi, *Il Paradiso degli Alberti,* x–xi); Garilli, 'Cultura e pubblico,' 4–7, 13–15, 31–3; and Balduino, 'Fortune e sfortune della novella italiana,' 158.
88 Feliciano, 'Justa Victoria,' ix–x. Although Feliciano's introduction is inspired by the *Filocolo,* his novella describing a wager placed on a woman's honour derives primarily from such medieval narratives as *Le roman dou roi Floire et de la belle Jehanne,* Boccaccio's tale of Zinevra (*Decameron,* 2.9), and the *Cantare di Madonna Elena.* On Feliciano's career see Baumgardner, 'Introduction' to *Novelle cinque,* 13–16.
89 On the structure and definition of 'Grasso legnaiuolo' and 'Bianco Alfani' see Bruni, *Sistemi critici e strutture narrative,* 122–37. For studies of the longer single novellas see Mario Martelli, 'Considerazioni sulla tradizione della novella spicciolata,' and Balduino, 'Fortune e sfortune,' 158–61. For a comprehensive list of the 'novelle spicciolate,' see Bessi, 'Il modello boccacciano,' 109–10.

90 For the problems of definition of these humanistic narratives, see Albanese, 'Da Petrarca a Piccolomini: Codificazione della novella uman- istica'; Pietragalla, 'Novella come romanzo: La *Historia de amore Camilli et Emiliae* di Francesco Florio'; and Balduino, 'Fortune e sfortune,' 158, 160. On the problems of definition of the novella in general see Quondam, ' "Limatura di rame" '; and Stewart, 'Boccaccio e la tradizione retorica.' Tonelli defines Piccolomini's *Historia* as an 'operetta' (also one of Bigolina's terms for *Urania*), and notes its links to Boccaccio's *Fiammetta* (*L'amore nella poesia, 173–6*). On the relationship between Piccolomini's narrative and *Urania*, see also Finucci, 2002, 43–5.

91 On the relationship between these works and *Urania*, see also Bigolina, ed. Nissen, 31–2. For a study of Caviceo's *Peregrino*, see Roush, 'Dante Ravennate and Boccaccio Ferrarese?' 551–9.

92 See also Caviceo, *Peregrino*, xxxvi, for the editor Vignali's account of the link between Caviceo and *Corbaccio*, although Vignali does not take note of the anti-erotic elements that the two works have in common. Caviceo's proem is rather complicated: the author first says that he dreams that he sees the ghost of Boccaccio, which in turn reminds him that he has earlier had a vision of the ghost of Peregrino; the author's account of this earlier visitation, addressed to Boccaccio's ghost, becomes the substance of the three books that follow. On the succession of ghosts in the proem see Roush, 'Dante Ravennate,' 554.

93 See Vignali's introduction to Caviceo, *Peregrino*, xvi–xvii, and Roush, 'Dante Ravennate,' 553.

94 On this aspect of *Fiammetta's* disclaimer, see Scordilis Brownlee, 'Cervantes,' 111–12.

95 For studies of Caviceo's notions of love and *questioni d'amore*, see Tonelli, *L'amore nella poesia*, 185–6, and Caviceo, *Peregrino*, xvi–xxi (Vignali's introduction).

96 For Vignali's list of the letters in the *Peregrino*, see Caviceo, *Peregrino*, liv–lv. In Bigolina's own time and region the true epistolary novel, describing a love affair entirely through letters exchanged by the participants, is repre- sented by Pasqualigo's *Delle lettere amorose libri due* (1563). On the episto- lary elements of the Renaissance dialogue, which doubtless also influenced Bigolina, see Forno, 'Il "libro animato," ' 251–9.

97 See Vignali's introduction, Caviceo, *Peregrino*, xxvii, xxxiii–iv.

98 This tendency also turns up occasionally in the Cinquecento novella; see for example Parabosco's *I diporti*, 1.1 and 1.2, which contain anachronistic references to 'tempi' (temples) and 'gli dei' (the gods), despite their settings in contemporary Christian cities.

99 For Peregrino's voyage to the underworld see 3.3–13, 244–59. For episodes of *questioni d'amore* in Caviceo's romance, see 1.38–44, 108–13, and 3.83–4, 340–2.

100 The relationship between Franco's *Filena* (or *Philena,* the Hellenized spelling that prevails in the original edition) and other Italian romances of the age is described by Albertazzi (*Romanzieri,* 37–46), Raya (*Storia,* 96–7), and Auzzas ('Narrativa veneta,' 135).

101 On the discovery and significance of *Phileto* (or *Fileto*), see Biadego's introduction in Corfino, *Phileto,* ix–xxvii; Raya, *Storia,* 96; Porcelli, *La novella del Cinquecento,* 98–101; and Auzzas, 'Narrativa veneta,' 134–5. Biadego provides the years 1497–1556 for this author (xii–xiii).

102 Such a disclaimer also appears in the opening octave of the first canto of Terracina's *Discorso,* wherein the author says she will not write of Scipio, Caesar, Achilles, Nero, or Aeneas, but rather of 'le Donne, i Cavalier, l'Arme, e gli Amori' (women, knights, arms, love affairs, 5 r–v). As in the case of writers of prose romances, Terracina feels she must take pains to distinguish her work, inspired by a chivalric romance (Ariosto's *Orlando furioso*), from true epic.

103 Because of these characteristics, as well as 'una più attenta analisi psicologica' (a more careful psychological analysis), Porcelli expresses the opinion that Corfino's romance is more pleasing to the taste of the modern reader ('è più gradevole al gusto del lettore moderno,' *La novella del Cinquecento,* 101).

104 For this work and its many editions see Albertazzi, *Romanzieri,* 71–82, and Raya, *Storia,* 94–5. For its characteristics as a prose romance, see also Auzzas, 'Narrativa veneta,' 135.

105 On the distinction between the novellas of northern Italy and those of Tuscany in this period, see Porcelli, *La novella del Cinquecento,* 12–13.

106 For Straparola's influence, see Bigolina, ed. Nissen, 26, 33–4 and n, 40–1n, 42–3 and n, 197n, 233n, 299n.

107 For these authors, see Auzzas, 'Narrativa veneta,' 125–8.

108 Parker discusses the link between wandering and erring (*errare/errore*) in Ariosto's romance: *Inescapable Romance,* 17–31.

109 For the hypothesis that Urania's wanderings reflect Bigolina's interest in novel-like self-determination, itself a reaction to Counter-Reformation restrictions, see Finucci, 2002, 59.

110 *Orlando furioso,* 1.7.2. On the significance of this verse for the *Furioso* as a whole, see Parker, *Inescapable Romance,* 20, and Ascoli, *Ariosto's Bitter Harmony,* 222–3, where it is discussed in the context of Ariosto's view of *giudizio.*

111 See Finucci, 2002, 45n, for a discussion of the parallels between *Fiammetta* and *Urania*. On Fiammetta's incapacity for action, see Scordilis Brownlee, 'Cervantes,' 119–20.

112 Bigolina, ed. Nissen, 34–5.

113 For possible references to *Orlando furioso*, some of which are tenuous at best, see Finucci, 2002, 55, 63, 90n, 101n, 112n, 127–8n, 136n, 151n, 172n, 176n; Bigolina, ed. Nissen, 39, 40n; Finucci, 2005, 32.

114 See Bigolina, ed. Nissen, 83n.

115 This formula may also be traced back to a somewhat similar antecedent in Boccaccio's *Filocolo:* 'Fatta la pistola, Florio piangendo la chiuse e suggellò' (having finished the letter, Florio, weeping, closed and sealed it, 3.21).

116 On this topic, see Bigolina, ed. Nissen, 33–5.

117 In his treatise on how to write novellas, Bonciani declared that a *novellatore* should only choose episodes that are necessary to the plot, without which 'l'azione sarebbe monca e imperfetta' (the action would be deficient and imperfect, *Lezione*, 153–4).

118 On this topic see Nissen, *Ethics of Retribution*, 29, 31–2.

119 For the Cumaean sibyl, see Boiardo, *Orlando innamorato*, II, 27.52–61. For Merlin, see Ariosto, *Orlando furioso*, 26.30–6 and 33.1–58; Cassandra's work is described in Ariosto, ibid., 46.80–98. See also Sannazaro, *Arcadia*, 19–20 (Judgment of Paris) and 101 (Mantegna). The narrative role of these artists' works will be discussed at greater length in chapter 3. On the rhetorical strategies of Sannazaro's artist, who never actually appears in *Arcadia* as a developed character, see Caruso, 'L'artista al bivio,' 163–70.

120 On the role of the artist as character in the novella, see Paul Watson, 'Cement of Fiction: Giovanni Boccaccio and the Painters of Florence'; Ciccuto, *Figure d'artista*, 57–104; and Land, *Viewer as Poet*, 5. On Sacchetti's satire of women by artists in *Trecentonovelle*, 136, see Simons, 'Portraiture, Portrayal, and Idealization,' 267. Doody notes that artists as characters in the novel (by which she means any longer work of prose fiction) were quite rare before the eighteenth century (*True Story*, 397).

121 See Nissen, *Ethics of Retribution*, 89–94. Most of these plots employ the common novella motif of the 'beffatore beffato' (the tricked trickster).

122 Bigolina, ed. Nissen, 19–20.

123 On Boccaccio's rather contrived names, which seem to provide a link to the ancient Greek romances, see Doody, *True Story*, 199–200.

124 Boccaccio, *De mulieribus claris*, 64. Finucci speculates that the name Clorina derives from Clori or Cloride (Chloris), and is meant to evoke the pastoral tradition (Finucci, 2002, 136n). For the relationship between

Urania and the Celestial Venus, which will be discussed in chapter 3, see Nissen, 'Subjects, Objects, Authors,' 25 and n.

125 Boccaccio, *De mulieribus claris*, 269. Ovid provides an early version of the story of Flora in *Fasti*, 5.193–378, wherein he says that she started out as a nymph with the Greek name 'Chloris' but became Flora, the goddess of flowers, after her marriage to the wind, Zephyrus (5.193; this transformation, with flowers spilling out of Chloris's mouth, is strikingly depicted on the right-hand side of Sandro Botticelli's *Primavera*). Ovid never refers to her as a prostitute. However, the Christian writer Lactantius offers the direct source to Boccaccio in this regard, lamenting the public nudity at Floralia celebrations and describing the Senate's artful mythological explanation of the prostitute Flora's origins (*Divine Institutes*, 1.20.1). Lactantius also mentions the name 'Chloris' that Ovid gives her, keeping the Greek spelling; Boccaccio's Latinized spelling 'Clora' does not derive from either source and thus might come from a corrupt reading, or else is his own invention.

126 Goffen, *Titian's Women*, 72. On the 'Flora Meretrix' in art, see also Lawner, *Lives of the Courtesans*, 97–102.

127 Betussi, *Libro . . . delle donne illustri*, 76r.

128 It may be significant that Christine de Pizan, who derives much from Boccaccio's *De mulieribus claris*, does not mention either Flora or Clora in the *Cité des dames*, most likely because she found the figure less than exemplary, a view Bigolina seems to have shared.

129 For examples of such visitations in Boccaccio's prose romances, see the epiphanies of Venus, Cupid, Mars, and Diana in *Filocolo*, 2.2–3, 2.42, 2.48, 2.57, 3.19, 3.38, and 4.137, as well as those of Venus and Tisiphone in *Fiammetta*, 1, 18–24, and 6, 125–6.

130 An exception to this might be claimed for Bigolina's numerous invocations or references to love, which sometimes has personified traits as Amore, the god of love (86, 108, 116, 178, 182, 186, 188, 194, 204, 254, 284). However, these references reflect little more than lyric or rhetorical convention, since Amore never makes a tangible appearance as a supernatural character in *Urania*.

131 For examples, see the eighth and ninth *questioni* (4.48, 4.51). On Bigolina's adaptation of the *questioni* topos, see Finucci, 2002, 55–7; 2005, 24–6.

132 Cf Capella's argument that women are more intelligent than men because of the association between Mercury, the planet of cleverness, and the sign of Virgo; moreover, the softness of women's bodies compared to men's is another indication of superior intelligence (*Della eccellenza e dignità delle donne*, 94). See also Domenichi, who repeats Capella's notion about the intellectual advantages of women's softer flesh (*La nobiltà delle donne*, 1, 15r–16r).

133 The motif of the knight who is angered at being shaken out of his love reverie while on horseback can be traced to Chrétien's *Lancelot* (526–7, vv 766–808).

134 For the numerous discussions of women in Latin or Italian that followed Boccaccio's *De mulieribus claris* and which precede the creation of *Urania*, see Jordan, *Renaissance Feminism*, 34–133; Benson, *Invention of the Renaissance Woman*, 9–122; and Cox, *Women's Writing in Italy*, 92–3. On Bigolina's relationship to these texts and to those that follow her, see Finucci, 2002, 57–63; 2005, 26–30.

135 On Capella, see Benson, *Invention*, 66–73; Jordan, *Renaissance Feminism*, 72–5; and Doglio's introduction to Capella, *Della eccellenza*, 30–6. The author's work was originally published under the name 'Capella,' the Latin term that he adopted in place of his actual name, 'Capra'; however, Doglio prefers the latter name for her edition.

136 Capella, *Delle eccellenza*, 89. See also Benson, *Invention*, 70–1.

137 On the other hand, Latin citations are quite common in the letters attributed to women in Lando's *Lettere*, so Bigolina could have had a recent model to follow for such displays of erudition on the part of women, if she had been so inclined. On the lack of emphasis on the oratorical skills of women in both early modern defences of women and the humanist educators, see Benson, *Invention*, 35. See also Cox, 'Seen but Not Heard,' 387–8, for the implications of women's education in conjunction with their roles in Renaissance dialogues.

138 See especially Castiglione, *Cortigiano*, 2.90–100, wherein Bernardo Bibbiena refutes the misogynists Gasparo Pallavicino and Ottaviano Fregoso. Subsequently, the debate over the worth of women continues off and on throughout Book 3. For the notion that Castiglione employs various strategies to restrict women within existing roles even while praising them, see Benson, *Invention*, 74–5. For a discussion of Castiglione's defence of women in the context of *Urania*, see Finucci, 2002, 44, 56, 107n.

139 On Domenichi's relationships with women authors and the place of *La nobiltà delle donne* among defences of women, see Cox, *Women's Writing in Italy*, 82–3, 92.

140 Domenichi attributes the fall of Troy to 'la pazzia de gli huomini' (men's insanity, *La nobiltà delle donne*, 2, 78r), saying that it was Paris who kidnapped Helen, not vice versa. For Bigolina's sympathetic view of Helen, see Bigolina, ed. Nissen, 148 and n.

141 On Lando's *Lettere*, see Jordan, *Renaissance Feminism*, 138–43. On the implications of Lando's probable part authorship of these letters, see Cox, *Women's Writing in Italy*, 83.

142 For further examples, see Lando, *Lettere,* 118v, 122r–123r, and 136r–137r.
143 See Bigolina, ed. Nissen, 150–3, and nn. Christine describes these figures
     in chapters 2.31–4. In 2.30, Christine introduces the idea that women have
     brought much that is good and useful into the world, whereas men continu-
     ally attribute evil to them. She then tells the stories of Judith and Holofernes
     (2.31), Esther and Ahasuerus (2.32), the Sabines (2.33), and Veturia and
     Coriolanus (2.34) as examples. Bigolina's point of departure is the same:
     'Inasmuch as women have been the cause of little evil, it remains for me to
     say how they have brought about many good and useful things' (Bigolina,
     ed. Nissen, 151); she then proceeds to provide the same four examples in the
     same exact sequence, although she does not treat them at as great a length.
144 Christine, *Cité des dames,* 2.47–9; Bigolina, ed. Nissen, 152–4. Concern
     about male brutality seems to be particularly common in defences of
     women written by women; see also Terracina's appeal to leaders of armies
     to be merciful to women and the weak in conquered lands ('A li cardinali,
     e sanguinosi capitani'), *Discorso,* 15, 25r–26r.
145 See Christine, *Cité des dames,* 2. 1–3, and Bigolina, ed. Nissen, 142.
146 Christine, *Cité des dames,* 198; translation by Brown-Grant (*Christine de
     Pizan and the Moral Defence of Women,* 80).
147 For Christine's prayer, which expresses doubt in her abilities, since so
     many male authorities have condemned women as inferior, see *Cité,* 1.1.
     Reason declares the divine origin of the allegories in 1.3. See Bigolina, ed.
     Nissen, 78, for the power of the heavens over Giudicio. Bigolina's allegory
     makes two passing references to God (64, 78), mentions heaven a few
     times as the origin of gifts bestowed upon humans (68, 78, 80), and oc-
     casionally calls himself (or his allegorical attributes) divine, in terms that
     sound more pagan than Christian (62, 78).
148 On Christine's use of theological authority to refute misogynists, see
     Brown-Grant, *Christine de Pizan and the Moral Defence of Women,* 142–6.
149 After her reference to the martyrs, Urania mentions the ancient sibyls,
     Sappho, Carmenta, Hortensia, the four daughters of 'Antione' (pos-
     sibly meant to be the Amazon queen Antiope), Penthesilea, Tamyris,
     Helen, Judith, Esther, the Sabine women, Veturia, and Circe (Bigolina,
     ed. Nissen, 140–53 and nn). All of these appear in various chapters of
     Christine's work. For speculation regarding the identity of 'Antione' see
     Bigolina, ed. Nissen, 143n. Finucci's proposal that the name refers to
     Amphion, king of Thebes, seems to be unfounded: not only did Amphion
     and Niobe have more than four daughters (seven, according to Ovid,
     Metamorphoses, 6.182), but these daughters, whose only role in the old
     tales was to be miserably slain by Artemis on account of Niobe's vain

boasting, can scarcely serve to exemplify the valiant warrior women whom Bigolina is describing in this passage; see Finucci, 2002, 118n, and 2005, 111n. For Amphion and Niobe, see Ovid, *Metamorphoses*, 6.146–312.

150 Ascoli, *Ariosto's Bitter Harmony*, 224. On the etymologies of ancient and early modern uses of the term see also Damisch, *Judgment of Paris*, 137, and Summers, *Judgment of Sense*, 22–3. For the biblical term κρίσις in conjunction with the moral crisis of the individual, who must judge correctly in order to bestow proper allegiance, see John 12:31.

2 Writing a Portrait

1 For the circumstances leading up to Aretino's flight to Venice, see Talvacchia, *Taking Positions*, 3–19.

2 See Mancini, *Lambert Sustris*, 2, and Freedman, *Titian's Portraits*, 10–17.

3 *Orlando furioso*, 46.14. Aretino's epitaph, in the church of San Luca in Venice, stresses particularly his ability to extract tribute from powerful people in spite of his humble origins; for the text of the epitaph, see Cosentini, *Una dama napoletana . . . Isabella Villamarina*, 57. For Aretino's career as an extortionist, see also his letter 3.124.

4 See Aretino's letter 2.131.

5 On the significance and popularity of Aretino's *Lettere*, see Palladino, 'Pietro Aretino,' 17–19; Cairns, *Pietro Aretino and the Republic of Venice*, 125–6; Freedman, *Titian's Portraits*, 13, 29–33; and Waddington, *Aretino's Satyr*, 47–58; as well as Procaccioli's introduction to Aretino's *Lettere* 1: 9–37.

6 On Aretino and Venetian print culture, see Waddington, *Aretino's Satyr*, 33–55.

7 The three letters to Bigolina are numbered 338, 339, and 353 in Procaccioli's modern critical edition; this numbering differs from that of the last complete edition of the *Lettere* before Procaccioli's, published in Paris in 1609 (cited in both of Finucci's editions of Bigolina's works). The letters are not numbered at all in the 1550 *princeps* of Book 5. For the complete texts and translations of Aretino's three letters to Bigolina, see Nissen, 'Giulia Bigolina and Aretino's *Lettere*,' in *In Dialogue with the Other Voice in Sixteenth-Century Italy*.

8 Datable references to Bigolina after the appearance of Book 5 of Aretino's *Lettere* include those of Angelo Leonico (1553), Mario Melechini (c. 1555), and Scardeone (1560). For Leonico, see Bigolina, ed. Nissen, 16–17. For Melechini, see Bigolina, ed. Nissen, 17–19 and nn; Finucci, 2002, 19, 33–6: Finucci, 2005, 8–9. In her earlier edition, Finucci intimates that Bigolina was actually the author of the work ascribed to Melechini, but without

evidence (33, 56, 64). Finucci also speculates that 'La novella di Giulia Camposanpiero' might have been written soon after 1545 on the basis of a datable watermark in the manuscript, but I believe it was more likely written after 1550, since Bigolina includes a sonnet riddle after her narrative, a vogue begun by Straparola in the first volume of the *Piacevoli notti*, which was published that year; see Finucci, 2005, 10, and Bigolina, ed. Nissen, 42–3 and n. The *Piacevoli notti* is not known to have been influential in manuscript form before 1550; see Straparola, lii–liii, for Donato Pirovano's commentary on the publication of this work.

9 References to such publicity seeking are evident in several letters sent to Aretino by his various acquaintances, which he included in Book 1 of the *Lettere;* see especially letters by Alessandro Piccolomini, Sperone Speroni, Ludovico Dolce, and Bernardino Daniello (*Lettere,* ed. Procaccioli 1: 486, 490, 503–5). See also Aretino's letter to Giovanni Agostino Cazza (2.107), in which we find a situation that appears to be analogous to Bigolina's: a writer who has not yet had occasion to meet Aretino sends him a letter and some poems, hoping for advice on how to develop his literary career; in this case, Aretino is quite happy to oblige. On the topic of Aretino publicizing the careers of other writers, see also Nissen, 'Giulia Bigolina and Aretino's *Lettere.*' For Aretino's efforts to promote the careers of novice artists, see Freedman, *Titian's Portraits,* 16.

10 For a list of the various artists with whom Aretino corresponded, see Freedman, *Titian's Portraits,* 13.

11 For a catalogue of Aretino's letters concerning creative women, and his attitudes towards them, see Nissen, 'Giulia Bigolina and Aretino's *Lettere.*'

12 Finucci, *The Lady Vanishes,* 17.

13 Aretino describes this habit frequently in Book 4 of the *Lettere;* see, for example, 4.295, wherein he boasts of his sexual prowess in middle age: 'ma io per me se stessi senza acoccarla quaranta volte il mese a questa e a quella ancilla, mi terrei arcispacciato' (but for my part, if I went without loosing a shaft forty times a month at this or that maidservant, I would consider myself quite done for, 4: 189). See also letters 4.275 and 4.434 concerning his relationship with his servant Lucietta, and Bigolina, ed. Nissen, 11–12 (concerning Aretino's letter 4.447, which also deals with this topic). Aretino's two daughters were born of his union with his housekeeper, Caterina Sandella, who was married to another of his servants; see Procaccioli's edition of the *Lettere,* 1991, 2: 1193n. Aretino was particularly proud of the fact that three of his former servants were known as 'le Aretine' (the Aretino women) because of their close association with him; see letters 3.124 and 3.229, and Lawner, *Lives of the Courtesans,* 65.

14 Berni associates food and sex in such poems as 'Capitolo dell'anguille,' 'Capitolo dei cardi,' 'Capitolo delle pesche' (Berni, *Rime*, 42–51). See also Aretino's own *Strambotti a la villanesca*, especially *strambotti* 37, 38, 43, 50, 54, 78, 82, 94, 128 (*Poesie varie*, 1: 187–210). These poems make the tone of raunchy satire in Aretino's second letter to Bigolina all the more apparent. Moreover, in his *Ragionamento* and *Dialogo*, Aretino refers to the aphrodisiacal qualities of truffles, cardoons, and other foods (64, 230–1). On the links between the imageries of food and sex in Renaissance literature see Toscan, *Le carnaval du langage*, 3: 1436–51 (fruit), 3: 1460–5 (salad), and 3: 1595–1621 (fish), as well as Pina Palma, 'Of Courtesans, Knights, Cooks and Writers: Food in the Renaissance,' and Bettella, *The Ugly Woman*, 101. For an example of fruits and vegetables as genitalia in a painting by Giovanni da Udine, see Tinagli, *Women in Italian Renaissance Art*, 129, and Waddington, *Aretino's Satyr*, 134, with an illustration in plate 5.

15 For examples of the commonplace Renaissance Neoplatonist discussions of beauty and the good, see Ficino, *Sopra lo amore*, 2.2, 30 and 5.1, 67–8; Leone Ebreo, *Dialoghi*, 220–8; Equicola, *Libro de natura de amore,* 343–4; Domenichi, *La nobiltà delle donne*, 1, 9v–10r; and Niccolò Franco, *Dialogo dove si ragiona delle Bellezze*, 7r–9r. In a similar vein, Speroni calls a man's physical features 'testimoni dell'anima' (revealers of the soul), and notes that for this reason a man with a pleasing aspect makes a better orator (*Dialogo della rettorica*, 680). See also Kristeller, *The Philosophy of M. Ficino*, 264–8.

16 Perella describes Aretino's satirical treatment of Neoplatonic motifs, including those expressed by Castiglione (*The Kiss Sacred and Profane*, 202–3). See also Waddington, *Aretino's Satyr*, 21–2.

17 For this aspect of Aretino's epistolary *oeuvre*, see Cairns, *Pietro Aretino*, 126–8.

18 In this context, it is well to remember Aretino's attitude towards what he considered to be upstart writers who strive for fame despite lack of talent, as expressed in one of the most memorable passages of the *Lettere*, the 'Dream of Parnassus' letter of 1537 (1.280). Here, in a parody of dream-vision literature, Aretino describes hack writers who want to climb Parnassus (i.e., make a career by attaching themselves to Venetian publishers), only to end up immersing themselves in a river of their own ink, like the grafters in the pitch in cantos 21–2 of Dante's *Inferno* (Aretino, *Lettere*, 1: 384–5). For a study of this letter, see Cairns, 242–4.

19 *Titian's Portraits*, 13–20.

20 See Petrarca, *Canzoniere*, 77, 78, and Land, *The Viewer as Poet*, 81–2.

21 Freedman, *Titian's Portraits*, 18.

22 For Aretino's interest in portraiture, see also Waddington, *Aretino's Satyr*, 57–90. Waddington notes that Aretino 'never saw the need to exalt the written portrait by denigrating the visual' (60), a view that Bigolina patently rejects.

23 See especially Dolce's celebrated citation of Ariosto's 'painting' of Alcina, *Dialogo della pittura*, 130–2. As will be noted in chapter 3, Dolce also has his speaker, Aretino, say that writers and painters are essentially the same, especially with regard to judging beauty (100).

24 On Aretino's use of the term *concetto*, see Freedman, *Titian's Portraits*, 26–9 and 84–7. For a study of the most celebrated applications of the term by Michelangelo, which provide an essential context for Aretino's usage, see Altizer, *Self and Symbolism in the Poetry of Michelangelo, John Donne, and Agrippa d'Aubigné*, 17–43.

25 *Titian's Portraits*, 18. For examples of Aretino's sonnets describing paintings in the *Lettere*, see 1.222, 2.197, 2.234, 2.421, 2.441, 3.38.

26 Famous examples can be found in letters 3.102 to Charles V, 5.454 to Agosto d'Adda, and 6.131 to Niccolò Molino. See also Freedman, *Titian's Portraits*, 26 (although her study does not use Procaccioli's numbering for the letters she cites but rather that of an earlier anthology).

27 For Aretino's works on the Index, see Waddington, *Aretino's Satyr*, 130–1 and 156.

28 For Salvatico, see Finucci, 2002, 27 and n, 37 and n, 47–50nn; and Bigolina, ed. Nissen, 12 and n, and 20.

29 Such ideas derive ultimately from classical art theory and practice; see Pliny, *Natural History*, 35.9 and 35.12. Statues of actual historical women (as opposed to goddesses, nymphs, or allegories) would have been extremely rare in either ancient or early modern times, as is evident in the story of the martyred courtesan Leaena, a defender of Athenian democracy, who could only be commemorated by a statue of a lion instead of her own likeness (Lawner, *Lives of the Courtesans*, 83). However, in Christine de Pizan's *Livre de la cité des dames*, Bigolina could have seen several references, presented as if they are historically attested, to women commemorated by statues (1.15, 1.21, 1.26, 1.30, 1.41).

30 Bigolina, ed. Nissen, 68–80. For the general belief that early modern portraiture had special powers of communication, including preservation of the memory of the dead, see Shearman, *Only Connect . . . Art and Spectator*, 108–9, and Cranston, *Poetics of Portraiture*, 54–61.

31 For the association between mirror images and portraiture, see Alberti's interpretation of the myth of Narcissus (*Della pittura*, 3: 46). See also Panofsky, *Idea*, 31–2 and 209n; Bann, *True Vine: On Visual Representation and*

the Western Tradition, 105–56; Beaujour, 'Some Paradoxes of Description,' 37; and Pardo, 'Artifice as Seduction in Titian,' 79–81. In his letter of 1545 to Marcantonio Morosini (*Lettere,* 3.265), Aretino says that if he had a portrait of himself as good as the one Titian made of Morosini, he would carry it around like a mirror. For the metaphorical value of the mirror image in medieval love poetry, see Frappier, *Histoire, mythe, et symboles,* 151–2.

32 On the topic of the supernatural in *Urania,* see Bigolina, ed. Nissen, 33–4.

33 For Bigolina's interest in the city of Salerno and its dynasty, see Bigolina, ed. Nissen, 19–20 and 85n.

34 In the face of a tradition which consistently demanded that a romance heroine be described as surpassingly beautiful, Bigolina dares to create a character who is explicitly said to be less attractive than others; this must be seen as yet another effort on her part to instil an element of realism into her narrative. Bettella notes that less attractive heroines did not begin to appear in novels until the mid-nineteenth century (*The Ugly Woman,* 188n), a trend that Bigolina seems to have anticipated by several centuries.

35 Plato, *Republic,* 10.1 (2: 425). On this passage, see also Summers, *Judgment of Sense,* 42. In fact, Plato condemns both painting and poetry for their inability to communicate anything beyond the superficial appearances of things (2: 425–33). On Plato's occasionally ambivalent views of the value of painting, see Summers, 32–3.

36 For portraiture as a memento of absent love, sustained by numerous classical examples, see Alberti, *Della pittura,* 44. See Ficino, *Sopra lo amore,* 6.6, 97 for the related notion that the eye, unlike the soul, can only appreciate the physical presence of objects. Niccolò Franco laments that no portrait could ever satisfy his sight's desire to contemplate constantly his beloved Filena (*Filena,* 15v–18v).

37 Panofsky notes Plato's consistent rejection of purely imitative representation (μιμητχή τέχη), meant to render only the sensory appearance of the material world, in favour of an artistic approach that might represent the Idea of the subject (*Idea,* 3–5); however, for Bigolina, portraiture seems to be nothing but imitative representation, without any redeeming characteristics: only literature can represent the Idea.

38 Since the days of Horace's 'ut pictura poesis,' the *paragone* between literature and the other arts had always focused on verse instead of prose; this is reflected in such early modern works as Leonardo's treatises defending painting, as well as Dolce's *Dialogo della pittura,* wherein Dolce makes a point of comparing Ariosto's verses to Titian's paintings (132; see also Rosand, 'Inventing Mythologies,' 36).

39 For Giovio's portrait collection, see Barocchi, 'L'invenzione,' 3: 2865–2918, and Freedman, *Titian's Women*, 15. For an extensive bibliography of studies of Isabella's collection, as well as an analysis of the role of artworks in her private rooms, see Bourne, 'Renaissance Husbands and Wives as Patrons of Art,' 93–9, 111–12n. See also Rose Marie San Juan, 'The Court Lady's Dilemma: Isabella d'Este and Art Collecting in the Renaissance.' On the rarity of art collections maintained by women, in the context of Isabella's Grotta and Studiolo, see Brown, 'A Ferrarese Lady and a Mantuan Marchesa,' 65, and Tinagli, *Women in Italian Renaissance Art*, 125–6. On the ethical implications of the kinds of art kept by early modern women in their private spaces, see Crum, 'Controlling Women or Women Controlled? Suggestions for Gender Roles and Visual Culture in the Italian Renaissance Palace,' 37–50.

40 For Cinquecento discussions of the classical motif of viewers falling in love with works of art, see Pino, 'Dialogo di pittura,' 105, and Varchi, *Lezzione della maggioranza delle arti*, 45–6. The idea is also expressed in one of Aretino's letters (5.303). Leonardo goes so far as to defend painting for its power to excite love passion in the viewer (*Paragone*, 65). For studies of amorous arousal among viewers (or creators) of artworks, for which the Pygmalion motif is a frequently cited archetype in early modern writings, see Freedberg, *Power of Images*, 317–77; Pardo, 'Artifice as Seduction in Titian,' 44–50; and Tinagli, *Women in Italian Renaissance Art*, 124–5, 132–5. For the notion that the Pygmalion motif may become an analogue for viewer response to art, see Land, *The Viewer as Poet*, 55–6. On the negative ethical implications of Pygmalion's love for his statue according to Christine de Pizan in *Epistre Othea*, see Brown-Grant, *Christine de Pizan and the Moral Defence of Women*, 68–9. The motif of falling in love with images is also quite widespread in folklore; see Thompson, *Motif-Index of Folk Literature*, T11.2 (5: 333).

41 For Titian's use of the term *poesie* see Padoan, *Momenti del rinascimento veneto*, 362–70, and Goffen, *Titian's Women*, 107. On the contemporary vogue for having portrait sitters impersonate historical, hagiographical, legendary, or mythological figures, see Cranston, *Poetics of Portraiture*, 86–94.

42 See the numerous illustrations in Damisch's *Judgment of Paris* for examples.

43 Goffen, *Titian's Women*, 153.

44 For an extensive list of depictions of the Judgment of Paris in both literature and the visual arts see Reid, *Oxford Guide to Classical Mythology in the Arts*, 2: 821–31.

45 The fall of Troy is explicitly linked to Venus's choice in Federigo Luigini's reference to the Judgment of Paris; the ideal woman described in his

dialogue is to be compared to Venus while she stood naked at the Judgment, 'per cui arse e cadde Troia' (for whom Troy burned and fell, *Il libro della bella donna*, 45–6). For the destructive implications of Paris's judgment in Christine de Pizan's *Epistre Othea*, see Brown-Grant *Christine de Pizan and the Moral Defence of Women*, 74.

46 On this topic, see Laurie Schneider Adams, 'Iconographic Aspects of the Gaze in Some Paintings by Titian,' and Goffen, *Titian's Women*, 136–69. For Titian's masterful use of glances to convey dramatic power, see Rosand, 'Inventing Mythologies,' 41–42.

47 See Adams, 'Iconographic Aspects of the Gaze in Some Paintings by Titian,' 226–7.

48 On the tendency of Cinquecento paintings to provide a more engaged and communicative relationship between viewers and painted subjects than had been the case in earlier art, a trend that Bigolina clearly wishes to portray in fictional terms in *Urania*, see Shearman, *Only Connect*, 108–48, and Robert Williams, *Art, Theory, and Culture in Sixteenth-Century Italy*, 5–14. See Goffen, *Titian's Women*, 277–8, for the significance of painted subjects gazing at one another, oblivious to the external viewer, in Titian's works. In her study of Sofonisba Anguissola, Garrard notes that the barrier between the viewer and the viewed in northern Italian art of this time is often reduced by forthright eye contact with the viewer on the part of the painted subjects (Garrard, 'Here's Looking at Me,' 558).

49 See Land, *Viewer as Poet*, 131, for a discussion of this letter as an illustration of a central tenet of Aretino's approach to art criticism, which is to communicate the viewer's response to the sight of the work of art.

50 For a discussion of Aretino's letter to Gambara, see Freedman, *Titian's Portraits*, 69–90. For the letter to Titian, see Land, *Viewer as Poet*, 132.

51 A close parallel to Bigolina's description of the duchess may also be found in the account of Ginevra's charms in Bandello's romance novella of Don Diego (1.27); here, however, Aretino's rhetorical style is taken seriously, not parodied (Bandello, 1: 337–8).

52 For Aretino's use of hyperbolic language in such descriptions see Freedman, *Titian's Portraits*, 20–2. On Aretino's tendency to use hyperbole in general, see Waddington, *Aretino's Satyr*, 51. On Aretino's use of imperatives to heighten the 'visibility' of his ekphraseis, see Palladino, 'Pietro Aretino: Orator and Art Theorist,' 133–4. Aretino's style for describing paintings was also imitated by some of his followers; see, for example, Lodovico Dolce's letter to Alessandro Contarini concerning Titian's *Venus and Adonis* (Dolce, *Dialogo della pittura*, 210–17). For a study of Dolce's letter,

with emphasis on its rhetorical style and erotic content, see Ginzburg, 'Titian, Ovid, and Sixteenth-Century Codes for Erotic Illustration,' 28–30.

53 See Rosand, 'Titian and the Critical Tradition,' 5. In the context of the prose romance, Titian is said to be the only painter capable of capturing perfectly the beauty of a woman in Franco's *Filena* (17v).

54 Padoan notes Titian's predilection for depictions of nude women, which he deliberately sought to render more erotic than had been the tendency of previous artists, even when treating the same subjects (*Momenti del rinascimento veneto*, 363–6). Arasse calls Titian's *Venus of Urbino* 'The archetypical female nude in Western painting' ('The *Venus of Urbino*,' 91).

55 Goffen, *Titian's Women*, 157–69. Ginzburg observes that 'we cannot ignore that contemporaries viewed Titian's mythological "poems" as explicitly erotic paintings. And the artist himself would have agreed' ('Titian, Ovid,' 28). Aretino acknowledges the erotic appeal of paintings of Venus in his letters 1.9 and 2.5, as well as in 6.475, wherein he tells Charles V that the emperor can satisfy both his spiritual and corporeal needs by gazing upon two of Titian's paintings in his possession, *The Trinity* and a nude Venus.

56 Adams, 'Iconographic Aspects of the Gaze,' 237. For the role of the colour red in Titian's erotic paintings, see also Adams, 230, 231, and 233; Rogers, 'Decorum of Women's Beauty,' 65; Goffen, *Titian's Women*, 35, 37, 75; and Freedman, *Titian's Portraits*, 78, 87. Cupid is shown carrying Venus's mantle, which is likewise red, in Sustris's *Judgment of Paris* in the Galleria Sabauda of Turin, although this work is thought to have been created after 1568 and thus might not have directly influenced Bigolina; for the date of this painting see Reid, *Oxford Guide to Classical Mythology*, 824. Doody remarks that a woman's red garment might serve as an indicator of feminine wickedness in the context of medieval romance, i.e., Boccaccio's *Filocolo*, wherein the unsuspecting red-garbed Biancifiore is set up to take the fall in Massamutino's plot to commit regicide with a poisoned peacock (*True Story*, 196).

57 For a much later 'failed Titian' in a novel, the artist Pellerin in Flaubert's *L'Éducation sentimentale*, see Doody, *True Story*, 397–8.

58 For Titian's self-promotion as a new Apelles, see Freedman, 'Titian and the Classical Heritage,' 192–201, and Land, 'Poetry and Anecdote,' 216–20.

59 Goffen, *Titian's Women*, 9.

60 Early modern fascination with the Campaspe story derives from Pliny's account in *Natural History*, 35.36, 86–7. See Castiglione's *Cortigiano* 1.52, 110, and 1.53, 112, for a well-known early modern account of Campaspe, and Dolce's *Dialogo della pittura* for the story as told by the interlocutor

Aretino (104). Neither Castiglione nor Dolce has his interlocutor express disapproval for Apelles, who falls in love with the woman while painting her in the nude. On Campaspe see also Lawner, *Lives of the Courtesans*, 86–8.

61 For evidence that Titian painted his mistresses, see also Land, 'Poetry and Anecdote,' 221.

62 Lawner provides evidence for the keeping of Venus images as private icons in intimate spaces (*Lives of the Courtesans*, 88).

63 For examples of this notion, see Aretino, *Lettere*, 1.114, 3.94, 3.102, and 4.487. See also Freedman, *Titian's Portraits*, 17. On the function of portraiture as memorial in this period, see Rosand, 'The Portrait, the Courtier, and Death,' 95–7.

64 See Palladino, 'Pietro Aretino,' 173–4, and Waddington, *Aretino's Satyr*, 61–9.

65 Freedman notes that Aretino took pleasure in seeing himself portrayed in nearly every artistic medium (*Titian's Portraits*, 35). See especially Aretino's letters to Marcolini (3.124), Francesco Cusano (3.94), and Iunio Petreo (3.229). On Aretino's obsession with his own portrayal, both in his writings and in the works of artists, see Palladino, 'Pietro Aretino,' 170–5.

66 On these works, see also Bigolina, ed. Nissen, 35 and n.

67 On the symbolism of mirrors in classical and medieval literature, with emphasis on mirrors as a means of self-judgment in the works of Alan of Lille, see Bradley, 'Backgrounds of the Title *Speculum* in Medieval Literature,' 111–12, and Shapiro, 'Mirror and Portrait,' 41–2. Bigolina is not the first to place a mirror within the face of an allegorical figure for the purpose of instruction in the arts: in the *Anticlaudianus* of Alan of Lille, the seven sisters of the arts are similarly instructed by the mirror-like face of Prudence (80). For the magic 'specchio di giustizia' (mirror of justice) in the *Peregrinaggio di tre giovani figliuoli del re di Serendippo*, in which the faces of malefactors appear black, see Armeno, *Peregrinaggio*, 33.

68 See Goffen, *Titian's Women*, 67, on the symbolism of mirrors in Titian's *Allegory of Vanity*. According to Charity Willard, Christine might have adopted the mirror of Reason from Vincent de Beauvais's *Speculum Historiale* (*Christine de Pisan*, 136–7). For the symbolic associations between mirrors and the beauty of women, as depicted in the artistry of early modern household objects, see Syson and Thornton, *Objects of Virtue*, 51–2. Lawner notes the frequent association of courtesans and mirrors in this moralistic 'Vanity' genre of early modern paintings (*Lives of the Courtesans*, 74, 198–9). Oiseuse (Idleness) carries an emblematic mirror in Guillaume de Lorris's *Roman de la rose* (v. 557). For the notion of 'specularity,' the reflexive

qualities of literary discourse in medieval romance, see Maddox, *Fictions of Identity in Medieval France*, 14–20.

69 On the topic of generic portraits of women in the sixteenth century and their lack of individual identities, see Cropper, 'Beauty of Woman,' 175–81; Garrard, 'Here's Looking at Me,' 568–70; and Woods-Marsden, *Renaissance Self-Portraiture*, 192.

70 For an analysis of the 'peculiar conflation of subject and object' in this painting, see Garrard, 'Here's Looking at Me,' 556–65. Garrard notes that Campi probably never actually painted Anguissola (565). On the significance of this painting, with its 'accomplished *invenzione*,' see also Woods-Marsden, *Renaissance Self-Portraiture*, 208–10.

71 Garrard has commented on Campi's subordinate position and the subtle criticism of him that Anguissola incorporates in this painting ('Here's Looking at Me,' 561–2).

72 Garrard, 'Here's Looking at Me,' 619. This judgment is echoed by Rose, who notes that Anguissola presents herself 'like a man' in her portraits, thereby eschewing the feminine attributes that would objectify her: 'the artist brings the pictorial focus to the mastery of her art, to the process rather than to the performer' ('Mirrors of Language, Mirrors of Self,' 42).

73 On the use of the term *storia* to designate medieval Italian chivalric narratives, see Allaire, *Andrea da Barberino and the Language of Chivalry*, 6.

74 On the concept of *invenzione*, see Panofsky, *Idea*, 51–66; Lee, *Ut pictura poesis*, 17–20: Barocchi, 'L'invenzione,' 3: 2401–2; and Land, *Viewer as Poet*, 104–11. In *Dialogo della pittura . . . l'Aretino*, Dolce allows his interlocutor, Aretino, to provide a definition of the relationship between *inventione* and *historia* that closely follows that of Alberti (126–8).

75 On the topic of women as portraitists, see Woods-Marsden, *Renaissance Self-Portraiture*, 9, 192–3. See also Jacobs, 'Woman's Capacity to Create: The Unusual Case of Sofonisba Anguissola,' 96–7, and Cranston, *Poetics of Portraiture*, 117–18, for the distinction between *ritrarre* and *imitare*.

76 For judgments of Anguissola's ability, including that of Giorgio Vasari, and the claim that she transcended the putative limits on her gender, see Jacobs, 'Woman's Capacity to Create,' 74–8, and Woods-Marsden, *Renaissance Self-Portraiture*, 196.

77 Woods-Marsden, *Renaissance Self-Portraiture*, 199.

78 Alberti, *Della pittura*, 72. On this aspect of Alberti's concept of *istoria*, see Cranston, *Poetics of Portraiture*, 52.

79 Rose, 'Mirrors of Language, Mirrors of Self,' 37–46.

80 Many of these claims are evident in Alberti's heartfelt paean to painting at the beginning of Book 2 of *Della pittura* (44–6). Later he speaks of the

intrinsic goodness and honesty of painting (48). On the notion that portraiture might serve as a substitute for an absent person in the works of Alberti and others; see Cranston, *Poetics of Portraiture*, 54–67.

81 For a discussion of Aretino's use of mirrors in Maco's failed attempt at self-fashioning, see Cranston, *Poetrics of Portraiture*, 150–1, and Waddington, introduction to *La Cortigiana*, 39–41.

82 The visual and conceptual innovations of this painting are discussed by Shapiro ('Mirror and Portrait,' 44), Woods-Marsden (*Renaissance Self-Portraiture*, 133–7), and Cranston (*Poetics of Portraiture*, 140–4). For evidence that Aretino himself owned the painting for a time, see Waddington, introduction to *La Cortigiana* 41.

3 Ekphrasis and the *Paragone*

1 Achilles Tatius, *Leucippe and Clitophon*, 3–5. On the response of the viewer to Tatius's fictional artwork, see Land, *Viewer as Poet*, 54. On Tatius's ekphrasis as a source for Titian's painted mythological eroticism, see Ginzburg, 'Titian, Ovid, and Sixteenth-Century Codes for Erotic Illustration,' 30–1. For the notion that this description of the painting of Europa invites the male reader to appreciate images of female victimization throughout Tatius's work (clearly a perspective that Bigolina would be inclined to satirize), see Haynes, *Fashioning the Feminine in the Greek Novel*, 57–8.

2 For the popularity of the sixteenth-century translations of these works, see Raya, *Storia dei generi letterari*, 91–3. Although the Renaissance Italian *volgarizzamenti* of classical romances were sometimes reworked, Coccio's rendering of *Leucippe and Clitophon* (1550) does not alter or embellish the three scenes of ekphrasis (1r–4r, 34r–36v, 57r–58v).

3 On the history of the use of the term, see Golahny, *Eye of the Poet*, 11–13. Golahny provides this definition: 'As presently applied, ekphrasis designates the text that expresses the poet-reader-viewer's reaction to actual or imagined works of art' (13). For Krieger, the shield of Achilles takes on an iconic value that allows for an extended study of the role of ekphrasis in Western literature (*Ekphrasis*, xiii–xvii). For a caveat on the overuse of the term in early modern studies, see Hope and McGrath, 'Artists and Humanists,' 169.

4 'Ut pictura poesis: erit quae si propius stes / te capiat magis, et quaedam si longius abstes' (a poem is like a painting: you will find one picture will attract you more / if you stand up close, another if you stand further back), Horace, *Ars poetica*, vv 361–2. For the prevalence of this phrase in the Renaissance, see Lee, *Ut pictura poesis*, 3–5.

5 Although no actual viewers appear in the narratives, Homer's mode of description does not seem to anticipate viewer response according to Land (*Viewer as Poet*, 36).

6 Land notes two distinct responses to Virgil's ekphrasis, that of the narrator and that of Aeneas himself (*Viewer as Poet*, 38, 61).

7 Ibid., 27. For Philostratus's notion that a painting is an illusion designed to evoke a specific viewer response, see ibid., 36.

8 On the deceptive naturalism of the paintings in Boccaccio's work, and their effect on the viewer who is made to appreciate their didactic import, see ibid., 62–4.

9 On the significance of Cupid's statue in the *Filocolo*, see Hollander, *Boccaccio's Two Venuses*, 37–8, and Grossvogel, *Ambiguity and Allusion in Boccaccio's Filocolo*, 182–4.

10 On the autobiographical elements of Sannazaro's romance, see Panizza, 'The Quattrocento,' 160–1.

11 For a study of Ariosto's rhetorical strategy for communicating the content of paintings through words, see Hulse, *Rule of Art*, 1–9. See Padoan, *Momenti del rinascimento veneto*, 356, for the notion that Ariosto's ekphraseis in *Orlando furioso* are more literary and rhetorical than pictorial, and thus are meant to illustrate the superiority of poetry to figurative art. Terracina provides a commentary on the ekphrasis of Rinaldo's cup (*Orlando furioso*, 33) in her own *Discorso*, 33, in order to demonstrate the superiority of literature, which can endure forever, to visual art, which is ephemeral (53r–54r).

12 Petrarca, *Canzoniere*, 77, 78. For a discussion of these sonnets and their imitators in Bigolina's time, see Varchi, *Lezzione della maggioranza delle arti*, 37–9.

13 For an example of Aretino's influence on poets who describe paintings, see Giovanni della Casa's two sonnets on a portrait by Titian (della Casa, *Rime*, 115–18). On Aretino's different treatment of paintings of male subjects as opposed to female in his sonnets, see Rogers, 'Sonnets on Female Portraits from Renaissance North Italy,' 297, 299.

14 Freedman, *Titian's Portraits*, 22–4

15 Ibid., 33.

16 On the relationship between Aretino's *Sonetti lussuriosi* and Romano's images see Tinagli, *Women in Italian Renaissance Art*, 126–7; Talvacchia, *Taking Positions*, 12–19, 198–227 (including sonnet texts); and Waddington, *Aretino's Satyr*, 23–30.

17 Aretino, *Il ragionamento*, 23. For a description of these frescoes, with emphasis on Aretino's painted parody of hagiography (the depiction of

the life of a prostitute he calls 'Saint Nafissa'), see Lawner, *Lives of the Courtesans,* 69.

18 For the interest in art criticism among the wider public, and the concept of the 'amateur tradition,' see Kristeller, *Renaissance Thought,* 184–5; Mendelsohn, *Paragoni,* xxiii–iv; and Robert Williams, *Art, Theory, and Culture in Sixteenth-Century Italy,* 1.

19 For art theorists writing before Bigolina or contemporaneously with her who discuss *giudizio,* see Castiglione, *Cortigiano,* 1.53 (112); Pino, *Dialogo di pittura,* 96–8 and 107 (where it is said to be a central element of the faculty of *disegno*); Varchi, *Lezzione,* 62–3 (citing Vasari) and 84 (citing Michelangelo); Vasari, *Le vite de' più eccellenti architetti, pittori, et scultori italiani,* 1: 12–14; and Dolce, *Dialogo della pittura,* 100–4. The concept is treated at length in a literary context by Giraldi Cinthio, *Discorsi intorno al comporre rivisti dall'autore,* 37–42. The development of the concept of judgment from classical times to the rise of early modern art theory is amply studied by Summers throughout *The Judgment of Sense.*

20 Examples of the *paragone* between painting and sculpture or ancient art in Titian's paintings are discussed by Goffen in *Titian's Women,* 44, 51–2, 107–69, and 273, and by Rosand in *Inventing Mythologies,* 44–5. See also Tinagli, *Women in Italian Renaissance Art,* 139–40.

21 Although the term 'low intellect' might reflect mere affected modesty, it is possible that Bigolina was influenced by the neo-Aristotelianism of Varchi, which divides the rational element of the soul into *ragione superiore* (the speculative or contemplative intellect) and *ragione inferiore,* the practical and creative intellect wherein the arts and poetry are said to flourish. See Varchi, *Lezzione,* 12–13, 15, 53; and Summers, *Judgment of Sense,* 276–7, for a discussion of Varchi's notion of differing levels of activity for the intellect.

22 On the prevalence of the Aristotelian doctrine of imitation in Renaissance painting and poetry see Lee, *Ut pictura poesis,* 3–15; Panofsky, *Idea,* 47–50; Barocchi, 'L'invenzione,' 2: 1525–7; Summers, *Judgment of Sense,* 12, 189 and *passim;* and Robert Williams, *Art, Theory, and Culture, passim,* especially 37–8, 43–5, and 77–8.

23 For discussions of these terms, see Panofsky, *Idea,* 66, 118–19; Altizer, *Self and Symbolism in the Poetry of Michelangelo, John Donne, and Agrippa d'Augigné,* ix–xi; Freedman, *Titian's Portraits,* 26–9; and Robert Williams, *Art, Theory, and Culture,* 36.

24 For the notion of the 'sister arts,' see Vasari, *Le vite,* 15; Lee, *Ut pictura poesis,* 67; Praz, *Mnemosyne,* 4–5; Kristeller, *Renaissance Thought,* 182–3; and Land, *Viewer as Poet,* 5. For Dolce, the poet and painter are 'quasi fratelli' (almost brothers, *Dialogo della pittura,* 96). On Titian's efforts to paint in

the fashion of poets, see Rosand, 'Inventing Mythologies.' Hulse discusses the development of ekphrasis and the *paragone* between painting and poetry as intricate and diverse forms of knowledge in the early modern period (*Rule of Art,* 9–24). On the innovative views of the relationship between painting and poetry that came to the fore in the late sixteenth century, which Bigolina anticipates to some extent, see Bolzoni, 'The Art of Memory and the Erotic Image in 16th and 17th Century Europe,' 108–11.

25 See Kristeller, *Renaissance Thought II,* 182–3. For examples of the *paragone* between the visual arts and poetry, see Mario Equicola, Francesco d'Olanda, and Giovambattista Gelli in Barocchi, *Scritti d'arte del Cinquecento,* 1: 259–60, 277–89, as well as Varchi, *Lezzione,* 53–9; Pino, *Dialogo di pittura,* 98, 109; and Dolce, *Dialogo della pittura,* 96–104. For the *paragone* in the ekphrasis of the ancient novel, see Doody, *True Story,* 398. See Cropper, 'Beauty of Woman,' 182–90, on the poetry/painting *paragone* in the context of portraits of women.

26 Speroni, *Dialogo della rettorica,* 648–9. Padoan notes a more subtle exaltation of poetry over the figurative arts in Ariosto's descriptions of Alcina (canto 7) and Angelica (canto 10) in *Orlando furioso,* since the poet appears to show a marked preference for literary metaphors over pictorial imagery (*Momenti del rinascimento veneto,* 347–9, 356–8).

27 On self-display in *Urania,* see Nissen, 'Subjects, Objects, Authors,' 24–7.

28 For the tendency of courtesans in this period to create elaborate mythological images of themselves, including Veronica Franco's self-identification as Venus, see Lawner, *Lives of the Courtesans,* 82. A letter attributed to Margherita degli Uberti Stanga, included in Lando's *Lettere,* provides a contemporary polemical take on the subject (109v–110r). Simons observes that any hint of sexuality in an early modern woman's portrait might lead her to risk being identified as a courtesan ('Portraiture, Portrayal, and Idealizations,' 276–7). See also Garrard, 'Here's Looking at Me,' 574–5. The self-identification with Venus is also recalled in Boccaccio's *Fiammetta,* where the misguided protagonist is pleased to have been compared to 'Ciprigna Venere' (Cyprian Venus) by women at the jousts (5, 87).

29 Goffen notes that it was considered improper in Venetian circles for women, wealthy or not, to commission paintings of themselves (*Titian's Women,* 59).

30 Damisch, *Judgment of Paris,* 188. On the Judgment of Paris in the arts, see also Bull, *Mirror of the Gods,* 343–8.

31 On the pervasive references to the episode of Zeuxis and the women of Croton in Cinquecento literature, see Panofsky, *Idea,* 15, 48–9. For the notion that Cinquecento portraiture involved a balance between individual

appearances and archetypes, with Zeuxis's story as a prime example, see Simons, 'Portraiture,' 310–11. Ariosto's Olimpia is another romance character who is said to be so beautiful that Zeuxis would only have needed her for a model, and thus may have served as an inspiration to Bigolina (*Orlando furioso*, 11.71).

32 On the unlikelihood that an artist would dare to depict a distinguished woman in the nude in this period, see Jones, 'What Venus Did with Mars,' 194; Rogers, 'Decorum of Women's Beauty,' 50–2; Goffen, 'Titian's *Sacred and Profane Love* and Marriage,' 113–14; and Goffen, *Titian's Women*, 36. On the use of mythological settings to justify nudity in painting, see Tinagli, *Women in Italian Renaissance Art*, 129, 132–7, and Rosand, 'So and So Reclining on her Couch,' 50. See Freedberg, *Titian's Portraits*, 360–1, for a discussion of the topic in the context of the *paragone:* painting was seen as more of a threat to morality than poetry when it came to the depiction of nudity. Trouble could arise even when artists wanted to appropriate the likeness of highborn women for clothed religious images; see Vasari's account of Fra Filippo Lippi, who could only have Lucrezia Buti pose as a model for a painting of the Virgin with great difficulty (*Le vite*, 1: 379–80).

33 For Bigolina's Princess of Poland, see Bigolina, ed. Nissen, 197n.

34 Caruso, 'L'artista al bivio,' 169–70, and Ovid, *Heroides*, 5 (Oenone to Paris), 35–6.

35 On nudity in depictions of the Judgment of Paris, both ancient and modern, see Damisch, *Judgment of Paris*, 133–4, 191; and Bull, *Mirror of the Gods*, 346–8. The nudity of all three goddesses is stressed by Ovid in *Heroides*, 17 (Helen to Paris): 'Tres tibi se nudas exhibuere deae' (three goddesses showed themselves nude to you), 118; it is also confirmed by Boccaccio: 'Que, ut aiunt, illi se . . . remotis vestibus Paridi monstravere' (who, as they say . . . showed themselves to Paris with their clothing removed), *Genealogie deorum gentilium*, 6.22, 1: 303; see also Boccaccio's *Comedia delle ninfe fiorentine*, 31, 770, and Castiglione, *Cortigiano* 3.2. On the particular iconographic problems of both literary and pictorial representations of the Judgment, see Caruso, 'L'artista al bivio,' 164. Caruso notes that the representation of the three goddesses in paintings of the Judgment routinely followed a '2 + 1' formula: one goddess is almost always shown from behind, the other two from the front (169–70). I would add that Bigolina, too, follows this formula, albeit in her own way: two goddesses are apparently shown clothed, the other seminude.

36 On Aretino's role in reshaping the concept of judgment, see Klein, *Form and Meaning*, 163; Palladino, 'Pietro Aretino: Orator and Art Theorist,' 96–100; and Waddington, *Aretino's Satyr*, 148–9. For Aretino as a mouthpiece of Dolce in *Dialogo della pittura*, see Summers, *Judgment of Sense*, 141–3.

37 Dolce, *Dialogo della pittura*, 102, trans. Roskill, 103. For Aretino's principal pronouncements on judgment as a speaker in Dolce's dialogue, see Dolce, 100–4.

38 See Aretino's letter 2.118 (to the sculptor Leone Leoni, dated 1539) for a discussion of *giudizio* and *discrezione* in conjunction with Michelangelo's painting technique (2: 130).

39 For Aretino's *giudizi* during these years, see Luzio, introduction to Aretino's *Pronostico satirico*, ix–xiv. Aretino boasts about his earlier prediction of the Sack of Rome in the proem to the *giudizio* of 1534 (Luzio, 3). See also Talvacchia, *Taking Positions*, 18.

40 Luzio, introduction to Aretino's *Pronostico*, xiii–xv.

41 Luzio, Aretino's *Pronostico*, 1–3.

42 For the unpublished letter of 1533 in which the 'iudicium' version of the inscription appears, and the controversy over which inscription the chain actually did bear, see Luzio, Aretino's *Pronostico*, 115–19, and Procaccioli, Aretino's *Lettere*, 1: 140n. For the version including the word 'mendacium,' see Aretino's letter to Francis I of 1533 (*Lettere*, 1.36) 1: 89, and also his *giudizio* of 1534 (Luzio, 16).

43 On this letter, see Lee, *Ut pictura poesis*, 38–9, and Land, *Viewer as Poet*, 139.

44 Boccaccio, *Teseida*, 472. For a study associating this passage with Boccaccio's condemnation of the Carnal Venus, with a special emphasis on the use of the term *giudicare* (to judge), see Hollander, *Boccaccio's Two Venuses*, 60. On the problematic aspects of Paris's choice, see Wind, *Pagan Mysteries in the Renaissance*, 82, 197.

45 Sallustius, *Concerning the Gods and the Universe*, 6–7; Ficino, *The Philebus Commentary*, 482–3; Fulgentius, *Mythologiae*, 2.1. See also Damisch, *Judgment of Paris*, 150–2; Wind, *Pagan Mysteries*, 270–1; and Kristeller, *The Philosophy of Marsilio Ficino*, 358–9, wherein the contrast between Minerva and Venus is particularly stressed.

46 Sannazaro, *Arcadia*, 19–20. For a study of the rhetorical strategies employed by Sannazaro's fictional painter of this Judgment scene, who must show Venus from the back because he has already made the other two goddesses so beautiful that Venus could not possibly surpass them, see Caruso, 'L'artista al bivio,' 163–6.

47 The Judgment of Paris in Christine's *oeuvre* is discussed by Blumenfeld-Kosinski, *Reading Myth* (175–6, 193, 198–200, 211–12). Christine declares herself to be the servant of Pallas in *Autres ballades*, 7 vv 25–8 (Christine de Pizan, *Oeuvres poétiques*, 1: 215).

48 See Damisch, *Judgment of Paris*, 183–5, and Brown-Grant, *Christine de Pizan and the Moral Defence of Women*, 72–4, for the ethical implications of Paris's choice in the *Epistre Othea*.

49 On the virtuousness of those who follow Pallas (Minerva), see also
    Fulgentius, *Mythologiae* (one of five works included in the anthology
    Fulgentius the Mythographer), 2.1, wherein the goddess is said to represent
    the choice of the contemplative life in the context of the Judgment of Paris,
    and Ficino, *Sopra lo amore*, 6.1 (89). Boccaccio presents the choice between
    Venus and Minerva with a certain irony in his Christian eclogue *Comedia
    delle ninfe fiorentine;* here the nymph Mopsa, an allegory of Wisdom, offers
    the gifts of Minerva as a means of enticing a youth to love her, but only
    succeeds when she shows him her body, subsequently becoming a devotee
    of Venus (18, 727–30). However, by the end of the work it becomes clear
    that Venus, when interpreted properly, actually represents the Christian
    love of the Trinity (41–2; see also Hollander, *Boccaccio's Two Venuses*, 74–7).
50 Bigolina seems to have derived this name from an enchantress, also known
    as 'la Savia Damigella,' who appears in certain Italian chivalric romances;
    see for instance *Tristiano Panciatichiano*, chapter 92, 128. For archaic defini-
    tions of the term, see *Dizionario etimologico italiano*, 1st ed., s.v. 'damigella.'
51 Lando, *Paradossi*, 229–30, wherein the author says he heard Villamarina
    declaim Latin verse. This work, published seven times between 1543 and
    1550, could easily have been familiar to Bigolina. Lando also includes a
    letter attributed to Villamarina in his *Lettere di molte valorose donne*, which
    shows her erudition (65r–v). Terracina devotes a canto to Villamarina in
    her *Discorso*, using her as an example to refute men who claim women
    cannot give good advice (27, 44r–45r); elsewhere she calls Villamarina
    'sagace' (shrewd), 9, 17r. Della Chiesa describes Villamarina as skilled in
    astrology and able to dispute with philosophers (*Theatro delle donne let-
    terate*, 193–4). For examples of Villamarina's poems, see Croce, *Aneddoti
    di varia letteratura*, 1: 330–8. For Villamarina's courtship with Ferrante
    Sanseverino, which is rather different from the fictional one Bigolina de-
    scribes, see Cosentini, *Una dama napoletana*, 20–1. It is interesting to note
    that Villamarina was said to have contributed her likeness to a painting,
    just as Bigolina has her duchess do; however, Villamarina was not painted
    as a mythological figure, but rather in the guise of the Virgin in a church in
    Naples, with the Prince beside her as Joseph, probably by the artist Andrea
    di Salerno; see Celano, *Delle notizie del bello, dell'antico, e del curioso della città
    di Napoli*, 3.7, 15–16. If Bigolina was aware of this, she doubtless considered
    it a wiser choice for a pose.
52 For the observation that Isabella d'Este had more portraits made of her-
    self than any of her contemporaries, male or female, see Goffen, *Titian's
    Women*, 87. On the scandalous assertion by Battista Fiera that Isabella
    might have posed nude for a painting, a story that could have influenced

Bigolina's creation of the duchess, see Jones, 'What Venus Did with Mars';
Tinagli, *Women in Italian Renaissance Art*, 126; and San Juan, 'The Court
Lady's Dilemma,' 334. On the problems inherent in the identification of
subjects in women's portraiture, see Cropper, 'Beauty of Woman,' 176–9,
and Goffen, *Titian's Women*, 45–63.

53 Alberti, *Della pittura*, 3: 90. On Alberti's standards for painters, derived
from Cicero's description of the ideal orator, see Lee, *Ut pictura poesis*,
17–18. Under the influence of the Counter-Reformation, artistic treatises
after Bigolina's time sometimes enjoined painters to use good judgment as
well as their intellect in their dealings with patrons, in order to keep them
happy, but these treatises tended to presuppose that the artist was acting
in good faith; see for example Gilio, *Dialogo*, 2: 18–19; Paleotti, *Discorso intorno*, 2: 122–3; and Armenini, *De' veri precetti della pittura*, 170–1, 233–7.

54 See Vasari for the idea that a painting should represent 'la intenzione del
pittore, e non le cose che e' non pensava' (the intention of the painter, and
not the things that he was not thinking, *Le vite*, 1: 59). Bigolina, defying the
norms of artistic decorum and inherently suspicious of the role of the visual arts in society, is far less willing to ascribe such moral authority to her
own painter.

55 The notion that attitudes towards artists were changing in this period, so
that artists were now held more responsible for the moral content of their
works than ever before, is described by Summers: 'Paintings and sculptures were thus newly subject to the same moral strictures as fantasies
and cogitations or even real acts themselves. A painting, like a sensation
or an image in the mind, might encourage piety or curiosity or lust, and
the artist who made an image was as praiseworthy or blameworthy as
the image itself, as liable to salvation or damnation as the viewer who
responds to it' (*Judgment of Sense*, 274). Bigolina lends dramatic life to this
new awareness in *Urania*.

56 For the notion that the 'theatrically managed' unveiling of the *Perseus*
statue in Benvenuto Cellini's autobiography emphasizes how works of
art should be seen as mere aesthetic objects occupying their own realm of
existence, see Mirollo, *Mannerism and Renaissance Poetry*, 109. This gesture,
which Cellini takes quite seriously, is treated ironically in Bigolina's work.
On the use of painted allegorical covers that had to be removed before
certain Renaissance portraits could be observed, see Cranston, *Poetics of
Portraiture in the Italian Renaissance*, 23–4; as Cranston notes, such covers
were a symptom of the prevailing tendency to 'structure viewing as a
process of revelation.' All this may be compared to Venus's revelation of
her body in Boccaccio's *Fiammetta* (called a 'semi-striptease' by Hollander,

Boccaccio's Two Venuses, 45), as she convinces Fiammetta to indulge in self-destructive, adulterous love (1, 18–19).

57 On Erasmus's recriminations against artists who depict biblical subjects in a licentious fashion in this work, and on his tendency to reveal 'a slight bias against artists as a species,' see Panofsky, *Erasmus and the Visual Arts,* 209–10. Politi, a bishop and early opponent of Luther, condemns on religious grounds those who claim that the display of mythological artworks may be justified by a legitimate desire to admire the artist's handiwork: even if these people were to demonstrate that they have no salacious motive in gazing upon the naked limbs of Venus or Diana or on images of Bacchanalian revels, Politi declares that their interest would still reveal an inclination towards superficiality and idle curiosity ('attamen vanitas esset & curiositas,' *Disputatio de Cultu,* columns 142–3). However, even a Counter-Reformation critic as authoritarian and doctrinaire as Gabriele Paleotti, always fearful that the faithful might be led astray by inappropriate interpretation of artworks, was inclined to absolve the artist of any blame; in his first sentence he says that patrons are a far bigger problem than artists (*Discorso intorno,* 2: 122), and that ultimately the Devil is responsible for artists' errors (2: 265–7). Book III of his treatise was meant to deal with 'le pitture lascive,' but was never published; however, the table of contents does survive, bearing hints that even here Paleotti would have imputed such works to an artist's licentiousness rather than to any malicious intent to deceive (2: 505–6). For the religious nature of the Counter-Reformation polemic against nudity in the arts, see Freedberg, 'Johannes Molanus on Provocative Paintings.'

58 Emilia's pilgrimage to the Holy House of the Blessed Virgin in Loreto, which is alluded to but not explicitly described, constitutes the principal exception (162–4, 168, 274). On the possibility that Bigolina was influenced by or responded to Counter-Reformation ideologies, see Finucci, 2002, 59, and 2005, 27–8, as well as Cox, *Women's Writing in Italy,* 123–5.

59 Goffen, *Titian's Women,* 125. On the use of mythological subjects to avoid accusations of indecency in early modern art, see Talvacchia, *Taking Positions,* 129–60.

60 Cropper, 'On Beautiful Women,' 385–8.

61 Ibid., 386. Cropper also notes here that the full-length *effictio,* such as Bigolina provides, is more typical of the romance than the lyric. The standard *descriptio* elements used by Petrarca are codified as rhetorical topoi by Speroni; see *Dialogo della rettorica,* 664–5.

62 For this terminology in Cinquecento sonnets describing portraits see Rogers, 'Sonnets on Female Portraits,' 291–2. Padoan traces the development of

Ariosto's *descriptiones mulierum* (those of Alcina, Angelica, and Olimpia) from the 1516 edition of the *Furioso* to that of 1532, noting a decrease in Ariosto's use of traditional literary metaphors in the later edition, as well as a heightened sensuality which Padoan attributes both to the influence of Titian and to Ariosto's newfound appreciation of the figurative arts (*Momenti del rinascimento veneto*, 358–62).

63 Cropper, 'Beauty of Woman,' 189–90. The idea that the image of a woman is the standard for beauty in general is expressed in Castiglione, *Cortigiano*, 1.52–4 (111–12), and Pino, *Dialogo di pittura*, 93–4, and is implied throughout the dialogues on beauty of Trissino, Firenzuola, Niccolò Franco, and Luigini. For studies of this topic see Cropper, 'On Beautiful Women'; Mirollo, *Mannerism and Renaissance Poetry*, 137–40; Rogers, 'Decorum of Women's Beauty'; Goffen, *Titian's Women*, 70, 126, 131, 239; and Bettella, 'Corpo di parti.' Rogers notes that sonnets describing portraits of women tend to extol an ideal of beauty or grace, as opposed to male portraits that emphasize the traits of the individual ('Sonnets on Female Portraits,' 297, 299). Tonelli goes so far as to categorize all the beautiful female characters of the Italian chivalrous epics in terms of how they are 'painted,' and which artist's style best captures them: Boiardo's women look like Correggio's, Ariosto's like Titian's, etc. (*L'amore nella poesia*, 169).

64 On the description of Emilia in the *Teseida*, see Cropper, 'On Beautiful Women,' 387; Bettella, *The Ugly Woman*, 84–6; and Gambera, 'Women and Walls,' 59–65.

65 For Alcina as an archetype of the literary description of the beautiful woman, see Dolce, *Dialogo della pittura*, 130–2.

66 Bettella, 'Corpo di parti,' 320.

67 Ibid., 320–5. Phileto too, in Corfino's romance, describes himself as having seen Medusa, when he concludes his description of the beautiful Euphrosine (*Phileto*, 30).

68 On the duality of the interlocutors in Leone's dialogue, and their possible interpretations, see Forno, 'Il "libro animato," ' 121–2.

69 On the rivalry between Aretino and Franco, see Waddington, *Aretino's Satyr*, 101–3.

70 On Buona's role in this dialogue, see Cox, 'Seen but Not Heard,' 391.

71 For a study of the Italian mock encomia, including the works of Berni, Firenzuola, Aretino, and others, see Bettella, *The Ugly Woman*, 82–127.

72 For an account of the role of women in Firenzuola's dialogue, see Smarr, *Joining the Conversation*, 14–16.

73 Boccaccio also changes the names of his tale tellers, to preserve their honour (*Decameron*, Introduction, 1: 29–30).

74 For studies of Urania's role in this episode, see Nissen, 'Motif of the Woman in Male Disguise,' 210–12, and Finucci, 2005, 24–30.

75 Firenzuola, *Dialogo della bellezze delle donne*, 587. For the translation, see Firenzuola, *On the Beauty of Women*, trans. Eisenbichler and Murray, 60. All translations of Firenzuola will be from this edition.

76 Rogers, 'Decorum of Women's Beauty,' 55.

77 Once more, it is essential to distinguish Bigolina's satire of this topos from those of rustic poets and followers of Berni who mock the traditional *descriptio mulieris* by deliberately presenting descriptions of unattractive women, as catalogued by Bettella in *The Ugly Woman*, cited above. Bigolina's satire involves a description of an *exceedingly attractive woman*.

78 Luigini, declaring that teeth should be described as pearls, provides an extensive list of examples from the works of various poets to prove his point (*Il libro della bella donna*, 28). See also Niccolò Franco, *Dialogo*, 36v.

79 Cropper, 'On Beautiful Women,' 389. The decorousness of the closed mouth in the blazon of female beauty is also suggested by Boccaccio in the *Comedia delle ninfe fiorentine;* although here the teeth of the two nymphs, hidden by their lips, are not described as pearls, nor are painted images explicitly evoked (9, 701–2).

80 Panofsky notes, in his study of Titian's *Sacred and Profane Love*, that the pairing of a clothed Venus with a nude one in a work of art 'was demonstrably familiar to a group of humanists and artists closely connected with Titian's own circle' (*Studies in Iconology*, 153). Bigolina might well have derived her own inspiration from her evident familiarity with these artists. On the controversy over Panofsky's assertion that *Sacred and Profane Love* depicts the two Venuses and is meant to be interpreted Neoplatonically, see Rosand, 'So and So Reclining on Her Couch,' 44–6. For the two Venuses, see also Bull, *Mirror of the Gods*, 192–3.

81 Boccaccio describes the two Venuses in *Genealogie deorum gentilium*, 3.22 and 3.23. Some Renaissance Neoplatonists are more inclined to ascribe lasciviousness to the Carnal Venus than is Ficino. Leone Ebreo acknowledges her generative function, but finds her morally problematic (*Dialoghi d'amore*, 129–33), whereas Betussi provides a radically dualistic view of the two Venuses (*Raverta*, 30). On Boccaccio's types of Venus, see also Rubin, 'Seductions of Antiquity,' 29–30.

82 For Ficino's two Venuses, see *Sopra lo amore*, 2.7, 6.5, 6.7–8 (39–40, 95, 99–103). On the two Venuses see also Panofsky, *Studies in Iconology*, 141–2 and 147–8, and Mendelsohn, *Paragoni*, 78, 246n. On the Venuses in *Urania* see Nissen, 'Subjects, Objects, Authors,' 25, 31n; Nissen, 'Giulia Bigolina

la prima romanziera italiana,' 62; as well as Bigolina, ed. Nissen, 37, and Finucci, 2002, 50.

83 Marion A. Wells notes the tension inherent in Ficino's scheme, given that both love of the body and love of the soul are said to derive from the sight of corporeal beauty, and yet love of the body is perforce still suspect; indeed Ficino ascribes something akin to the disease of love-melancholy to excessive love for the beauty of the body; see Wells, *Secret Wound*, 52–3.

84 Pico, *Commento sopra una canzone d'amore*, 105–6, 152–5. On Pico's Venuses, see also Panofsky, *Studies in Iconology*, 144–5n.

85 Firenzuola, *Dialogo*, 566. Italian has two adjectives that derive from the name Venus, *venusto* (referring to an idealized concept of beauty) and *venereo* (meaning sensual, lustful, lascivious, or venereal). For Firenzuola, the first clearly pertains to the Celestial Venus, whereas the second (the only one having a cognate in current English usage) designates the Carnal Venus.

86 For this aspect of the *Fiammetta*, see the Prologue (3–4), chapter 1 (25), chapter 5 (58), and especially the envoi addressed to the book itself (chapter 9, 157–9).

87 On the topic of 'literary reflectivity' in the *Filocolo*, see Grieve, *Floire and Blancheflor and the European Romance*, 123–33. For the *Filocolo* as both literary object and 'galeotto,' see also Kirkham, *Fabulous Vernacular*, 76–134.

88 Grossvogel, *Ambiguity and Allusion*, 243–4.

4 The Sight of the Beautiful

1 On the pervasive early modern interest in psychological or sense theory, see Park, 'Organic Soul,' 457–8. For overviews of Renaissance love dialogues see Forno, 'Il "libro animato," ' 113–24; Vianello, *Il 'giardino' delle parole*, 9–72; and Cox, *Renaissance Dialogue*.

2 This debate, which mostly grew out of Aristotle's pronouncements on the soul, is summarized by Knowles (*Evolution of Medieval Thought*, 206–18), and by Douglas in the context of one of the last of the Aristotelian scholastics, Pietro Pomponazzi (*Philosophy and Psychology of Pietro Pomponazzi*, 140–70).

3 On the efforts of the bishop of Padua in 1489 to suppress the debates among the Averroists of the university concerning the unity of the intellect, see Nardi, *Saggi sull'aristotelismo padovano*, 153–5. For the role of Padua in the development of Italian secular Aristotelianism see also Kristeller, *Renaissance Thought II*, 117–18, and Randall, introduction to Pomponazzi's *On the Immortality of the Soul*, 258–60.

4 For a study of the internal and external senses and their relationship to the process of judgment, see Summers, *Judgment of Sense*, 27–8.

5 Reisch, *Margarita philosophica nova*, 2.10.2–4 (484–6); Pomponazzi, *Pomponatius in libros de anima*, 126–32. For the wax impression simile in Aristotle, see *De anima*, 2.12, 137. Reisch adopts the same simile in 2.11.3 (510). According to Summers, Aristotle's simile emphasizes his materialist definition of sensation, as opposed to an early modern tendency to link sensation to interior visions, which implies a role for judgment in the process of sensation (*Judgment of Sense*, 27).

6 Castiglione likewise stresses, in terms not dissimilar to Bigolina's, the complete reliance of imagination on the external senses (*Cortigiano*, 4.67, 328). See Land, *Viewer as Poet*, for the notion that imagination sometimes referred to the capacity of the soul to create (or even 'paint') internal images when stimulated by the senses (19–20).

7 For the tendency of both psychology and ethics to combine with other disciplines, and thus transcend cloistered academic debate (especially in conjunction with the widespread use of printing after 1500), see Park, 'Organic Soul,' 457.

8 For Pomponazzi the will strives towards the Good, but he does not mention the Beautiful in this context: 'Obiectum re formale intellectus est Ens, et verum obiectum voluntatis est Bonum' (the object of the intellect as a thing of substance is Being, and the true object of the will is the Good; *Pomponatius in libros de anima*, 126). For Pomponazzi's concept of the soul as essentially material, even as it participates in immateriality, see Douglas, *Philosophy and Psychology*, 217–18. For the typically Averroistic notion of the distinction between the material, mortal 'cogitative' soul and the purely spiritual (and therefore deathless) 'possible Intellect' see Nardi, *Saggi sull' aristotelismo*, 180–1; Randall, introduction to Pomponazzi's *Immortality*, 260–1; and Kessler, 'Intellective Soul,' 489. Bigolina herself is indifferent to the Aristotelian subdivisions of the intellect into such entities as 'possible,' 'cogitative,' or 'active,' which were much discussed in the academies: for her, there is only one intellect, an immaterial thing that is apparently unique to each individual. The idea of the immaterial soul is also expressed in one text that Bigolina clearly knew, Christine de Pizan's *Livre de la cité des dames* (1.9).

9 On Aristotle's codification of women as inherently inferior in *De generatione animalium*, see Maclean, *Renaissance Notion of Women*, 8–9, 28–46.

10 According to Panofsky, this mid-sixteenth-century art concept, distantly derived from the Platonic theory of Ideas, was most clearly expressed by Vasari in the 1568 edition of the *Vite* (*Idea*, 60–3).

11 Aristotle, *De sensu*, 219. The notion is also reflected in Speroni's *Dialogo della rettorica*, wherein rhetoric and poetry, the arts best suited to delight the intellect–'arti delle parole, istrumenti dell'intelletto' (arts of words, instruments of the intellect) – are said to enter the body through the ears (649).

12 For Ficino's view that all earthly beauty ultimately derives from God and the supernal realm of Ideas, see Kristeller, *Philosophy of Marsilio Ficino*, 266–9.

13 In terms of the *paragone*, Bigolina's views are exactly opposite to those of Leonardo da Vinci, who denigrates hearing (and thus poetry) in order to exalt sight as the 'miglior senso' (better sense, *Paragone*, 237).

14 Such a view is also sustained by the classical Neoplatonist Plotinus in the *Enneads*: 'Beauty addresses itself chiefly to sight; but there is a beauty for hearing too' (1.6, 56).

15 For a study of the role of the senses in Ficino's dialogue, with emphasis on the implications of the division between higher and lower senses, see Musacchio, 'Role of the Senses in Mario Equicola's Philosophy of Love,' 89–91. See also Kristeller, *Philosophy of Marsilio Ficino*, 265–6.

16 For Cattani's references to the Venuses and types of beauty, see also *I tre libri d'amore*, 55 and 85–8.

17 On Bembo's efforts to evoke the egalitarian tone of Petrarca's *Canzoniere* in the *Asolani*, and thereby make Neoplatonic notions more accessible to a non-academic audience that might also include women, see Vianello, *Il 'giardino,'* 29–30. On the role of women in Bembo's dialogue, see also Smarr, *Joining the Conversation*, 10–14.

18 For an early source for the story of Stesichorus, see Plato, *Phaedrus*, 460–3.

19 For Cicero's influence on Quattrocento dialogues, see Marsh, *Quattrocento Dialogue*, 2–23. For the concept of debate *in utramque partem* see also Cox, *Renaissance Dialogue*, 62–3. Vianello notes the lack of true dialectic, and therefore any single voice of authority, in Bembo's *Asolani* (*Il 'giardino,'* 28). For the notion that all three of the male speakers in the *Asolani* reflect different (and to some extent, equally valid) attitudes of Bembo himself, see Scrivano, 'Nelle pieghe del dialogare bembesco,' 107.

20 For a comparison between Castiglione and Bigolina with regard to the topos of the book as portrait, see Finucci, 2002, 94n. Saccone provides a useful summary of the many studies of Castiglione's motif of portraiture, as well as his own analysis of the *Cortigiano* as both treatise and portrait ('Portrait of the Courtier in Castiglione,' 329–30).

21 However, according to Padoan, this passage shows Castiglione's distrust of painting as the art form least able to provide a true portrait (*Commedia rinascimentale veneta*, 354). For a study of Castiglione's 'portrait' and the notion of the commemoration of the dead in Renaissance portraiture, see Rosand, 'The Portrait, the Courtier, and Death.'

22 On the implications of Apelles's ability to capture idealized feminine beauty in Castiglione's story of Campaspe, see Cropper, 'Beauty of Woman,' 181.

23 In this regard Bigolina may have been influenced by Speroni, who asserts that the arts of rhetoric and poetry bring more delight to the intellect through the ears than music (*Dialogo della rettorica*, 649).

24 See Musacchio, ' Role of the Senses,' 94–5, for a discussion of the materialistic aspects of Equicola's essentially Aristotelian view of the soul, as well as his appreciation of the soul's ability to partake in sensual experience, which stands at odds with Ficino's Neoplatonism. On the differences between the Aristotelian and Neoplatonic views of the soul's relationship to lower bodily appetites in the context of Renaissance dialogues, see Russell and Merry, introduction to *Dialogue on the Infinity of Love*, 31, and Buranello, 'Figura meretricis,' 59–60.

25 For an extended passage in Melechini's dialogue that is closely paraphrased, when not cited verbatim, from the opening passages of Leone's *Primo dialogo* concerning the definition of love, see Besançon, Bibliothéque Municipale MS. 597 57v–66r (corresponding to Leone, *Dialoghi*, 5–13). Melechini gives the part of Filone to his speaker Coraro, while the speakers Bigolina and Perenotto take turns repeating the words of Sofia. On Bigolina as speaker in Melechini's dialogue, see Bigolina, ed. Nissen, 17–19, and Finucci, 2002, 19, 35–6.

26 On the realistic and allegorical characteristics of Leone's Sofia, see Smarr, *Joining the Conversation*, 16, 20, 114.

27 On the classical origins of Leone's views, see Summers, *Judgment of Sense*, 33–4.

28 Speroni, *Dialogo d'amore*, 2: 538–9. Speroni also employs alimentary metaphors in his description of how the intellect appreciates the arts of painting and music in *Dialogo della rettorica* (677). For Pliny's anecdote, see *Natural History*, 8.54 (3: 91). For Titian's adoption of this image as a symbol of his ability to create an art that can surpass nature, see Garrard, ' "Art More Powerful Than Nature," ' 243–7. See Bigolina, ed. Nissen, 94, for her own use of alimentary metaphor.

29 On the possible links between Speroni and Bigolina, see Finucci, 2002, 22, 36–7, and Bigolina, ed. Nissen, 44.

30 Finucci notes that Bigolina embraces Speroni's view of the inherent infe-
riority of portrait painting in this passage, but does not address the part
exalting Titian (2005, 83n). For an analysis of Speroni's passage in conjunction with Titian's reputed ability to outdo nature in his art, see Garrard,
' "Art More Powerful Than Nature," ' 242.

31 Aretino, *Lettere*, 2.445. On the somewhat libertine roles of courtesan poets
such as Baffa and d'Aragona in love dialogues, as opposed to Bigolina's
more discreet participation in Melechini's *A ragionar d'amore*, see Finucci,
2002, 35–6, and 2005, 9; on this aspect of the courtesan poets see also
Russell and Merry, introduction to *Dialogue on the Infinity of Love*, 32. Baffa's
role here stands at odds with that of Leonora, another of Betussi's female
dialogue participants, who is described as a lover of wisdom (Betussi,
Leonora, 308), and who plays a leading role in the conversations over which
she presides.

32 In his *Leonora*, Betussi appears to give equal status to sight and hearing, the
only two external senses (as opposed to the internal sense of mind) that
can participate in the appreciation of true beauty (336–7).

33 See especially Michelangelo's sonnet 'Non ha l'ottimo artista alcun concetto' and his madrigal 'Sì come per levar, donna, si pone' *(Rime)*.

34 The exaltation of the powers of portraiture to delight the sense of sight, so
evident in Aretino's *Lettere*, is also reflected in Speroni's *Dialogo della rettorica*: here Speroni compares oratory to a noble painting of the truth that
delights our minds, just as the sense of sight is accustomed to take delight
in real portraits ('de' ritratti materiali suol dilettarsi la vista,' 680).

35 On d'Aragona's role as interlocutor in her own dialogue, see Russell and
Merry, introduction to *Dialogue on the Infinity of Love*, 32–41, and Smarr,
Joining the Conversation, 106–7, 111–17, as well as Curtis-Wendtland,
'Conversing on Love.' For her role in Speroni's *Dialogo d'amore*, see
Buranello, '*Figura meretricis*,' 54–63, and Smarr, 106–11.

36 'Tu déi sapere, figliuola, che comunemente niuno amare possiamo, se
prima agli occhi nostri non piace; onde la prima cosa che si dee fare da
chi innamorar si vuole debba essere il cercar di persona la quale aggradi
agli occhi suoi.' (You must know, daughter, that we usually cannot love
someone unless first he pleases our eyes; therefore the first thing that must
be done by someone who wishes to fall in love is seek out the person who
gives pleasure to her eyes'): Gottifredi, *Specchio d'amore*, 254.

37 In this regard Bigolina finds something of a kindred spirit in the epi-
grammatist Andrea Alciati, whose emblem numbered 188, 'Mentem, non
formam, plus pollere' (The mind, not beauty, is the more worthy; trans.
J. Moffitt), is accompanied by an illustration of a fox contemplating a very

naturalistically rendered simulacrum of a human head, only to note that even though it looks so perfect, it has no brain, and thus no real value (*Book of Emblems*, 219). As Bigolina does in *Urania*, Alciati diminishes the importance of beauty by presenting it in the form of a mere effigy.

38 According to Carlo Ginzburg, the senses were often associated with specific sins in confession manuals; however, condemnations of the sense that facilitated the sin of lust did not emphasize sight over touch until the later sixteenth century, when the widespread printing of sensual images began to be regarded as a grave problem ('Titian, Ovid, and Sixteenth-Century Codes for Erotic Illustration,' 32–3). Once more, it would seem that Bigolina anticipates a trend. On the ethical implications of the contrasting types of gaze inspired by art images, especially images of Venus, see Rubin, 'Seductions of Antiquity,' 36–8.

39 Lynn Lawner has remarked upon the Renaissance tendency to regard the sight of beauty, especially as it is embodied in the visual arts, as a civilizing influence: 'Much of Renaissance art could be termed a "defense of Phryne" (i.e. the Greek courtesan who posed nude as Venus for Praxiteles and Apelles) in the sense that the display of physical beauty becomes one of man's highest purposes' (*Lives of the Courtesans*, 93).

40 Lacan, *Four Fundamental Concepts of Psycho-Analysis*, 84.

41 Junkerman, 'Lady and the Laurel,' 52. As I have argued elsewhere, Junkerman's notion that Giorgione's painting seems to illustrate the perils of the literary woman who might choose the wrong mode of self-display may be profitably compared to Bigolina's creation of her authorial persona in *Urania* (Nissen, 'Subjects, Objects, Authors,' 25–7).

42 See Goffen, *Titian's Women*, 133–6.

43 See ibid., 115. Here Goffen observes that Titian was constantly motivated by the various *paragoni* between the arts, throughout his career.

44 Goffen emphasizes this aspect in these specific works; see *Titian's Women*, 39, 45, 79, 148.

45 On this topic see Adams, 'Iconographic Aspects of the Gaze in Some Paintings by Titian,' 225–6.

46 In 'Artemisia and Susanna,' Garrard observes, 'Few artistic themes have offered so satisfying an opportunity for legitimized voyeurism as Susanna and the Elders' (149). The same could well be said of the Judgment of Paris.

47 Stampa, *Rime*, 55 ('Voi che 'n marmi, in colori, in bronzo, in cera') and 56 ('Ritraggete poi me da l'altra parte').

48 On Henri's visit to Franco, and her commemoration of the event in writing, see Rosenthal, *Honest Courtesan*, 102–11.

49 Veronica Franco, *Lettere*, 30; trans. Jones and Rosenthal, 24.

50 Veronica Franco, *Lettere*, 69; trans. Jones and Rosenthal, 37. On the portraits of Franco described by the poet, see Croce, *Aneddoti di varia letteratura*, 2: 1–11.
51 Veronica Franco, *Lettere*, 32; trans. Jones and Rosenthal, 27–8.

5 Kissing the Wild Woman

1 Nancy Vickers finds a similar notion of the fearful otherness implicit in the sight of a reflected image in the context of Ovid's Actaeon ('Body Remembered,' 107).
2 For wild people in Thompson's *Motif-Index of Folk Literature*, see motifs B240.3, D92, D812.9, D1719.2, F567, F567.1, F610.1, F611.1.3, G671, G672, M301.1, P55, R1, and T93.1. Bartra notes that medieval writers tended to avoid theological explanations for wild men, preferring instead to describe them in psychological or sociological terms: they were not made wild by God, but rather by circumstance (*Wild Men in the Looking Glass*, 90). See also Bernheimer, *Wild Men in the Middle Ages*, 8–9, and 19. On medieval speculation concerning the souls of wild people and their potential for redemption, see White, *Tropics of Discourse*, 161–5. Vitullo discusses the more permanent type of wild man as a stock character in medieval Italian epics (*Chivalric Epic in Medieval Italy*, 51–61).
3 On the wild man's classical origins, see Bartra, *Wild Men*, 12–36. Classical naturalists such as Pliny often described the exotic human types said to live in distant lands, the so called Plinian races (Friedman, *Monstrous Races in Medieval Art and Thought*, 7). For medieval associations with demons or witches, see Bartra, 118–24.
4 On the role of wild folk in festivals, plays, and pageants, with special emphasis on a famous description of a festival that occurred in Padua in 1208, see Bernheimer, *Wild Men*, 50–84. Even in the revived Carnival celebrations in Venice, which began in the 1980s, I have seen numerous 'wild men' wearing costumes made of myriad strips of black plastic to simulate a shaggy coat of fur. See Bartra, *Wild Men*, 104, for the role of the wild figures in heraldry.
5 Janet Smarr has noted a similar moral distinction between the sexes in Marguerite de Navarre's *Heptaméron;* here women are said to be more civilized than men on account of the latter's tendency to view violence and lust as virtues (*Joining the Conversation*, 197–8).
6 The motif of the despondent hero who adopts a wild life dates back to the mid-twelfth century at least, to the experiences of Merlin in Geoffrey of Monmouth's *Vita Merlini;* however, Merlin grieves for his dead brothers, not a lost love. On the psychic element of romance, and its associations

with feminine love-melancholy in the context of the *Orlando furioso*, see Wells, *Secret Wound*, 97–8. The motif of the rejected male lover who seeks voluntary exile as a means of overcoming love-melancholy also appears in the Italian novella tradition, established therein by Boccaccio's tale of Tedaldo degli Elisei (*Decameron*, 3.7); see also Parabosco's novella of Gilberto, *I diporti*, 2.2. In both of these stories, the lover eventually resolves his crisis by returning to his native city in disguise, just as Urania does.

7 Segre, *Fuori del mondo*, 91–3. Segre also provides a list of romance characters who exhibit this behaviour, including some motivated by other emotional stresses besides love (*Fuori del mondo*, 91).

8 Chrétien de Troyes, *Yvain*, in *Oeuvres*, 407, vv 2798–9. For the link between this episode and the medieval medical notion that sufferers from melancholy tend to seek solitude, see Duggan, *Romances of Chrétien de Troyes*, 162.

9 Bartra, *Wild Men*, 136. For the episode of Yvain's wildness, see Chrétien de Troyes, *Oeuvres*, 407–12, vv 2804–3021. On the implications of Yvain's wildness see also Le Goff, *Medieval Imagination*, 114–31, and Duggan, *Romances*, 158–64. The protagonist of the twelfth-century French romance *Partonopeu de Blois*, overcome with shame at having angered his lover, likewise lives as an animal in the woods until he is rescued (vv 5499–6067).

10 See *Roman de Tristan en prose*, ed. Curtis, 3: 871, for Tristan's initial mad scene, after he has come to imagine that Iseut has betrayed him. See *Roman de Tristan en prose*, ed. Ménard, 1.168, for the continuation of the narrative, including a description of Tristan as a wild man who eats raw meat and is so changed that he is unrecognizable. The episode of this character's madness in the *Tristano Panciatichiano*, which is more amply developed than the corresponding scene in the French prose romance (*Tristano*, 294–8, 310–14), is described extensively throughout Heijkant's article 'Tristan pilosus.'

11 For the characteristics of Tristan's madness in the *Folie* texts, see Segre, *Fuori del mondo*, 89–90, and Heijkant, 'Tristan pilosus,' 241.

12 Petrarca, *Canzoniere*, sonnet 35, v.1. On the poet's recurring search for solitude in wild places, and its often illusory benefits, see Radcliffe-Umstead, 'Petrarch and the Freedom to Be Alone,' 236–7.

13 For the prevalence in the Italian novella of the motif of the disappointed lover who becomes a wild man in the woods, see Rotunda, *Motif-Index of the Italian Novella in Prose*, 188 (motif T93.1).

14 Segre, *Fuori del mondo*, 91–2. Heijkant also applies these dichotomies to Tristano in the *Tristano Panciatichiano* ('Tristan pilosus,' 240).

15 The first three books of Bandello's *Novelle*, including 186 stories, were published in Lucca in 1554, roughly the time when Bigolina was composing *Urania*.

16 On the lack of narrative unity in this tale's 'vasta trama' (vast plot), see Porcelli, *La novella del Cinquecento*, 34.

17 Bandello, *Opere*, 1: 353. The recognition by hairy birthmark is a standard feature of medieval romance; see *Le roman dou roi Flore et de la belle Jehanne*, 421–2, and Boccaccio's story of Zinevra, whose name is a variant of Ginevra and thus might have served as an inspiration to Bandello (*Decameron*, 2.9; 1: 291, 292); see also Feliciano's 'Justa Victoria' (xviii). On the links between Boccaccio's Zinevra and Urania see Nissen, 'Motif of the Woman in Male Disguise,' 210–14.

18 On the topic of the special sufferings of lovers endowed with a 'gentle heart,' in the context of the poetry of the *dolce stil novo*, see Valency, *In Praise of Love*, 234, 245.

19 Boccaccio, *filocolo*, 4.17, 323–4, and *Decameron*, Introduction, 1: 40–2; Bembo, *Asolani*, 1.4–5.

20 Ariosto, *Orlando furioso*, 32.35. On the parallels between Bradamante's experiences and those of Urania, see Finucci, 2002, 112n, 127–8n.

21 Bigolina, ed. Nissen, 108, 132. Fileno too, in Boccaccio's *Filocolo*, releases his reins and allows his horse to wander for a time (3.33, 243–4).

22 Ariosto, *Orlando furioso*, 32.69; Bigolina, ed., Nissen, 162–4.

23 Bigolina, ed. Nissen, 40. Indeed, many participants in the sixteenth-century quarrels over the propriety of romance thought it was indecorous for a distinguished nobleman such as Orlando to be depicted as insane for love; see Scordilis Brownlee, 'Cervantes as Reader of Ariosto,' 220–1. However, readers of the time would have recognized that Ariosto's ironic vision could not possibly have been transferred effectively to Bigolina's female protagonist.

24 Wells, *Secret Wound*, 98. On romance love-melancholy as hysteria, see also Wells, 23, 103.

25 Ovid, *Remedia amoris*, 193, trans. J.H. Mozley. Ovid's notion that exertions can cure lovesickness is also evoked by Boccaccio's Fiammetta in chapter 3 of the *Fiammetta* (44), while in Corfino's *Phileto* the protagonist likewise decides to travel to ease the grief of exile from his beloved (61).

26 On the hairiness of the wild protagonist in the *Tristano Panciatichiano*, which contrasts with analogous episodes in the older French texts from which this work derives, see Heijkant, 'Tristan pilosus,' 241–2. On the hairiness of both romance and hagiographic wild people, see Nissen, 'Hagiographic Romance.'

27 For the wild behaviour of this saint, see Charles Allyn Williams, 'Oriental Affinities of the Legend of the Hairy Anchorite,' 10–12; Bartra, *Wild Men*, 73–5; and Heijkant, 'Tristan pilosus,' 240–1.

28 Nissen, 'Motif of the Woman in Male Disguise,' 211–13.

29 Trans. Musa and Bondanella, 98.

30 Trans. Musa and Bondanella, 99.

31 Segre notes that darkened skin is a common element in the romance process of becoming unrecognizable (*Fuori del mondo*, 91). Boccaccio doubtless
mentions it in the case of his wild woman in order to emphasize the degree
of her transformation, since it violates the standard aesthetic of the literary
description of the lovely woman, whose skin was ever as white as snow
or alabaster. On the significance of Beritola's wild characteristics, and their
comparison with those of characters in romance and hagiographic narratives, see Nissen, 'Hagiographic Romance.' Boccaccio provides a similar
account of a marooned character, Archimenide, who is reduced to a wild
existence until he is rescued in *Comedia delle ninfe fiorentine*, 38, 809–10.

32 On the tendency of certain literary wild men, such as the protagonist of the
Tristano Panciatichiano, to eat herbs instead of meat, see Heijkant, 'Tristan
pilosus,' 240–1; in this respect, Beritola is not entirely unique.

33 On the ambiguities implicit in the characters of both the prince and
Clorina, see Bigolina, ed. Nissen, 38–9, and n.

34 Stith Thompson calls the contest for the hand of a princess, with tasks
assigned to the suitors (motif H335), 'one of the most usual situations in
folktales' (*The Folktale*, 153). However, as in certain other plot situations,
Bigolina makes a point of reversing the genders of the characters involved.
See Thompson, *Motif-Index*, 105–8, for folkloristic motifs involving tasks
or quests, and also Rotunda, *Motif-Index of the Italian Novella*, 22, for these
motifs in the Italian novella tradition.

35 *Inferno*, 33, v. 58. For possible sources for this scene, see also Bigolina, ed.
Nissen, 233n and 235n.

36 Bernheimer describes the rise of artistic depictions of wild people in idyllic
family groups in the late Quattrocento and early Cinquecento: hirsute husbands are typically shown returning with game to their wives and children
in caves or sylvan settings, or else wild couples are portrayed as revelling
in their natural existence (*Wild Men*, 155–8). Bigolina's creation of a loyal
and loving wild couple seems to reflect this trend.

37 Bartra summarizes the medieval view of the place of the wild man that
Bigolina would seem to have inherited: 'The environment, the *habitat*,
of the wild man was made up of that unique and slippery notion of nature that medieval culture recreated from the Greeks. Nature was not
simply the sum of animal, mineral, and vegetable: it was a space
invented by culture to establish a network of significations supposedly
external to society, but which permitted reflection upon the meaning of
history and the life of men on earth ... The wild man preserved a relationship with nature that, by analogy, prescribed a canon of social and

psychological behavior: he fused or confounded himself with its sylvan surroundings. He was a natural man, symmetrically opposed to the social Christian man' (*Wild Men*, 96). On this subject see also White, *Tropics of Discourse*, 165–8.

38 Padoan finds this same theme of the lover's need for courage, ultimately descended from Boccaccio, in two sixteenth-century comedies, Bernardo Dovizi da Bibbiena's *Cassaria*, and *l'Anconitana* by Bigolina's fellow Paduan Beolco (*Momenti del rinascimento veneto*, 281).

39 Bernheimer refers to depictions of Luxuria as a hairy hag with pendulous breasts, as in the twelfth-century abbey church in Moissac (*Wild Men*, 39). However, emblem 72 in Alciati's *Emblemata* describes Luxuria as a very masculine faun, with the supposedly aphrodisiac colewort entwined around his head: 'Immodicae Veneris symbola certa refert' (He provides certain symbols of unbridled Venus; *Book of Emblems*, 91). Thus, Luxuria could be depicted as either a wild woman or a wild man, and indeed Bigolina herself has the lusty reprobate Menandro take the form of a faun in Fabio's dream (ed. Nissen, 242).

40 Indeed, Alciati's emblem for 'Natura' is Pan, of whom he says that the goatlike lower regions symbolize the propagation of the human species through copulation, in the fashion of animals (emblem 97, *Book of Emblems*, 117). For Alciati, the very image of nature was a wild man whose god-like virtues, confined to his upper half, could never completely dominate his bestial lower half. This is the usual pattern of Greek mythological anthropomorphism, with the human part uppermost and the animal part below; see also the vision of Clorina as a serpent-woman in Fabio's dream; Bigolina, ed. Nissen, 242.

41 Although Bigolina's wild woman shows great devotion to her mate, she is also said to be inordinately fond of men in general ('imperciò ch'ella smisuratamente dietro gli huomini si struggeva,' Bigolina, ed. Nissen, 236).

42 In folktales, kissing most often occurs in the contex of breaking enchantments in order to liberate someone from a repulsive transformation; see Thompson, *The Folktale*, 98, and von Franz, *Psychological Meaning of Redemption Motifs in Fairytales*, 115. Boiardo provides an example of this in *Orlando innamorato*, when Brandimarte must overcome fear in order to kiss a fearsome serpent, which is then transformed into the fairy Febosilla (II, 26.4–14). This motif may have provided some inspiration to Bigolina. For the classical notion (subsequently adopted by Christian moralists) that kissing, as a sign of *passio amoris* (love passion), was a particularly feminine characteristic, leading to a 'derangement of faculties' and thus unworthy of a man, see Perella, *The Kiss Sacred and Profane*, 88–9. It would seem that

Bigolina regards the Femina Salvatica's unrestrained kissing in similar terms: such behaviour is appropriate only for a 'wild woman.' See Charles Allyn Williams, 12–15, for the ancient pagan motif of sexual union with a wild man as a means to break an enchantment, which may have some affinities here.

43 Trans. Roche-Mahdi, Heldris, *Silence*, 275.

44 On this likelihood, see Roche-Mahdi's note to line 3559 (Heldris, *Silence*, 325).

45 Heldris, *Silence*, 306–8. For an analogous scene of the wild Merlin laughing because he knows of a queen's hidden adultery, see Geoffrey of Monmouth, *Vita Merlini*, 65.

46 Straparola, *Le piacevoli notti*, 4.1, 1: 249. For the influence of Straparola on Bigolina, see Bigolina, ed. Nissen, 33–4 and n. Donato Pirovano, Straparola's most recent and authoritative editor, does not mention *Silence* in his note on the sources of the tale of Costanza/Costanzo, despite the evident parallels (1: 246n).

47 Straparola, *Piacevoli notti*, 1: 260, and Bigolina, ed. Nissen, 232–4 and n, 40–1n.

48 For additional examples of this motif in narratives by Boccaccio and others, see Nissen, 'Motif of the Woman in Male Disguise,' 203–5.

49 For the influence of Straparola, *Piacevoli notti*, 5.1, on Bigolina, see Bigolina, ed. Nissen, 34n and 233n. Bigolina appropriates Straparola's motif of the boy who furtively approaches a captive wild man in a royal palace (Straparola, 5.1, 327; Bigolina, ed. Nissen, 232–4), which is well established in folklore; for examples see also the Grimms' tale 'Iron Hans' (Grimm, *Complete Fairy Tales*, 443–8) and Sierra's Swedish tale 'The Wild Man' (*Quests and Spells*, 17–24).

50 For the Sileni, see Bartra, *Wild Men*, 19–20. For ancient accounts of captured wild men, see Bernheimer, *Wild Men*, 87.

51 See Bernheimer, *Wild Men*, 121–2, for commentary on this episode.

52 Ibid., 122–5, 135–41, and Bartra, *Wild Men*, 104.

53 Finucci notes that this episode resembles a sort of 'upside down' version of Ariosto's account of Norandino and the monstrous orc (*Orlando furioso*, 17.29–65). Norandino must rescue his wife, Lucina, from the eyeless orc, which eats men and imprisons women, distinguishing one from the other by sense of smell. Rather like Urania, Norandino must disguise his scent by smearing himself with rancid goat fat (Finucci, 2005, 32).

54 Here, Bigolina reverses the ancient misogynist notion that typically associated malodorousness with women, not with men; on this topic see Gambera, 'Women and Walls,' 61–2, and Bettella, *The Ugly Woman*, 22–5.

55 Genesis 27: 1–40. On Esau as a wild man and other wild men in the
Old Testament, see Bartra, *Wild Men*, 45–7. For the characteristics of the
Hebrew concept of the wild man see White, *Tropics of Discourse*, 160–4.
The sense of smell as an ultimate identifier is also evident in the New
Testament: the saved will be known by the sweet odour of Christ, whereas
the damned will smell of death (2 Corinthians 2: 14–16).

56 Smell is also the most significant sense in Dante's episode of the dream
of the Siren, or 'femmina balba' (*Purgatorio*, 19, vv 1–33): the apparition's
stench is what finally awakens the poet from sleep, and reveals to him
the Siren's true nature. Here too smell appears to 'trump' vision. On the
allegorical significance of the Siren's odour, see Yavneh, 'Dante's "dolce
serena" and the Monstrosity of the Female Body,' 110, 116, 118; and
Gambera, 'Women and Walls,' 48. See also Boccaccio's own tale of a wild
woman, in which Giannotto confirms that he has indeed found his long-
lost mother, Beritola, by sense of smell ('pur nondimeno conobbe incon-
tanente l'odor materno'), even after he has failed to recognize her by sight
(*Decameron*, 2.6, 1: 218). For sources for this motif see Branca's note on the
passage, *Decameron*, 1: 218.

57 Cervantes, *The Ingenious Hidalgo Don Quixote de la Mancha*, trans. John
Rutherford, 208.

58 Bartra, *Wild Men*, 200–1. Segre declares Cervantes' episode of Cardenio to
be the last gasp of 'follia cavalleresca' (*Fuori del mondo*, 92–3).

Conclusion

1 Bigolina's letter to Francesco Barozzi, which includes an almost comical mini-essay on the perils of presumptuousness, is described by
Finucci, 2002, 20–1 and n, and Bigolina, ed. Nissen, 14–16, wherein may
be found a translation of the letter into English. In the letter, Bigolina
humbly requests two extra tickets to see a comedy. On the topic of audacity in Bigolina's 'Novella di Giulia Camposanpiero,' see Bigolina, ed.
Nissen, 45–50.

2 Christine de Pizan also includes references to her own uniqueness and inclination to learning, likewise placed in the mouths of her allegories (*Livre
de la cité des dames*, 1.3, 2.36). These passages appear to have influenced
Bigolina. For this motif, see also Terracina's vivid passage on her inner
conflict between desire to learn and fear of failure: 'Ma d'imparar tant'ho
le voglie intente / che spesso per timor n'arco le ciglia / e timorosa ogni
martir sopporto, / e d'errar sempre hebbi gia il viso smorto' (So much does
my desire incline toward learning, that often I knit my brows in fear, and
fearful, I endure every suffering, and once my face was always pale at the

thought of error; *Discorso sopra il principio di tutti i canti di Orlando furioso,* 46.6, 5–8).

3 On this topic, and the 'sly narcissistic gesture' that this passage implies, see also Finucci, 2005, 83–4n. On the perceived need for early modern women writers to belittle themselves for their lack of rhetorical skills, see Bassanese, 'Selling the Self,' 70–1, and Bigolina, ed. Nissen, 45–6.

4 In any event, the greatest controversy over painting, which primarily emphasized nudity in religious works rather than in mythological paintings, did not occur until the Council of Trent issued its decree on images in 1563, several years after the likely date of *Urania.* For the decree and resulting controversy see Freedberg, 'Johannes Molanus on Provocative Paintings,' 369.

5 Collodi, *Le avventure di Pinocchio,* chapter 3, 11, and chapter 5, 18–19.

6 Ovid, *Metamorphoses,* 15, vv 875–9. For the appearance of the motif in a widely distributed book of Bigolina's time, see also Alciati's emblem 132 ('Ex litterarum studiis immortalitem acquiri,' acquiring immortality from the study of literature; *Book of Emblems,* 156).

7 The only sixteenth-century manuscript of *Urania,* Trivulziana 88, appears to be a professionally prepared presentation copy, made specifically for the person to whom it was dedicated, since Salvatico's initials are inscribed on the leather of the cover; see Bigolina, ed. Nissen, 25, 50.

8 Archivio di Stato di Padova, Archivio notarile 829, 65r–66r, included here in the Appendix. This codex contains the third book of Antonio Villani's collected legal documents, spanning the years 1563–6. Villani's Latin preface to the will appears on 64r. On the certainty that this document is an autograph, see the opening paragraph, as well as Bigolina, ed. Nissen, 5.

Appendix

1 *item* (Latin, 'likewise, in addition')
2 Iesus Hominem Salvator (Latin, 'Jesus the Saviour of Mankind')
3 Abbreviation of Veneto dialect term *formento (frumento),* 'wheat' (Boerio, *Dizionario del dialetto veneto* s.v.).
4 Variant of Veneto dialect term *intimele,* 'pillowcases' (Boerio, *Dizionario del dialetto veneto* s.v.).
5 Another variant of 'Vicomercato,' the family of Bigolina's husband; as has been noted, in other documents in the Padua archive it is also spelled 'Vilmercato.'
6 There is an apparent scribal error here on Bigolina's part; the name appears as 'Matia,' an improbable name for a woman.

Bibliography

Manuscript Sources

Bassano del Grappa, Biblioteca Civica. *Novellieri, materiali bibliografici*. Vol. 4. Manoscritti autografici di Bartolommeo Gamba. 5 vols.
Besançon, Bibliothèque Municipale. MS 597. Mario Melechini, *A ragionar d'amore*.
Padua, Archivio di Stato di Padova. Archivio Notarile, vol. 829. *Abbreviature di Antonio Villani notaio, 1563–1566*.
Padua, Archivio di Stato di Padova. Archivio Notarile, vol. 4830.
Padua, Archivio di Stato di Padova. Archivio Notarile, vol. 4839.
Padua, Biblioteca Civica. MS 1239 XV. Cesare Malfatti, *Cronichetta ovvero epitome delle famiglie che ora sono nella città di Padoa, composta nel 1538*.
Venice, Biblioteca Marciana. MS It. Classe XI, Codici 59–60. 2 vols. Apostolo Zeno, *Zibaldoni*.

Primary Sources

Alan of Lille. *Anticlaudianus*. Ed. and trans. James Sheridan. Toronto: Pontifical Institute of Medieval Studies, 1973.
Alberti, Leon Battista. *Della pittura*. Ed. Cecil Grayson. Vol. 3 of *Opere volgari*. Bari: Laterza, 1973.
Alciati, Andrea. *A Book of Emblems: The Emblematum Liber in Latin and English*. Ed. and trans. John F. Moffitt. Jefferson, NC: McFarland, 2004.
Aretino, Pietro. *Cortigiana; Opera nova; Pronostico; Il testamento dell'elefante; Farza*. Ed. Angelo Romano. Milan: Rizzoli, 1989.
– *Lettere*. 6 vols. Ed. Paolo Procaccioli. Edizione nazionale delle opere di Pietro Aretino 4. Rome: Salerno Editrice, 1997–2002.

– *Poesie varie.* Ed. Giovanni Aquilecchia and Angelo Romano. Edizione
  nazionale delle opere di Pietro Aretino 1. Rome: Salerno Editrice, 1992.
– *Ragionamento; Dialogo.* Ed. Paolo Procaccioli. Milan: Garzanti, 2005.
Ariosto, Ludovico. *Orlando furioso.* Ed. Marcello Turchi. 2 vols. Milan:
  Garzanti, 1984.
Aristotle. *On the Soul; Parva naturalia; On Breath.* In *Aristotle in Twenty-three
  Volumes.* Vol. 8. Trans. W.S. Hett. Cambridge, MA: Harvard University
  Press, 1986.
Armenini, Giovanni Battista. *De' veri precetti della pittura.* Ed. Marina Gorreri.
  Turin: Einaudi, 1988.
Armeno, Cristoforo. *Peregrinaggio di tre giovani figliuoli del re di Serendippo.* Ed.
  Renzo Bragantini. Rome: Salerno Editrice, 2000.
Bandello, Matteo. *Tutte le opere di Matteo Bandello.* Ed. Francesco Flora. 2 vols.
  Milan: Mondadori, 1966.
Bembo, Pietro. *Gli Asolani.* Ed. Giorgio Dilemmi. Florence: Accademia della
  Crusca, 1991.
Berni, Francesco. *Poesie e prose.* Ed. Ezio Chiorboli. Florence: Olschki, 1934.
Betussi, Giuseppe. *Libro de M. Giovanni Boccaccio delle donne illustre.* Venice:
  Nicolini da Sabbio, 1547.
– *Il Raverta; La Leonora.* Ed. Giuseppe Zonta. In *Trattati d'amore del Cinquecento.*
  Bari: Laterza, 1912. 3–150; 307–50.
Bigolina, Giulia. *Urania: The Story of a Young Woman's Love, & The Novella of
  Giulia Camposanpiero and Thesibaldo Vitaliani.* Ed. and trans. Christopher
  Nissen. Medieval and Renaissance Texts and Studies, vol. 262. Tempe:
  Arizona Center for Medieval and Renaissance Studies, 2004.
Boccaccio, Giovanni. *Comedia delle ninfe fiorentine.* Ed. Antonio Enzo Quaglio.
  Vol. 2 of *Tutte le opere di Giovanni Boccaccio.* Ed. Vittore Branca. Milan:
  Mondadori, 1964. 665–835.
– *Corbaccio.* Ed. Pier Giorgio Ricci. Classici Ricciardi 44. Turin: Einaudi, 1977.
– *Decameron.* 2 vols. Ed.Vittore Branca. Einaudi classici 99. Turin:
  Einaudi, 1992.
– *Decameron.* Trans. Mark Musa and Peter Bondanella. New York:
  Norton, 1982.
– *Elegia di madonna Fiammetta.* Ed. Carlo Salinari and Natalino Sapegno.
  Classici Ricciardi 10. Turin: Einaudi, 1976.
– *Famous Women (De mulieribus claris).* Ed. and trans. Virginia Brown.
  I Tatti Renaissance Library 1. Cambridge, MA: Harvard University
  Press, 2001.
– *Filocolo.* Ed. Antonio Enzo Quaglio. Milan: Mondadori, 1998.

– *Genealogie deorum gentilium libri.* 2 vols. Ed. Vincenzo Romano. Bari: Laterza, 1951.

– *Teseida delle nozze di Emilia.* Ed. Alberto Limentani. Milan: Mondadori, 1992.

Boethius. *The Consolation of Philosophy.* Ed. and trans. V.E. Watts. New York: Penguin, 1981.

Boiardo, Matteo Maria. *Orlando innamorato.* 2 vols. Ed. Giuseppe Anceschi. Milan: Garzanti, 2003.

Bonciani, Francesco. *Lezione sopra il comporre delle novelle.* Ed. Bernard Weinberg. Vol. 3 of *Trattati di poetica e retorica del Cinquecento.* Bari: Laterza, 1972. 135–65.

Cantare di Madonna Elena. Ed. Giovanni Fontana. Florence: La Crusca, 1992.

Capella (Capra), Galeazzo Flavio. *Della eccellenza e dignità delle donne.* Ed. Maria Luisa Doglio. Biblioteca del Cinquecento 40. Rome: Bulzoni, 2001.

Castiglione, Baldassare. *Il libro del cortigiano.* Ed. Giulio Carnazzi. Milan: Biblioteca Universale Rizzoli, 2000.

Cattaneo, Silvan. *Dodici giornate.* Vol. 1 of *Salò e la sua Riviera descritta da Silvan Cattaneo e da Bongianni Grattarolo.* Venice: Tommasini, 1745.

Cattani da Diacceto, Francesco. *I tre libri d'amore di M. Francesco Cattani da Diacceto, Filosafo et gentil'huomo Fiorentino, con un Panegerico all'amore, et con la vita del detto autore, fatta da M. Benedetto Varchi.* Venice: Giolito, 1561.

Caviceo, Iacopo. *Il peregrino di M. Giacopo Caviceo da Parma.* Venice: Nicolini da Sabio, 1547.

– *Il peregrino.* Ed. Luigi Vignali. Rome: La Fenice Edizioni, 1993.

Cervantes Saavedra, Miguel de. *Don Quixote de la Mancha.* Ed. Francisco Rico and Joaquín Forradellas. Biblioteca Clásica 50. Barcelona: Instituto Cervantes, 1999.

– *The Ingenious Hidalgo Don Quixote de la Mancha.* Trans. John Rutherford. London: Penguin, 2000.

Chariton. *Chaereas and Callirhoe.* Ed. and trans. B.P. Reardon. *Collected Ancient Greek Novels.* Berkeley: University of California Press, 1989. 17–124.

Chrétien de Troyes. *Oeuvres complètes.* Ed. Anne Berthelot, Peter F. Dembowski, Daniel Poirion, Karl D. Uitti, and Philippe Walter. Paris: Gallimard, 1994.

Christine de Pizan. *Epistre Othea.* Ed. Gabrielle Parussa. Geneva: Droz, 1999.

– *Le livre de la cité des dames.* Ed. Patrizia Caraffi and Earl Jeffrey Richards. Milan: Luni, 1997.

– *Oeuvres poétiques de Christine de Pisan.* 3 vols. Ed. Maurice Roy, 1886. Reprint, New York: Johnson Reprint Corporation, 1965.

Collodi, Carlo. *Le avventure di Pinocchio*. Milan: La Biblioteca Ideale Tascabile, 1995.

Colonna, Francesco. *Hypnerotomachia Poliphili*. 1499. Reprint, New York: Garland, 1976.

I compassionevoli avvenimenti di Erasto. Venice: Comin da Trino, 1563.

Corfino, Lodovico. *Istoria di Phileto veronese*. Ed. Giuseppe Biadego. Livorno: Giusti, 1899.

Dante Alighieri. *De vulgari eloquentia*. Ed. Pier Vincenzo Mengaldo. In *Opere minori*, vol. 2. Milan: Ricciardi, 1979.

– *Inferno*. Ed. Natalino Sapegno. Florence: La Nuova Italia, 1984.

– *Paradiso*. Ed. Natalino Sapegno. Florence: La Nuova Italia, 1981.

d'Aragona, Tullia. *Dialogo della infinità d'amore*. Ed. Giuseppe Zonta. *Trattati d'amore del Cinquecento*. Bari: Laterza, 1912. 185–243.

della Casa, Giovanni. *Rime*. Ed. Roberto Fedi. Milan: Biblioteca Universale Rizzoli, 1993.

della Chiesa, Francesco Agostino. *Theatro delle donne letterate. Con un breve discorso della preminenza, e perfettione del sesso donnesco*. Mondovì: Gislandi, 1620.

de Lorris, Guillaume, and Jean de Meun. *Le roman de la rose*. 2 vols. Ed. Félix Lecoy. Paris: Honoré Champion, 1966.

Dolce, Lodovico. *Dialogo della pittura intitolato l'Aretino*. Ed. and trans. Mark W. Roskill. Renaissance Society of America Reprint Texts 10. Toronto: University of Toronto Press, 2000.

Domenichi, Lodovico. *La nobiltà delle donne*. Venice: Giolito, 1549.

Equicola, Mario. *La redazione manoscritta del Libro de natura de amore di Mario Equicola*. Ed. Laura Ricci. Rome: Bulzoni, 1999.

Feliciano, Felice. 'Justa Victoria.' In *Catalogo dei novellieri italiani in prosa*. 2 vols. Ed. Giovanni Papanti. Livorno: Vigo, 1871.

Ficino, Marsilio. *The Philebus Commentary*. Ed. and trans. Michael J.B. Allen. Berkeley: University of California Press, 1975.

– *Sopra lo amore ovvero convito di Platone*. Ed. Giuseppe Rensi. Testi e documenti vol. 131. Milan: SE, 2003.

Firenzuola, Agnolo. *Dialogo delle bellezze delle donne*. Ed. Adriano Seroni. In *Opere*. Florence: Sansoni, 1971. 519–96.

– *On the Beauty of Women*. Trans. Konrad Eisenbichler and Jacqueline Murray. Philadelphia: University of Pennsylvania Press, 1992.

La Folie Tristan de Berne. Ed. Joseph Bédier. Paris: Firmin-Didot, 1907. Reprint New York: Johnson Reprint Corporation, 1965.

Franco, Niccolò. *Dialogo dove si ragiona delle Bellezze*. Casale di Monferrato: Guidone, 1542.

– *La Philena di M. Nicolo Franco. Historia amorosa ultimamente composta.* Mantua: Ruffinelli, 1547.

Franco, Veronica. *Lettere.* Ed. Stefano Bianchi. Rome: Salerno Editrice, 1998.

– *Poems and Selected Letters.* Ed. and trans. Ann Rosalind Jones and Margaret F. Rosenthal. Chicago: University of Chicago Press, 1998.

Fulgentius. *Fulgentius the Mythographer.* Trans. Leslie George Whitbread. Columbus: Ohio State University Press, 1971.

Geoffrey of Monmouth. *Life of Merlin (Vita Merlini).* Ed. and trans. Basil Clarke. Cardiff: University of Wales Press, 1973.

Gherardi da Prato, Giovanni. *Il Paradiso degli Alberti.* Ed. Antonio Lanza. Rome: Salerno Editrice, 1975.

Gilio, Giovanni Andrea. *Dialogo di M. Giovanni Andrea Gilio da Fabriano degli errori de' pittori circa l'istorie.* 3 vols. Ed. Paola Barocchi. In *Trattati d'arte nel Cinquecento.* Bari: Laterza, 1961.

Giovanni Fiorentino. *Il Pecorone.* Ed. Enzo Esposito. Ravenna: Longo, 1974.

Giraldi Cinthio, Giovan Battista. *Discorsi intorno al comporre rivisti dall'autore nell'esemplare ferrarese Cl. I 90.* Ed. Susanna Villari. Messina: Centro Interdepartimentale di Studi Umanistici, 2002.

Gottifredi, Bartolomeo. *Specchio d'amore. Dialogo di Messer Bartolomeo Gottifredi nel Gottifredi nel quale alle giovani s'insegna innamorarsi.* Ed. Giuseppe Zonta. *Trattati d'amore del Cinquecento.* Bari: Laterza, 1912. 249–304.

Grazzini, Antonfrancesco. *Le cene.* Ed. Ettore Mazzali. Milan: Rizzoli, 1989.

Grimm, Jacob, and Wilhelm Grimm. *The Complete Fairy Tales of the Brothers Grimm.* Trans. Jack Zipes. New York: Bantam, 1992.

Heldris de Cornualle. *Silence: A Thirteenth Century French Romance.* Ed. and trans. Sarah Roche-Mahdi. East Lansing: Michigan State University Press, 1999.

Heliodorus of Emesa. *Istoria delle cose etiopiche d'Eliodoro.* Ed. and trans. Leonardo Ghini. Venice: Giolito, 1556.

Hélisenne de Crenne. *Les Angoysses douloureuses qui procédent d'amours.* Ed. Paule Demats. Paris: Les belles lettres, 1968.

Horace. *Ars poetica.* Ed. and trans. Burton Raffel. Albany: State University of New York Press, 1974.

Istoria di due nobilissimi amanti Ottinello e Giulia. Ed. Goffredo Bellonci. *Novelle italiane dalle origini al cinquecento.* Milan: Lucarini, 1986. 558–69.

Lactantius. *Divine Institutes.* Trans. Anthony Bowen and Peter Garnsey. Liverpool: Liverpool University Press, 2003.

Lando, Ortensio. *Lettere di molte valorose donne, nelle quali chiaramente appare non esser ne di eloquentia ne di dottrina alli huomini inferiori.* Venice: Giolito, 1549.

– *Paradossi cioè sentenze fuori del comun parere.* Ed. Antonio Corsaro. Studi e testi del rinascimento europeo vol. 8. Rome: Edizioni di storia e letteratura, 2000.

Leonardo da Vinci. *Paragone: A Comparison of the Arts by Leonardo da Vinci.* Ed. and trans. Irma A. Richter. London: Oxford University Press, 1949.

Leone Ebreo. *Dialoghi d'amore.* Ed. Santino Caramella. Bari: Laterza, 1929.

Leonico, Angelo. *L'amore di Troilo, et Griseida, ove si tratta in buona parte la guerra di Troia.* Venice: Gerardo, 1553.

Lestoire de Merlin. Ed. H. Oskar Sommer. Vol. 2 of *The Vulgate Versions of the Arthurian Romances.* Washington: Carnegie Institute of Washington, 1908.

Longus. *Daphnis and Chloe.* Ed. and trans. Paul Turner. London: Penguin, 1989.

Luigini, Federigo. *Il libro della bella donna.* 1863. Reprint, Bologna: Forni, 1974.

Manetti, Antonio. 'La novella del Grasso legnaiuolo.' Ed. Paolo Procaccioli. Milan: Garzanti, 1998.

Marie de France. *Lais.* Ed. A. Ewert. Oxford: Blackwell, 1965.

Masenetti, Giovanni Maria. *Il divino oracolo in lode dei nuovi sposi del 1548 e di tutte le belle gentildonne padovane.* Venice: n.p., 1548.

Michelangelo Buonarroti. *Rime.* Ed. Enzo Noè Girardi. Bari: Laterza, 1967.

'La novella del Bianco Alfani.' Ed. Aldo Borlenghi. In *Novelle del Quattrocento.* Milano: Rizzoli, 1962. 315–36.

Ovid. *Ars amatoria.* Ed. and trans. J.H. Mozley. In *Ovid in Six Volumes,* vol. 2, *The Art of Love, and Other Poems.* Cambridge, MA: Harvard University Press, 1985. 11–175.

– *Fasti.* Ed. and trans. James George Frazer. Loeb Classical Library 253. Cambridge, MA: Harvard University Press, 2003.

– *Heroides and Amores.* Trans. Grant Showerman. Cambridge, MA: Harvard University Press, 1958.

– *Metamorphoses.* 2 vols. Ed. and trans. Frank Justus Miller. Loeb Classical Library 42–3. Cambridge MA: Harvard University Press, 2005.

– *Remedia amoris.* Ed. and trans. J.H. Mozley. In *Ovid in Six Volumes,* vol. 2, *The Art of Love, and Other Poems.* Cambridge, MA: Harvard University Press, 1985. 177–233.

Paleotti, Gabriele. *Discorso intorno alle imagini sacre e profane.* Ed. Paola Barocchi. Vol. 2 of *Trattati d'arte del Cinquecento.* Bari: Laterza, 1961.

Parabosco, Girolamo. *I diporti.* Ed. Giuseppe Gigli and Fausto Nicolini. Bari: Laterza, 1912.

Partonopeu de Blois. A French Romance of the Twelfth Century. 2 vols. Ed. Joseph Gildea. Villanova, PA: Villanova University Press, 1967.

Pasqualigo, Luigi. *Delle lettere amorose libri due.* Venice: Rampazetto, 1563.

Petrarca, Francesco. *Canzoniere.* Ed. Gianfranco Contini. Turin: Einaudi, 1964.

– *Trionfi*. Ed. Guido Bezzola. Milan: Rizzoli, 1984.

Philostratus the Elder; Philostratus the Younger. *Imagines*. Ed. and trans. Arthur Fairbanks. Cambridge, MA: Harvard University Press, 1979.

Piccolomini, Enea Silvio. *Historia de duobus amantibus*. Ed. and trans. Gioachino Chiarini. In *Novelle italiane. Il Quattrocento*. Milan: Garzanti, 1982. 131–237.

Pico della Mirandola. *Commento sopra una canzone d'amore*. Ed. Paolo de Angelis. Palermo: Novecento, 1994.

Pino, Paolo. *Dialogo di pittura*. Ed. Susanna Falabella. Rome: Lithos, 2000.

Plato. *Phaedrus*. In *Plato in Twelve Volumes*. Vol. 1. Ed. and trans. Harold North Fowler. Cambridge, MA: Harvard University Press, 2001.

– *The Republic*. 2 vols. Trans. Paul Shorey. Cambridge, MA: Harvard University Press, 1956.

– *Symposium*. In *Plato in Twelve Volumes*. Vol. 3. Ed. and trans. W.R.M. Lamb. Cambridge, MA: Harvard University Press, 1983.

Pliny. *Natural History*. 10 vols. Ed. and trans. H. Rackham. Cambridge, MA: Harvard University Press, 1952.

Plotinus. *The Enneads*. Trans. Stephen MacKenna. London: Faber, 1969.

Politi, Ambrogio Catarino. *Disputatio R.P.F. Ambrosii Catharini Politi episcopi minoriensis de cultu & adoratione imaginum*. In *Enarrationes R.P.F. Ambrosii Catharini Politi senensis archiepiscopi compsani in quinque priora capita libri geneseos*. Rome: Antonius Bladus, 1552. Columns 121–44.

Pomponazzi, Pietro. *Pomponatius in libros de anima*. In *La psicologia di Pietro Pomponazzi secondo un manoscritto inedito dell'Angelica di Roma*. Ed. Luigi Ferri. Rome: Salviucci, 1876.

Pucci, Antonio. *Madonna Lionessa*. In *Fiore di leggende. Cantari antichi*. Ed. Ezio Levi. Scrittori d'Italia no. 64, Series 1: Cantari leggendari. Bari: Laterza, 1914. 217–27.

Reisch, Gregorius. *Margarita philosophica nova*. 3 vols. Ed. Lucia Andreini. Analecta Cartusiana 179. Salzburg: Institut für Anglistik und Amerikanistik, Universität Salzburg, 2002.

Le roman de Tristan en prose. 3 vols. Ed. Renée L. Curtis. Cambridge: Brewer, 1985.

Le roman de Tristan en prose. 6 vols. Ed. Philippe Ménard. Geneva: Droz, 1987–93.

Roman dou roi Flore et de la belle Jehanne. Ed. L.J.N. Monmerqué and Francisque Michel. In *Théatre Français du moyen âge*. Paris: Firmin-Didot, 1885. 417–30.

Sacchetti, Franco. *Il Trecentonovelle*. Ed. Antonio Lanza. Florence: Sansoni, 1984.

Sallustius. *Concerning the Gods and the Universe*. Ed. and trans. Arthur Darby Nock. Hildesheim: Georg Olms, 1966.

Sannazaro, Jacopo. *Arcadia*. Ed. Alfredo Mauro. In *Opere volgari*. Bari: Laterza, 1961. 1–132.

Shakespeare, William. *Sonnets*. Ed. Douglas Bush. In *The Complete Pelican Shakespeare: The Histories and the Non-Dramatic Poetry*. Ed. Alfred Harbage. Harmondsworth: Penguin, 1981.

Speroni, Sperone. *Dialogo d'amore*. Ed. Mario Pozzi. Vol. 2 of *Trattatisti del Cinquecento*. Milan: Ricciardi, 1996. 511–63.

– *Dialogo della dignità delle donne*. Ed. Mario Pozzi. Vol. 2 of *Trattatisti del Cinquecento*. Milan: Ricciardi, 1996. 565–584.

– *Dialogo della rettorica*. Ed. Mario Pozzi. Vol. 2 of *Trattatisti del Cinquecento*. Milan: Ricciardi, 1996. 637–682.

Stampa, Gaspara. *Rime*. Ed. Gustavo Rodolfo Ceriello. Milan: Rizzoli, 1976.

Straparola, Giovan Francesco. *Le piacevoli notti*. 2 vols. Ed. Donato Pirovano. I novellieri italiani vol. 29. Rome: Salerno Editrice, 2000.

Tatius, Achilles. *Achille Tazio Alessandrino dell'amore di Leucippe et di Clitophonte: Nuovamente tradotto dalla lingua greca*. Ed. and trans. Francesco Angelo Coccio. Venice: Nicolini da Sabio, 1551.

– *Leucippe and Clitophon*. Ed. and trans. Tim Whitmarsh. Oxford: Oxford University Press, 2001.

Terracina, Laura. *Discorso sopra il principio di tutti i canti di Orlando furioso*. Venice: Giolito, 1554.

– *Rime della Signora Laura Terracina*. Venice: Giolito, 1554.

Trissino, Gian Giorgio. *I ritratti*. Ed. Willi Hirdt. In *Gian Giorgio Trissinos Porträt der Isabella d'Este: Ein Beitrag zur Lukian-Rezeption in Italien*. Heidelberg: Carl Winter Universitätsverlag, 1981. 19–28.

Il Tristano Panciatichiano. Ed. and trans. Gloria Allaire. Arthurian Archives, Italian Literature 1. Cambridge: Brewer, 2002.

Varchi, Benedetto. *Lezzione della maggioranza delle arti*. Ed. Paola Barocchi. In *Pittura e scultura nel Cinquecento*. Livorno: Sillabe, 1998. 11–59.

Vasari, Giorgio. *Le vite de' più eccellenti architetti, pittori, et scultori italiani, da Cimabue insino a' tempi nostri (nell'edizione per i tipi di Lorenzo Torrentino, Firenze 1550)*. 2 vols. Ed. Luciano Bellosi and Aldo Rossi. Turin: Einaudi, 1986.

Virgil. *The Aeneid of Virgil: A Verse Translation*. Ed. and trans. Allen Mandelbaum. Berkeley: University of California Press, 1981.

Wilde, Oscar. *The Picture of Dorian Gray and Selected Stories*. Ed. Gary Schmidgall. New York: Penguin, 1995.

Wroth, Lady Mary. *The First Part of the Countess of Montgomery's Urania*. Ed. Josephine A. Roberts. Binghamton, NY: Medieval and Renaissance Texts and Studies, 1995.

Secondary Sources

Adams, Laurie Schneider. 'Iconographic Aspects of the Gaze in Some Paintings by Titian.' In *The Cambridge Companion to Titian*. Ed. Patricia Meilman. Cambridge: Cambridge University Press, 2004. 225–40.

Albanese, Gabriella. 'Da Petrarca a Piccolomini: Codificazione della novella umanistica.' In *Favole parabole istorie. Le forme della scrittura novellistica dal medioevo al rinascimento. Atti del Convegno di Pisa 26–28 ottobre 1998*. Ed. Gabriella Albanese, Lucia Battaglia Ricci, and Rossella Bessi. Rome: Salerno Editrice, 2000. 257–307.

Albertazzi, Adolfo. *Romanzieri e romanzi del Cinquecento e del Seicento*. Bologna: Zanichelli, 1891.

Allaire, Gloria. *Andrea da Barberino and the Language of Chivalry*. Gainesville: University Press of Florida, 1997.

Altizer, Alma B. *Self and Symbolism in the Poetry of Michelangelo, John Donne, and Agrippa d'Aubigné*. The Hague: Martinus Nijhoff, 1973.

Arasse, Daniel. 'The *Venus of Urbino*, or the Archetype of a Glance.' In *Titian's Venus of Urbino*. Ed. Rona Goffen. Cambridge: Cambridge University Press, 1997. 91–107.

Ascoli, Albert Russell. *Ariosto's Bitter Harmony: Crisis and Evasion in the Italian Renaissance*. Princeton: Princeton University Press, 1987.

Auzzas, Ginetta. 'La narrativa veneta nella prima metà del Cinquecento.' In *Storia della cultura veneta*. 6 vols. Ed. Girolamo Arnaldi and Manlio Pastore Stocchi. Vicenza: Neri Pozza, 1976–86. 3: 99–138.

Bakhtin, Mikhail Mikhailovich. *The Dialogic Imagination*. Trans. Caryl Emerson and Michael Holquist. Austin: University of Texas Press, 1982.

Balduino, Armando. 'Fortune e sfortune della novella italiana fra tardo Trecento e primo Cinquecento.' In *La nouvelle. Formation, codification et rayonnement d'un genre médiéval. Actes du Colloque International de Montréal-McGill University, 14–16 octobre 1982*. Ed. Michelangelo Picone, Giuseppe Di Stefano, and Pamela D. Stewart. Montreal: Plato Academic Press, 1983. 155–73.

Ballarin, Alessandro. 'Profilo di Lamberto d'Amsterdam (Lamberto Sustris).' *Arte veneta* 16 (1962): 61–81.

Bann, Stephen. *The True Vine: On Visual Representation and the Western Tradition*. Cambridge: Cambridge University Press, 1989.

Baratto, Mario. *Realtà e stile nel Decameron*. Rome: Riuniti, 1984.

Barocchi, Paola. 'L'invenzione.' In vol 3. of *Scritti d'arte del Cinquecento*. 3 vols. Ed. Paola Barocchi. Milan: Ricciardi, 1971–7. 2401–2.

Bartra, Roger. *Wild Men in the Looking Glass: The Mythic Origins of European Otherness.* Trans. Carl T. Berrisford. Ann Arbor: University of Michigan Press, 1994.

Bassanese, Fiora A. 'Selling the Self; or, the Epistolary Production of Renaissance Courtesans.' In *Italian Women Writers from the Renaissance to the Present: Revising the Canon.* Ed. Maria Ornella Marotti. University Park: Pennsylvania State University Press, 1996. 69–82.

Battaglia, Salvatore. *Giovanni Boccaccio e la riforma della narrativa.* Naples: Liguori, 1969.

Baumgardner, George H. Introduction to *Novelle Cinque: Tales from the Veneto.* Ed. and trans. George H. Baumgardner. Barre, MA: Imprint Society, 1974.

Beaujour, Michel. 'Some Paradoxes of Description.' *Yale French Studies* 61 (1981): 27–59.

Bendinelli Predelli, Maria. 'Dal cantare romanzesco al cantare novellistico: Vicissitudini di una forma.' In *La nouvelle: Genése, codification et rayonnement d'un genre médiévale. Actes du Colloque International de Montréal (McGill University, 14–16 octobre 1982.* Ed. Michelangelo Picone, Giuseppe di Stefano, and Pamela D. Stewart. Montreal: Plato Academic Press, 1983. 174–88.

Benson, Pamela Joseph. *The Invention of the Renaissance Woman.* University Park: University of Pennsylvania Press, 1992.

Berger, Harry, Jr. 'Fictions of the Pose: Facing the Gaze of Early Modern Portraiture.' *Representations* 46 (1994): 87–120.

Bernheimer, Richard. *Wild Men in the Middle Ages: A Study in Art, Sentiment, and Demonology.* New York: Octagon Books, 1970.

Bessi, Rossella. 'Il modello boccacciano nella spicciolata toscana tra fine Trecento e tardo Quattrocento.' In *Dal primato allo scacco. I modelli narrativi italiani tra Trecento e Seicento.* Ed. Gian Maria Anselmi. Rome: Carocci, 1998. 107–23.

Bettella, Patrizia. 'Corpo di parti: Ambiguità e frammentarietà nella rappresentazione della bellezza femminile nei ritratti di Trissino e Firenzuola.' *Forum Italicum* 33, 2 (1999): 319–35.

– *The Ugly Woman: Transgressive Aesthetic Models in Italian Poetry from the Middle Ages to the Baroque.* Toronto: University of Toronto Press, 2005.

Blumenfeld-Kosinski, Renate. *Reading Myth: Classical Mythology and Its Interpretations in Medieval French Literature.* Stanford: Stanford University Press, 1997.

Boerio, Giuseppe. *Dizionario del dialetto veneto.* Venice: Cecchini, 1867.

Bolzoni, Lina. 'The Art of Memory and the Erotic Image in 16th and 17th Century Europe: The Example of Giovan Battista della Porta.' In *Eros and Anteros: The Medical Traditions of Love in the Renaissance.* Ed. Donald A.

Beecher and Massimo Ciavolella. University of Toronto Italian Studies 9. Ottawa: Dovehouse Editions, 1992. 103–22.

Borromeo, Anton Maria. *Notizia de' novellieri italiani posseduti dal conte Anton Maria Borromeo, gentiluomo padovano, con alcune novelle inedite.* Bassano: Remondini, 1794.

Bourne, Molly. 'Renaissance Husbands and Wives as Patrons of Art: The *Camerini* of Isabella d'Este and Francesco II Gonzaga.' In *Beyond Isabella: Secular Women Patrons of Art in Renaissance Italy.* Ed. Sheryl E. Reiss and David G. Wilkins. Kirksville, MO: Truman State University Press, 2001. 93–123.

Bradley, Sister Ritamary. 'Backgrounds of the Title *Speculum* in Medieval Literature.' *Speculum* 29, 1 (1954): 100–15.

Branca, Vittore. *Giovanni Boccaccio. Profilo biografico.* Florence: Sansoni, 1997.

Brown, Clifford M. 'A Ferrarese Lady and a Mantuan Marchesa: The Art and Antiquities Collections of Isabella d'Este Gonzaga (1474–1539).' In *Women and Art in Early Modern Europe: Patrons, Collectors, and Connoisseurs.* Ed. Cynthia Lawrence. University Park: Pennsylvania State University Press, 1998. 53–71.

Brown-Grant, Rosalind. *Christine de Pizan and the Moral Defence of Women: Reading Beyond Gender.* Cambridge: Cambridge University Press, 1999.

– Introduction and translation to *The Book of the City of Ladies* by Christine de Pizan. London: Penguin, 1999.

Brownlee, Kevin, and Marina Scordilis Brownlee. Introduction to *Romance: Generic Transformation from Chrétien de Troyes to Cervantes.* Hanover, NH: University Press of New England, 1985.

Bruni, Francesco. *Sistemi critici e strutture narrative. Ricerche sulla cultura fiorentina del rinascimento.* Naples: Liguori, 1969.

Bull, Malcolm. *The Mirror of the Gods.* Oxford: Oxford University Press, 2005.

Buranello, Robert. '*Figura meretricis*: Tullia d'Aragona in Sperone Speroni's *Dialogo d'amore.*' *Spunti e ricerche* 15 (2000): 53–68.

Cairns, Christopher. *Pietro Aretino and the Republic of Venice: Researches on Aretino and His Circle in Venice, 1527–1556.* Florence: Olschki, 1985.

Caruso, Carlo. 'L'artista al bivio: Venere àntica e venere pòstica nel Giudizio di Paride.' *Italian Studies* 60, 2 (2005): 163–77.

Celano, Carlo. *Delle notizie del bello, dell'antico e del curioso della città di Napoli per i signori forastieri.* 3 vols. Naples: Paci, 1724.

Ciccuto, Marcello. *Figure d'artista.* Letteratura italiana antica 3. Fiesole: Cadmo, 2002.

Cosentini, Laura. *Una dama napoletana del XVI secolo: Isabella Villamarina, Principessa di Salerno.* Trani: Vecchio, 1896.

Cox, Virginia. *The Renaissance Dialogue: Literary Dialogue in Its Social and Political Contexts, Castiglione to Galileo*. Cambridge Studies in Renaissance Literature and Culture 2. Cambridge: Cambridge University Press, 1992.

– 'Seen but Not Heard: The Role of Women Speakers in Cinquecento Literary Dialogue.' In *Women in Italian Renaissance Culture and Society*. Ed. Letizia Panizza. Oxford: European Humanities Research Centre, University of Oxford, 2000. 385–400.

– *Women's Writing in Italy, 1400–1650*. Baltimore: Johns Hopkins University Press, 2008.

Cranston, Jodi. *The Poetics of Portraiture in the Italian Renaissance*. Cambridge: Cambridge University Press, 2000.

Croce, Benedetto. *Aneddoti di varia letteratura*. 4 vols. Bari: Laterza, 1953.

Cropper, Elizabeth. 'On Beautiful Women, Parmigianino, *Petrarchismo*, and the Vernacular Style.' *Art Bulletin* 58 (1976): 374–94.

– 'The Beauty of Woman: Problems in the Rhetoric of Renaissance Portraiture.' In *Rewriting the Renaissance: The Discourses of Sexual Difference in Early Modern Europe*. Ed. Margaret W. Ferguson, Maureen Quilligan, and Nancy J. Vickers. Chicago: University of Chicago Press, 1986. 175–90.

Crum, Roger J. 'Controlling Women or Women Controlled? Suggestions for Gender Roles and Visual Culture in the Italian Renaissance Palace.' In *Beyond Isabella: Secular Women Patrons of Art in Renaissance Italy*. Ed. Sheryl E. Weiss and David G. Wilkins. Kirksville, MO: Truman State University Press, 2001. 37–50.

Curtis-Wendlandt, Lisa. 'Conversing on Love: Text and Subtext in Tullia d'Aragona's *Dialogo della infinita d'amore*.' *Hypatia* 19, 4 (2004): 75–96.

Damisch, Hubert. *The Judgment of Paris*. Translated by John Goodman. Chicago: University of Chicago Press, 1996.

Doody, Margaret Anne. *The True Story of the Novel*. New Brunswick, NJ: Rutgers University Press, 1997.

Douglas, Andrew Halliday. *The Philosophy and Psychology of Pietro Pomponazzi*. Hildesheim: Olms, 1962.

Duggan, Joseph. *The Romances of Chrétien de Troyes*. New Haven: Yale University Press, 2001.

Finucci, Valeria. *The Lady Vanishes: Subjectivity and Representation in Castiglione and Ariosto*. Stanford: Stanford University Press, 1992.

– Introduction to *Urania*, by Giulia Bigolina. Ed. Valeria Finucci. Rome: Bulzoni, 2002.

– Introduction to *Urania: A Romance*. Ed. and trans. Valeria Finucci. Chicago: University of Chicago Press, 2005.

Forin, Elda Martellozzo. *La bottega dei fratelli Mazzoleni, orologiai in Padova (1569)*. Padua: Il Prato, 2005.

Formiciova, Tamara. 'Nuove attribuzioni di quadri dell'Ermitage a Lambert Sustris.' *Arte veneta* 32 (1978): 182–6.

Forno, Carla. *Il 'libro animato': Teoria e scrittura del dialogo nel Cinquecento*. Turin: Tirrenia Stampatori, 1992.

Frappier, Jean. *Histoire, mythes et symboles. Etudes de littérature française*. Geneva: Droz, 1976.

Freedberg, David. 'Johannes Molanus on Provocative Paintings.' *Journal of the Warburg and Courtauld Institutes* 34 (1971): 229–45.

– *The Power of Images: Studies in the History and Theory of Response*. Chicago: University of Chicago Press, 1989.

Freedman, Luba. 'Titian and the Classical Heritage.' In *The Cambridge Companion to Titian*. Ed. Patricia Meilman. Cambridge: Cambridge University Press, 2004. 183–202.

– *Titian's Portraits through Aretino's Lens*. University Park: Pennsylvania State University Press, 1995.

Friedman, John Block. *The Monstrous Races in Medieval Art and Thought*. Cambridge, MA: Harvard University Press, 1981.

Frye, Northrop. *Anatomy of Criticism: Four Essays*. Princeton: Princeton University Press, 1973.

Fuchs, Barbara. *Romance*. New York: Routledge, 2004.

Gambera, Disa. 'Women and Walls: Boccaccio's *Teseida* and the Edifice of Dante's Poetry.' In *Boccaccio and Feminist Criticism*. Ed. Thomas C. Stillinger and F. Regina Psaki. Studi e Testi 8. Chapel Hill: Annali d'Italianistica, 2006. 39–68.

Garilli, Francesco. 'Cultura e pubblico nel *Paradiso degli Alberti*.' *Giornale storico della letteratura italiana* 149 (1972): 1–47.

Garrard, Mary D. ' "Art More Powerful Than Nature"? Titian's Motto Reconsidered.' In *The Cambridge Companion to Titian*. Ed. Patricia Meilman. Cambridge: Cambridge University Press, 2004. 241–61.

– 'Artemisia and Susanna.' In *Feminism and Art History: Questioning the Litany*. Ed. Norma Broude and Mary D. Garrard. New York: Harper and Row, 1982. 146–71.

– 'Here's Looking at Me: Sofonisba Anguissola and the Problem of the Woman Artist.' *Renaissance Quarterly* 47, 3 (1994), 556–622.

Geremia, Lino. *La leggenda ritrovata. Viaggio nella piccola, grande storia della comunità di Santa Croce Bigolina di Cittadella*. Cittadella: Continuos, 2005.

Giamatti, A. Bartlett. *Exile and Change in Renaissance Literature*. New Haven: Yale University Press, 1984.

Ginzburg, Carlo. 'Titian, Ovid, and Sixteenth-Century Codes for Erotic Illustration.' In *Titian's Venus of Urbino*. Ed. Rona Goffen. Cambridge: Cambridge University Press, 1997. 23–36.

Goffen, Rona. 'Titian's *Sacred and Profane Love* and Marriage.' In *The Expanding Discourse: Feminism and Art History*. Ed. Norma Broude and Mary D. Garrard. New York: Icon Editions, 1992. 110–25.

– *Titian's Women*. New Haven: Yale University Press, 1997.

Golahny, Amy, ed. *The Eye of the Poet: Studies in the Reciprocity of the Visual and Literary Arts from the Renaissance to the Present*. Lewisburg: Bucknell University Press, 1996.

Grieve, Patricia E. *Floire and Blancheflor and the European Romance*. Cambridge: Cambridge University Press, 1997.

Grossvogel, Steven. *Ambiguity and Allusion in Boccaccio's Filocolo*. Florence: Olschki, 1992.

Guglielmi, Guido. 'Una novella non esemplare del *Decameron*.' *Forum Italicum* 14 (1980): 32–55.

Haynes, Katharine. *Fashioning the Feminine in the Greek Novel*. London: Routledge, 2003.

Heijkant, Marie-José. 'Tristan pilosus: La folie de l'heros dans le *Tristano Panciatichiano*.' In *Tristan-Tristant: Mélanges en l'honneur de Danielle Buschinger à l'occasion de son 60éme anniversaire*. Trans. Sabine Raaijmakers Costa. Ed. André Crépin and Wolfgang Spiewok. Greifswald: Reineke-Verlag, 1996. 231–42.

Heiserman, Arthur. *The Novel before the Novel: Essays and Discussions about the Beginnings of Prose Fiction in the West*. Chicago: The University of Chicago Press, 1977.

Hollander, Robert. *Boccaccio's Two Venuses*. New York: Columbia University Press, 1977.

Hope, Charles, and Elizabeth McGrath. 'Artists and Humanists.' In *The Cambridge Companion to Renaissance Humanism*. Ed. Jill Kraye. Cambridge: Cambridge University Press, 1996. 161–88.

Hulse, Clark. *The Rule of Art: Literature and Painting in the Renaissance*. Chicago: University of Chicago Press, 1990.

Jacobs, Fredrika H. 'Woman's Capacity to Create: The Unusual Case of Sofonisba Anguissola.' *Renaissance Quarterly* 47, 1 (1994): 74–101.

Jones, Roger. 'What Venus Did with Mars: Battista Fiera and Mantegna's "Parnassus." ' *Journal of the Warburg and Courtauld Institutes* 44 (1981): 193–8.

Jordan, Constance. *Renaissance Feminism: Literary Texts and Political Models*. Ithaca: Cornell University Press, 1990.

Junkerman, Anne Christine. 'The Lady and the Laurel: Gender and Meaning in Giorgione's Laura.' *The Oxford Art Journal* 16, 1 (1993): 49–58.

Kessler, Eckhard. 'The Intellective Soul.' In *The Cambridge History of Renaissance Philosophy*. Ed. Charles B. Schmitt, Quentin Skinner, Eckhard Kessler, and Jill Kraye. Cambridge: Cambridge University Press, 1990. 485–534.

Kirkham, Victoria. *Fabulous Vernacular: Boccaccio's Filocolo and the Art of Medieval Fiction*. Ann Arbor: University of Michigan, 2001.

Klein, Robert. *Form and Meaning: Essays on the Renaissance and Modern Art.* Trans. Madeline Jay and Leon Weseltier. New York: Viking, 1979.

Knowles, David. *The Evolution of Medieval Thought*. New York: Vintage Books, 1962.

Krieger, Murray. *Ekphrasis: The Illusion of the Natural Sign*. Baltimore: Johns Hopkins University Press, 1992.

Kristeller, Paul Oskar. *The Philosophy of Marsilio Ficino*. Trans. Virginia Conant. Gloucester: Peter Smith, 1964.

– *Renaissance Thought II: Papers on Humanism and the Arts*. New York: Harper and Row, 1965.

Lacan, Jacques. *The Four Fundamental Concepts of Psycho-Analysis*. Ed. Jacques-Alain Miller. Trans. Alan Sheridan. New York: Norton, 1978.

Land, Norman E. 'Poetry and Anecdote in Carlo Ridolfi's *Life of Titian*.' In *The Cambridge Companion to Titian*. Ed. Patricia Meilman. Cambridge: Cambridge University Press, 2004. 205–24.

– *The Viewer as Poet: The Renaissance Response to Art*. University Park: Pennsylvania State University Press, 1994.

Lawner, Lynn. *Lives of the Courtesans: Portraits of the Renaissance*. New York: Rizzoli, 1987.

Lee, Rensselaer W. *Ut pictura poesis: The Humanistic Theory of Painting*. New York: Norton, 1967.

Le Goff, Jacques. *The Medieval Imagination*. Trans. Arthur Goldhammer. Chicago: University of Chicago Press, 1988.

Lovarini, Emilio. *Studi sul Ruzzante e la letteratura pavana*. Padua: Antenore, 1965.

Luzio, Alessandro. Introduction to *Un pronostico satirico di Pietro Aretino*. By Pietro Aretino. Bergamo: Istituto italiano d'arti grafiche, 1900.

Maclean, Ian. *The Renaissance Notion of Woman: A Study in the Fortunes of Scholasticism and Medical Science in European Intellectual Life*. Cambridge: Cambridge University Press, 1980.

McLeod, Glenda. *Virtue and Venom: Catalogs of Women from Antiquity to the Renaissance*. Ann Arbor: University of Michigan Press, 1991.

Maddox, Donald. *Fictions of Identity in Medieval France*. Cambridge: Cambridge University Press, 2000.

Mancini, Vincenzo. *Lambert Sustris a Padova. La Villa Bigolin a Selvazzano.* Selvazzano Dentro: Biblioteca Pubblica Comunale, Centro Culturale, 1993.

Marsh, David. *The Quattrocento Dialogue: Classical Tradition and Humanist Innovation.* Cambridge, MA: Harvard University Press, 1980.

Martelli, Mario. 'Considerazioni sulla tradizione della novella spicciolata.' In *La novella italiana. Atti del Convegno di Caprarola 19–24 settembre 1988.* 2 vols. Rome: Salerno Editrice, 1989. 1: 215–44.

Mendelsohn, Leatrice. *Paragoni: Benedetto Varchi's Due Lezzioni and Cinquecento Art Theory.* Studies in the Fine Arts: Art Theory, vol. 6. Ann Arbor: University of Michigan Press, 1982.

Meneghetti, Maria Luisa. 'Il romanzo.' In *La letteratura romanza medievale.* Ed. Costanzo di Girolamo. Bologna: Il Mulino, 1994. 127–91.

Mirollo, James V. *Mannerism and Renaissance Poetry: Concept, Mode, Inner Design.* New Haven: Yale University Press, 1984.

Musacchio, Enrico. 'The Role of the Senses in Mario Equicola's Philosophy of Love.' In *Eros and Anteros: The Medical Traditions of Love in the Renaissance.* Ed. Donald A. Beecher and Massimo Ciavolella. University of Toronto Italian Studies vol. 9. Ottawa: Dovehouse Editions, 1992. 87–101.

Muscetta, Carlo. *Boccaccio.* Bari: Laterza, 1981.

Nardi, Bruno. *Saggi sull'aristotelismo padovano dal secolo XIV al XVI.* Studi sulla tradizione aristotelica nel Veneto vol. 1. Florence: Sansoni, 1958.

Niccoli, Gabriel. 'Autobiography and Fiction in Veronica Franco's Epistolary Narrative.' *Canadian Journal of Italian Studies* 16, 47 (1993): 129–42.

Nissen, Christopher. *Ethics of Retribution in the Decameron and the Late Medieval Italian Novella: Beyond the Circle.* Lewiston, NY: Mellen, 1993.

– 'Giulia Bigolina and Aretino's *Lettere*.' In *In Dialogue with the Other Voice in Sixteenth-Century Italy: Literary and Social Contexts for Women's Writing.* Ed. Julie D. Campbell and Maria Galli Stampino. The Other Voice in Early Modern Europe, vol. 58. Toronto: Centre for Reformation and Renaissance Studies Publications, 2011.

– 'Giulia Bigolina la prima romanziera italiana.' Trans. Rossella Consiglio. *Alta Padovana* 4 (2005): 50–64.

– 'Hagiographic Romance and the Wild Life in Boccaccio's Novella of Beritola (*Decameron* II, 6).' *Italica.* Forthcoming.

– 'The Motif of the Woman in Male Disguise from Boccaccio to Bigolina.' In *The Italian Novella.* Ed. Gloria Allaire. New York: Routledge, 2003. 201–17.

– 'Subjects, Objects, Authors: The Portraiture of Women in Giulia Bigolina's *Urania*.' *Italian Culture* 18 (2000): 15–31.

Padoan, Giorgio. *La commedia rinascimentale veneta.* Vicenza: Neri Pozza, 1982.

– *Momenti del rinascimento veneto.* Padua: Antenore, 1978. 347–70.

Pagliano, Graziella. 'Il motivo del travestimento di genere nella novellistica e nel teatro italiano del rinascimento.' In *Abito e identità. Ricerche di storia letteraria e culturale*. Ed. Cristina Giorcelli. Rome: Edizioni Associate, 1995. 23–94.

Palladino, Lora Anne. 'Pietro Aretino: Orator and Art Theorist.' PhD diss., Yale University, 1981.

Palma, Pina. 'Of Courtesans, Knights, Cooks and Writers: Food in the Renaissance.' *MLN* 119, 1 (2004): 37–51.

Panizza, Letizia. 'The Quattrocento.' In *The Cambridge History of Italian Literature*. Ed. Peter Brand and Lino Pertile. Cambridge: Cambridge University Press, 1999.

Panofsky, Erwin. 'Erasmus and the Visual Arts.' *Journal of the Warburg and Courtauld Institutes.* 32 (1969): 200–7.

– *Idea: A Concept in Art Theory*. Trans. Joseph J.S. Peake. Columbia: University of South Carolina Press, 1968.

– *Studies in Iconology*. New York: Harper and Row, 1967.

Pardo, Mary. 'Artifice as Seduction in Titian.' In *Sexuality and Gender in Early Modern Europe: Institutions, Texts, Images*. Ed. James Grantham Turner. Cambridge: Cambridge University Press, 1993. 55–89.

Park, Katharine. 'The Organic Soul.' In *The Cambridge History of Renaissance Philosophy*. Ed. Charles B. Schmitt, Quentin Skinner, Eckhard Kessler, and Jill Kraye. Cambridge: Cambridge University Press, 1990. 464–84.

Parker, Patricia A. *Inescapable Romance: Studies in the Poetics of a Mode*. Princeton: Princeton University Press, 1979.

Passano, Giambattista. *Novellieri italiani in prosa*. 2nd ed. Turin: Paravia, 1878.

Perella, Nicholas J. *The Kiss Sacred and Profane: An Interpretative History of Kiss Symbolism and Related Religio-Erotic Themes*. Berkeley: University of California Press, 1969.

Pietragalla, Daniela. 'Novella come romanzo: La 'Historia de amore Camilli et Emiliae' di Francesco Florio.' In *Favole parabole istorie. Le forme della scrittura novellistica dal medioevo al rinascimento. Atti del Convegno di Pisa 26–28 ottobre 1998*. Ed. Gabriella Albanese, Lucia Battaglia Ricci, and Rossella Bessi. Rome: Salerno Editrice, 2000. 359–77.

Porcelli, Bruno. *Dante maggiore e Boccaccio minore. Strutture e modelli*. Pisa: Giardini, 1987.

– *La novella del Cinquecento*. Letteratura Italiana Laterza 22. Bari: Laterza, 1973.

Praz, Mario. *Mnemosyne: The Parallel between Literature and the Visual Arts*. Bollingen Series XXXV, vol. 16. Princeton: Princeton University Press, 1974.

Procaccioli, Paolo. Introduction to *Lettere*, by Pietro Aretino. 2 vols. Milan: Rizzoli, 1991.

Quondam, Amedeo. ' "Limatura di rame": Qualche riflessione sulla novella nel sistema del classicismo.' In *Favole parabole istorie. Le forme della scrittura novellistica dal medioevo al rinascimento. Atti del Convegno di Pisa 26–28 ottobre 1998.* Ed. Gabriella Albanese, Lucia Battaglia Ricci, and Rossella Bessi. Rome: Salerno Editrice, 2000. 543–57.

Radcliff-Umstead, Douglas. 'Petrarch and the Freedom to Be Alone.' In *Francis Petrarch, Six Centuries Later: A Symposium.* Ed. Aldo Scaglione. Chapel Hill: University of North Carolina Department of Romance Languages, 1975. 236–48.

Randall, John Herman. Introduction to *On the Immortality of the Soul,* by Pietro Pomponazzi. In *The Renaissance Philosophy of Man.* Ed. Ernst Cassirer, Paul Oskar Kristeller, and John Herman Randall. Chicago: University of Chicago Press, 1948. 257–79.

Raya, Gino. *Storia dei generi letterari: Il romanzo.* Milan: Vallardi, 1950.

Reardon, B.P. Introduction to *The Collected Ancient Greek Novels.* Ed. B.P.Reardon. Berkeley: University of California Press, 1989.

Reid, Jane Davidson. *The Oxford Guide to Classical Mythology in the Arts, 1300–1990s.* 2 vols. New York: Oxford University Press, 1993.

Richardson, Brian. 'The Cinquecento: Prose.' In *The Cambridge History of Italian Literature.* Ed. Peter Brand and Lino Pertile. Cambridge: Cambridge University Press, 1999.

Richardson, Francis L. *Andrea Schiavone.* Oxford: Clarendon, 1980.

Rogers, Mary. 'The Decorum of Women's Beauty: Trissino, Firenzuola, Luigini and the Representation of Women in Sixteenth-Century Painting.' *Renaissance Studies* 2, 1 (1988): 47–75.

– 'Sonnets on Female Portraits from Renaissance North Italy.' *Word and Image* 2, 4 (1986): 291–305.

Rosand, David. 'Inventing Mythologies: The Painter's Poetry.' In *The Cambridge Companion to Titian.* Ed. Patricia Meilman. Cambridge: Cambridge University Press, 2004. 35–57.

– 'The Portrait, the Courtier, and Death.' In *Castiglione: The Ideal and the Real in Renaissance Culture.* Ed. Robert W. Hanning and David Rosand. New Haven: Yale University Press, 1983. 91–130.

– 'So and So Reclining on Her Couch.' In *Titian's Venus of Urbino.* Ed. Rona Goffen. Cambridge: Cambridge University Press, 1997. 37–62.

– 'Titian and the Critical Tradition.' In *Titian: His World and His Legacy.* Ed. David Rosand. New York: Columbia University Press, 1982. 1–39.

Rose, Judith. 'Mirrors of Language, Mirrors of Self: The Conceptualization of Artistic Identity in Gaspara Stampa and Sofonisba Anguissola.' In *Maternal*

Measures: Figuring Caregiving in the Early Modern Period. Ed. Naomi J. Miller and Naomi Yavneh. Aldershot: Ashgate, 2000. 29–48.

Rosenthal, Margaret F. *The Honest Courtesan: Veronica Franco, Citizen and Writer in Sixteenth-Century Venice.* Chicago: University of Chicago Press, 1992.

Rotunda, D.P. *Motif-Index of the Italian Novella in Prose.* Indiana University Publications Folklore Series no. 2. Bloomington: Indiana University Publications, 1942.

Roush, Sherry. 'Dante Ravennate and Boccaccio Ferrarese? Post-Mortem Residency and the Attack on Florentine Literary Hegemony, 1480–1520.' *Viator* 35 (2004): 543–62.

Rubin, Patricia. 'The Seductions of Antiquity.' In *Manifestations of Venus: Art and Sexuality.* Ed. Caroline Arscott and Katie Scott. Manchester: Manchester University Press, 2000. 24–38.

Russell, Rinaldina, and Bruce Merry. Introduction to *Dialogue on the Infinity of Love,* by Tullia d'Aragona. Ed. Rinaldina Russell and Bruce Merry. Chicago: University of Chicago Press, 1997.

Saccone, Eduardo. 'The Portrait of the Courtier in Castiglione.' In *The Book of the Courtier, The Singleton Translation.* Ed. Daniel Javitch. New York: Norton, 2002. 328–9.

Salwa, Piotr. ' "Il Paradiso degli Alberti": La novella impigliata.' In *La novella italiana. Atti del Convegno di Caprarola, 19–24 settembre 1988.* 2 vols. Rome: Salerno, 1989. 755–69.

Samuels, Richard S. 'Benedetto Varchi, the Accademia degli Infiammati, and the Origins of the Italian Academic Movement.' *Italian Quarterly* 29, 4 (1976): 599–634.

San Juan, Rose Marie. 'The Court Lady's Dilemma: Isabella d'Este and Art Collecting in the Renaissance.' In *The Italian Renaissance.* Ed. Paula Findlen. Oxford: Blackwell, 2002.

Scardeone, Bernardino. *Historiae de urbis Patavii antiquitate, et claris civibus patavinis libri tres.* 1560. Reprint, Bologna: Forni, 1979.

Scordilis Brownlee, Marina. 'Cervantes as Reader of Ariosto.' In *Romance: Generic Transformation from Chrétien de Troyes to Cervantes.* Ed. Kevin Brownlee and Marina Scordilis Brownlee. Hanover, NH: University Press of New England, 1985. 220–37.

– 'The Counterfeit Muse: Ovid, Boccaccio, Juan de Flores.' In *Discourses of Authority in Medieval and Renaissance Literature.* Ed. Kevin Brownlee and Walter Stephens. Hanover, NH: University Press of New England, 1989. 109–27.

Scrivano, Riccardo. 'Nelle pieghe del dialogare bembesco.' In *Il dialogo. Scambi e passaggi della parola.* Ed. Giulio Ferroni. Palermo: Sellerio, 1985. 101–9.

Segre, Cesare. *Fuori del mondo. I modelli nella follia e nelle immagini dell'aldilà.* Turin: Einaudi, 1990.
– 'La novella e i generi letterari.' In *La novella italiana. Atti del Convegno di Caprarola, 19–24 settembre 1988.* 2 vols. Biblioteca di filologia e critica vol. 3. Rome: Salerno Editrice, 1989. 1: 47–57.
– *Le strutture e il tempo.* Turin: Einaudi, 1974.
Shapiro, Marianne. 'Mirror and Portrait: The Structure of *Il libro del cortigiano.*' *The Journal of Medieval and Renaissance Studies* 5, 1 (1975): 37–62.
Shearman, John. *Only Connect . . . Art and Spectator in the Italian Renaissance.* The National Gallery of Art, Bollingen Series 37. Princeton: Princeton University Press, 1992.
Sierra, Judy, ed. *Quests and Spells: Fairy Tales from the European Oral Tradition.* Ashland, OR: Kaminski, 1994.
Simons, Patricia. 'Portraiture, Portrayal, and Idealization: Ambiguous Individualism in Representations of Renaissance Women.' In *Languages and Images of Renaissance Italy.* Ed. Alison Brown. Oxford: Clarendon, 1995. 263–311.
Smarr, Janet Levarie. *Joining the Conversation: Dialogues by Renaissance Women.* Ann Arbor: University of Michigan Press, 2005.
Stevens, John. *Medieval Romances: Themes and Approaches.* London: Hutchinson, 1973.
Stewart, Pamela D. 'Boccaccio e la tradizione retorica. La definizione della novella come genere letterario.' *Stanford Italian Review* 1, 1 (1979): 67–74.
Summers, David. *The Judgment of Sense: Renaissance Naturalism and the Rise of Aesthetics.* Cambridge: Cambridge University Press, 1987.
Swennen Ruthenberg, Myriam. 'Coming Full Circle: Romance as *Romanzo* in Elsa Morante's *L'isola di Arturo.*' In *Modern Retellings of Chivalric Texts.* Ed. Gloria Allaire. Aldershot: Ashgate, 1999. 147–63.
Syson, Luke, and Dora Thornton. *Objects of Virtue: Art in Renaissance Italy.* Los Angeles: J. Paul Getty Museum, 2001.
Talvacchia, Bette. *Taking Positions: On the Erotic in Renaissance Culture.* Princeton: Princeton University Press, 1999.
Thompson, Stith. *The Folktale.* Berkeley: University of California Press, 1977.
– *Motif-Index of Folk Literature.* 6 vols. Bloomington: Indiana University Press, 1957.
Tiffany, Sharon W., and Kathleen J. Adams. *The Wild Woman: An Inquiry into the Anthropology of an Idea.* Cambridge, MA: Schenkman, 1985.
Tinagli, Paola. *Women in Italian Renaissance Art: Gender, Representation, Identity.* Manchester: Manchester University Press, 1997.
Tonelli, Luigi. *L'amore nella poesia e nel pensiero del rinascimento.* Florence: Sansoni, 1933.

Toscan, Jean. *Le carnaval du langage. Le lexique érotique des poètes de l'équivoque de Burchiello à Marino, XV–XVII siècles.* 4 vols. Lille: Presses Universitaires de Lille, 1981.

Valency, Maurice. *In Praise of Love: An Introduction to the Love Poetry of the Renaissance.* New York: Schocken, 1982.

Veronese, Emilia, and Elisabetta Dalla Francesca, eds. *Acta graduum academicorum gymnasii Patavini ab anno 1551 ad annum 1561.* Fonti per la storia dell'Università di Padova 16. Rome: Antenore, 2001.

Vianello, Valerio. *Il 'giardino' delle parole. Itinerari di scrittura e modelli letterari nel dialogo cinquecentesco.* Rome: Jouvence, 1993.

Vickers, Nancy J. 'The Body Re-membered: Petrarchan Lyric and the Strategies of Description.' In *Mimesis: From Mirror to Method, Augustine to Descartes.* Ed. John D. Lyons and Stephen G. Nichols, Jr. Hanover, NH: University Press of New England, 1982. 100–9.

Vinaver, Eugène. *The Rise of Romance.* Oxford: Clarendon, 1971.

Viola, Raffaello. *Due saggi di letteratura pavana, seguiti da una ontologia di testi del Ruzzante e del Magagnò con la traduzione italiana.* Padua: Liviana, 1948.

Vitale, Maurizio. *La questione della lingua.* Palermo: Palumbo, 1978.

Vitullo, Juliann. *The Chivalric Epic in Medieval Italy.* Gainesville: The University Press of Florida, 2000.

von Franz, Marie-Louise. *The Psychological Meaning of Redemption Motifs in Fairytales.* Toronto: Inner City Books, 1980.

Waddington, Raymond B. *Aretino's Satyr: Sexuality, Satire, and Self-Projection in Sixteenth-Century Literature and Art.* Toronto: University of Toronto Press, 2004.

– Introduction to *Cortigiana*, by Pietro Aretino. Trans. Douglas Campbell and Leonard G. Sbrocchi. Carleton Renaissance Plays in Translation 38. Ottawa: Dovehouse, 2003.

Watson, Paul F. 'The Cement of Fiction: Giovanni Boccaccio and the Painters of Florence.' *MLN* 99, 1 (1984): 43–64.

Wellek, René, and Austin Warren. *Theory of Literature.* 3rd ed. New York: Harcourt, Brace and World, 1970.

Wells, Marion A. *The Secret Wound: Love Melancholy and Early Modern Romance.* Stanford: Stanford University Press, 2007.

Wetzel, Hermann H. 'Premesse per una storia del genere della novella. La novella romanza dal Due al Seicento.' In *La novella italiana. Atti del Convegno di Caprarola 19–24 settembre 1988.* 2 vols. Rome: Salerno, 1989. 1: 265–81.

White, Hayden. *Tropics of Discourse: Essays in Cultural Criticism.* Baltimore: Johns Hopkins University Press, 1992.

Willard, Charity. *Christine de Pisan: Her Life and Works.* New York: Persea, 1984.

Williams, Charles Allyn. 'Oriental Affinities of the Legend of the Hairy Anchorite.' *University of Illinois Studies in Language and Literature* 10, 2 (1925): 5–56.

Williams, Robert. *Art, Theory, and Culture in Sixteenth-Century Italy: From Techne to Metatechne.* Cambridge: Cambridge University Press, 1997.

Wind, Edgar. *Pagan Mysteries in the Renaissance: An Exploration of Philosophical and Mystical Sources of Iconography in Renaissance Art.* New York: Norton, 1968.

Woods-Marsden, Joanna. *Renaissance Self-Portraiture: The Visual Construction of Identity and the Social Status of the Artist.* New Haven: Yale University Press, 1998.

Yavneh, Naomi. 'Dante's "dolce serena" and the Monstrosity of the Female Body.' In *Monsters in the Italian Literary Imagination.* Ed. Keala Jewell. Detroit: Wayne State University Press, 2001. 109–36.

Yenal, Edith. *Christine de Pizan: A Bibliography.* 2nd ed. Scarecrow Author Bibliographies 63. Metuchen, NJ: Scarecrow Press, 1989.

Zatti, Sergio. 'Il mercante sulla ruota: La seconda giornata.' In *Lectura Boccaccii Turicensis: Introduzione al Decameron.* Ed. Michelangelo Picone and Margherita Mesirca. Florence: Cesati, 2004. 79–97.

Zumthor, Paul. *Toward a Medieval Poetics.* Trans. Philip Bennett. Minneapolis: University of Minnesota Press, 1992.

Index

Mancini, Vincenzo, 14, 62, 242n, 244n
Manetti, Antonio, 37
Mantegna, Andrea, 49, 106, 253n
Mantua, 43, 62
Manutius, Aldus, 106
Marcolini, Francesco, 14, 62, 265n
Marfisa (in Ariosto's *Orlando furioso*), 199
Marguerite de Navarre (*Heptaméron*), 284n
Marie de France: *Guigemar* of, 105; *Lanval* of, 31
Marinella, Lucrezia, 2
Marmorina, 105
Mars, 254n
Marsh, David, 280n
Marsuppini (in Ficino's *Sopra lo amore*), 154
Martelli, Mario, 250n
Martini, Simone, 73, 107
Masenetti, Giovanni Maria, 15, 64, 245n
Massamutino (in Boccaccio's *Filocolo*), 264n
Medoro (in Ariosto's *Orlando furioso*), 199, 219–20
Medusa, 125, 276n
Melechini, Mario, 164, 243n, 257n, 281n, 282n
Menandro (character in *Urania*), 26, 28, 52, 191, 206, 288n
Mendelsohn, Leatrice, 269n, 277n
Mendoza, Don Diego de, 92
Meneghetti, Maria Luisa, 246n, 248n, 249n
Mercury, 254n
Merlin, 31, 49, 190, 203, 205, 211–15, 253n, 284n, 289n
Messer Maco (in Aretino's *Cortigiana*), 99, 267n

Michelangelo Buonarroti, 89, 115–17, 160, 172, 260n, 272n, 282n
Minerva (Pallas), 82–3, 102–3, 113–14, 119–21, 272n, 273n
Mino (in Sacchetti's *Trecentonovelle* 84), 49
Mirabello, 12–13
Mirollo, James V., 274n, 276n
mirrors, 58, 80, 94–5, 98–100, 189–90, 260n, 261n, 265n, 267n
Moissac, 288n
Molino, Niccolò, 260n
Mopsa (in Boccaccio's *Comedia delle ninfe fiorentine*), 273n
Morosini, Marcantonio, 261n
Moses, 126
Musacchio, Enrico, 280n, 281n
Muscetta, Carlo, 250n

Naples, 12, 19, 25, 33, 88–9, 197, 198, 202, 273n
Narcissus, 18, 260n
Nardi, Bruno, 278n, 279n
Neoplatonism, 8, 69, 72, 79, 118, 126, 128, 130–5, 137–8, 147–8, 151, 153–5, 159, 162, 167, 170, 173–4, 183, 259n, 277n, 280n, 281n
Nero (Nero Claudius Caesar), 252n
New Testament, 257n, 290n
Niccoli, Gabriel, 185, 187–8
Nissen, Christopher, 242n, 248n, 251n, 253n, 257n, 258n, 270n, 277–8n, 281n, 283n, 286n, 287n, 289n, 290n
Norandino and Lucina (*Orlando furioso* 17), 289n
novel, 1, 17, 19, 22, 32, 33, 38, 44–5, 52, 103–4, 247n, 248n, 251n, 252n
novella, 3, 17–18, 21, 23–4, 31, 33, 36, 43–4, 47–51, 61, 77, 143, 225, 241n, 246n, 250n, 251n, 285n, 287n, 289n

Rose, Judith, 266n
Rosenthal, Margaret, 187, 283n
Rota, Giovannibattista, 13, 244n
Rotunda, D.P., 285n, 287n
Roush, Sherry, 251n
Rubin, Patricia, 277n, 283n
Rubinetto (in Straparola's *Piacevoli notti* 5.1), 215
Ruggiero (in Ariosto's *Orlando furioso*), 125, 199–200
Russell, Rinaldina, and Bruce Merry, 281n, 282n

Sabine women, 58, 256n
Sacchetti, Franco (*Trecentonovelle*), 49, 122, 253n
Saccone, Eduardo, 280n
St John Lateran, 105
Sainte-Maure, Benôit de, 18
Salerno, 12, 25–6, 28, 30, 36, 46–7, 78, 85, 89, 182, 191–2, 196, 206, 208–10, 217, 261n
Salerno Editrice, 36
Salinari, Carlo, 250n
Sallustius (Gaius Sallustius Crispus), 118, 272n
Salvatico, Bartolomeo, 9, 24, 45, 75–6, 142, 144, 149, 176, 189, 191, 198, 216, 219, 227, 243n, 260n, 291n
Salwa, Piotr, 250n
Sandella, Catarina, 258n
San Juan, Rose Marie, 262n, 274n
San Luca (church in Venice), 257n
Sannazaro, Jacopo, 22, 31, 37, 49, 106, 118, 201–2, 253n, 268n, 272n
Sannio (in Franco's *Filena*), 41–2
Sanseverino, Ferrante, 51, 92, 120, 273n
Sansovino, Iacopo, 14, 129
Santa Croce Bigolina, 12, 244n

Sapegno, Natalino, 33, 249n, 250n
Sappho, 256n
Sartre, Jean Paul, 178
Savia Damigella (in *Urania*), 28–9, 47, 57, 88–9, 120–1, 139, 176, 273n
Scardeone, Bernardino, 11, 13, 17, 24, 242n, 243–4n, 245n, 246n, 257n
Scipio (Publius Cornelius Scipio Africanus), 252n
Scipio's ghost (in Caviceo's *Peregrino*), 39, 48
Scordilis-Brownlee, Marina, 246n, 249n, 250n, 251n, 253n, 286n
Scrivano, Riccardo, 280n
Sebastiano da Longiano, Fausto, 115
Segre, Cesare, 9, 34, 192, 194, 196, 246n, 247n, 250n, 285n, 287n, 290n
Selvaggia (in Firenzuola's *Delle bellezze delle donne*), 132–4
Selvazzano, 12
Seneca (Lucius Annaeus Seneca): *Phaedra* of, 33–4, 250n
Sermoneta, Girolamo, 117
Servi (Paduan church), 12
Shakespeare, William, 129–30
Shapiro, Marianne, 265n, 267n
Shearman, John, 260n, 263n
sibyls, 58, 256n; of Cumae, 49, 107, 253n
Sidney, Sir Philip, 19
Sierra, Judy, 289n
Sigismund I, 114
Silence (in Heldris's *Roman de Silence*), 31, 212–14, 216
Sileni, 215, 289n
Simons, Patricia, 121, 130, 253n, 270n
Sincero (in Sannazaro's *Arcadia*), 201–2
Siren (in Dante's *Purgatorio* 19), 290n
Sistine Chapel, 116–17

Ingram Content Group UK Ltd.
Milton Keynes UK
UKHW040727240423
420680UK00001B/12